Civil Procedure in Italy

Civil Procedure in Italy

Third Edition

Michele Angelo Lupoi

This book was originally published as a monograph in the International Encyclopaedia of Laws/Civil Procedure.

Founding Editor: Roger Blanpain
General Editor: Frank Hendrickx
Volume Editor: Piet Taelman

Wolters Kluwer

Published by:
Kluwer Law International B.V.
PO Box 316
2400 AH Alphen aan den Rijn
The Netherlands
E-mail: international-sales@wolterskluwer.com
Website: lrus.wolterskluwer.com

Sold and distributed in North, Central and South America by:
Wolters Kluwer Legal & Regulatory U.S.
7201 McKinney Circle
Frederick, MD 21704
United States of America
Email: customer.service@wolterskluwer.com

Sold and distributed in all other countries by:
Air Business Subscriptions
Rockwood House
Haywards Heath
West Sussex
RH16 3DH
United Kingdom
Email: international-customerservice@wolterskluwer.com

ISBN 978-90-411-9574-6

e-Book: ISBN 978-90-411-9575-3
web-PDF: ISBN 978-90-411-9576-0

The Author

Prof. Michele Angelo Lupoi was born in Rome in 1967. He studied Law at the University of Bologna, Italy where he graduated in 1991, with a thesis in Civil Procedural Law on matters of international jurisdiction. In 1996, he discussed his doctorate thesis on international lis pendens, and in 2000 he was appointed as researcher in the Faculty of Law at the University of Bologna.

In 2004, he became an associate professor at the University of Bologna, where he currently teaches Civil Procedural Law, Insolvency Law and European Judicial Cooperation (in English) at the School of Law. He is the coordinator of the *Corso di studio magistrale in Giurisprudenza* of the School of Law of the University of Bologna at Ravenna.

He has published a book on transnational conflicts of jurisdictions in 2002 and several volumes and essays in matters of international and comparative procedural law, insolvency, matrimonial proceedings, trust law and other procedural topics.

He has been a visiting scholar at Cornell Law School, Ithaca, NY (1997–1998) and three times at Roger Williams University School of Law, Bristol, RI (2000, 2001 and 2008).

He also practises civil and family law in Bologna.

The Author

Table of Contents

List of Abbreviations

App.	Court of Appeal
AJCL	American Journal of Comparative Law
Cass.	*Corte di cassazione*
CC	*Codice civile (Civil Code)*
Corte cost.	*Corte costituzionale (Constitutional Court)*
CG	*Il corriere giuridico*
CPC	*Codice di procedura civile (Civil Procedural Code)*
CP CG	*Codice penale (Criminal Code) Il corriere giudico*
CPP	*Codice di procedura penale (Criminal Procedural Code)*
CSM	*Consiglio superiore della Magistratura*
CTU	*Consulente tecnico d'ufficio (Court-Appointed Expert)*
Decr.	Decree (decreto)
DF	*Il diritto di famiglia e delle persone*
DL	*Decreto-legge*
DLGS	*Decreto legislativo*
DPR	*Decreto del Presidente della Repubblica (President of the Republic's Decree)*
ECHR	European Convention of Human Rights
ECJ	European Court of Justice
FD	*Famiglia e diritto*
FI	*Foro italiano*
FM	*Famiglia e minori*
GC	*Giustizia civile*
GCM	*Giustizia civile – Massimario*
GD	*Guida al diritto*
GI	*Giurisprudenza italiana*
GM	*Giurisprudenza di merito*

List of Abbreviations

GPC	*Il giusto processo civile*
IJPL	*International Journal of Procedural Law*
ILJ	*The Italian Law Journal*
MP	Member of Parliament
NLCC	*Le nuove leggi civili commentate*
PM	*Pubblico ministero*
RA	*Rivista dell'arbitrato*
RD	*Regio decreto (Royal Decree)*
RDC	*Rivista di diritto civile*
RDI	*Rivista di diritto internazionale*
RDP	*Rivista di diritto processuale*
RDIPP	*Rivista di diritto internazionale privato e processuale*
RTDPC	*Rivista trimestrale di diritto e procedura civile*
SU	*Sezioni unite (Full Chamber of the Cassazione)*
TAR	*Tribunale amministrativo regionale (Regional Administrative* tribunal)
Trib.	*Tribunale (main Court of First Instance)*
Trib. min.	*Tribunale per i minorenni (main Court of First Instance for minors)*
ULR	Uniform Law Review

General Introduction

§1. General Background: The Italian Constitutional, Political and Legal System

1. Italy is a Parliamentary Republic since the end of World War II, when a referendum abolished the monarchy[1] on 2 June 1946. On the same date, a national assembly was elected to start drafting a new Constitution, which finally entered into force on 1 January 1948.

The Italian Constitution is a compromise between the communism, socialist, liberal and Catholic traditions, in a common effort to build a new democratic order after the dark years of the Fascist regime. It is grounded on fundamental principles of freedom and solidarity, with a strong social orientation. The Constitution puts to the forefront the citizen's role, both as an individual and as a member of free associations and entities of all kinds (political parties, trade unions and so on). As a matter of fact, the formulation of Article 1 is quite eloquent: 'Italy is a democratic Republic, based on labour. The people are sovereign, in compliance with the forms and limits set by the Constitution.'

As concerns us here, after the Fascist dictatorship, a very strong effort was put into ensuring the autonomy and the independence of the judiciary and in safeguarding some fundamental principles of (procedural) freedom, especially in the criminal field.

The first part of the Constitution sets the fundamental principles of the Republic (Articles 1–12); the second deals with the rights and duties of the citizens, in the personal, social, economic and political fields, respectively (Articles 13–55), most notably personal, political and religious freedom and access to justice; finally, the third part hands out the basic rules of the republican order, as concerns the Parliament, the President of the Republic, the Government, the Judiciary (Articles 101–113) and so on.

The mechanisms to reform the Constitution are rather complex and require very large parliamentary majorities (*maggioranze qualificate*).[2] This might explain why rather few innovations have been made to the Constitution's original text since 1948.[3] While the main reforms have concerned the territorial organization of the State, with the institution of regional governments (*regioni*) and the distribution of

1. For a historic overview of Constitutional law in Italy *see* G. De Vergottini, *Diritto costituzionale*, 115 et seq. (2d ed., Cedam 2000).
2. Unlike other countries, Italy is based on a written and rigid Constitution.
3. *See* De Vergottini, *supra*, 199 et seq.

the State functions between the central and the local bodies (in a move towards a quasi-federal organization), as concerns us here, it is worth mentioning the Constitutional law which modified Article 111 of the Constitution in matters of fundamental procedural guarantees, establishing the principle of the *giusto processo* (fair trial) (*see infra*, paragraphs 59 et seq.). In recent years, changes of the Constitutional provisions concerning the Judiciary have been proposed, raising rather spirited controversies in Parliament and in the society at large. As a matter of fact, the problematic relation between the political power and the judiciary in Italy is well documented.

2. General political elections are held every five years, with a semi-majority electoral mechanism. The history of electoral laws in Italy is particularly troubled. An earlier law, approved among heated controversies, basically imposing on the voters a rigid list of candidates selected by the political parties, was declared unconstitutional by the Constitutional Court, in the decision No. 1 of 13 January 2014, as concerned both the 'majority premium' awarded to the coalition which obtained more votes and to the 'blocked' lists of candidates, insomuch as they distorted the principle of representativeness of the electorate. A new statute concerning the election of the *Camera dei deputati* was therefore approved in 2015 (Law No. 52, the so-called *Italicum*). Also this new regulation, however, was recently found to be partially unconstitutional by the Constitutional Court in its decision of 9 February 2017, No. 35. Among heated controvercies, another electoral law (the so-called *Rosatellum*) was hastily approved at the end of October 2017: the next general elections of 2018 will be therefore governed by this new regulation, which mixes both majority and proportional aspects and encourages parties to form electoral coalitions in order to gain some premium Members of Parliament if their coalition obtains more than 40% of the votes..

In the past twenty years, a bipolar political system had formed, with an alternation of centre-left and centre-right governments. Recently, however, a third political movement has appeared on the scene, making the scenario more complicated than usual and the risk of ungovernability after new elections more real.

The Parliament is composed of two Chambers, the *Senato* and the *Camera*. There are 315 elected senators (six of them elected by Italian citizens living abroad) (Article 57). Former presidents of the Republic become honorary senators for life. Also, the President of the Republic may appoint five honorary senators for life, for their high social, scientific, artistic and literary merits (Article 59). The *Camera* has 630 elected members (*deputati*). Italian citizens may elect *deputati* when they become 18 years old, but they are entitled to vote for the *Senato* only when they reach 25 years of age. Different age limits also apply to be eligible as a candidate for either the *Senato* or the *Camera*.

Any new State law must be approved by a majority of both Chambers, and this makes the legislative process rather slow and sometimes frustrating (Article 70). A proposal for the abolition of the Senate is currently under discussion.

The Prime Minister is appointed by the President of the Republic and chooses the Ministers of the Government. The Government must obtain a confidence vote from both the Chambers at the beginning of its mandate. A parliamentary majority must sustain the Government during the entire mandate.

3. Since the 1970s, many functions, prerogatives and powers have been transferred from the State to the territorial political entities into which Italy is divided on a decreasing scale: regions (*regioni*), provinces (*province*) and municipalities (*comuni*). Local administrations are elected every five years with a majority system. Functional conflicts between different organs of the State, the State and a region or different regions are solved by the Constitutional Court. In recent years, reforms have been enacted to implement a more 'federalistic' organization of the State, especially as concerns the local tax systems.

In recent times, the existence of 'provinces' as autonomous intermediate territorial entities started being questioned and in April 2014 they were subject to a reform which did not abolish them but turned them into different entities ('*enti di secondo livello*'), i.e., assemblies whose components (the mayors of the municipalities inside the territory of each province) are no longer directly elected by the Italian voters. A *consiglio provinciale* (provincial council) also exists, whose members are elected among the local administrators in second level elections. These new entities have competence in areas such as school housing, environmental protection, local transportation and so forth. Ten former provinces, moreover, have been transformed in 2014 in '*città metropolitane*' (metropolitan cities) (Turin, Rome, Milan, Venice, Genova, Bologna, Florence, Bari, Naples and Reggio Calabria), second level representative bodies which have the same territorial and subject-matter jurisdiction of the provinces they took the place of.

4. Italy is a civil law country. As such, written statutes enacted by Parliament or other bodies exercising primary or secondary legislative functions are the main sources of the law. In the civil law tradition, certainty and foreseeableness of the rule of law are considered fundamental guarantees of freedom for the citizens. The role of unwritten law and practices, however, especially in certain sectors, should not be underestimated.

The sources of law in Italy are organized along a hierarchic structure: rules formed at a higher level, therefore, always prevail over lower ones (*lex superior derogat inferiori*). Relations and conflicts between different sources of equal standing are solved according to a temporal (*lex posterior derogat anteriori*) and a subject-matter factor (*lex specialis derogat generali*).

5. The basic source of law in Italy is the Constitution (and the subsequent Constitutional laws).[4] The Constitutional Court[5] is in charge, *inter alia*, of reviewing alleged violations of Constitutional rules and principles by any 'lower' normative provision. This is an exclusive jurisdiction: no other form of judicial review is admitted even though it is now quite common for judges in Italy to give legal provisions a 'constitutionally oriented' interpretation; in other words, when doubts arise, rules are generally interpreted in a way which makes them compatible with

4. That is, Acts of Parliament enacted with the special mechanisms and majorities provided for by Art. 138 Const. *See* para. 1.
5. Whose main functions and composition are governed by Arts 134 et seq. Const.

the Constitution. As a matter of fact, the Constitutional Court itself expects ordinary judges to try and give legal provisions a meaning which makes them compatible with the Constitution, before remitting the case to the Court: *interpretatio secundum constitutionem.*[6]

Access to the Constitutional Court is not open to the general public outside of already pending proceedings; in other words, it is not possible to file a petition directly to the court alleging a violation of the Constitution in a statutory provision. On the contrary, a constitutional issue must be raised in pending judicial proceedings; if that issue is deemed to be relevant for the decision of the case at hand and not prima facie ungrounded, the judge will refer it to the Constitutional Court, which will then decide upon it (for more details *see infra*, paragraph 299).

6. Below the Constitutional level, the primary source of law in Italy is the *legge ordinaria* (ordinary law), enacted by Parliament with the procedures established in Articles 70 et seq. of the Constitution,[7] which, *inter alia*, require a majority vote of the same text by both Chambers.

There are, however, other (frequently used) normative instruments which are given the same authority as the *legge ordinaria*:

(a) a *decreto-legge* (DL) can be enacted by the Government in extraordinary cases of necessity and urgency, in compliance with Article 77 of the Constitution.[8] Its effects are only provisional, since it must be confirmed and implemented into an act of Parliament within sixty days. In practice, *decreti-legge* are often used by the executive to bypass the slow law-making parliamentary process, sometimes with a substantial abuse of power; at the implementing state, the original contents of the *decreto-legge* may of course be changed by Parliament;
(b) *decreto legislativo* (DLGS) is another act of the Government (Article 76 of the Constitution); unlike the *decreto-legge*, however, the *decreto legislativo* is enacted following a specific delegation by the Parliament to the Executive (*legge delega*), providing the main guidelines the Government must follow and the goals to achieve. *Decreti legislativi* are often employed in very technical areas, which require detailed and analytical rules. In recent years, they have been used many times in the civil procedural field. When they are enacted, *decreti legislativi* do not require further approval by Parliament. However, if the Government does not respect the guidelines set by Parliament or (as it often happens) rules are inserted in the *decreto* which go beyond those guidelines (*eccesso di delega*), the Constitutional Court may be called to strike out those rules as unconstitutional.

7. The civil law tradition is rooted in the idea of the code, that is, a statute which provides for an organic and extensive set of rules for all the main areas of the law. In Italy, a Civil Code (CC), a Civil Procedural Code (CPC), a Criminal Code (CP)

6. *Corte Cost.* 10 Feb. 2006, n. 57, *ord.*
7. Or by the regions (*leggi regionali*), within their subject-matter normative jurisdiction.
8. Some subject-matters, however, can never be regulated by a *decreto-legge*.

and a Criminal Procedural Code (CPP) exist. Originally enacted in the 1940s,[9] all of them have gone through more or less profound changes and innovations in the past seventy years.[10] Even though they still represent the main point of reference in their respective areas of operation, it must be remarked that the ideal of the code has been in crisis for a while; many laws, statutes and acts have been enacted over the past decades in areas previously contained in the codes, so that now entire sectors of the law are disciplined outside of them (e.g., labour law). The influence of European law and the need to implement directives into national law in rather specific sectors, in an often-fragmentary fashion, has increased this tendency to 'evade' from the code.

In the past few years, moreover, a new idea of 'mini-code' has emerged in the form of pieces of legislation providing sectorial regulations for certain specific matters: for example, the 'Code for private insurance contracts'[11] and the 'Consumer code'[12] (*see infra*, paragraph 39). Most often, these mini-codes ('testi unici') collect together (and innovate on) previously existing provisions, dispersed in several different pieces of legislation. Some of these 'special' codes contain important procedural provisions (e.g., the new rule on class actions: Article 140*bis* of the Consumer code, *see* at paragraphs 361 et seq.).

Within their legislative functions defined by the Constitution, also Italian regions enjoy legislative powers to enact *leggi regionali* Regions have no power to enact statutes in civil procedural matters.

8. Below the ordinary law level, various sources of secondary law can be found, such as regulations, enacted by the Government or by other public bodies and Constitutional organs to implement ordinary rules and administrative orders (*ordinanze amministrative*).

9. The Italian legal system also admits unwritten sources of law, namely practices and customs (*usi*),[13] which consist of constantly and generally repeated behaviours, followed by the members of a community in the persuasion that they are legally binding. In other words, an objective element (the so-called *longa repetitio*) must mix with a subjective one (the *opinio juris*) to grant a custom a normative character. Customs, however, can never prevail over conflicting legal rules (*contra legem*). In practice, usages are most often employed in sectors where no or few legal

---

9. In particular, on the history of the civil code *see* P. Rescigno 'Introduzione', in *Trattato di diritto privato*, ed. P. Rescigno, 2nd edn (Turin: Utet, 1999), 7 et seq.
10. For example, the CPP was completely redrafted at the end of the 1980s, the whole family law part of the CC was revolutionized in the 1970s, some criminal felonies have been eliminated and some new added in the CP, and so on.
11. DLGS No. 209 of 7 Sep. 2005. *See* S. Amorosino & L. Desiderio (eds), *Il nuovo codice della assicurazioni. Commento sistematico* (Milan: Giuffrè, 2006).
12. DLGS No. 206, of 6 Sep. 20005, No. 206. *See* V. Cuffaro (ed.), *Codice del consumo* (Milan: Giuffrè, 2006).
13. A. Giuliani, 'Le disposizioni sulla legge in generale – Gli articoli da 1 a 15', in *Trattato di diritto privato*, ed. Rescigno *supra*, 407 et seq.

provisions exist, especially in commercial law, at the local,[14] national or international level. Chambers of Commerce keep records of most local usages and customs.

10. Judicial decisions are not a source of law in Italy. As a matter of fact, the stare decisis doctrine is not followed and judicial decisions (even the ones rendered by the Italian Supreme Court) do not enjoy a binding authority in proceedings other than the ones in which they are rendered. Case law, including the decisions if the Supreme Court, only has a persuasive authority for other judges. As a matter of fact, every Italian judge is entitled to 'disagree' with the *Cassazione* decisions and to give legal provisions based on his or her own interpretation. This leads to conflicting and sometimes very contradictory case law and to several different judicial interpretations of the same rules. The *Cassazione* itself plays a part in this interpretative fragmentation, since different sections of the Supreme Court (and sometimes even different panels within the same section) are known to render decisions which conflict with each other. Until recently, single sections of the *Cassazione* could also disagree with decisions rendered by the full chamber of the Supreme Court.

The 2006 reform of proceedings before the Court of Cassation (*see infra*, paragraphs 258 et seq.), however, has tried to change this situation and to avoid that single sections of the Supreme Court render decisions which conflict with the principles of law previously formulated by the full chamber of the Court itself (*sezioni unite*): today, therefore, single sections, should they disagree with a full chambers decisions on a specific issue of law, are compelled to abstain from deciding the case and to refer it to the *sezioni unite*.

By introducing this 'soft' binding relation between single sections and the full chamber of the Court, an attempt has been made to render the case law of the *Cassazione* less unpredictable and more coherent.

On the other hand, in order to encourage lower courts to follow the precedents of the *Cassazione*, in 2009, a new Article 360*bis* was inserted in the CPC, introducing the so-called *Cassazione* filter (*filtro in Cassazione*), according to which an appeal before the Supreme Court is considered inadmissible if the second instance judge duly applied the case law of the *Cassazione* and the appellant does not show any good reason to *change* such case law (*see* paragraphs 264, 268).

Even though judicial decisions do not enjoy a formal normative character, undeniably Italian judges (and especially the Supreme Court) give a fundamental contribution in completing the legal system by interpreting existing rules, filling lacunae and updating existing provisions to the ever-evolving spirit of the times.[15] Several instances are known, moreover, of (controversial) judicial decisions giving a 'creative' interpretation of statutory provisions.

14. For example, the commercial practices concerning the sale of farm animals within a given province.
15. S. Chiarloni, 'Ruolo della giurisprudenza e attività creative di nuovo diritto', RTDPC (2002): 1; L.P. Comoglio & V. Carnevale, 'Il ruolo della giurisprudenza e i metodi di uniformazione del diritto in Italia', RDP (2004): 1037; M. Taruffo, 'Precedente e giurisprudenza', RTDPC (2007): 709.

11. In the exercise of the judicial function, the interpretation of the rule of law and the terms and notions used therein is one of the courts' primary tasks.[16] From this point of view, the literal formulation of a rule is the main epistemological factor from which any judicial analysis should depart.

However, legal interpretation should also go beyond the strict meaning of the words used in a provision, taking into consideration, among other factors, the lawmaker's intentions and aims when such provision was originally drafted, the framework of any relevant constitutional principle, a balance of conflicting interests, the changes in the society after a statutory rule was enacted and so forth.

In the interpretation of civil law, recourse is also often made to analogy[17] or to the fundamental principles of the system to fill in any lacuna; in other words, a case may be decided by referring to legal or judicial solutions given for similar cases. However, analogy may never be made in relation to statutory rules having an extraordinary nature.

12. Also, the opinion of the legal authors (*dottrina*) is not a source of law; it is however fundamental for both practitioners and academics to analyse and criticize the existing rules and case law, in an effort to influence the future developments of both the legislative and the judicial powers. Interestingly, the Law on the Judicial Order expressly forbids Italian judges from quoting academic writing in the reasoning of their decisions. Usually, therefore, a judgment will only make a generic reference to 'the prevalent doctrine' or employ other similar expressions to acknowledge the contribution of the scientific community to the interpretation of the rule of law.

§2. Delimitation of the Subject-Matter

I. Definition of the Term 'Civil Procedure'

13. Civil procedure (*diritto processuale civile*) is the branch of the law which deals with the regulation of civil judicial proceedings as opposed to other forms of judicial proceedings (e.g., criminal or administrative).

In civil proceedings, subjective rights (*diritti soggettivi*) or personal status of the parties are adjudicated upon or enforced by the judge. In this context, subjective rights can be defined as those juridical positions which are immediately and directly safeguarded by the legal order (as opposed to the so-called *interessi legittimi*, *see infra*, paragraph 19).

16. *See* N. Picardi, 'La funzione del giudice nell'interpretazione e nell'applicazione del diritto', GC (2003): II, 363.
17. *See* A. Giuliani, *supra*, 429 et seq.; Cricenti, 'L'analogia come regola di giustificazione delle decisioni giudiziarie: il modello italiano', *Eur. dir. priv.* (1998): 551.

14. Not only private parties but also a public administration can sue or be sued in civil proceedings when the claim does not refer to the administration's authoritative powers.[18] It must also be pointed out that even purely private disputes may have public interest connotations (e.g., proceedings on a personal status) with several procedural implications.[19]

15. Civil proceedings may be defined as the tool devised by the State to safeguard and protect subjective rights, in order to grant social peace, avoid self-justice and ensure certainty and predictability of the rule of law. Different forms of judicial protection of subjective rights may be applied for, depending on the type of judicial remedy required in the given case. On a general level, one must distinguish between proceedings in which the existence of a subjective right or a personal status is ascertained, with a decision on the merits of the case (*azione/processi di cognizione*)[20] and those – which usually presuppose and are a consequence of the former – where such a decision on the merits is enforced (*azione/processi di esecuzione*). In between, the so-called *azione cautelare* can be found, that is, judicial activity to grant interim measures to safeguard the efficient fulfilment of both the *azione di cognizione* and the *azione di esecuzione*, through provisional decisions which either preserve or anticipate the effects of the other two forms of actions.

Processi di cognizione, moreover, are traditionally divided into proceedings where a subjective right is ascertained through an exhaustive cognition of the relevant facts (*processi di cognizione piena*) and those where the decision is based on summary information or evidence (and sometimes, no evidence at all) (*processi di cognizione sommaria*).

16. Not every model of proceedings is exhaustively disciplined by the law. As a matter of fact, the code of civil procedure regulates, in very fine details, only (the so-called) ordinary cognizance proceedings (*procedimento ordinario di cognizione*) at first instance before the *Tribunale* (i.e., the main Court of First Instance): whenever lacunae are found in the regulation of other special or summary proceedings, those general rules may be referred to. Recent legislation appears to grant the judge more discretion in organizing the course of some 'special' proceedings (e.g., *procedimento sommario*, *see* paragraphs 343 et seq.), as an attempt to make them faster and more efficient.

II. Notion of Civil Jurisdiction: Distinctions (and Similarities) with Other Types of Procedures (Administrative, Criminal)

17. According to Article 102 of the Constitution, jurisdiction to adjudicate is conferred to 'ordinary magistrates' established by law and organized according to

18. *See* P. Virga, *La tutela giurisdizionale nei confronti della pubblica amministrazione*, 4th edn (Milan: Giuffrè, 2003).
19. For example, intervention of the *Pubblico Ministero*.
20. For further details, *see* paras 174 et seq.

the rules of the judicial order.[21] Ordinary courts are opposed to special or extraordinary courts, whose institution is expressly prohibited by Article 102(2) of the Constitution.[22] Only the creation of specialized sections within ordinary courts is allowed by the Constitution (*see infra*, paragraph 89).

18. The distinction between criminal and civil jurisdiction appears clear enough: criminal proceedings concern the establishment and the punishment of felonies analytically identified in the Criminal Code (CP) and in the criminal legislation, both in the private interest of the damaged or hurt person and in the public interest of the State to grant peace to the society and sanction violations of the law. Criminal proceedings do not solve disputes: they are centred around the sanction delivered by the court on the offender, not the right of the victim to compensation for the damage suffered. This does not exclude however that the damaged person may participate in criminal proceedings (*costituzione di parte civile*) and obtain (at least partial) compensation for the loss suffered (*provisionale*) therein.[23] It has to be remarked, however, that the start of criminal proceedings against the wrongdoer does not prevent the victim from starting autonomous parallel civil proceedings in order to get compensation for his or her damage. Only when a specific election is made to move the civil action into the criminal one, must the civil proceedings be discontinued.[24]

19. Administrative disputes are adjudicated by an autonomous (special) administrative courts system, based on administrative regional tribunals (*tribunali amministrativi regionali*: TAR),[25] that is, courts of first instance at the regional level, and one *Consiglio di Stato*, in Rome, which, *inter alia*, works as a Court of Appeal against the decisions rendered by the TAR.

In administrative proceedings, the defendant is a public administration or a public entity or body and the petitioner's claim is based on juridical positions different from subjective rights, the so-called *interessi legittimi*.[26] These legitimate interests are a peculiarity of the Italian legal system. They express the special relation between the administrative powers and the public at large and can roughly be described as the interests of the citizen in the proper exercise of the administrative function on the part of the public powers. The classic exemplification is of someone who takes part in a public examination: he or she does not have a subjective right to pass the examination but only an interest in the examination being held in a fair and impartial way so that when such interest is violated he or she can bring a suit to have an act of the administration revoked or annulled (and possibly have the administration perform some related specific action).

---

21. *RD* No. 12 of 31 Jan. 1941.
22. As a reaction against the notorious special Tribunals established by the Fascist regime before World War II.
23. In other words, the exercise of the civil action in criminal proceedings (*esercizio in sede penale dell'azione civile*) depends on the party's own free choice.
24. More details in M.A. Zumpano, *Rapporti tra processo civile e processo penale* (Turin: Giappichelli, 2000).
25. Established by Law No. 1034 of 1971.
26. As to the origins of *interessi legittimi* in the Italian legal order *see* G.F. Ricci, *Principi di diritto processuale generale*, 3rd edn (Turin: Giappichelli, 2001), 51 et seq.

The distinction between *diritti soggettivi* and *interessi legittimi* is sometimes rather hard to pin down so that a reaction against the very notion of *interessi legittimi* (and the whole separate administrative court system) can be noted in recent legal literature.

In certain subject-matters, moreover, civil and administrative courts enjoy exclusive jurisdiction, thus making the jurisdictional issue easier to solve.

20. Administrative proceedings have traditionally been regulated by specific statutes (sometimes with express reference to the rules of the CPC), most notably Law No. 2248 of 20 March 1865 and Law No. 205 of 21 July 2000.

This area of procedural law was completely redrafted by DLGS No. 104 of 2 July 2010, introducing a 'mini-code' for administrative proceedings.[27] Further modifications were brought by DLGS No. 195 of 2011.[28]

21. As a general rule, a public administration can always be sued before a civil court for an alleged violation of a subjective right. The civil judge, however, can never directly modify or revoke an act of a public body or compel the administration to perform an action; in case of successful civil proceedings, if the administration does not voluntarily comply with the court's decision, specific administrative proceedings have to be brought to enforce it (*giudizio di ottemperanza*), now regulated by Articles 112 et seq. of DLGS No. 104 of 2010.

22. In Italian procedural academic writing there is no consensus as to the definition of civil jurisdiction, in particular in relation to other non-judicial 'procedures' which lead to 'decisions' (e.g., the acts of a public authority). Over the years, many views have been expressed and the debate is still quite open. With a certain degree of approximation, it can be said that the civil judicial function aims at solving disputes over subjective rights and personal status, through the application and the establishment of the rule of law, therefore safeguarding (or aiming at safeguarding) social peace. What makes the exercise of civil jurisdiction different from other forms of dispute resolution or decision making is the role of the judge as a third and impartial adjudicator, with no interests of his or her own in the solution of the dispute.

The judge complies with such high task from a position which is both secondary and substitutive;[29] in other words, judicial adjudication of a dispute is the *extrema ratio*, when the parties cannot or will not autonomously find an out-of-court settlement or otherwise compose their differences. When conflict erupts, the parties cannot make their own justice, but they have to refer to the courts.

In this light, the efficient, prompt and inexpensive functioning of the machinery of justice is a fundamental aspect of any civilized and fair society. This is why, at

27. GD 31(2010): 8 et seq.
28. GD 1 (2012): 28 et seq.
29. It has to be remarked, however, that part of the judicial function has a primary character, insomuch as, as concerns certain institutions and situations, the parties could never achieve the aim they pursue outside of judicial proceedings, the classic example, in Italy, being a divorce.

least in Italy, as in several other countries, the crisis of civil justice really is the crisis of the legal system at large: when fast and efficient adjudication of a dispute cannot be granted, the citizens lose their confidence in the institutions, and the whole social texture is endangered. While the so-called Alternative Dispute Resolution (ADR) can bring some relief, they cannot be considered as a substitute for the adjudication of the parties' rights through the State court's system or as a miraculous solution for the problems of civil justice.

The Italian lawmaker, however, in an attempt to reduce the workload of the courts, has made it mandatory from 21 March 2011, to try and mediate several types of civil disputes before enabling the plaintiff to bring the case before the court (*condizione di procedibilità*) (Article 5, DLGS No. 28 of 2010, *see infra*, paragraphs 52, 202, 451 et seq.). Recent legislation, moreover, introduced Article 185*bis* in the CPC, allowing the judge to make settlement proposals to the parties in the course of the proceedings (*see* paragraph 215) and in 2014 a new form of ADR was introduced, also functioning, in certain cases, as a *condizione di procedibilità* for pecuniary claims (*negoziazione assistita*: Articles 2 et seq., DL No. 132 of 2014, *see* Part XII).

23. In civil, criminal and administrative proceedings, some common characteristics can be found, most notably, the position of the judge as not only an impartial but also a 'disinterested' adjudicator.

Impartiality is not a peculiar feature of the judicial function; also the public administration, as a matter of fact, should always act in compliance with the best interest of the law even when pursuing his or her own aims and interests. The judge, on the other hand, has (or should have) no interest whatsoever in the outcome of the dispute (*terzietà*), which he or she decides only for the superior sake of justice and the rule of law.

24. Judicial cognizance proceedings of all kinds aim at establishing a degree of legal certainty to put an end to a situation of 'legal uncertainty' and to the dispute arising therefrom. Res judicata grants the immutability of a judicial decision's effects, preventing every court from further examining cases already adjudicated upon (*ne bis in idem*) and putting an end to litigation.

25. In varying degrees, all judicial proceedings are governed by the principle *audiatur et altera pars* ('let the other party be heard too') (*principio del contraddittorio*),[30] according to which the judge can never render a decision before all the parties have had the chance to be heard and defend themselves before him or her.[31] This right to be heard is arguably more intensively carried out in full cognition proceedings, where, as a matter of fact, at every stage of the procedure, all the parties must be able to effectively raise their claims, objections and defences before the court.

---

30. N. Picardi, 'Audiatur et altera pars'. Le matrici storico-culturali del contraddittorio', RTDPC (2003): 7.
31. And when a decision has to be given ex parte, the parties must anyway be subsequently heard in order to confirm or revoke such decision.

26. The adjudication of disputes over subjective rights is another peculiarity of civil proceedings, especially vis-à-vis criminal proceedings (where no real 'dispute' exists). Civil proceedings are usually initiated and brought to an end by the subjects whose rights fall to be adjudicated therein (*principio di impulso di parte*), the exceptions being the (limited) cases where the *Pubblico Ministero* may bring a civil action and cases of 'extraordinary standing' (*legittimazione straordinaria*).

In criminal proceedings, on the other hand, the judicial initiative rests entirely in the hands of the *Pubblico Ministero*, on his or her own initiative or the damaged person's petition (*querela di parte*). The PM is under a constitutional duty (Article 112 of the Constitution), whenever he or she receives a *notitia criminis* (i.e., the report that a crime is likely to have been committed) to start the criminal action (or rather, to start investigations to verify if such action should be brought forth: *indagini preliminari*). A criminal action, therefore, can never be freely disposed of in the strict sense of the expression.

III. Separate Court Systems and Rules of Procedure

27. As we have already seen, different courts systems exist for civil, criminal and administrative disputes respectively. Each court's system follows its own procedural rules; even if they are inspired by the same fundamental constitutional principles, and some common elements can be found, they tend to follow different patterns.

28. Some 'special' courts must also be mentioned to complete the picture:

- tax and revenue disputes fall to be adjudicated by special tax commissions (*Commissioni tributarie*), composed of judges and laymen with a specialization in financial and tax law (*see* DPR No. 636 of 26 October 1972).[32] Proceedings before the commissions are governed by the ordinary procedural rules of the CPC as applicable;
- the *Corte dei conti*, established by Law No. 800 of 14 August 1862, has, *inter alia*, jurisdictional functions in matters of accounting liability within the public administration and as concerns war and ordinary pensions. It now adjudicates cases on a regional basis;[33]
- the *Tribunale* (*regionale* and *superiore*) *delle acque pubbliche* (RD No. 1775 of 11 December 1933), also with a regional structure, has jurisdiction to adjudicate on public water rights;[34]
- the Constitutional Court (*Corte costituzionale*) performs a fundamental task in reviewing the constitutionality of ordinary and secondary legal provisions.

32. About this, I refer to Ricci, *supra*, 61 et seq.
33. *See* L. Montesano & G. Arieta, *Trattato di diritto processuale civile* (Padua: Cedam, 2001), 24.
34. On 11 Nov. 2002, *DL* No. 251 was approved, providing for, *inter alia*, the abolition of the *Tribunali delle acque pubbliche*; however, this specific provision was left out of the final conversion Law No. 1 of 10 Jan. 2003, and these *Tribunali* are therefore still vested with their jurisdiction.

29. It must be mentioned that also the *Consiglio superiore della Magistratura* (CSM, High Council of the Judiciary) and the National Bar Council (*Consiglio nazionale forense*) are considered to perform a jurisdictional activity when they exercise their disciplinary powers vis-à-vis magistrates and lawyers, respectively.[35]

IV. Different Models of Civil Proceedings

30. Even within civil jurisdiction, different procedures are followed, depending on the subject-matter of the dispute and\or the function of the type of proceedings chosen by the plaintiff. As a matter of fact, as it was pointed out already, a distinction must be drawn between full-cognizance proceedings, where the court's decision is released after an exhaustive evidence-gathering phase, granting the parties the chance to prove their respective cases, in an adversary mode; and summary proceedings, where a decision is rendered either without taking any evidence at all or after a summary ascertainment of the relevant facts, or on the basis of limited specific evidence. Against this background, the existence of different models for both ordinary and summary proceedings must be acknowledged in the context of the general basic model of proceedings at first instance before the *Tribunale*. As a matter of fact, Italian legislation provides for several different models of civil proceedings, in relation to the subject-matter of the disputes. Apart from those found in both the Code of Civil Procedure (CPC) and CC, a variety of types of proceedings can be found in special legislation.[36] The scenario therefore is very fragmented and sometimes confusing for both the lawyers and the judges. In an attempt to reduce the number of special proceedings available and simplify the situation, DLGS No. 150 of 2011, which entered into force on 6 October 2011, was enacted[37]: as many as twenty-eight special proceedings were redrafted, bringing each one of them within the boundaries of a general procedural 'model' (specifically, either ordinary, labour or summary proceedings, or rather, an adapted version of these 'models') This procedural simplification, however, did not really reach its aims, since, in reality the special proceedings converted into one of the three general models still maintain specific provisions. Moreover, the reform of 2011 did not consider the vast majority of special proceedings, in particular those found in the CC or in the CPC or which concern, among others, insolvency, family, minors, industrial property, consumer disputes. On the positive side, these special proceedings now are regulated in a comprehensive piece of legislation, which makes the life of both lawyers and judges easier.

The main procedural models available under Italian legislation are the following:

– labour and social security disputes are full-cognizance proceedings which follow the so-called *rito del lavoro*, that is, a more concentrated and fast procedure,

35. For a full list of all minor jurisdictional bodies *see* Montesano, Arieta, *supra*, 29.
36. V.P. Porreca, 'Il decreto legislativo sulla semplificazione dei riti: qualche osservazione iniziale', <www.judicium.it>, 1.
37. C. Consolo, 'Prime osservazioni introduttive sul d. lgs. n. 150/2011 di riordino (e relativa "semplificazione") dei riti settoriali', CG (2011): 1485.

where the parties' cases are however exhaustively ascertained. Unlike other countries, no autonomous labour courts exist in Italy. Until the 1990s, subject-matter competence was granted to a specific section of the *pretura* (*pretura del lavoro*) with its own offices, clerks and magistrates. After the elimination of the *pretura* in 1998, all labour and social security disputes entered into the subject-matter competence of a specific division of the Tribunale (*sezione lavoro del tribunale*);

- disputes concerning contracts of lease and free-loan of urban immovable properties or businesses (Article 447*bis* CPC) are subject to full-cognizance proceedings, to which a special concentrated procedure applies (*rito locatizio*), roughly based on the *rito del lavoro* (*see supra*). No specific section of the *Tribunale* has been created to handle these disputes;
- *legge* No. 69 of 18 June 2009 introduced a new procedural model for disputes where little evidence needs being gathered in order for the judge to decide (*procedimento sommario di cognizione*, Articles 702*bis* et seq. CPC, *see* paragraphs 343 et seq.);
- non-contentious jurisdiction (*giurisdizione volontaria*)[38] is administered by ordinary civil judges, but it is considered to have an administrative nature; here, the judge does not adjudicate disputes over rights; rather, he or she governs situations where relevant private and public interests are at stake;[39] a wide variety of proceedings fall within this category, in many different areas of the law (among others, family law, personal capacity, company law and so on). The codes and other statutes[40] usually provide for some peculiar procedural provision for each specific type of *azione volontaria*, which apply in combination with the general guidelines provided for by the code of civil procedure in the section dedicated to chambers proceedings (*see infra*, paragraphs 352 et seq.);
- disputes over most family and status matters are subject to specific procedures provided for by the CPC, the CC and other statutes. It is beyond the point of this monograph to enter into the details of these extremely variegated actions, especially since they are deeply influenced by their substantive content. Most notably, in the framework of ordinary proceedings before the *Tribunale*, legal separations and divorce proceedings are subject to some very specific rules (*see infra*, paragraphs 335 et seq.).Law No. 6 of 9 January 2004 has, *inter alia*, introduced new procedural provisions for the appointment of *amministratori di sostegno*[41] in favour of persons who, without being not in full possession of their faculties, because of some physical or psychological disability or infirmity appear to be wholly or partially unable to take care of their own interests;[42]
- small-claims disputes before the justice of the peace are subject to a special procedure, with a stronger stress on orality and less procedural preclusions.

38. *See* A. Jannuzzi, *Manuale della volontaria giurisdizione*, 8th edn (Milan: Giuffrè, 2000).
39. For example, the appointment of a guardian to a minor.
40. *See*, e.g., Arts 25–33 of DLGS No. 5 of 17 Jan. 2003, on company non-contentious proceedings.
41. *See* F. Danovi, 'Il procedimento per la nomina dell'amministratore di sostegno (L. 9 gennaio 2004, n. 6)', RDP (2004): 797; M.A. Lupoi, 'Profili processuali del rapporto tra l'amministrazione di sostegno e le altre misure di protezione dell'incapace', *Familia* (2006): 361.
42. G. Bonilini & A. Chizzini, *L'amministrazione di sostegno*, 2nd edn (Padua: Cedam, 2007).

§3. SOURCES OF CIVIL PROCEDURAL LAW

I. The Constitution

31. The Constitution sets the fundamental procedural rights and guarantees for every type of judicial proceedings. These superior provisions prevail over any lower rule and can be referred to both in the interpretation of positive law and in filling up legal lacunae. *See infra* for an analysis of the procedural guarantees provided for by the Constitution in relation to civil proceedings.

II. The Code of Civil Procedure and Its Reforms: Other Procedural Statutes

32. The code of civil procedure contains a comprehensive set of rules for civil proceedings in Italy.[43] As compared to other European countries, Italy's move towards the codification of (procedural) law came, rather late, in 1865, after the political unification of the nation.[44] The first post-unitarian code of civil procedure of 1865 was basically based on the former codes of Piedmont and rather old-fashioned as compared to the French model.[45]

After decades of discussions and projects,[46] the present code[47] entered into force on 21 April 1942, a rather hard time for justice (and the whole world at large). It was originally inspired by the three basic principles of procedure enunciated by Giuseppe Chiovenda, the father of Italian modern civil procedure: orality,[48] concentration and immediacy. Therefore, in order for the proceedings to be concentrated and speedy, rather strict preclusions were established with a major role played by oral over written defences. The post-war period, however, was not the right time for such an innovative system to meet with a positive reaction from the forensic community, especially since Italian lawyers traditionally opposed procedural preclusions of any kind. By 1950, under pressure from the lawyers' lobby, the basic characters of this new procedural system were reformed,[49] with the elimination of the so very much disliked preclusions. This has produced many negative side-effects, some still felt today in the chronic backlog of the courts.

43. *See* N. Trocker, '*Italian Civil Justice, an Introduction*', in *Civil justic in Italy*, 1 et seq. (M. De Cristofaro & N. Trocker eds., Jigakusha 2010).
44. Some of the small States into which Italy was previously divided had their own codes; however, other regions applied foreign codes, like Lombardia, ruled by the Austrians. For more details *see* L.P. Comoglio, C. Ferri & M. Taruffo, *Lezioni sul processo civile*, 2nd edn (Bologna: Il Mulino, 1998), 33 et seq.
45. For a historical overview, *see* N. Picardi, 'Il bicentenario del codice di procedura civile in Italia. Origine, evoluzione e crisi del monopolio statuale della procedura', in *Studi in onore di Modestino Acone*, vol. I (Naples: Jovene, 2010), 185 et seq.
46. *See* C. Mandrioli, *Corso di diritto processuale civile*, 10th edn, vol. I (Turin: Giappichelli, 1995), 425 et seq. and L.P. Comoglio, C. Ferri & M. Taruffo, *supra*, 39 et seq.
47. *RD* No. 1443 of 28 Oct. 1940.
48. *See* Vocino, 'Oralità del processo (diritto processuale civile)', in *Enciclopedia del diritto*, vol. XXX (Milan: Giuffè, 1980), 592 et seq.
49. Law No. 581 of 14 Jul. 1950 and *DPR* No. 657 of 18 Oct. 1950.

33. The code of civil procedure is composed of four books: the first sets down common principles for all civil judicial activities, with a particular focus on ordinary cognizance proceedings; the second book deals with ordinary cognizance proceedings (*processo di cognizione ordinario*), the third with enforcement of decisions and other enforcement titles and the fourth with a mixed bag of particular cognizance proceedings (for labour, lease contracts, legal separation disputes), summary proceedings (*decreto ingiuntivo*, interim relief and so on), alternative disputes resolution systems (arbitration). As an appendix to the code, one must also consider the *disposizioni di attuazione* (implementing provisions),[50] which regulate the fine details of some of the mechanisms to which the code refers.

34. Between the 1950s and the 1980s, only sectorial innovations were introduced in the code. Arguably, in these matters, the most important pieces of legislation of the times were the Divorce Act of 1970,[51] which introduced divorce and divorce proceedings in Italy, and the new provisions on labour disputes of 1973,[52] which radically innovated and substituted the previous rules contained in the code.[53]

A wide debate was, however, developing concerning structural reforms of the judicial system, in order to face the ever-growing crisis of civil justice. Initial plans to draft a new code of civil procedure were, however, soon shelved and less ambitious projects to reform the existing code started to circulate. Finally, Law No. 353 of 26 November 1990 was enacted, with some major innovations to the CPC, most notably a new preclusions system for ordinary proceedings at first instance and an increased role for the single trial judge of the *Tribunale*. This reform met with a lot of hostility especially from the lawyers. Entry into force (as a whole) of Law 353/90, originally scheduled for 1 January 1992, kept on being postponed until mid-1995. Moreover, the lawyers' reaction against the reform was so fierce[54] that its original rules only were effective for a few weeks, before being somehow 'toned down' by a further act of Parliament which diluted the preclusions and time limits for the defendant and reorganized the initial phase of the proceedings.[55]

Most new provisions brought by Law No. 353/90 only applied to proceedings started (at first instance) on or after 2 May 1995. Proceedings pending at that date were still subject to the so-called *vecchio rito* (old procedure), that is, to the original rules of the code of 1942, as reformed in 1950, as well as to some minor provisions of the law 353/90. In an attempt to deal with the backlog of such 'old procedure' disputes, special sections within the tribunals were eventually instituted (*sezioni stralcio*)[56] for several years, with laymen appointed as judges (*giudici onorari*

50. RD No. 1368 of 18 Dec. 1941.
51. Law No. 898 of 1 Dec. 1970, as reformed by Law No. 74 of 6 Mar. 1987.
52. Law No. 533 of 11 Aug. 1973.
53. Other minor procedural provisions are contained in Law No. 532 of 8 Aug. 1977, Law No. 793 of 18 Oct. 1977 and Law No. 399 of 30 Jul. 1984.
54. A strike went on for weeks, to have the new system of preclusions changed.
55. *See* F. Cabrini, M.A., Lupoi, in: Carpi, Taruffo (eds), *Commentario breve al codice di procedura civile, Appendice di aggiornamento* (Padua, Cedam, 1996).
56. Law No. 27 of 22 Jul. 1997.

aggregati: *GOA*). In practice, for many different reasons, these *sezioni stralcio* did not prove to be an efficient and effective solution to the backlog problem.

35. The reform of 1990 was immediately followed by another very innovative piece of legislation, that is, Law No. 374 of 21 November 1991, instituting the *giudici di pace* (justices of the peace) as small-claim courts of first instance, taking the place of the *giudice conciliatore*, with a wider competence and specific procedural rules (*see infra*, paragraph 156). Also this law entered into force after many delays in 1995.

36. The final part of the 1990s was characterized by many important procedural reforms:

– the introduction of the single monocratic judge at first instance (DLGS No. 51 of 19 February 1998):[57] the *pretura* (an intermediate Court of First Instance between the *conciliatore* and the *Tribunale*) was eliminated, and the disputes pending therein transferred to the *Tribunale*; moreover, proceedings before the *Tribunale* were drastically reformed. In the code of 1942, any dispute before the tribunal fell to be decided by a panel of three judges (the so-called *collegio*), after a single judge of the panel (the *giudice istruttore*) had prepared the case, in particular, gathering the necessary evidence, so that the dispute came before the panel only when it was ready to be decided (at least in part). Already the reform of 1990 had introduced, for many disputes, the so-called *giudice monocratico*, that is, a single judge to both instruct and decide the case. The panel decision, however, was still, so to speak, the rule. *DLGS* 51/98 drastically reformed the situation, thereby relegating the role of the panel decision to important but (comparatively) few disputes, listed in Article 50*bis* CPC, and leaving all the other litigation to the monocratic judge;

  This reform has been rather well accepted, especially since the elimination of the *pretura* has made redundant many of the competence problems posed by the previous co-existence of as many as three courts of first instance, even if it must be remarked that a panel decision could grant more careful consideration of a case. It must be pointed out, however, that expectations that this reform would help reduce the courts' backlog have proved to be unrealistic;
– the transfer of the subject-matter competence for (most) public labour disputes from the administrative to the ordinary civil courts (DLGS No. 80 of 31 March 1998), which already had competence for private labour disputes. This concentration of hundreds of thousands of disputes has obviously created a congestion of the courts, both at first instance and at the appeal level;
– a first reform of arbitration (Law No. 25 of 5 January 1994): the old rules of the code, originally influenced by an heavy anti-arbitration bias, were abrogated with a comprehensive reform of both domestic and international arbitration, characterized by a favour for this ADR method, promoting substantial equivalence between a judgment and an arbitration award (*see infra*, paragraphs 429 et seq.);

57. More details in L.P. Comoglio, C. Ferri & M. Taruffo, *supra*, 181.

– the partial reform of the judicial sale of immovable assets (Law No. 302 of 3 August 1998), most notably with the possibility for the court to delegate the sale of seized goods to a public notary.

37. The reforms of the 1990s have been followed by a continuous flow of reforms, which tried to solve the problems of Italian civil procedural law, most notably the exceedingly long duration of the proceedings. The CPC of 1940 was actually never completely revised but, reform after reform, most of its original provisions have been more or less extensively modified and new rules have entered it. Moreover, many new statutes have been enacted alongside the code, in the context of the so-called de-codification process.

In its recent efforts at amending the Italian procedural system, the lawmaker does not appear to be following a strategic plan, preferring a 'patchwork approach', touching several different institutions and parts of the code in a piecemeal way. The main motivator for the last waves of procedural reforms has been the need to reduce the exceedingly long duration of civil proceedings in Italy. The Italian lawmaker has approached this most important problem with the incantation that the time required to obtain a judgment in Italy could be reduced by simply intervening on the procedural mechanisms rather than through a radical intervention at the structural level. Crucially, no new investments have been made in the judicial service, preferring 'zero-budget' reforms of procedural provisions. Not surprisingly, these latest reforms do not appear to have solved the problems faced by Italian civil justice. As a matter of fact, changing the procedural mechanisms is not enough to reduce the delay in the adjudication of cases and the courts backlog, especially since, at the decision stage, disputes still have to be solved on an individual basis and the time a judge needs to render his decision may not be reduced by statute. One positive factor to take into consideration in this context, however, is the extremely high productivity rate of Italian judges in recent statistics. Together with some beneficial effects deriving from the newly introduced ADR preliminary systems, this appears to have led, in recent times, to a small but encouraging decrease in the courts' backlog.[58]

The first main wave of reforms came in the years 2005 and 2006, with what has been defined as a tsunami of procedural legislation, mainly in an attempt to shorten the duration of civil proceedings.[59] The legislator's ideas, however, were far from clear and as many as three different statutes were promulgated, in the space of a few months, before the new reforms could be deemed ready to enter into force, on 1 March 2006. In particular, mention must be made to Law No. 80 of 14 May 2005, Law No. 263 of 28 December 2005 and Law No. 52 of 24 February 2006; from here on, I will refer to these pieces of legislation as the reforms of 2005–2006.

These statutes touched upon many rules in the code of civil procedure, especially in relation to special cognizance proceedings, interim relief and enforcement

58. *See also* R- Caponi, 'The performance of the Italian civil justice system: an empirical assessment', ILJ (2016): 15.

59. *See* F. Carpi, 'Linee di tendenza delle recenti riforme processuali', RTDPC (2006): 849; M. De Cristofaro, 'Il nuovo processo civile "competitivo" secondo la l. 80/2005', RTDPC (2006): 171; F.P. Luiso & B. Sassani, *La riforma del processo civile. Commentario breve agli articoli riformati del codice di procedura civile* (Milan: Giuffrè, 2006).

proceedings. As a general rule, these new provisions only apply to proceedings brought on or after 1 March 2006. With some limited exceptions, cases already pending at that date continue to follow the old rules (i.e., the CPC as reformed in 1990, *see supra*, paragraph 34). The reform of enforcement proceedings, however, has been granted an immediate application also to pending cases where the sale of the seized goods had not yet been authorized by the judge.[60]

In the months and years following the reform of 2005–2006, some other important procedural reforms have been enacted. Already in February 2006, DLGS No. 40 brought throughout reforms of both the proceedings before the Court of Cassation and arbitration. Some of the new rules on the *Cassazione*, however, proved to be rather problematic and unpopular. As a matter of fact, after a few years, Law No. 69 of 18 June 2009, *inter alia*, brought further extensive innovations to these types of proceedings.

Law No. 69 also introduced several reforms to other parts of the CPC. The new provisions, as a rule, only apply to proceedings started from July 2009.[61]

As a matter of fact, today, in Italian civil courts, proceedings may be subject to several different sets of provisions, depending, in general, on the law applicable at the time the claim was first brought at first instance. This, of course, is rather confusing for practitioners and judges.

The rules of the CPC were further modified by Law No. 183 of 2010 (the so-called *Collegato lavoro*) in relation to labour proceedings, in the context of a wider reform of labour law.

Since 2011, a continuous stream of legislative reforms has poured out of Parliament. The lawmaker, strenuously trying to reduce the duration of civil proceedings but without a well-defined action-plan, started drafting several pieces of legislation concerning different aspects of civil justice.[62] The general guidelines of such ‘reforms’ can be identified as improving the efficiency of judicial resources and reducing the courts’ backlog by making it more expensive to litigate and by limiting access to the appeal level. Several of the innovations thus introduced proved to be very controversial among lawyers who have protested at various levels alleging that they lead to a denial of justice.[63]

In recent years, the lawmaker’s attention seems to be concentrated on enforcement proceedings, which have been subject to several piecemeal innovations.

---

60. *See* F. Cordopatri, ‘Le nuove norme sull’esecuzione forzata’, RDP (2005): 755.
61. R. Caponi, *Italian Civil Justice Reform 2009* (ZZPint 2009); M.A. Lupoi, *Recent Developments in Italian Civil Procedure Law*, 3 Civ. Proc. Rev. 25 (2012).
62. Concerning the recent legislative ‘technique’ in procedural matters *see* B. Capponi, ‘Il diritto processuale civile “non sostenibile”’, RTDPC (2013): 855.
63. On this recent wave of procedural reforms, *see* R. Martino & A. Panzarola (eds), *Commentario alle riforme del processo civile dalla semplificazione dei riti al decreto sviluppo* (Turin: Giappichelli, 2013); R. De Nictolis, *Riti speciali di cognizione. Commentario al d. lgs. 1° settembre 2011, n. 150* (Bologna: Zanichelli, 2012); C. Vellani, ‘I processi civili dopo le manovre di stabilizzazione finanziaria e di sviluppo del 2011’, RTDPC (2012): 345.

38. Other important rules or principles of civil procedure (or rules relating to the civil judicial system) can be found outside the CPC, in statutes and other acts of Parliament. It is impossible (and possibly pointless) to refer to them all. Some of them, however, are particularly important and deserve being mentioned here:

– RD No. 12 of 30 January 1941, which regulates the courts' judicial system in Italy (*ordinamento giudiziario*) and the subsequent legislation (*see infra*, paragraphs 83 et seq.).
– The procedural rules contained in the Insolvency Act of 1942,[64] as extensively modified by DLGS No. 5 of 9 January 2006[65] and DLGS No. 169 of 12 September 2007.[66] In Italy, insolvency law is considered as an autonomous branch of the law, somehow in between commercial and civil procedural law. Without entering into any detail, it must be pointed out that special bankruptcy sections (*sezioni fallimentari*) are instituted in the *Tribunali* to deal with insolvency proceedings. A comprehensive reform of the existing proceedings in this area of the law is expected in the near future, after Law No. 155 of 19 October 2017 delegated the Government to reform the substantial and procedural aspects of enterprises crisis and insolvency.
– The reform of private and procedural international law (Law No. 218 of 31 May 1995):[67] this statute provided for a new comprehensive set of rules for the matters at hand, previously split between the preliminary part of the CC (private international law) and the code of civil procedure (procedural international law). As concerns us here, Articles 2–5 CPC (on international jurisdiction of the Italian courts) and Articles 796–805 CPC (on recognition and enforcement of foreign decisions, the so-called *delibazione*) were abrogated and substituted for Articles 3–11 and 64–72 of l. 218/95 respectively (*see infra*, paragraphs 139 et seq. and 423 et seq.).
– The establishment of a procedural mechanism to grant compensation for unreasonably long delays in the adjudication of a dispute (Law No. 89 of 24 March 2001, the so-called *legge Pinto*) (*see infra*, paragraph 65).
– The introduction of a 'testo unico', gathering together all the relevant provisions in matters of legal costs, judicial fees and legal aid formerly dispersed in several different pieces of legislation (DPR No. 115 of 2002).[68]
– The regulation of mediation in civil and commercial matters: DLGS No. 28 of March 2010 (*see* paragraphs 450 et seq.).

64. *RD* No. 267 of 16 Mar. 1942 (*legge fallimentare*).
65. *See* A. Jorio & M. Fabiani (eds), *Il nuovo diritto fallimentare* (Bologna: Zanichelli, 2006); M. Fabiani, 'Le trasformazioni della legge fallimentare', FI (2005): V, 153.
66. *See La nuova legge fallimentare. L'analisi del Rd 267/1942 alla luce dell'ultimo dlgs correttivo*, GD *Dossier mensile*, 2007, No. 9.
67. *See* 'Riforma del sistema italiano di diritto internazionale privato: l. 31 maggio 1995, n. 218, Commentario', RDIPP (1995): 905 et seq.; S. Bariatti (ed.), 'Riforma del sistema italiano di diritto internazionale privato', NLCC (1996): 877 et seq.
68. *See Il Testo Unico delle spese di giustizia. Le norme, le novità e l'analisi degli esperti*, GD *Dossier mensile*, 2002, No. 7.

39. It has to be noticed that, in recent years, almost every piece of Italian legislation dealing with new matters or institutions has also introduced sectorial procedural provisions (e.g., concerning specific remedies or ADR mechanisms). It is impossible here to mention every relevant rule or statute; suffice then to briefly refer to the following:

- DLGS No. 68 of 9 April 2003, on the harmonization of certain aspects of copyright law, developing ADR mechanisms (Article 35) and introducing specific forms of interim relief, including a version of the French *astreinte* (Article 24).[69]
- DLGS No. 70 of 9 April 2003, dealing with certain aspects of electronic commerce, whose Article 19 provides for voluntary ADR mechanisms.
- DLGS No. 168 of 27 June 2003, instituting specialized sections in some *Tribunali* and courts of appeal to deal with disputes over industrial and intellectual property rights; in disputes falling in this subject-matter, *DLGS* No. 30 of 10 February 2005 ('Code of industrial property rights'), at Article 134, basically provided for the application of the so-called *processo societario* (*DLGS* 5/2003). This provision, however, was soon deemed to be unconstitutional,[70] since the relevant delegating statute[71] only did authorize the Government to reform the substantive aspects of industrial property rights and not the procedural ones also.
- DLGS No. 196 of 30 June 2003 (the so-called Privacy code),[72] whose Article 52 concerns the protection of personal data contained in judicial decisions and arbitral awards.
- DLGS No. 215 of 9 July 2003, on the equal treatments of persons, irrespective of their race and ethnic origin.[73]
- DLGS No. 216 of 9 July 2003, on the equal treatment of workers, providing for rules on the judicial protection of rights (Article 4) and on the legal standing of trade unions to bring actions to protect the workers' rights (Article 5).[74]
- DLGS No. 82 of 7 March 2005, as modified by *DLGS* No. 159 of 4 April 2006 (the so-called E-governance code), whose Articles 20 et seq. contain provisions on the evidentiary value of electronic documents and electronic signatures.
- DLGS No. 206 of 6 September 2005 (the so-called Consumer Code), with procedural provisions referring to advertisement claims (Article 26), the legal standing of consumer associations, consumer actions, interim relief, ADR mechanisms (Articles 136–141).
- DLGS No. 209 of 7 September 2005 (the so-called Code for private insurance contracts), establishing new extra-judicial devices for the speedy determination of road accidents damages.

---

69. M. Barbuto, *L'inibitoria ad alta efficacia deterrente*, GD 19 (2003): 62.
70. *Corte cost.* 17 May 2007, n. 170, *Merito*, 2007, No. 6, 27; *see* B. Sassani, 'Eccessi di delega, rito societario e proprietà industriale', <www.judicium.it>.
71. Law No. 273 of 12 Dec. 2002.
72. *See Il codice della privacy. Le novità del Dlgs 196/2003 e i commenti degli esperti*, GD *Dossier mensile*, 2003, No. 8.
73. *See* M. Gentile, 'Attribuita la legittimazione ad agire in giudizio alle associazioni iscritte nell'apposito registro', GD 37 (2003): 25.
74. *See* F. Ciampi, 'Con la relazione alla Commissione europea una verifica sull'efficacia delle norme', GD 37 (2003): 39.

- Law No. 54 of 8 February 2006, on parental rights, introducing the so-called joint custody of minors as well as several procedural remedies and provisions for custody and alimony proceedings.[75]
- Law No. 67 of 1 March 2006, for the safeguard of persons with disabilities against discriminations, with provisions concerning legal standing, judicial proceedings and burden of the proof.
- DLGS No. 198 of 11 April 2006, No. 198 (the so-called Code for equal opportunities between men and women),[76] with specific provisions (Articles 36 et seq.) on legal standing, special procedures, interim relief.
- Law No. 99 of 23 July 2009, which introduced a completely revised Article 140*bis* in the Consumer Code, on class actions (*see* paragraphs 361 et seq.).
- Law No. 219 of 10 December 2012 and DLGS No. 154 of 28 December 2013, revising the status of children born out of wedlock in order to treat them on an equal footing as children born of married parents, introducing, in particular, new rules as to the subject-matter jurisdiction of ordinary and juvenile Tribunals and provisions as to the hearing of a child's opinion in the course of judicial proceedings.[77]
- DL No. 13 of 17 February 2017 converted into Law No. 46 of 13 April 2017, creating specialized sections within the *Tribunali* to deal with international protection and immigration cases.

III. European Sources of Procedural Law

40. When dealing with sources of procedural law in Italy today, it must be remarked that, after the Amsterdam Treaty, procedural matters fall within the scope of European law, insomuch as the Union intervention in this area of the law is necessary for the proper functioning of the Common Market, in compliance with the subsidiarity principle. These issues are now regulated by Articles 67 et seq. of the Lisbon Treaty.

41. Several European regulations have already been implemented in various important areas of civil procedure. When a regulation enters into force, it is self-executing and automatically prevails over conflicting domestic provisions within its scope of application. Community regulations concern transnational proceedings, that is, civil proceedings where some 'foreign' community element is present. It is easy to foresee, however, that, within the current movement towards harmonization of both substantial and procedural law in Europe and worldwide, the Member States

---

75. *See* M.A. Lupoi, 'Aspetti processuali della normativa sull'affidamento condiviso', RTDPC (2006): 1063.
76. *See* I. Tricomi, 'Un intervento di semplificazione necessario che dimentica le competenze del Titolo V', GD 28 (2006): 41.
77. *See* M.A. Lupoi, 'Il procedimento della crisi tra genitori non coniugati avanti al tribunale ordinario', RTDPC (2013): 1289; L. Querzola, 'Riforma della filiazione e processo: nuove sfumature delle categorie giuridiche tradizionali?', RTDPC (2013): 1041; F. Tommaseo, 'I procedimenti de potestate e la nuova legge sulla filiazione', RDP (2013): 558.

will tend to uniform their domestic rules to the ones applicable vis-à-vis other Member States.

The procedural regulations approved this far are:

- Regulation No. 1346/2000 of 29 May 2000,[78] on insolvency proceedings,[79] which entered into force on 31 May 2002; since 26 June 2017, however, the recast Regulation No. 2015/848, of 20 May 2015 is applicable.
- Regulation No. 1347/2000 of 29 May 2000,[80] on jurisdiction and recognition, and enforcement of judgments in matrimonial and parental responsibility matters, which entered into force on 31 May 2001;[81] this regulation has been substituted for by Regulation No. 2201/03 of 27 November 2003 (Brussels II*bis*),[82] which entered into force on 1 August 2004, but whose rules are applied only as of 1 March 2005.[83]

---

78. A. Fumagalli, 'Il regolamento comunitario sulle procedure di insolvenza', RDP (2001): 677; R. Caponi, 'Il regolamento comunitario sulle procedure di insolvenza', FI (2002): V, 220; E. Consalvi, 'Recognition and Enforcement of Judgments under the EC Regulation on Insolvency Proceedings', <www.judicium.it>; E. Frascaroli Santi, 'Prospettive di riforma del sistema concorsuale italiano e incidenza del regolamento comunitario sulle procedure di insolvenza', in *Studi in memoria di Angelo Bonsignori*, vol. II (Milan: Giuffrè, 2004), 1167; M.A. Lupoi, 'Conflitti di giurisdizioni e di decisioni nel regolamento sulle procedure di insolvenza; il caso 'Eurofood' e non solo', RTDPC (2005): 1393; C. Punzi, 'Le procedure d'insolvenza transfrontaliere nell'Unione europea', RDP (2003): 997.
79. GD 25 (2000): 106; the Regulation is based on the Brussels Convention of 23 Nov. 1995, about which *see* Carbone, 'Il c. d. fallimento internazionale tra riforma italiana del diritto internazionale privato e normativa di diritto uniforme', *Diritto del commercio inter-nazionale* (1998): 633; P. Gottwald, 'Le insolvenze transfrontaliere: tendenza e soluzioni europee e mondiali', RTDPC (1999): 149.
80. In OJEC, L. 160, 30 Jun. 2000, 9 et seq.
81. *See* M.A. Lupoi *Brussels II: New Rules for Transnational Matrimonial Disputes*, in *Essays on Transnational and Comparative Civil Procedure* 105–154 (Carpi & Lupoi ed. Giappichelli 2001).
82. G. Biagioni, 'Il nuovo regolamento comunitario sulla giurisdizione e sull'efficacia delle decisioni in materia matrimoniale e di responsabilità dei genitori', RDI (2004): 991; M. De Cristofaro, in Bonilini, Chizzini, Confortini (eds), *Codice ipertestuale di separazione e divorzio. Commentario con banca dati di giurisprudenza e legislazione* (Turin: Utet, 2005, 895); F. Salerno, 'I criteri di giurisdizione comunitari in materia matrimoniale', RDIPP (2007): 63; Tomasi, 'Doppia cittadinanza e giurisdizione in materia matrimoniale nel Reg. no. 2201/2003 ("Bruxelles II bis")', *Int'l lis* 4 (2008): 13.
83. Italian case law on this Regulation is already quite rich. For example, as concerns the rules on jurisdiction, *see Trib.* Brindisi 1 Aug. 2006, *decr.*, RDIPP, 207, 438, on Art. 12(3); *Cass. SU* 2 Nov. 2007, n. 23030, RDIPP, 2009, 104; *App.* Bologna 6 May 2008, n. 686, <www.giuraemilia.it>, on Art. 8; *Trib. min.* Catania 23 Jul. 2008, *decr.*, FM, 2008, No. 11, 89; *Trib.* Belluno 6 Mar. 2009, n. 106, FD, 2010, 179, *App.* Caltanissetta 4 May 2009, FM, 2009, No. 6, 54; *Trib. min.* Genova 11 Dec. 2009, *decr.*, FM, 2010, No. 9, 61, on Art. 15; *Cass. SU* 17 febbraio 2010, n. 3680, *ord.*, RTDPC, 2010, 750; *Trib.* Varese 4 Oct. 2010, *decr.*, <www.ilcaso.it>, on Art. 10; *Trib.* Belluno 5 Nov. 2010, n. 221, FM, 2011, No. 1, 45. With reference to abduction of minors, *see Trib. min.* Cagliari 26 Nov. 2007, n. 590, FM, 2008, No. 2, 16; *Cass.* 27 May 2008, n. 13829, RDIPP, 2009, 416; *Cass.* 7 Jul. 2008, n. 18614, GI, 2009, 1110; *Trib. min.* Emilia Romagna 7 May 2009, FD, 2010, 38. On recognition of foreign decisions in Italy, *see App.* Milano 19 Aug. 2006, *decr.*, RDIPP, 2007, 739, on Art. 42; *Cass.* 20 Dec. 2006, n. 27188, RDIPP, 2007, 1093; *Trib.* Bari 9 Dec. 2007, GM, 2010, 659; *Trib.* Bari 27 Apr. 2009, FD, 2009, 852; *Cass.* 16 Oct. 2009, n. 22093, RDIPP, 2010, 463; *Cass. SU* 21 Oct. 2009, n. 22238, RDIPP, 2010, 474.

– Regulation No. 1348/2000 of 29 May 2000,[84] on service and communication of judicial and extra-judicial acts in civil and commercial matters,[85] which entered into force on 31 May 2001; from 13 November 2008, this Regulation has been substituted for by Regulation No. 1393/2007, of 13 November 2007.[86]
– Regulation No. 1206/2001 of 28 May 2001, on the taking of evidence abroad in civil and commercial matters,[87] which entered into force on 1 July 2001 (but whose rules began to be applied, for the most part, only from 1 January 2004).[88]
– Regulation No. 805/2004 of 21 April 2004, introducing a European enforcement order for uncontested claims, which entered into force on 21 January 2005 but is applied only as of 21 October 2005, with the exceptions of Articles 30–32.[89]
– Regulation No. 1896/2006 of 12 December 2006, introducing harmonized proceedings for a European payment order, which entered into force on 31 December 2006 but are applied only from 12 December 2008, with the exception of Articles 28–31, applicable since 12 June 2008;[90] Italy has not yet adopted a

---

84. P. Biavati, 'Notificazioni e comunicazioni in Europa', RTDPC (2002): 501; M. De Cristofaro, 'La nuova disciplina delle notificazioni infracomunitarie in materia civile', *Studium juris* (2001): 517; F. Cordopatri, 'Note sul regolamento CE n. 1348/2000 del Consiglio del 29 maggio 2000, relativo alla notificazione e alla comunicazione negli Stati membri degli atti giudiziari ed extragiudiziali in materia civile o commerciale', in *Studi in memoria di Angelo Monsignori, supra*, vol. I, 309; F. Tommaseo, 'Sulle notificazioni internazionali nello spazio giuridico europeo', RDP (2005): 407.
85. GD 24 (200): 110. The Regulation is based on the convention of 26 May 1997, *International litigation procedure*, 1998, 693.
86. S.A. Villata, 'Il regolamento C.E. n. 1393/2007 sulle notificazioni di atti giudiziari nell'ambito degli Stati membri', RDP (2009): 153.
87. OJEC, L-174, 27 Jun. 2001, 1 et seq.
88. C. Besso, *Taking of Evidence Abroad: From the 1970 Hague Convention to the 2001 European Regulation*, in *International Civil Litigation in Europe and Relations with Third States* (A. Nuyts & N. Watté eds, Bruxelles 2005); P. Biavati, 'Problemi aperti in materia di assunzione delle prove civili in Europa', RTDPC (2005): 425; R. Bonatti, 'Sovranità nazionale e leggi processuali nell'armonizzazione del diritto delle prove in Europa', RTDP (2004): 211; A. Giussani, 'L'esibizione di documenti situati nello spazio giuridico europeo', RTDPC (2002): 867; N. Trocker, 'Note sul regolamento n. 1206/2001 relativo all'assunzione delle prove in materia civile o commerciale', RDI (2003): 670; Ubertazzi, 'Il regolamento comunitario sulle prove e la descrizione della contraffazione', RDIPP (2008): 689.
89. P. Biavati, *Some Remarks About the European Regulation Creating an Enforcement Order for Uncontested Claims*, in *Essays in Honour of Konstantinos D. Kerameus*, vol. I, 75 (AthensBruxelles 2009); N. Boschiero, *The Forthcoming European Enforcement Order. Towards a European Law Enforcement Area*, RDI 394 (2003); G. Campeis & A. De Pauli, 'Prime riflessioni sul titolo esecutivo europeo per i crediti non contestati (regolamento n. 805/2004/CE)', GC (2004), II, 529; F. Carpi, 'L'ordine di pagamento europeo tra efficacia della tutela e garanzia della difesa', RDP (2002): 688; C. Crifò, *First Steps Towards the Harmonisation of Civil Procedure: The Regulation Creating a European Enforcement Order for Uncontested Claims*, Civ. just. quar. 200 (2005); G. Olivieri, 'Il titolo esecutivo europeo (qualche considerazione sul Reg. CE 805/ 2004 del 21 aprile 2004)', <www.judicium.it>. Italian case law on this Regulation is still rather scarce: *see Trib.* Milan 30 Nov. 2007, *decr.*, FI, 2009, I, 936; *Trib.* La Spezia 7 Feb. 2008, *ord.*, RDIPP, 2009, 735; *Trib.* Milan 23 Apr. 2008, *ord.*, FI, 2009, I, 936; *Trib.* Mantova 24 Sep. 2009, RDIPP, 2010, 149; *Trib.* Monza 1 Febbraio 2010, <www.ilcaso.it>.
90. G. Porcelli, 'La 'nuova' proposta di procedimento europeo di ingiunzione di pagamento', RTDPC (2006): 1259; G. Campeis & A. De Pauli, 'Prime riflessioni sul procedimento europeo di ingiunzione di pagamento (regolamento n. 1896/2006/CE)', GC (2007): II, 355; A. Carratta, 'Il procedimento ingiuntivo europeo e la "comunitarizzazione" del diritto processuale civile', RDP (2007): 1514; E. D'Alessandro, *Choosing among the Three Regulations Creating a European Enforcement*

national statute to coordinate the provisions of the European Regulation with the internal rules of procedure. Therefore, courts are filling the gaps of Regulation No. 1896 with rather different solutions, especially as concerns the procedural phase following the opposition of the debtor and the passage to the ascertainment of the merits of the credit.[91]

- Regulation No. 861/2007 of 11 July 2007, introducing uniform European rules for small-claims proceedings, applicable since 1 January 2009.[92]
- Regulation No. 4/2009 of 18 December 2008, on jurisdiction, applicable law, recognition and enforcement of decisions, and cooperation in matters of alimony obligations, applicable since 18 June 2011.[93]
- Regulation No. 650/2012, of 4 July 2012, on jurisdiction, applicable law, recognition and enforcement of decisions and acceptance and enforcement of authentic instruments in matters of succession and on the creation of a European Certificate of Succession, applicable since 17 August 2015.[94]
- Regulation No. 1215/2012 of 12 December 2012, on jurisdiction, recognition and enforcement of decisions in civil and commercial matters, applicable since

---

Order (EEO Regulation, EOP Regulation, ESCP Regulation): Practical Guidelines, 1 Int'lis 39 (2010); M.A. Lupoi, 'Di crediti non contestati e procedimenti di ingiunzione: le ultime tappe dell'armonizzazione processuale in Europa', RTDPC (2008): 171; A. Mondini, 'Il Regolamento (CE) 12 dicembre 2006, n. 1896, sul procedimento europeo d'ingiunzione di pagamento in materia di controversie transfrontaliere, civili o commerciali', <www.judicium.it>.

91. For an example, *see Trib.* Piacenza 18 Sep. 2010, <www.giuraemilia.it>.

92. J.P. Cortés Diéguez, *Does the Proposed European Procedure Enhance the Resolution of Small Claims?*, Civ. just. quar. 83 (2008); E. D'Alessandro, *Choosing among the Three Regulations Creating a European Enforcement Order (EEO Regulation, EOP Regulation, ESCP Regulation): Practical Guidelines*, 1 Int'lis 39 (2010); A. Leandro, 'Il procedimento europeo per le controversie di modesta entità', RDI (2009): 65; V. Pozzi, 'Il rito bagattellare europeo', RTDPC (2008): 611; X. Kramer, *Harmonisation of Procedures in Europe: The Proposal for a European Small Claims Procedure*, Int'l lis 109 (2006).

93. P. Franzina, 'Sul *forum necessitatis* nello spazio giudiziario europeo', RDI (2009): 1121; A. Malatesta, 'La convenzione e il protocollo dell'Aja del 2007 in materia di alimenti', RDIPP (2009): 829; A. Pancaldi, 'La disciplina processualcivilistica delle obbligazioni alimentari alla luce del nuovo regolamento Ce n. 4 del 2009', RDPC (2010): 1353; Pocar &Viarenzo, 'Il regolamento (CE) n. 4/2009 in materia di obbligazioni alimentari', RDIPP (2009): 805.

94. Leandro (ed), *Il diritto internazionale privato europeo delle successioni mortis causa*, (Milan: Giuffrè, 2013); T. Ballarino, 'Il nuovo regolamento europeo sulle successioni', RDI (2013): 1116; A. Bonomi, 'Successions internationales – conflits de lois et de jurisdictions', Recueil des cours de l'academie de droit international de la Haye (2010): 71; E. Calò, 'L'inarrestabile declino della cittadinanza altrui: il Regolamento (UE) n. 650/2012 del 4 luglio 2012', CG (2013): 549.

January 2015[95] recasting and taking the place of Regulation No. 44/2011, of 22 December 2000.[96]

- Regulation No. 655/2014 of 15 May 2014, establishing a European account preservation order procedure to facilitate cross-border debt recovery in civil and commercial matters, applicable since January 2017.

§4. General Features of the Administration of Justice in Civil Matters

I. Characteristics of the Procedure

42. Civil proceedings can be defined as a chain of connected and consequent acts and orders, which starts with a party's claim and ends with the judge's decision. In between, the subject-matter of the dispute must be, so to speak, prepared for judgment in compliance with the contradiction principle, that is, by granting the counterpart the chance to fully and effectively resist the plaintiff's action and raise defences and/or related claims and for both parties to prove the facts on which their respective claims are based.

43. Civil proceedings are governed by several most important principles which shape the very notion of civil justice in Italy. Most of them have now been incorporated into Constitutional provisions and may be considered as fundamental rights of the individual. It is therefore necessary to analyse them in some depth.

---

95. F. Pocar & Viarengo & F. Villata, *Recasting Brussels I* (Cedam 2012); P. Biavati, *Judicial Cooperation in Europe: Is Exequatur Still Necessary??*, IJPL 403 (2011); F. Carpi, 'L'esecutorietà delle sentenze e l'opposizione nel regolamento n. 44 del 2001 e le recenti modifiche', RTDPC (20113): 59; E. D'Alessandro, 'Il titolo esecutivo europeo nel sistema del regolamento n. 1215/2012', in RDP (2013): 1044; M. De Cristofaro, *The Abolition of Exequatur Proceedings: Speeding Up the Free Movement of Judgments While Preserving the Rights of the Defense*, IJPL 432 (2011); P. Franzina, *The Proposed New Rule of Special Jurisdiction Regarding Rights In Rem in Moveable Property: A Good Option for a Reformed Brussels I Regulation?*, Dir. comm. int. 789 (2011); C. Honorati, *Provisional Measures and the Recast of Brussles I Regulation: A Missed Opportunity for a Better Ruling*, RDIPP 525 (2012); A. Leandro, 'Prime osservazioni sul regolamento (UE) n. 1215/2012 ("Bruxelles I bis")', GPC (2013): 583; O. Lopes Pegna, 'Il regime di circolazione delle decisioni nel regolamento (UE) n. 1215/2012 ("Bruxelles I-bis")', RDI (2013): 1206; M.A. Lupoi, 'La nuova disciplina della litispendenza e della connessione tra cause nel regolamento Ue n. 1215 del 2012', RTDPC (2013): 1425; L. Querzola, 'Il nuovo sistema delle misure provvisorie e cautelari nel reg. Ue n. 1215 del 2012, RTDPC (2012): 1479; L. Radicati di Brozolo, *Arbitration and the Draft Revised Brussels I Regulation: Seeds of Home Country Control and of Harmonization?* 7 IJPL 423 (2011); C. Silvestri, 'Recasting Brussels I: il nuovo regolamento n. 1215 del 2012', RTDPC (2013): 677.

96. *See* E. Merlin, 'Riconoscimento ed esecutività della decisione straniera nel Regolamento "Bruxelles I"', RDP (2001): 433; E. Merlin, 'Novità sui criteri di giurisdizione nel Regolamento CE "Bruxelles I"', *Int'l lis* (2002/03): 1, 40; F. Salerno, *Giurisdizione ed efficacia delle decisioni straniere nel regolamento (CE) n. 44/2001 (La revisione della convenzione di Bruxelles del 1968)*, 3rd edn (Padua: Cedam, 2006); A. Mansi, *Il giudice italiano e le controversie europee* (Milan: Giuffrè, 2004); M.A. Lupoi in: F. Carpi, M. Taruffo (eds), *Commentario breve al codice di procedura civile*, 6th edn (Padua: Cedam, 2009), 2875 et seq.

A. *Principle of Party Control over the Proceedings* (Principio Dispositivo)

44. This is the fundamental principle of Italian civil procedure, and it effectively provides the foundation of civil justice in Italy. In compliance with the *principio dispositivo*, it is possible to say that civil proceedings have an adversary character, and that the parties are put to the forefront of the dispute. As a matter of fact, the judge can neither take the initiative to start proceedings ex officio nor bring new facts into the materials of the case of his or her own motion. In other words, civil proceedings, while implying very serious public policies (insomuch as the exercised jurisdiction is one of the main functions of the State), concern private interests and, as such, should put the parties at their forefront. In recent years, moreover, the idea spread that the whole notion of civil jurisdiction is no longer connected with the sovereignty of the State but rather with the private interests of the parties that such fundamental function is aimed at protecting and safeguarding.

The *principio dispositivo* has two facets: the first, refers to the control of the parties over the subject-matter and the continuance of the dispute; the second, to the control of the parties over the evidence on which the dispute will be decided. Since they have different contents, implications and solutions, each must be considered autonomously.

1. The Parties' Control over the Dispute

45. Civil proceedings in Italy can never start on the court's own motion (*ne procedat judex* ex officio). This is an absolute principle, so very much so that, in order to grant the State's control over situations where important public policies are at stake, *Pubblico Ministero* had to be granted standing to bring or resist a claim. The *Pubblico Ministero* is a judge who may start a civil action or take part in civil proceedings in the superior interests of the State, as a party, without any adjudicating power (*see infra*, paragraphs 95 et seq.).

Apart from the (limited) cases where the law grants right of action to the *Pubblico ministero*, only a party's petition can set the wheels of civil justice in motion (*principio della domanda*), and only the parties can make the trial proceed from one step to the next, until its natural end, the judgment (*principio dell'impulso di parte*); if they agree to do so, as a general rule, they can at any moment (implicitly or explicitly) discontinue the proceedings, with no possibility for the court of rendering judgment anyway (*rinuncia agli atti*).

46. The parties are the masters of the procedure; also only they can determine the objective scope of the dispute through the claims, objections and counter-claims they raise against each other in their respective briefs. Never can the judge introduce claims and facts in the proceedings of his or her own motion. This is an absolute corollary of the *principio dispositivo* in the context at hand; the judge is *tabula rasa* vis-à-vis the subject-matter of the dispute, and he or she can only adjudicate on the rights, claims, facts which the parties themselves have brought into the proceedings through their official acts. Accordingly, Article 112 CPC clearly states that the judge must perform its adjudicating function within the limits of the parties' requests only (*corrispondenza tra il chiesto e il pronunciato*).[97] If he or she violates this provision, the decision can be appealed against (*vizio di ultrapetizione*). A necessary corollary of this principle is that the judge is under a duty to decide the whole case at hand, at least insomuch as deciding on some issues is not made useless by the previous solution of a preliminary or absorbing issue or claim. Also, if he or she omits deciding upon a specific claim or defence, can the decision be appealed against (*omissione di pronuncia*).

The judge may, at certain conditions, order joinder of a third party on his or her own motion, but this is not an exception to the principles exposed so far, since it is for the parties and the parties only to extend their defences and claims against the third party (and vice versa).

In the context of the *principio dispositivo*, it is the judge's role, however, to ensure that the proceedings are conducted promptly and loyally by the parties, to supervise the evidence-gathering phase and to, finally, apply the law to the facts of the case as alleged (and proved: *see infra*) by the parties.

47. The Italian procedural system is governed by the principle *iura novit curia*, which means that it is for the judge to find, interpret and apply the appropriate rule of law for the dispute at hand. In theory, a party's claim can be accepted even if no mention is made therein to specific rules and provisions, as long as the relevant facts are alleged and proved, and the party has sufficiently specified the kind of order (*petitum*) he or she demands to the court. In practice, it is always wise for the party to point out to the court the rules which he or she deems applicable to his or her case and anyway to provide the judge with case law, precedents and doctrine's opinions concerning the provisions to be applied.

The *iura novit curia* principles applies not only to national legal provisions, but also to European ones and to those derived from international Treaties. Moreover, Article 14 of Law No. 218/95[98] now expressly states that also the content of foreign law must be ascertained ex officio by the judge. In order to gather the necessary information to perform this quite difficult task, the judge may require an expert's opinion (e.g., from a foreign academic or a professor of comparative law) or apply to the offices of the Ministry of Justice. Only when the judge is not in the position to determine the actual contents of foreign law, can he or she apply Italian law by default.

2. The Parties' Control over Evidence

48. According to Article 115 CPC, in his or her decision, the judge may only rely on the evidence provided for either by the parties or by the *Pubblico Ministero*,

97. *See* A. Carratta & M. Taruffo, 'Poteri del giudice', in *Commentario del Codice di Procedura Civile*, ed. S. Chiarloni (Bologna: Zanichelli, 2011), 1 et seq.
98. Ivaldi, 'In tema di applicazione giudiziale del diritto straniero', RDIPP (2010): 585, F. Pocar, 'Sulle conseguenze della mancata conoscenza del diritto straniero richiamato dalla norma di conflitto', in *Collisio legum, Studi di diritto internazionale privato per Gerardo Broggini* (Milan: Giuffrè, 1997), 413; I. Queirolo, 'Conoscenza del diritto straniero e contraddizioni della giurisprudenza italiana', RDIPP (2010): 603.

unless the law states otherwise.[99] As a general rule, then, the *principio dispositivo* implies that the judge cannot gather evidence on his or her own motion to ascertain the facts to which the parties have referred to in their defences. In connection with the burden of the proof principle, therefore, the parties succeed or fail only on the strength and persuasiveness of the evidence that they themselves bring into the proceedings.

As Article 115(1) CPC makes clear, however, in this context, the *principio dispositivo* is not as absolute as in the determination of the subject-matter of the dispute (*see supra*). As a matter of fact, when the law allows him or her, the judge can gather evidence on his or her own motion; and in Italian civil procedure, these powers ex officio, even in ordinary proceedings, have expanded over the years, as we shall *see infra*.

In other words, Italian civil procedure has an adversary character, with some inquisitorial elements: namely, the role of the *Pubblico Ministero* as concerns the scope, and continuance of the dispute and the powers which the court can exercise ex officio in the evidence-gathering phase.

In this context, it cannot be said that the ascertainment of the 'truth' is an absolute aim of civil proceedings.[100] It has to be pointed out, however, that Article 281*bis* CPC expressly confers a power to the judge to hear the testimony of persons which the parties made references to and who are likely to know 'the truth'. While the philosophic relevance of this provision should probably not be overestimated, the rule at hand helps understand that the court must not exercise its official evidentiary powers simply to override the burden of the proof principle.

B. Principle of Judicial Economy (Principio dell'Economia dei Giudizi) *and* Ne Bis in Idem

49. It is both in the public and in the private interest that justice be delivered promptly and as inexpensively as possible, avoiding any duplication of judicial activity and putting an end to litigation without conflicting decisions.[101]

The machinery of justice is costly for the State which must grant its proper and efficient functioning; in this light, useless judicial activity is a waste of public time and money. Also for the parties, however, to take part in never-ending litigation is costly, time-wasting and stressful.

The principle of procedural economy is probably the main interpretative standard used by the courts in the interpretation of procedural provisions today: as a matter of fact, judges will tend to apply and interpret the law in such a way as to avoid delaying the continuation of the proceedings. Quite controversially, this principle

99. *See* M. Taruffo & M. Taruffo, *supra*, 447 et seq.

100. It must be pointed out that, in the Italian juridical community, a debate does indeed go on concerning the relation between civil proceedings and the ascertainment of the truth. For a recent analysis of the various positions, *see* L. Dittrich, 'La ricerca della verità nel processo civile: profili evolutivi in tema di prova testimoniale, consulenza tecnica e fatto notorio', RDP (2011): 108.

101. *See* L.P. Comoglio, Il principio di economia processuale (Padua: Cedam, 1980).

also falls to be mentioned in contexts where the interpretation of procedural rules leads to the discontinuance or the striking out of the case.[102]

When two or more decisions are rendered in separate proceedings which conflict with each other, the whole system of justice is defeated, both at the theoretic level (because different outcomes of the same or related claims show the intrinsic fallacy of court-administered justice) and at the practical level (since it might be impossible to enforce decisions which conflict with each other and, anyway, time, energies and money have been spent to no avail).

As concerns us here, therefore, it is a primary goal of the system to make sure that the parties' dispute, however complex, be adjudicated in one set of proceedings, with one decision only. Achieving these results proves particularly difficult when the case is very complex, and more than two parties are involved. As we shall see, the code provides for many devices in order to: (*a*) bring together related claims by one or more plaintiffs against one or more defendants (*cumulo oggettivo e soggettivo di cause*); (*b*) consolidate related actions brought before the same or different courts (*riunione di cause*); (*c*) avoid duplicative litigation (*litispendenza* and *continenza di cause*); (*d*) prevent conflicting decisions; (*e*) allow joinder of third parties in the proceedings (*intervento di terzi*); (*f*) grant the concentration of appeal proceedings (*principio dell'unitarietà dell'impugnazione, impugnazioni incidentali*); and (*g*) avoid any useless judicial activity.[103]

C. *Principles of Orality, Immediacy and Concentration* (Principi dell'Oralità, dell'Immediatezza e della Concentrazione)

50. The ideal that civil proceedings should be inspired by the principles of orality, immediacy and concentration was first enunciated by Giuseppe Chiovenda at the start of the 1900s, and even today it is widely considered as the optimum goal for a civil procedural system to achieve.

In other words, according to this ideal, civil proceedings should grant an immediate contact between the parties and the judge, based on oral argument and defences, in the course of a concentrated set of hearings (if not in one hearing only). In particular, it is deemed fundamental that the judge who gathers the evidence in the instructing phase is also the same judge who releases the final judgment. In practice, not every dispute is liable to be adjudicated under these three principles, especially today that the law is becoming more and more technical and sectorial. Recent reforms, moreover, tend to limit the role of orality in civil proceedings in Italy.

As a matter of fact, complicated disputes (either in fact or in law) do not lend themselves well to oral defences, but rather require lengthy and articulated written expositions, for the sake of both the judge and the counterpart(s) (in compliance with the right to an effective reply). Oral presentation of cases requires more time than that the dramatic backlog of Italian courts can afford.

---

102. According to R. Caponi, *European Minimum Standards for Courts. Independence, Specialization, Efficiency. A Glance from Italy*, in *Festschrift fur Professor Nikolaos K. Klamaris* 155 (Sakkoulas Publications 2016), this approach is at odds with the principle of efficiency of civil procedure.
103. For example, denying the gathering of unnecessary evidence.

In a practical perspective, concentration of the proceedings is also severely lacking in Italy: the backlog of Italian courts simply makes it impossible to concentrate the various hearings in which a dispute is articulated[104] within short delays from each other. Moreover, the right to be heard and to reply to the counterpart contentions conflicts with concentration, in-so-much as, at every step of the procedure, time limits should be granted to the parties to arrange their defences and reactions. Interestingly, however, in 2009, the so-called calendar of the proceedings has been introduced (*see* paragraph 314), in an attempt to make the evidence-gathering phase more concentrated and less diluted.

All in all, today, the three Chiovenda's principles are but an aspiration. In practice, in proceedings before the *Tribunale*, the role of written defences is much wider than that of oral presentations.[105] Immediacy is usually lost in the confusion of very crowded hearings, where many cases are simultaneously heard.[106] Concentration is simply unattainable, since proceedings at first instance last an average of three to five years. Even the reform of labour proceedings, specifically introduced in 1973 to implement the principles of orality, immediacy and concentration, has (at least partially) failed. It is true that labour disputes may be adjudicated at the end of just one hearing; it is also true, however, that in certain tribunals, several months (and sometimes years) elapse between the filing of the plaintiff's petition and the appearance of the parties before the court.

II. Fundamental Guarantees

51. The judicial function should be exercised in compliance with fundamental procedural rights and guarantees for the parties. It is possible today to define a notion of 'fair civil trial' on the basis of some important international Treaties and of domestic legislation.

At the international level, reference must be made to Article 6(1) of the European Convention of Human Rights (ECHR) and now to Article 47 of the Nice Fundamental Rights Charter of the EU of 7 December 2000. At the domestic level, the provisions of the Constitution have to be considered.

In a way, the notion of fair trial is all inclusive, and from it every other procedural guarantee is originated. It is, however, possible and convenient to separate such notion from other guarantees which are its logical antecedent.

A. *Right of Action (Access to Justice)*

52. Article 24(1) of the Italian Constitution grants to everyone (*tutti*) access to justice in order to safeguard his or her own subjective rights and legitimate interests.

104. Nowadays, in many *Tribunali*, it is quite common for hearings to be fixed within six to twelve months apart from each other.
105. *See*, e.g., Arts 163, 167, 183, 190 CPC.
106. The possible turnover of the instructing judges in the course of a case is also an important element to take into account.

In other words, every individual or legal person, irrespective of nationality, religion, political belief, sex or race, can start proceedings before Italian courts to have his or her own rights vindicated. This right of action is granted against the administrative powers too, before both ordinary and administrative tribunals.

A party's right of action can never be eliminated or too narrowly restricted, so that its exercise becomes in practice too difficult or costly or subject to an excessive delay. In several occasions, for instance, the Constitutional Court declared unconstitutional statutory provisions that made arbitration mandatory in certain types of disputes, since they were considered to be in violation of Article 24 of the Constitution, insomuch as they prevented parties from going to court and obliging them to take part in an arbitration they never consented to in the first place. In other cases, on the other hand, the Constitutional Court concluded that requiring the parties to try and mediate their dispute as a preliminary condition for being allowed to file their claim before the judge was in compliance with the constitutional right of action, as long as the attempt to mediate did not limit access to the courts for an excessive period of time.

This notion of 'restricted access to justice' (*azione condizionata*) is very important today, after DLGS No. 28 of 2010 made a preliminary attempt to mediate a case a precondition to starting judicial proceedings in some types of civil and commercial disputes (*see* paragraph 202). Arguably, a mandatory attempt to mediate is not unconstitutional as concerns the delay it might cause to the start of the action in court, as long as a three months' time limit to the duration of mediation proceedings is statutorily set as in the case at hand. The real problem of mandatory mediation as it was originally introduced by DLGS No. 28 of 2010 lied with its costs, which could be rather high when the value of the case was not small and the parties to the dispute numerous. It was therefore submitted that the Constitutional Court could find this economic implications in violation of some Constitutional fundamental rights, such as the right of access to justice and the principle of equality. When the original rules of DLGS No. 28 were partially redrafted by *DL* 21 June 2013, No. 69, implemented by Law No. 98 of 9 August 2013, however, this aspect underwent a throughout reform (*see* paragraph 202), so that now any possible Constitutional problem from this point of view appears to be solved.[107]

53. The right of action is correlated with the duty of the judge to adjudicate a case (*dovere decisorio del giudice*): as a matter of fact, when a claim is filed, the judge must render a decision, with no possibility to abstain from judgment. On the other hand, of course, the plaintiff can only aspire to a decision on the merits, not necessarily in his or her favour. In civil proceedings, right of action is necessarily connected with a substantial right which allegedly needs to be vindicated, but the former exists irrespective of the actual existence of the latter; in other words, the right of action has a (partially) abstract character. As a matter of fact, the existence

---

107. On access to court and its limitation through financial burdens *see* N. Trocker, *Civil Procedure as a Part of the Constitutional Project: The Fundamental Guarantees of the Parties*, in *Civil Justice in Italy* 57 (M. De Cristofaro & N. Trocker eds, Jigakusha 2010).

of the right on which the claim is based will be ascertained at the end of the proceedings by the judge. At the moment the proceedings start, on the other hand, the plaintiff only asserts that he or she is suing for an allegedly existing right.

54. Also, the defendant has a right of action in proceedings started by his or her counterpart; at certain conditions, the law allows the defendant to raise an autonomous (but connected) counter-claim (*domanda riconvenzionale*: Article 36 CPC), which the court is under a duty to adjudicate, too.

B. Right to an Effective Remedy

55. To grant access to justice proves rather useless if, in practice, the system cannot provide for an effective relief. The right to an effective remedy, that is, a remedy which offers adequate and full compensation to the parties, is by any right a fundamental part of the right of action; in other words, it is not enough to grant access to the courts when the system cannot provide for actual justice. A remedy is effective when it is timely and can exhaustively satisfy the petitioner's demands of justice. From this point of view, the length of the proceedings and the crisis of enforcement procedures are two of the main problems in Italian justice today.[108]

C. Right of the Defence

56. In civil proceedings, the mirror image of the right of action is the right of the defence, that is, the defendant's right to effectively contest the plaintiff's claim, to have the latter's petition denied. According to Article 24(2) of the Constitution, such right is inviolable at every stage of the proceedings.

57. On a wider scale, it could be argued that the right of the defence is the one and basic procedural guarantee, both for the plaintiff and for the defendant. Undoubtedly, the right of the defence concerns all the parties of the proceedings, whatever their position might be, at any stage of the procedure. The right of the defence is the all-inclusive procedural guarantee, the basic idea being that a fair decision presupposes the effective participation of all the interested parties to the procedure in which it was rendered.

58. On a smaller level, from the defendant's point of view, the right of the defence basically consists in the possibility to contest the facts on which the plaintiff's claim is based, to raise defences (*eccezioni*) against such claim and to prove the facts on which those defences are based. In this perspective, the right to bring evidence into the proceedings is a fundamental part of the right of the defence; in other words, the party must be able to effectively demonstrate that his or her case

108. *See* N. Trocker, *Civil Procedure as a Part of the Constitutional Project: The Fundamental Guarantees of the Parties*, *supra*, 58.

is grounded (*diritto a difendersi provando*).[109] In order to be effective, moreover, the right of the defence requires the law or the judge to give the parties enough time to respond to another party's claim or petition.

D. *Right to a Fair Trial*

59. As we have seen, the Constitution, after a reform in 1999, expressly states that the judicial function is implemented through fair trial, following the path originally traced by Article 6 ECHR: as a matter of fact, the revised Article 111(1) Constitution[110] makes it clear that fair trial (*giusto processo*), regulated by law, is the necessary instrument for exercising judicial protection of rights. There is no exhaustive list of the elements which compose the notion of fair trial, which, by all accounts, should be considered as a general clause, subject to developments and integrations in compliance with the 'spirit of the times'. It is, however, possible to identify the following sub-guarantees as being part of the notion of fair trial.

1. Right to Be Heard (*Principio del Contraddittorio*)

60. After the redrafting of Article 111 Constitution in 1999, the right of the parties to be heard is now affirmed and protected at the highest level. Article 111 also specifies that any proceedings must grant the *principio del contraddittorio* between the parties on an equal footing.

The basic notion is that the right to be heard concerns the relations among the parties, and it implies the right for each party to reply to any claim, defence or petition brought by the other party before the decision is rendered.

However, it is now also recognized that the right to be heard should be effective in the relationship between the parties and the judge, so that the former should always be allowed to argue and present their defences towards any objection or issue raised by the latter of his or her own motion, before he or she renders his or her decision on such matters.[111]

61. The two different notions of 'right to be heard' mentioned in paragraph 60 are now both enunciated in Article 101 CPC. This provision, in its original formulation, enucleates the *principio del contraddittorio* (*audiatur et altera pars* principle), according to which, unless otherwise stated by the law, the judge can never decide a claim if the party against whom such claim is raised neither was summoned nor appeared before the court. In other words, it is a fundamental principle

109. *See* N. Trocker, *Civil Procedure as a Part of the Constitutional Project: The Fundamental Guarantees of the Parties*, *supra*, 61.
110. By Constitutional Law No. 2 of 23 Nov. 1999.
111. *See* L. Montesano, 'La garanzia costituzionale del contraddittorio e i giudizi civili di "terza via"', RDP (2000): 929; N. Picardi, '"Audiatur et altera pars". Le matrici storico-culturali del contraddittorio', RTDPC (2003): 7.

of Italian procedure that no decision can be lawfully rendered before all the interested parties have been enabled to present their defences. This does not require the summoned party to actually participate actively in the proceedings: what the law requires is that he or she has had at least the chance to do so, through regular and timely service of the originating petition. After receiving such notice, a defendant always has the prerogative to decide not to file a defence. This will not of course block the course of the case, but certain specific provisions on default proceedings will apply. The law, exceptionally, allows ex parte decisions in certain situation. However, such deviation from the general principle is only a temporary one: as a matter of fact, specific procedural mechanisms always put the counterpart in the position to defend his or her case and oppose the judge's decision after the latter has been granted, and eventually have such order revoked or modified (*contraddittorio differito*).

62. The right to be heard must of course be granted at the initial stage of the proceedings. The original petition should, therefore, be timely served on the defendant, so that he or she may fully arrange his or her defences before appearing in court. At the very first hearing, if the defendant has not filed a defence and has not appeared before the court, the judge must check the regularity of service of the claim and order for it to be renovated if it is found faulty. And even when service is regular, the petition might present faults which made it impossible for the defendant to appear before the court (e.g., the date of the hearing might not be specified) or to timely arrange his or her defence (e.g., the ninety-day time limit between service and the first hearing has not been respected by the plaintiff).[112] When this happens, the judge must order the petition to be corrected and/or integrated and served again on the defendant. Only when this has been complied with by the plaintiff, can the judge declare the defendant in default and proceed with the case.

But even when the defendant files a defence, at certain conditions, before trial can proceed, in compliance with Article 164 CPC, he or she can require the plaintiff's petition to be integrated or corrected or apply for an extension of the time limit to file a defence (e.g., if the original claim did not warn the defendant to file his or her defence at least twenty days before the hearing in order not to be precluded from raising counter-claims).[113]

63. The right to be heard must also be implemented and protected throughout the proceedings, at all levels and in every circumstance, since any step of the procedure must be taken after all the interested parties have had a chance to express their own point of view. This is recognized by the code, which, for example, always grants that, for every party's written brief (*memoria*), the counterpart has the right to deposit a written reply (*replica*); or that a party may have his or her own witnesses to testify on the same circumstances as the counterpart's witnesses (*testi a riprova*); or that the party may appoint his or her own expert (*consulente tecnico di parte*) to participate in the activities of the court-appointed expert (CTU), and so on.

112. Article 164 CPC.
113. Article 163 No. 7 CPC.

Moreover, the new formulation of Article 101 CPC, as revised in 2009, also makes it clear that the parties have a right not to be subject to 'surprise' decisions from the judges; it is indeed surprising for the litigants (and a violation of their right to be heard) when the final judgment is taken on grounds and issues which were neither raised nor debated among them in the course of the proceedings. Such situation might take place in relation to the legal qualification of the relevant facts (as a matter of fact, the judge is always free to apply the legal provisions he or she deems more appropriate for the given case, irrespective of the qualifications given by the parties) or to procedural or substantial issues which the law allows the judge to raise of his or her own motion.

The new text of Article 101(2) CPC, therefore, now forbids such 'surprise' decisions, insomuch as it requires the judge, when he or she decides to raise an issue of his or her own motion, to always give the parties a time limit to file a brief and a reply on such matters, before he or she may render his or her judgment. The rational of this new provision is that the parties should always be enabled to try and 'change the mind' of the judge before the latter gives his or her decision.[114]

2. Right to a Speedy Trial

64. In order for judicial relief to be effective, it must be timely. The very notion of fair trial implies speedy proceedings. Most often, as a matter of fact, late justice is no justice at all. This is clearly recognized by Article 6(1) ECHR, Article 47 Nice Charter and Article 111(2) of the Italian Constitution, according to which 'the law ensures the reasonable duration of the proceedings'.[115] Despite the strong statement contained therein, however, this appears to be a rather ineffective provision.

It is a well-known fact that Italian civil proceedings tend to be exceedingly long. Actually, the expression 'Italian torpedo' was invented to reflect how litigants, in the transnational setting, could bog down their litigation by filing their claim in Italy.[116] There are many reasons for this situation and not many of them are related to the procedural rules themselves: there are simply too many disputes, too few (or too ineffectively used) judges,[117] too many lawyers, too much backlog[118] and congestion and too many delays. Most of all, more money should be invested by the State to grant the efficient functioning of the machinery of justice.

114. Buoncristiani, 'Il nuovo art. 101, comma 2°, c. p. c. sul contraddittorio e sui rapporti tra parti e giudice', RDP (2010): 399; Giadi, 'Il principio del contraddittorio e la nullità della sentenza della "terza via"', RDP (2010): 826; A. Proto Pisani, 'Appunti su questioni rilevabili d'ufficio e principio del contraddittorio', FI (2010): V, 301.

115. N. Tommaseo, 'Durata irragionevole del processo e diritto all'equa riparazione nella giurisprudenza della Corte di Strasburgo e nella legge Pinto', in *Studi in memoria di Angelo Bonsignori* (Milano: Giuffrè, 2004), tome I, 737; N. Trocker, 'Il nuovo articolo 111 della costituzione e il "giusto processo" in materia civile: profili generali', RTDPC (2001): 381; N. Trocker, 'Dal "giusto processo" all'effettività dei rimedi: l''azione' nell'elaborazione della Corte europea dei diritti dell'uomo (parte II)', RTDPC (2007): 439.

116. R. Caponi, *The Performance of the Italian Civil Justice System: An Empirical Assessment*, ILJ 15 (2016).

117. About 2,765 career judges examine civil cases at first and second instance: R. Caponi, *supra*, 19.

In the past twenty-five years, the Italian lawmaker has indeed tried to improve the situation through continuous reforms of the existing procedural rules: the results, however, have proved rather discouraging. As a matter of fact, changing the procedural mechanisms is not enough, in itself, to reduce the delay in the adjudication of cases and the courts backlog, especially since, at the decision stage, disputes still have to be solved on an individual basis and the time a judge needs to render his or her decision may not be reduced by statute.

In recent reforms, the lawmaker has also tried to introduce alternative remedies and measures aimed at making civil proceedings more effective. For instance, it is worth mentioning here the adoption, in 2009, of a form of *astreinte* (Article 614*bis* CPC), that is, a court's order which should induce a debtor to voluntarily comply with a judicial decision, under threat of (mounting) pecuniary sanctions in case of failure to do so. Apparently, however, this new remedy in practice is neither very commonly applied for nor granted.

The need for a structural reform is felt, even though few certainties exist as to the direction to take and the changes to bring; and maybe even that would prove ineffective, against the Italian cultural and social context. In other words, right now, the law simply appears unable to ensure the reasonable duration of civil proceedings.

In order to try and solve this critical situation, the lawmaker has recently turned to ADR, introducing, for example, a preliminary mandatory attempt at mediation for several types of civil proceedings, effective as of 21 March 2011 (*see* paragraph 202). Moreover, at the institutional level, DL No. 98 of 6 July 2011, implemented by Law No. 111 of 15 July 2011, in an attempt to grant more efficiency to the activities of judicial offices, introduced the so-called programme for the management of pending civil, administrative and tax cases. Basically, every year, the Presidents of every judicial office will have to hand out the guidelines for the future activities of their office, in particular, planning the handling of backlog, taking into consideration the stream of new cases. As an example, the programme should point out priorities in dealing with pending cases, taking into consideration their subject-matter and their starting date. Every year, moreover, the programme should make a balance of the implementation of the previous year programme. Failure to comply with the objectives set out in the programme may have negative effects on the career of the magistrates involved. On the other hand, compliance with the programme should lead to financial benefits for the relevant judicial office.

65. For several decades, Italy has been constantly ruled against by the European Court of Human Rights for violation of the 'reasonable delay' principle of Article 6 ECHR, so that, in the European Court's circles, an 'Italian problem' in these concerns is said to exist.

---

118. It must be remarked, however, that in recent years the number of pending cases is decreasing, possibly as a consequence of the economic crisis and increasing costs for bringing cases to the courts. *See also* R. Caponi, *supra*, 23; R. Caponi, *European Minimum Standards for Courts. Independence, Specialization, Efficiency. A Glance from Italy*, in *Festschrift fur Professor Nikolaos K. Klamaris* 164 (Sakkoulas Publications 2016) for some data and statistics.

In 2001, the *legge Pinto* (*see supra*, paragraph 38) tried to bring a solution to such dramatic situation, by granting a national remedy to the parties who demand compensation for unreasonably long proceedings.[119] This national remedy effectively aspires at substituting recourse to the European Court, under the subsidiarity principle. The case law of the Courts of Appeal and the *Corte di cassazione* is now quite extensive.[120] As a matter of fact, an unforeseen side-effect of the remedy brought by *Legge Pinto* is a massive amount of litigation about the excessive length of proceedings which is now congesting every Court of Appeal, bringing more delays to an already critical situation. In 2012, therefore, Legge Pinto went through an extensive revision with the not so covert aim of restricting and making less palatable the use of the remedies provided therein.[121]

The time-standards for the evaluation of the excessive delay in the dispatching of a dispute are now statutorily set: three years at first instance, two years at the appeal level, one year before the Supreme Court. The reasonable duration of enforcement proceedings has been set at three years, and at six years for insolvency proceedings. The 'reasonable time limit' is considered respected, however, when a case is disposed of with an irrevocable decision within six years.

The reform of 2012 also set forth several exclusions from the right to be indemnified for the excessive length of proceedings: in particular, the remedy provided for by *Legge Pinto* may not be invoked now by a party who was sanctioned for abuse of process under Article 96 CPC (*see* paragraph 180) or which unreasonably refused a settlement proposal (*see* paragraph 458) or which anyway abused of her procedural rights, leading to an unjustified delay in the solution of the case.

Following the guidelines of Article 2 of the law, the complexity of the case, the behaviour of the parties and of any other authority involved in the dispute must be considered and evaluated.

The amount of damages which may be awarded in compliance with this national remedy is rather symbolic, and the remedy itself has been considered quite ineffective. The European Court for Human Rights has therefore ruled that such remedy cannot hinder the parties from still bringing a recourse to the Court in Strasbourg in compliance with the ECHR.[122] The situation has possibly worsened after the revision of *Legge Pinto* of 2012, which fixed the amount paid by the State between Euros (EUR) 500.00 and EUR 1,500.00 for each year exceeding the reasonable

119. The political rationale behind the noble ideals is to reduce the flow of petitions to the European Court – with the practical result of congesting the national Courts of Appeal! *See* C. Besso et al., *Misure accelleratorie e riparatorie contro l'irragionevole durata dei processi* (Turin: Giappichelli, 2002); A. Martino, 'Sul diritto all'equa riparazione in caso di violazione del termine ragionevole del processo (legge 24 marzo 2001, n. 89)', RDP (2001): 1068; S. Pellegrini, *Il processo civile e la civile giustizia* (Padua: Cedam, 2005).

120. More details in Bertuzzi, 'Violazione del principio della ragionevole durata del processo e diritto all'equa riparazione', GM (2001): 1153 et seq.; Morozzo Della Rocca, 'L'equa riparazione per irragionevole durata del processo nelle prime decisioni della Cassazione', GC (2003): I, 702.

121. C. Consolo & M. Negri, 'Ipoteche di costituzionalità sulle ultime modifiche alla legge Pinto: varie aporie dell'indennizzo municipale per durata irragionevole del processo (all'epoca della – supposta – spending review)', CG (2013): 1429; F, Ghirga, 'Considerazioni critiche sulle recenti modifiche della c.d. Legge Pinto', RDP (2013): 1021.

122. *See* ECHR 19 Dec. 2002, *D & G*, 2003, 73; Didone, 'La Cassazione, la legge Pinto e la Corte europea dei diritti dell'uomo', RTDPC (2004): 193.

length of the proceedings as statutorily defined (*see* above), depending on the outcome of the dispute, the behaviour of both the judge and the parties, the nature of the interests at stake, the value of the case. The indemnity paid by the State, however, may never exceed the value of the right as ascertained by the judge.[123]

The revision of 2012 also concerned the procedural mechanisms to apply for the indemnity provided by *Legge Pinto*. The petition must now be addressed to the President of the Court of Appeal, against the Ministry of Justice, within six months from the end of the relevant proceedings.[124] The President will then release a decree ex parte, which may either allow or deny the petition. In the first instance, an indemnity is awarded in compliance with the guidelines set by *Legge Pinto* (*see* above). The claimant may either accept the decree or oppose it before the Court of Appeal, who will decide with a three-judge panel, in chambers (*see* paragraphs 351 et seq.). The decree awarding an indemnity must also be served on the Ministry within thirty days or it will become ineffective and no further petition will be allowed.

Legge Pinto went through another important revision in 2015,[125] which severely reduced the chances for a party to be compensated for the excessive duration of civil proceedings.[126] A new Article 1*bis* was brought into the statute, stating that a party has the right to apply for *rimedi preventivi* (preventive remedies) in order to avoid a violation of the 'reasonable delay' principle set forth in Article 6 of the ECHR. Parties who have applied for such *rimedi preventivi* but still have suffered a damage deriving from the unreasonable duration of the proceedings are entitled to an equitable compensation. The *rimedi preventivi* to which Article 1*bis* refers are listed in Article 1*ter* (e.g., bringing the claim as a summary proceeding under Article 702*bis* CPC – *see* paragraphs 343 et seq. – and applying for a procedural switch from ordinary to summary proceedings under Article 183*bis* CPC – *see* paragraph 215). The downside of this 'right' is that, under the new Article 2, paragraph 1 of *Legge Pinto*, a claim for equitable compensation brought by a party who has not applied for *rimedi preventivi* under Article 1*ter* is considered inadmissible. In other words, a party who does not prove to have tried to use any of the devices which could fasten the course of the proceedings, may not later on complain about the excessive length of the trial. This new system forces lawyers to at least apply for acceleratory procedural devices. Should they fail to do so, they could arguably be tried for professional liability by their unsatisfied client, who was refused access to the compensatory remedies of *Legge Pinto*.

---

123. *App*. Reggio Calabria 8 Apr. 2013, CG (2013): 1422 found that this new restriction could violate Art. 117(3) Const. and applied for a ruling from the Constitutional Court.
124. Previously, the law allowed such a petition to be brought even while the relevant proceedings were still pending: *App*. Bari 18 Mar. 2013, CG (2013): 1420 argued that this revision could be unconstitutional and submitted a petition for constitutional review to the Constitutional Court.
125. Law 28 Dec. 2015, n. 208, the so-called *Legge di stabilità 2016*; *See* M.A. Lupoi, *Nowhere Fast? Shortcuts to Judgment in Recent Italian Procedural Legislation*, in *Ways of Implementation of the Right to Civil Proceedings Within a Reasonable Time* 304 (Vilnius Universitetas 2016).
126. *See* G. Buffone, 'Legge Pinto: ridotte le ipotesi di accesso al risarcimento', GD 6 (2016): 63.

E. Impartiality and Independence of the Courts

66. The very notion of jurisdictional function implies that the judge who decides a case must be an impartial adjudicator;[127,128] that the parties should be equal before the law; that the court must apply the law to the facts of the case with no undue (internal or external) influences and pressures.

The judge must be (and appear to be) impartial in order for the society at large to have confidence in the judicial system, accept the courts' decisions and have faith in the rule of law. In other words, for the parties of the dispute, the impartiality of the judge is a fundamental guarantee of fairness and justice.

67. According to Article 51 CPC, the judge is under a duty to abstain from deciding a case (*astensione obbligatoria*) if:[129]

- he or she has an interest in the dispute or in another dispute concerning the same juridical issue;
- he or she, or his or her spouse is a relative,[130] is affiliated or living or has friendly relations with one of the parties or one of their solicitors;
- he or she, or his or her spouse is involved in pending litigation, is on bad or unfriendly terms with one of the parties or one of her solicitors, is either a debtor or a creditor of one of the parties or one of its solicitors;
- at any stage of the litigation, he or she counselled or represented one of the parties in the dispute, deposed as a witness, was on the adjudicating panel in another instance of the case or as an arbitrator or was appointed as a court expert;
- he or she is a guardian, a representative, an agent or an employer of one of the parties or has managing powers in an association, committee or company which has an interest in the dispute.

68. In any other case, the judge may discretionally and voluntarily abstain[131] from the case if serious reasons for doing so exist (*astensione facoltativa*).

69. Whenever one of the grounds for compulsory abstention exists and the judge does not voluntarily abstain, each party may challenge the judge (*ricusazione*), by filing a petition and presenting the specific reasons and evidence at least two days before the hearing. The proceedings are automatically stayed, while a three-judge panel of the *Tribunale* renders its decision, after hearing the challenged judge and

127. *See* A. Gustapane, L'autonomia e l'indipendenza della magistratura ordinaria nel sistema costituzionale italiano (Milan: Giuffrè, 1999); S. Bartole, Il potere giudiziario (Bologna: Mulino, 2006); G. Scarselli, Ordinamento giudiziario e forense, 3rd edn (Milano: Giuffrè, 2010), 35 et seq.; P. Biavati, 'L'organizzazione della giustizia civile', in La giustizia civile e penale in Italia, ed. P. Biavati et al. (Bologna: il Mulino, 2008), 187; R. Caponi, *European Minimum Standards for Courts. Independence, Specialization, Efficiency. A Glance from Italy*, in *Festschrift fur Professor Nikolaos K. Klamaris* 158 (Sakkoulas Publications 2016).
128. Article 111(2) Const.
129. *See also* L. Dittrich, *Incompatibilità, astensione e ricusazione del giudice civile* (Padua: Cedam, 1991).
130. Up to the fourth degree of kindred.
131. Discretionary abstention must be authorized as per Art. 51(2) CPC.

gathering any relevant evidence. The court's order may not be appealed against.[132] If the challenge is allowed, the court appoints a new judge who takes the place of the original one. If the petition is denied, the applying party will be fined.[133]

70. A judge is impartial when he or she is independent; in other words when he or she only responds to the law (and his or her conscience) and is free from any juridical, political or corporative tie.

71. First of all, the judge must be independent from any other State function and power. The separation of the three fundamental powers has been clearly affirmed in the Italian Constitution: as concerns us here, Article 101(2) states that judges are only subject to the law and Article 104(1) expressly qualifies the Judiciary as an autonomous and independent order. Article 108(2) extends the independence guarantee to special jurisdictions and to all the laymen taking part in the administration of justice.

72. The CSM (High Council of the Judiciary)[134] is the judiciary self-government body.[135] It is chaired by the President of the Republic, and the first President and the *Procuratore generale* of the *Corte di cassazione* sit in it by right.[136] The twenty-four other members of the CSM are elected as follows: two-thirds by ordinary magistrates, one-third by the Parliament (among university professors in juridical matters and lawyers with at least fifteen years of practice).[137] A Vice-President is appointed among the members elected by Parliament.

The Constitution provides for the guidelines which govern the activities, the functions and the prerogatives of the CSM. The *Consiglio*, in compliance with the law on the judiciary order (*ordinamento giudiziario*), is in charge of appointing, promoting, transferring and sanctioning the magistrates (Article 105 Const.).[138] On the other hand, it is for the Minister of Justice to organize and manage all the services related to the administration of justice (Article 110 Const.).

---

132. A. Panzarola, *La ricusazione del giudice civile. Il problema della impugnabilità della decisione* (Bari: Cacucci, 2008).
133. Article 54(3) CPC. The amount of this fine is right now rather symbolic (no more than EUR 250.00, after a reform in 2009).
134. *See* G. Scarselli, *supra*, 85 et seq.; R. Caponi, *European Minimum Standards for Courts. Independence, Specialization, Efficiency. A Glance from Italy*, in *Festschrift fur Professor Nikolaos K. Klamaris* 159 (Sakkoulas Publications 2016).
135. For a critical analysis of the role of the CSM in the crisis of Italian justice *see* G. Di Federico, 'Il contributo del CSM alla crisi della giustizia', in *Le novità in materia di ordinamento giudiziario* (BUP: Bologna, 2013): 5.
136. Article 104(2)(3) Const.
137. These elected members stay in office for four years.
138. For a collection of the CSM disciplinary decisions *see* Ricciotti & Mariucci (eds), *Deontologia giudiziaria*, II volumes (Padua: Cedam, 1995).

73. The judge should also be independent of other judges, in the sense that he or she should perform his or her office responding only to the law and his or her conscience. From this point of view, in Italy, no stare decisis principle exists (*see* paragraph 10) and all judges are at the same level; any distinction between them being based on their different functions only.[139]

F. Establishment of Courts by Law (Garanzia del Giudice Naturale)

74. Nobody can be drawn away from his or her natural judge provided by the law: this principle is enunciated by Article 25(1) of the Constitution, which enucleates the so-called parties' right to the *giudice naturale*. This guarantee is particularly relevant in criminal proceedings, but it has an impact on civil proceedings also.

75. Prima facie, as concerns us here, this provision forbids any undue dismissal, denial or transfer of jurisdiction or venue in compliance with rules which entered into force after the date when proceedings were started. As Articles 5 and 10 CPC and 10 of Law 218/95 make clear, to ensure certainty and foreseeableness of the forum, both competence and jurisdiction must be determined taking into consideration the factual and juridical background in force at the moment the original petition was brought. Moreover, the Constitutional provision also forbids the creation of extraordinary courts or tribunals.

76. At a deeper level, recent studies have questioned the very notion of 'natural judge' in the transnational context, coming to the conclusion that, as concerns international jurisdiction, this notion must be interpreted as requiring some close connection to exist between the court and the dispute in order to avoid the exercise of exorbitant fora. It is submitted that, in connection with the right to an effective remedy and to an effective defence, this notion might allow Italian courts to dismiss their jurisdiction in transnational disputes when such close connection is clearly lacking.[140]

G. Right to a Reasoned Decision

77. According to Article 111(6) of the Constitution, every judicial decision must be reasoned. As we shall see, the Code of Civil Procedure requires every judgment to expose the reasons of the decision (*motivazione*); also orders (*ordinanze*) must be at least succinctly reasoned. The decision's reasons concern both the issues of fact (*quaestio facti*) and the issues of law (*quaestio iuris*) adjudicated upon.

78. On a Constitutional level, stating that every decision should be reasoned is a means to granting democratic control over judicial activities; moreover, by making his or her reason to judgment clear, the judge becomes liable for his or her own

139. Article 107(3) Const.
140. *See* M.A. Lupoi, *Conflitti transnazionali di giurisdizioni* (Milan: Giuffrè, 2002).

decision. As concerns the public at large, when a judgment is seriously and convincingly reasoned, confidence in the judiciary and acceptance of its decisions can be ensured; as concerns the parties to the dispute, to know the reasons why the decision was rendered is fundamental to bring an appeal against it.

It has to be remarked, however, that the right to a reasoned decision has not been extended to the transnational level, so that foreign decisions may be recognized and enforced in Italy even when they are not reasoned.[141]

Moreover, it is widely acknowledged in Italy today that the need to write the reasons for judgment is one of the main reasons for the courts' backlog. Accordingly, the lawmaker has introduced rules encouraging judges to write more concise decisions (*see* paragraph 230). New rules enabling courts to reason their decisions only upon the parties specific request are presently been discussed.

H. Right to Bring an Appeal (Diritto all'Impugnazione)

79. The Italian Constitution does not provide for a constitutional right to bring an appeal (*appello*) against a judgment of first instance.[142] In other words, the Italian constitutional system does not grant a right to the so-called double level of jurisdiction (*doppio grado di giurisdizione*). Such double level of adjudication on the merits, however, is recognized by the code of civil procedure (Articles 339 et seq.); this means that, unlikely as it might be, it would be possible for the lawmaker to eliminate the appeal with no need to modify the text of the Constitution beforehand. The lawmaker could also decide to limit the right of a second level appeal to certain decisions only. For instance, until 2006, equity decisions of the *giudice di pace* could not be appealed before the *Tribunale*. Such restrictions to a second level appeal, however, are not popular and most existing cases have been repealed, since a first instance decision who cannot be appealed against may anyway be brought before the *Cassazione* (Supreme Court) (*see* paragraph 80), whose caseload is therefore increased. In 2012, however, access to the appeal level has been restricted through the introduction of the so-called filter to the appeal (*filtro in appello*) (*see* paragraph 250).

80. The Constitution, as a matter of fact, grants the parties the right to file a petition (*ricorso straordinario*) to the *Corte di cassazione* against any judgment (*rectius*, decision) which, in the civil field, adjudicates upon a subjective right and is not subject to any other form of review: Article 111(7).[143] This constitutional right of access to the Supreme Court is one of the reasons for the *Cassazione*'s dramatic backlog. It also represents a major obstacle to any reform of the appeal system based, for example, on leave to appeal to the *Cassazione*.

As a matter of fact, in order to establish any effective filter to the Supreme Court, the Constitution needs to be changed, and this is rather unlikely to happen in the

141. *See*, e.g., *Cass.* 13 Mar. 1993, n. 3029, RDIPP, 1994, 124.
142. *See* Liebman, 'Il giudizio d'appello e la Costituzione', RDP (1980): 401 et seq.
143. Article 111(7) Const.

short term. In 2009, however, an attempt was made at introducing a preliminary selection of cases brought before the *Cassazione* (*see* paragraph 264).

I. Principle of the Administration of Justice in Open Court (Principio di Pubblicità dei Giudizi)

81. This is not an absolute principle in Italian civil procedure. On the contrary, public hearings are nowadays almost an exception. Article 128 CPC states that the hearing in which a case is discussed (*udienza di discussione*) is open to the public, unless the court decides otherwise, on public order or public security grounds. This provision, however, is now very seldom applied in ordinary civil proceedings at first instance, where the final discussion hearing hardly ever takes place.

82. Hearings before the trial judge are never public[144] and neither are hearings in chambers. Hearings before the Court of Appeal and the *Corte di Cassazione*, on the other hand, are usually public. All courts' judgments are public too.

At the open hearing, the public must not bear weapons, express approval or disapproval, nor cause any disturbance.[145]

144. Article 84 *disp. att.* CPC.
145. Article 129 CPC.

Part I. Judicial Organization

Chapter 1. The Courts and Their Members

§1. Courts

I. Introduction

83. The Constitution provides for the fundamental principles concerning the judicial function and the Judiciary.[146,147] Some of those principles have already been analysed in the previous pages. In the next paragraphs the picture will be completed.

In a democratic vision of society, Article 101(1) of the Constitution states that justice is administrated in the people's name. In compliance with this provision, every judgment is rendered 'in the name of the Italian people'. Of course, this does not mean that the judges are 'representative' of the people nor that they, in adjudicating cases, should take into consideration the 'will' of the majority. On the contrary, reference is made here to the fact that judges decide cases in the exercise of a fundamental public function. A necessary corollary of this is the fact that the judge must be wholly independent and subject to the law only, as Article 101(2) points out (*see supra*).

The judicial function is performed by ordinary magistrates, according to the rules of the so-called judicial order.

Apart from the basic rules set by the Constitution, more specific provisions as to the administration and management of the courts, and the status of the persons working therein are found in RD No. 12 of 30 January 1942 and in other statutes.

In recent years, however, the *ordinamento giudiziario* has been extensively reformed by some rather controversial pieces of legislation.[148] While it is beyond the scope of this monograph to enter into the details of these regulations, it is worth mentioning the most relevant legislation in force at the moment:

---

146. *See* L. Chieffi, *La magistratura. Origine del modello costituzionale e prospettive di riforma* (Naples: Jovene, 1998); G. Di Federico (ed.), *Manuale di ordinamento giudiziario* (Padua: Cedam, 2004).
147. *See* N. Trocker, *The Court System*, in *Civil justic in Italy*, 19 (M. De Cristofaro & N. Trocker eds, Jigakusha 2010).
148. For the latest developments, *see* G. Finocchiaro, 'Guida rapida al nuovo ordinamento giudiziario. Prima lettura della legge 111/2007', GD 34 (2007) (insert); Finocchiaro, G., 'Dei tirocini formativi e dell'ufficio per il processo', RDP (2015): 961. *See also* 'Dieci anni di riforme dell'ordinamento giudiziario', FI (2016): V, 157.

- DLGS No. 109 of 23 February 2006, as modified by Law No. 269 of 24 October 2006, on disciplinary sanctions against magistrates and the relevant procedural provisions.[149]
- DLGS No. 106 of 20 February 2006, as modified by Law No. 269 of 24 October 2006, on the reorganization of the Office of the *Pubblico Ministero*.
- DLGS No. 26 of 30 January 2006, as modified by Law No. 111 of 30 July 2007, establishing the Superior School for the Judiciary and setting provisions about the formation of judges.
- DLGS No. 160 of 5 April 2006, as modified by Law No. 111 of 30 July 2007 and by Law 197 of 25 October 2016, introducing new provisions for the access to the Judiciary.
- Law No. 24 of 22 February 2010, providing for urgent measures concerning the functionality of the judiciary system.
- DL No. 179 of 18 October 2012 (converted into Law No. 221 of 17 December 2012) and DL No. 90 of 24 June 2014 (converted into Law No. 114 of 11 August 2014), establishing the '*Ufficio per il processo*', i.e., a staff supporting the individual judge in his activities; in particular, this staff is composed also of law graduates apprentices (*tirocinanti*) (*see infra* § 85).[150]

II. Structure of the Court System

84. The Judiciary can be described as a pyramid-shaped structure, which develops along bureaucratic vertical lines.[151]

As concerns civil courts, after the reform of 1998 which eliminated the *pretura*, only two courts of first instance exist in Italy today.

The justice of the peace (*giudice di pace*)[152] is an honorary judge, instituted by Law No. 374 of 21 November 1991, to adjudicate small (civil and criminal) claims and matters. The offices of the justice of the peace used to be spread over the national territory, more or less in each municipality (*comune*) but, in an attempt at reviewing the expenses of the State, DLGS 7 September 2012 No. 156 cut down many of the court's offices located in smaller towns (whose workload was transferred to surviving offices).[153] In 2016, however, some of these offices have been reinstated, with the relevant municipalities agreeing to finance their activities. In the same year, a process of reform of the status of these honorary judges has controversially started.[154]

Proceedings before the justice of the peace are meant to be fast, mostly oral, with a stress on conciliation. The trial is conducted and the decision taken by a single judge (*see* paragraph 333).

149. *See* D. Potetti, 'La figura normativa del magistrato scorretto', GM (2011): 892.
150. G. Finocchiaro, 'Dei tirocini formativi e dell'ufficio per il processo', RDP (2015): 973.
151. *See* G. Scarselli, *supra*, 134 et seq.
152. *See* D. Cavallini, 'Il giudice di pace nell'ordinamento giudiziario: il difficile rapporto tra legge speciale e normative generali', RTDPC (2006): 1219.
153. *See* G. Costantino, 'La revisione delle circoscrizioni giudiziarie', RDP (2012): 1567.
154. *See* in particular, Law No. 57 of 28 Apr. 2016 and DLGS No. 92, of 31 May 2016.

85. Apart from certain cases where the Court of Appeal is exceptionally granted jurisdiction to adjudicate cases at first instance (e.g.,: recognition and enforcement of foreign judgments), all the disputes not falling within the subject-matter and value competence of the justice of the peace (*see infra*, paragraph 156) are adjudicated by the *Tribunale*, which functions as the main first instance court in civil matters as well as judge of appeal for appeals against the decisions of the justice of the peace.[155] After the abolition of the *preture*, a *Tribunale* used to be normally structured in a main seat (usually, in the capital city of a province) and one or more *sezioni distaccate* (detached sections), which had taken the place of some of the busiest *preture*. However, in the implementation of a spending-review policy, *DLGS* 7 September 2012 No. 155 reshaped the territorial distribution of *Tribunali* across the country, eliminating all of the *sezioni distaccate* (whose caseload was incorporated in that of the main seat) and several *Tribunali* located in minor towns.[156] The reform brought by *DLGS* No. 51 of 1998 has completed the separation between disputes which are to be decided by a single judge of the *Tribunale* (*giudice monocratico*) – the vast majority – and disputes which must be decided by a three-judge panel (*collegio*). Article 50*bis* CPC hands down the list of the so-called *cause collegiali*, which can be roughly summarized as follows: (*a*) disputes which require the participation of the *Pubblico Ministero*; (*b*) some disputes relating to insolvency proceedings; (*c*) disputes falling within the competence of the specialized sections of the *Tribunale* (*sezioni specializzate*); (*d*) some disputes relating to the deliberations and to the liability of the administrators of incorporated companies; (*e*) litigation concerning contested wills and the adjudication of hereditary rights of legitimate heirs; (*f*) disputes concerning the civil liability of magistrates; and (*g*) chambers proceedings, unless otherwise stated. Today, also most industrial and intellectual property[157] disputes fall to be adjudicated by a three-judge panel.

Since 2015, a project was launched at the Ministry of Justice in order to implement the so-called *Ufficio per il processo* (office for the proceedings) which tries to innovate judicial offices by revising the organizing schemes of both the judges and the court's clerks. Basically, courts are encouraged to start organizing structures with support staff for the judge and its activities. This support staff is mainly composed by law graduate trainees, whose functions vary from searching juridical literature and jurisprudential precedents to writing reports, helping the judge organizing his hearings, elaborating statistic data and so forth.[158]

---

155. Article 339 CPC was reformed in 2006: now, even decisions rendered by the *giudice di pace* in the exercise of its equitable jurisdiction (i.e., in disputes having a value of EUR 1,200.00 or less) may be appealed against, but only as concerns alleged violations of either procedural, constitutional and community law or the subject-matter fundamental principles.

156. G. Costantino, *supra*, 1567. Some detached sections on the Italian islands of Ischia, Lipari and Elba have been later reinstated (on a temporary basis) by DLGS 19 Feb. 2014, n. 14.

157. Article 2(1) of DLGS No. 168 of 2003.

158. More details may be found at this link: https://www.giustizia.it/giustizia/it/mg_2_9_2.page; G. Finocchiaro, 'Dei tirocini formativi e dell'ufficio per il processo', RDP (2015): 961. *See also* N. Graziano, 'Entra in scena il giudice coordinatore e referente dei Got', GD 11 (2017): 24.

86. Courts of Appeal are courts of second instance, for appeals against the decisions of the *Tribunale*. They have functional territorial competence over the *Tribunali* located within their circuit (on a regional or multi-provincial scale). They also have very limited first instance competence, for example, as concerns recognition and enforcement of foreign decisions.[159]

After the reform of Law No. 353/90, every procedural activity before the Court of Appeal should be performed by a panel of three judges.

87. The *Corte di cassazione* is the Italian Supreme Court, located in Rome.[160] It is the court of last instance for appeals against decisions of the Courts of Appeal (or other decisions which are not subject to ordinary appeal). Its main function is to grant the strict observance and uniform interpretation of the law (*nomofilachia*).[161] Therefore, it only deals with juridical issues and not with the ascertainment and evaluation of the relevant facts of the case (*giudizio di legittimità*). Thus, the *Cassazione* does not (usually) decide the merits of a case: as a general rule, when a petition for review is allowed (*giudizio rescindente*), and a new decision must be drafted to substitute the original one (*giudizio rescissorio*), the case is remitted to a lower court (*giudice di rinvio*). At least in theory, it is therefore possible for a case to be brought before the *Cassazione* more than once.

The *Cassazione* is also in charge of solving conflicts of jurisdiction in the domestic and the transnational setting and conflicts of competence within the Italian ordinary courts system.

88. The *Cassazione* is divided in several 'chambers' (*sezioni*), which deal with different subject-matters. Usually, a panel of five judges (*sezione semplice*) will decide a case; matters of jurisdiction, however, must normally be decided by a special panel of nine judges (*sezioni unite*). However, a case may be assigned to a *sezione semplice* if the *sezioni unite* have already decided upon the same jurisdictional issue.[162]

The court also decides in *sezioni unite* when it is necessary to solve conflicting precedents given by different *sezioni semplici* on issues of law or when very important legal questions have to be addressed. Even in a procedural system where the Supreme Court's decisions are not binding, decisions rendered by the *sezioni unite* of the *Cassazione* have particular importance and bear a lot of persuasive weight on lower-instance judges, who normally follow them.

It must also be pointed out that Article 374(3) CPC, as revised in 2006, puts an obligation on a *sezione semplice* to refer the decision of a case to the full chambers of the Court whenever the former does not agree with a principle of law set forth by

159. *See* L. Montesano & G. Arieta, *Trattato di diritto processuale*, vol. I, tome I (Padua: Cedam, 2001), 199 et seq.
160. Before 1923, Italy had as many as five regional courts of cassation (Turin, Florence, Rome, Naples, Palermo: *see* R. Caponi, *Italian Civil Justice Reform 2009* (*ZZPint* 2009). On the history of the *Cassazione see* L.P. Comoglio, C. Ferri & M. Taruffo, *Lezioni sul processo civile*, 2nd edn (Bologna: Il Mulino, 1998), 833 et seq.
161. *See* Visalli, 'La logica del giudice e la funzione uniformatrice della Cassazione', RDC (1998), I, 705; G. Scarselli, *supra*, 234 et seq.
162. Article 374(1) CPC, as revised in 2006.

the latter in a previous judgment;[163] even though no stare decisis principle has been adopted as such, this new provision should make the case law of the *Cassazione* more consistent.

It has to be observed, however, that it is not exceptional for conflicting *sezioni unite* decisions to be rendered on the same legal issue even within a short time of each other.

Generally speaking, the case law of the *Cassazione* is often rather contradictory and its exemplary value is often scarce.[164]

89. As allowed by Article 102(2) of the Constitution, in civil matters, some specialized (autonomous) sections (*sezioni specializzate*) exist to deal with specific disputes with the cooperation of laymen and honorary magistrates.[165]

Mention must be made here of the juvenile courts (*Tribunali per i minorenni*), that is, *Tribunali* with special jurisdiction in matters concerning minors (both civil and criminal).[166] However, Law No. 219 of 2012 (*see* paragraph 39) greatly reduced the jurisdiction of these *Tribunali* in civil matters. In particular, as a rule, parental responsibility and maintenance disputes must now be brought before the ordinary *Tribunale*. These courts are located in every region and a specific section of the Court of Appeal exists to adjudicate appeals against their decisions. The adjudicating panels are composed of both professional judges and experts in juvenile matters acting as lay judges.

Certain agrarian disputes are to be decided by the specialized agricultural sections (*sezioni specializzate agrarie*) within ordinary *Tribunali* and Courts of Appeal.

DLGS No. 168 of 27 June 2003 instituted specialized chambers in some *Tribunali* and Courts of Appeal to deal with disputes over industrial and intellectual property rights.[167] In an attempt at improving judicial activities in a very sensitive area of civil litigation, DL No. 1 of 24 January 2012, implemented by Law No. 27 of 24 March 2012, created 'Specialized chambers for business disputes' which basically took the place (and absorbed the subject-matter competence) of these specialized chambers for intellectual and industrial property disputes, with an extended competence over class actions (*see* paragraphs 361 et seq.) and a variety of company disputes.[168] These new 'Chambers for business disputes' have been created (and became operational in September 2012) in Tribunals and Courts of Appeals located

163. *See* M. Taruffo, 'Una riforma della Cassazione civile?', RTDPC (2006): 755.
164. As R. Caponi, 'Italian Civil Justice Reform 2009', *ZZPint* (2009), writes: 'Instead of being a source of guidance, the Court is often a source of confusion for lower courts (…) This encourages the increase in the number of reviews, because there is always the hope that they will meet a favourable decision, possibly due to the court being distracted or due to a conscious revirement.'
165. *See* G. Scarselli, *supra*, 138 et seq.; R. Caponi, *European Minimum Standards for Courts. Independence, Specialization, Efficiency. A Glance from Italy*, in *Festschrift fur Professor Nikolaos K. Klamaris* 169 (Sakkoulas Publications 2016).
166. For example, certain decisions over custody rights of children born out of wedlock.
167. *See* G. Casaburi, 'Le sezioni distrettuali della proprietà intellettuale ed industriale. Perché poi non si dica "peccato"', *Dir. ind.* (2003): 207; G. Bonelli, 'Sezioni specializzate di diritto industriale: speranze o illusioni?', *Dir. ind.* (2004): 105 G. Casaburi, 'L'istituzione delle sezioni specializzate per la proprietà industriale ed intellettuale: (prime) istruzioni per l'uso', *Dir. ind.* (2003): 405.
168. *See* F. Santagada, 'Sezioni specializzate per l'impresa, accelerazione dei processi e competitività delle imprese', RDP (2012): 1269.

in the capital of each region (with some exceptions: e.g., as concerns Val d'Aosta, venue is granted to the courts in Turin). This innovation has been criticized for bringing courts away from the parties involved in the dispute. Moreover, in order to start proceedings in this would-be elite chambers, the parties have to pay a court fee which is double than the average one (*see* paragraph 304). With a rather controversial (and indeed hardly rational) innovation brought by DL No. 145 of 23 December 2013, implemented by Law No. 9 of 21 February 2014, whenever a company whose main seat is located abroad sues or is sued before the *Tribunale delle imprese*, special venue rules apply and only nine courts have competence for the whole of Italy (e.g.: the special chamber of Rome 'covers' five different regions: Marche, Toscana, Abruzzo, Umbria, Lazio).[169] Apparently, the *ratio legis* is that foreign companies should thus find litigating in Italy more 'competitive'.

In order to the deal with the dramatic increase of migrants reaching the Italian territory and of the related civil actions for asylum applications and immigration disputes, DL No. 13 of 17 February 2017, converted into Law No. 46 of 13 April 2017, instituted specialized sections within the *Tribunali* to deal with the growing numbers of international protection and immigration cases. This new piece of legislation also introduced specific procedural rules which arguably restrict some rights of the defence. These new sections have only been operating for a few months so it is too early to verify their functioning.

Finally, specialized sections are instituted within some Courts of Appeal to adjudicate upon public waters rights (*Tribunali regionali delle acque pubbliche*).

III. Administration of the Court: The Auxiliaries of the Judge

90. From the administrative point of view, a court is composed by the magistrates and all the personnel and employees working therein, all of which are part of the judiciary order. Administration and management of the courts is a task of the Ministry of Justice.

91. Among the court's personnel, mention must be made of the *cancelliere* (clerk of the court) who is in charge of very important functions not only as an auxiliary of the judge (e.g., taking care of the written report of hearings or supervising the redaction of the text of the judge's orders and decisions, which he or she also signs),[170] but also of his or her own (e.g., as concerns the judicial sale of moveable assets, the management of the files of the cases, communications to the parties and so on).

92. Another auxiliary of the judge is the *ufficiale giudiziario* (bailiff), an official of the Ministry of Justice who performs many fundamental tasks within the

169. *See* M. Farina, 'Brevi note sul Tribunale delle società con sede all'estero (art. 10 D. l. 145\2013)', <www.judicium.it>.
170. *See* Arts 57–58 CPC.

administration of justice, most notably as concerns enforcement of decisions (seizure) and service on the parties of court orders or parties' documents (*notifiche*).[171]

93. Both the *cancelliere* and the *ufficiale giudiziario* are under a civil liability when they refuse to perform their functions without good reason or when they perform a vitiated act in bad faith or with fraud.[172]

94. Other auxiliaries of the judge are: (*a*) the court-appointed guardian, in charge of keeping and sometimes managing seized or attached goods, with a right to be remunerated (at given conditions) (Articles 65 et seq. CPC); (*b*) the CTU, who gives opinions on technical issues; (*c*) translators and interpreters, to whom the judge may recur when needed.

IV. The *Pubblico Ministero* (*'Ministère Public'*)

95. Italian civil proceedings are adversary in character, and the court can never start proceedings ex officio. For certain situations, however, it was deemed necessary to preserve some public power of control and/or intervention. To respect the adversarial nature of the proceedings, and the impartial and independent character of the jurisdictional function, the *Pubblico Ministero* (PM) was thus also given an active role in civil proceedings.

The *Pubblico Ministero* is a professional judge,[173] but he or she belongs to a different branch (*magistratura requirente*) than the magistrates who adjudicate disputes (*magistrature decidente*). His or her main function, of course, is to play the role of the public prosecution in criminal proceedings but also in civil proceedings does he or she have a (not marginal) position in verifying the correct application of the law and the proper administration of justice, in safeguarding the interests and rights of the State, and of juridical and incapacitated persons or minors.

96. In cases where the law so expressly states, the PM can start civil proceedings (PM *attore*) (Article 69 CPC). Here, the PM is by all accounts a plaintiff who sues on behalf of the State to safeguard situations characterized by very strong public policies.[174]

97. Moreover, Article 70 CPC lists the specific cases where intervention of the PM in civil proceedings started by the parties is a validity prerequisite of the entire procedure (*intervento necessario*):[175] (*a*) actions which the PM himself or herself could have started in compliance with Article 69 CPC; (*b*) matrimonial litigation;

---

171. *See* Art. 59 CPC.
172. Article 60 CPC.
173. Therefore, all the prerogatives and duties of the adjudicating judge extend to the PM as well, who is not a representative of the executive power.
174. For example, to have a person incapacitated and put under the custody of a guardian.
175. In these disputes, the PM intervention is obtained through a communication of the court to the PM.

(*c*) status and personal capacity cases; (*d*) whenever the law so requires;[176] (*e*) before the *Corte di Cassazione*, in cases provided for by the law.[177]

Moreover, the PM may voluntarily join any proceedings in which he or she believes a public interest is at stake (*intervento volontario*).

98. In disputes which the PM himself or herself has started (or in those which he or she could have started), he or she has the very same powers of the parties as concerns the allegations of facts and evidence, right of appeal, possibility to request interim relief and so forth.

More limited powers can be exercised in disputes in which the PM has a simple right of joinder: he or she may file documents, require evidence and present conclusions within the limits of the parties' claims, with no possibility to widen the objective subject-matter of the dispute. Usually, no right of appeal exists in these contexts, with the exception of (some) matrimonial disputes.[178]

Before the *Cassazione*, the PM only presents his or her own conclusions as to whether allow or dismiss the parties' appeals.

99. Since he or she represents, so to speak, the public interests, the PM can of course abstain from participating in the proceedings on the same grounds as the adjudicating judge (*astensione*); he or she can never, however, be challenged by the parties (Article 73 CPC).

V. Appointment of Judges

100. Both career judges and laymen or honorary judges belong to the Judiciary (*ordine giudiziario*).[179] As a matter of fact, Article 106(2) of the Constitution refers to the law on the *ordinamento giudiziario* in order to provide for the conditions of appointment of honorary judges, who may assume any function which a single ordinary judge may perform.

---

176. For example, *querela di falso*, *see infra*, paras 310 et seq.

177. Article 70 CPC was modified by *DL* No. 69 of 21 Jun. 2013, implemented by Law No. 98 of 9 Aug. 2013, so that now the participation of the PM in proceedings before the *Cassazione* is not always required but only in certain cases, under statutory provisions: *see* R. Russo, 'Il p.m. presso la S.C. civile! Chi era costui? Appunti sugli artt. 75 e 81 del d.l. n. 69 del 2013', <www.judicium.it>. For an application of the new rule *see*, e.g., *Cass.*, 20 Jan. 2014, n. 1089, GD 10 (2014): 24, ruling that the *Pubblico ministero*'s participation in the public hearings of the so-called '*sezione filtro*' is no longer mandatory but the *Pubblico Ministero* always has the prerogative to participate in those hearings in which he deems a public interest to be at stake, under Art. 70(3) CPC.

178. Article 72(3)(4)(5) CPC.

179. G. Finocchiaro, 'L'accesso in magistratura nella nuova legge sull'ordinamento giudiziario', RDP (2009): 1491; G. Finocchiaro, *Access to the Judiciary under the New Italian Law on the Judiciary System: Critical Remarks*, in *Access to Justice and the Judiciary. Towards New European Standards of Affordability, Quality and Efficiency of Civil Adjudication* 119 (Uzelac & Van Rhee eds, Interstentia 2009); M.A. Lupoi, *Between Tradition and Innovation: The Formation of a Jurist in Italy*, in *The Reception and Transmission of Civl Procedural Law in the Global Society* 112 (M. Deguchi & M. Storme eds, Maklu 2008); G. Scarselli, *supra*, 145 et seq.; P. Biavati, D. Cavallini, R. Orlandi, Assetti della giustizia civile e penale in Italia (Bologna: Il Mulino, 2016), 19.

101. Honorary judges are non-career magistrates who perform some very important judicial functions, traditionally acting as *Giudici di pace* (*see* paragraph 102) or as deputy judges, within the *Tribunale* (*see* paragraph 102), the *Tribunale per i minorenni* and the *Corte d'appello.*[180] They belong to the judicial order along with career judges, and their appointment is allowed (even if not imposed) by the provisions of Article 106(2) Const. Their role is now considered to be essential in order for the civil justice system to operate. In 2016, the Parliament approved Law No. 57 of 28 April, in order to delegate the Government to draft new rules and directives of a reform of the status and the organization of honorary judges. The Government implemented that *legge delega* with DLGS No. 116 of 13 July 2017, introducing a comprehensive reform of both honorary judges and *Giudici di pace*..

102. Until the reform of July 2017, the *Giudice di pace* (justice of the peace) was an honorary judge in charge of adjudicating small claims, a layman who was part of the judicial order so that he or she was subject to all the compatible rules and provisions which apply to professional magistrates. The original idea behind the institution of this honorary judge was that he or she should have been the expression of the society more than a technician of the law. In practice, in the light of the requisites for appointment,[181] more than a simple legal education was required and his or her equitable jurisdiction was limited to cases having a value of not more than EUR 1,100.00: Article 113(2) CPC.[182] His or her office was only temporary,[183] but not gratuitous; a fee was provided for every day he or she held hearings and for every decision rendered or judicial settlement agreed before him or her.

Only Italian citizens could be appointed. Originally, only senior persons could aspire to become justices of the peace; the age limits were however drastically lowered by Law No. 673 of 6 December 1994: until the reform of 2017, a candidate should be at least 30 and not more than 70 years old. A candidate should leave any subordinate employment, both public and private, before he or she could be appointed. Moreover, a candidate should hold a university degree in law and have passed the bar exam.

Also until the reform of July 2017, *Giudici onorari di Tribunale* (GOT) were very widely used, to perform some of the tasks of professional judges of the *Tribunale.*[184] They were appointed by decree of the Ministry of Justice, in compliance with a deliberation of the CSM, upon a proposal of the competent Judiciary Council. In order to be appointed as a *GOT,* the Italian citizenship and a law degree were required. Their position was a temporary one, for a maximum of two mandates (six

180. *See* G. Scarselli, *supra*, 259; P. Biavati, D. Cavallini, R. Orlandi, *supra*, 38 et seq.; R. Caponi, *The Performance of the Italian Civil Justice System: An Empirical Assessment*, ILJ 19 (2016).
181. As revised by Law No. 259 of 14 Nov. 2002.
182. Recently, those powers have even been excluded in any dispute concerning mass contracts governed by Art. 1342 CC: Art. 113(2) CPC as revised by Law No. 63 of 7 Apr. 2003.
183. A *giudice di pace* may serve for no more than 14 years, up to the age of 75.
184. L. Dittrich, 'La 'microriforma' del procedimento di nomina, conferma e revoca dei giudici onorari di tribunale (d. m. 26 settembre 2007)', RDP (2008): 745; F.P. Luiso, 'Magistratura togata, magistratura onoraria, "altra" giustizia', <www.judicium.it>; F.P. Luiso, 'La magistratura onoraria', RTDPC (2008): 355; G. Scarselli, *supra*, 261 et seq.

years in total). The criteria and the procedures for their appointment were revised by a DM of 3 June 2009.

Another type of honorary judge, the auxiliary appeal judge, moreover, was created by DL No. 69 of 21 June 2013, implemented by Law No. 98 of 9 August 2013, in order to try and support Court of Appeal judges in dealing with the massive backlog of appeal litigation, by taking part in the hearings and deciding cases. Retired magistrates, university professors, lawyers may apply for this new position. A total of 400 auxiliary appeal judges will be appointed for five years, with the task to write at least ninety decisions a year, for a compensation of EUR 200.00 *per* decision, up to a maximum of EUR 20,000.00 per year.

103. Law No. 116 of 13 July 2017 introduced a completely new regulation of first instance honorary judges, basically unifying the two previously existing figures of the *Giudice di pace* and of the *Giudice onorario di Tribunale* (*see* paragraph 102) and introducing the new figure of the *Giudice onorario di pace* (honorary justice of the peace), a sort of hybrid figure which will act either as a first instance judge for small claims (the proper *Giudice di pace*) or as an auxiliary of professional judges in the Tribunali.

In order to eventually be appointed as a *Giudice onorario di pace*, a candidate (who must be at least 27 years old) must first be selected by the CSM, upon a proposal from the local Council of the Judiciary. After such selection, the candidate enters into a six-month internship in a *Tribunale*, within the *Ufficio per il processo* (*see* paragraph 45). He or she must also attend at least thirty hours of both theoretical and practical courses organized by the *Scuola superiore della Magistratura.* During this internship, candidates will not receive any form of remuneration. At the end of the internship, the CSM will select the best candidates and appoint them as *Giudici onorari di pace*. After such appointment, a *Giudice onorario di pace* will act either as a proper *Giudice di pace* (i.e., a first instance judge for small claims) or as a member of the *Ufficio per il processo* of a *Tribunale*, to support and coaudivate professional judges, performing important activities such as the preparation of a case to be discussed by the judge, the collection of existing case law, the gathering of evidence, the issue of simpler orders.

The appointment as an honorary magistrate lasts for four years but it can be confirmed for a second four-years mandate. However, there are no preclusions for a *Giudice onorario di pace* to perform other employment of professional activities (with certain incompatibilities concening the exercise of the legal profession within the judicial office the honorary magistrate belongs to).

An honorary magistrate's remuneration will be composed of both a fixed part and a variable part, based upon his or her performance.

104. To be qualified as a professional judge (*giudice togato*), a magistrate must have taken and passed the State exam referred to in Article 106(1) Constitution When such examination is successfully passed, a candidate is appointed for life as a judge.[185]

185. Exceptionally, *emeritus* University professors or lawyers with at least 15 years of practice, upon designation by the *CSM*, can be appointed as judges of the *Corte di cassazione*: Art. 106(3) Const.

The *ordinamento giudiziario* (i.e., the basic rules concerning a judge's appointment, functions, status and career) has lately been subject to several (rather controversial) reforms (*see supra*, paragraph 83). In particular, DLGS No. 160 of 5 April 2006,[186] setting new rules for accessing the Judiciary, has subsequently been largely modified by *legge* No. 111 of 30 July 2007.[187]

Judges are civil servants; to become one, therefore, Article 97(3) of the Constitution requires passing a State exam. Before the exam, a would-be judge's training has a wholly theoretical character, with little or no practical experiences in judicial offices. Periodically, upon the CSM deliberation, according to the vacant seats and the general needs, national examinations are fixed, to appoint a given number of magistrates.

To take the State exam, the following requirements must now be complied with:

- a law degree (after a university course of at least four years) and (alternatively);
- a diploma from a Specialization School for the legal professions, established *ex* Article 16 *DLGS* No. 398 of 1997 (*see infra*) or a diploma for attending a two-year course in a Specialization School established in compliance with DPR 10 March 1982, No. 162);
- a doctorate degree in a juridical subject;
- a qualification to practise the forensic profession;
- having been an honorary magistrate for at least six years;
- having concluded a stage in a judicial office or an eighteen-month professional apprenticeship in the Avvocatura dello Stato, in compliance with Article 73 of DL No. 69 of 21 June 2013, as modified by DL No. 90 of 24 June 2014, converted into Law No. 114 of 11 August 2014.[188]

Also some categories of public servants, administrative judges, university professors, lawyers and state attorneys are entitled to take the exam to become a judge.

Italian citizenship is also required as well as an irreproachable morality and conduct.

The exam (which a candidate may fail for a maximum of three times) is divided into a written part, with essays in civil, criminal and administrative law, and an oral part on eleven group of subjects, including one foreign language.

After the exam, a twelve-month apprenticeship (*tirocinio*) in judicial offices takes place. Trainee judges (the so-called MOT: *magistrato ordinario in tirocinio*) must spend one month of their *tirocinio* attending courses at the *Scuola superiore della Magistratura* (the Magistrates' Higher School) in Scandicci, near Florence.

After they take on their functions, magistrates voluntarily may take part in a permanent training path, organized, at the moment, by the CSM, though a scientific Committee composed of both judges and university professors, with both national

186. In GD 23 (2006): 12.

187. In GD 33 (2007): 8. *See* C. Vellani, 'Interventi in ambito processualcivilistico nella XV legislatura', RTDPC (2008): 1079.

188. G. Finocchiaro, 'Dei tirocini formativi e dell'ufficio per il processo', RDP (2015), 961.

and local initiatives. A *Scuola superiore della magistratura* has also been created for the formation and the bringing up-to-date of judges.[189]

Moreover, every four years, a judge has to undergo a professional evaluation, concerning his or her ability, productivity, care and commitment. In case of a negative outcome of these evaluations, a judge's salary will not be increased, and he or she may be compelled to take qualification courses or given new functions or be excluded from directive tasks or specific functions. After several negative outcomes, a judge will be removed from service.

§2. Members of the Judiciary

I. Introduction

105. The Judiciary is composed of all the (professional and honorary: *see* above) magistrates, performing both adjudicating (*magistratura decidente*) and investigating (*magistratura requirente*) functions. Some of the characteristics and guarantees of the members of the judiciary have already been examined.[190] It must be added that, as a guarantee of their independence and impartiality, judges are irremovable (Article 107 of the Constitution), that is, they cannot be dismissed or transferred from their office without their consent or a deliberation of the *CSM*. Some exceptions, however, exist: ex officio transfers of a judge may be disposed, most notably when some reason of incompatibility exists.

II. Incompatibilities

106. Being a justice of the peace is incompatible with being a member of Parliament (MP) and of local political or control bodies and entities, a minister of any confession, a directive or executive member of a political party.[191] It is also incompatible with having professional relationships with insurance companies or banks.

Lawyers can now[192] become justices of the peace in the same circuit in which they exercise their professional practise; they cannot however defend cases before their own office nor take up at higher instances cases which were previously adjudicated by their own office.

107. Articles 16, 18 and 19 of the basic law on the judiciary order (RD No. 12 of 1941) list the judge's incompatibilities, which a judge is under a duty to disclose and which can be roughly summarized as follows:

189. Rordorf, 'La scuola superiore della magistratura', FI (2008): V, 268.
190. For example, independence, *see supra*, paras 66 et seq.
191. Article 8 Law No. 374/91.
192. The original preclusion has been abrogated.

- with some exceptions,[193] a judge may not perform other (public or private) professional or commercial activities; he or she may however perform liberal activities which do not require enlistment in a professional list;[194]
- a judge may not sit in the same territorial court in which one of his or her relatives practises law;
- with some exceptions, judges with three degrees of kinship of each other cannot sit in the same court;
- moreover, all the ordinary incompatibilities for public servants extend to magistrates.

Honorary judges are subject to an extended regime of incompatibilities, especially when they also practise as lawyers. For example, a very strict regime is provided for lawyers who are appointed as auxiliary appeal judges in compliance with DL No. 69 of 2013 (*see* paragraph 102), as concerns their relations with the parties of the dispute or their lawyers. Moreover, they cannot serve as honorary judges in the Court of Appeal of the judicial district in which they are registered as lawyers.

III. End of Functions

108. Justices of the peace are only temporary: they stay in office for a maximum of fourteen years, up to the age of 75. Honorary judges of the *Tribunale* are also temporary: their office lasts five years, with a possible extension of one more year only.

109. After the reform of 2017 (*see* paragraph 103) the newly created *Giudice onorario di pace* also have a temporary appointment, for a maximum of two four-year mandates, with an age limit of 70.

110. Ordinary professional judges terminate their service when they reach retirement age, voluntarily resign from office, are dismissed[195] or are expelled from service. This of course complies with the notion that the Italian judge is a public servant and a part of a bureaucratic structure.

IV. Discipline and Civil Liability of Judges

111. Taking part in one of the main functions of the State is a challenging task, and it is important that judges always behave properly, both in the exercise of their

193. For example, being a MP or an arbitrator – in arbitrations in which a public administration is involved.
194. For example, being a novelist or a contributor to a review.
195. For example, if the judge loses the Italian citizenship.

functions and in their personal life.[196] Disciplinary sanctions[197] can therefore be imposed by the CSM, on the initiative of the Minister of Justice when a judge: (*a*) fails to perform his or her duties; (*b*) behaves in such a way as to be deemed untrustworthy; or (*c*) undermines the prestige of the Judiciary.

112. After long debates, Law No. 117 of 13 April 1988 introduced a civil liability system for magistrates in Italy.[198] In the light of the critical remarks of the European Commission against that system, a new regulation was enacted by Law No. 18 of 27 February 2015.

It is thus possible for any person to sue the Italian State for both pecuniary and non-pecuniary damages caused by a judge acting in serious fault (*colpa grave*)[199] or with malice (*dolo*) or in cases of denial of justice (*diniego di giustizia*). Such denial of justice recurs when a deadline for the judge to perform a certain judicial activity has elapsed, the interested party has filed a petition for the performance of the relevant activity and thirty days have since then expired in vain without any justified reason.

The claim for damages deriving from a judge's civil liability is brought against the Prime Minister but only after all of the ordinary appeals or the other remedies provided against the relevant decision or order have been used. The claim must be brought within three years since the moment the action is legally allowed. When a party's claim is allowed and damages are awarded, the State must recover the money thus spent from the liable judge: the latter, however, must not be sentenced to pay more than half his net yearly salary (unless he is found to have acted with malice).

A liable judge will also undergo a disciplinary action. He may also be charged with a criminal felony, if that is the case.

---

196. Cavallini & Giangiacomo, *Magistrati onorari e responsabilità disciplinare* (Milan: Giuffrè, 2009); N. Picardi, 'Responsabilità civile del giudice e dello Stato giudice', in *La giurisdizione nell'esperienza giurisprudenziale contemporanea*, ed. R. Martino (Milan: Giuffrè, 2008), 341 et seq.
197. The possible sanctions are: *ammonimento* (admonishment), *censura* (formal blame), *perdita dell'anzianità* (loss of seniority), transfer ex officio, loss of salary, removal and dismissal.
198. On the (civil) liability of the judge in a historical and comparative perspective, *see* A. Giuliani & N. Picardi, *La responsabilità del giudice* (Milan: Giuffrè, 1987).
199. Under the revised rules, 'colpa grave' recurs:

    - in cases of clear violation of European and Italian law; in this regard, the clarity and precision of the rules violated by the judge are considered, as well as the seriousness and inexcusableness of the violation. With specific reference to a manifest violation of European Union law, failure to comply with the obligation to refer a preliminary question of interpretation to the Court of justice under Article 267(3) of the Treaty on the functioning of the European Union as well as the conflict between the judge's act or decision vis-à-vis the interpretation granted by the European Court of Justice are considered;
    - when the relevant facts and evidence are misinterpreted;
    - when a fact is considered to be true when its existence is undeniably negated by the documents of the file of the case;
    - when a fact is considered to be false when its existence is undeniably affirmed by the documents of the file of the case;
    - when a provisional measure is granted outside of its legal limits or without reasons.

Chapter 2. The Bar

§1. Exercise of the Legal Profession

I. Conditions for Admission

113. The legal profession in Italy has been organized and ruled for a long time by the so-called Forensic Professional Law No. 36 of 22 January 1934 (*legge professionale forense*).[200,201] After debates which lasted for decades, finally the Parliament approved a new *legge professionale*, namely Law No. 247 of 31 December 2012.[202]

The traditional distinction between *avvocati* and *procuratori* (which had lost much of its significance over the years) has finally been eliminated by Law No. 27 of 24 February 1997, and every candidate who passes the bar exam now immediately becomes *avvocato*.

There is no professional distinction between litigation lawyers and lawyers who mostly perform extra-judicial activities, nor do Italian *avvocati* specialize as plaintiff rather than defence lawyers.

114. In order to exercise the legal profession in Italy, it is necessary to be registered in a specific list (*albo professionale*),[203] kept and managed by the *Ordine degli avvocati* (Bar Association), organized in both national and local structures. A different *albo* (and a local Bar Association) exists for each *Tribunale*, and it is possible for a lawyer to be enlisted in only a single local *albo* at any given moment. A lawyer however may practise in the whole Italian territory, irrespective of the local *albo* he or she is registered in.

115. To become a lawyer and to be enlisted as such in the professional list,[204] according to the new rules established by decree No. 70 of 17 March 2016 of the Ministry of Justice, after taking a university law degree[205] (*laurea magistrale in Giurisprudenza*), the prospective lawyer must preliminary complete an eighteen-month apprenticeship (the so-called *pratica forense*) under the directions of a qualified and experienced lawyer. An apprentice is now expected to stay at least twenty

---

200. *See* G. Scarselli, *supra*, 337 et seq.
201. M.A. Lupoi, 'Between Tradition and Innovation: the Formation of a Jurist in Italy', *supra*, 110.
202. *See* R. Danovi, *La nuova legge professionale forense* (Milan: Giuffrè, 2014). This new statute required several further regulations and decrees in order for its provisions to be fully implemented. For example, decree of the Ministry of Justice of 14 Feb. 2017, No. 34 established a regulation for the constitution of arbitral and ADR institutions (*Camere arbitrali di conciliazione e degli organismi di risoluzione alternative delle controversie*) within each Bar Association (*see* G. Finocchiaro, 'Le strutture esistenti possono adeguarsi sino a ottobre 2017', GD 16 (2017): 18); on 17 Mar. 2016, moreover, decree No. 70 of the Minisitry of Justice set the new rules concerning the apprenticeship (*tirocinio*) which a law graduate must attend in order to gain access the Bar exam.
203. It is a criminal felony to practice the legal profession without the necessary titles or using forged titles (Art. 348 CP).
204. Special conditions of enlistment exist, however, for specific categories, e.g., University professors or certain magistrates.
205. From an Italian University or a foreign degree confirmed or recognized in Italy.

hours a week in a law office or at least to operate for the same amount of hours under a lawyer's direct supervision (Article 3, decree No. 70 of 2016), attending at least twenty court hearings every six months and actively performing judicial tasks, like the writing of legal opinions and judicial briefs, under the supervision and control of the local Bar Association. Moreover, an apprentice is required to take part in mandatory eighteen-month formative courses organized under Article 43 of the new professional Law No. 247 of 2012. It is also possible for an apprentice to spend a six-month training in a law office in another Member State of the European Union (Article 6, decree No. 70 of 2016). A period of training may also be spent in a judicial office. A year of such practice can be substituted for the participation in ad hoc courses at the so-called Schools for Forensic Specialization, established by the Law Schools, with the collaboration of both magistrates and lawyers. Forensic Schools (*Scuole forensi*), in compliance with Article 29(1), lett. (*c*) of Law No. 247 of 2012, have now also been created by Bar Associations, in the light of Regulation No. 3 of 20 June 2014, drafted by the National Forensic Council (*Consiglio nazionale forense*). Moreover, the possibility has now been introduced for Law School students to perform their first six months of apprenticeship during their final University year (Article 5 of decree No. 70 of 2016).

At the end of this apprenticeship, it is possible to take the State exam, which is held once a year.

The bar exam, at the moment,[206] is organized both at the national and at the local level: the Ministry of Justice provides for the same tests nationwide, but candidates are organized in several Commissions, one for each Italian Court of Appeal.

The exam is composed of both a written and an oral part. The written part is made up of three tests over three consecutive days; candidates must deliver a civil and a criminal law opinion (*pareri*)[207] and write a judicial brief (*atto giudiziale*). The new professional law of 2012 (*see* paragraph 113) made this part of the exam much tougher for the candidates since it forbids them from using codes which also refer to the case law (*codici commentati*). From 2018,[208] therefore, only simple codes and statutory provisions will be available during the written part of the exam.

For the oral part, after the reform of the *legge professionale* of 2012, the candidate must study five mandatory juridical subjects (legal ethics, civil law, criminal law, civil procedural law, criminal procedural law) and two of his or her own choice (within a fixed list).

Passing the written part is a prerequisite for moving on to the oral part of the exam. As a whole, the examination process can take as many as twelve to fifteen months.

After passing the bar exam, until very recently, no form of continuing legal education was formally imposed on a lawyer (if not as a deontological duty towards his

---

206. The Bar exam rules have been revised by Law No. 180 of 18 Jul. 2003: the main innovation is represented by the fact that the candidates' written essays are now corrected by a Commission sitting in a Court of Appeal different from the one they belong to, in order to try and put an end to certain abuses and malpractices of the past. *See* E. Sacchettini, 'Per la "supercommissione" del ministero un ruolo di coordinamento e di controllo', GD 31 (2003): 21 et seq.
207. For every subject, two choices of title are given.
208. This deadline, however, has already been postponed several times: *see* R. Danovi, 'Per gli avvocati i "nuovi" esami non cominciano mai', GD 15 (2017): 8.

or her clients). The situation, however, following the indications of many commentators,[209] has changed in 2007, when the Italian Bar Association approved a regulation[210] which made it compulsory for lawyers to be engaged in an ongoing professional training. The new *legge professionale* of 2012 confirms (Article 11) that a lawyer has the duty to update his or her professional skills. Over the course of every three years, from the beginning of 2008, Italian lawyers are required to earn as many as sixty 'credits' (nine in relation to legal ethics)[211] by attending 'formative events' approved by the national or the local Bar Associations. A very intense formative activity is performed by Forensic Schools organized by the Bar Associations, both at the local and national level. The new law of 2012 excluded certain categories of lawyers from such formative duties (e.g., senior lawyers, with a practice of more than twenty-five years or who are older than 60).

116. Apart from passing the Bar exam, the following conditions must be complied with, in order to be enlisted in an *albo professionale*: (*a*) Italian citizenship;[212] (*b*) unrestricted exercise of civil rights; and (*c*) irreproachable conduct. To reside within the circuit of *Tribunale* in whose *albo* the candidate wants to be enlisted, however, is no longer required.[213]

If all the necessary conditions exist, registration in the list for the professional Bar Association is a mandatory activity and not a discretionary one in order to practise as a lawyer.

Within thirty days of enlistment, the lawyer must appear before the court and take an oath to perform his or her duties with diligence and honourableness, in the interest of justice.

Nowadays, a lawyer enlisted in the *albo* of a specific *Tribunale* can practise and defend cases all over the national territory. Of course, when a lawyer defends cases outside his or her circuit, he or she will usually need to rely on local lawyers too, at least as concerns his or her domicile of election (i.e., the address where all the court's communications will be sent to).

117. Special professional lists exist for:

- lawyers who are also employees of public bodies and entities;
- lawyers who are also full-time university professors;

209. *See* A. Mariani Marini, 'Contro le resistenza sull'aggiornamento nasce la Scuola superiore degli avvocati', GD 24 (2007): 11. For a comparative perspective, *see* F. Carpi & G. Di Federico, *The Education and Training of Judges and Lawyers*, in *Role and Organization of Judges and Lawyers in Contemporary Societies. IXth World Conference on Procedural Law, Coimbra-Lison (Portugal) 25/31-VIII-1991* 405 et seq. (Pessoa Vaz ed., 1995).
210. The first version of the regulation was approved on 18 Jan. 2007 (*see La previdenza forense*, No. 2, 2007, 124); a revised version was then approved on 16 Jul. 2007 (*see* GD 30 (2007): 88).
211. The total number of credits that lawyers are supposed to earn every three years was reduced in 2014.
212. This condition does not apply to nationals of the European Union: Law No. 146 of 22 Feb. 1994.
213. Law No. 14 of 3 Feb. 2003.

- lawyers who can defend cases before the *Corte di cassazione* (*avvocati cassazionisti*);[214] this category includes at least 30,000 lawyers. It is argued that such a large number of lawyers admitted to argue before the Supreme Court is one of the reasons for the enormous workload of the Cassazione;[215]
- trainee practising lawyers (*praticanti*);
- trainee practising lawyers (*praticanti con patrocinio*) who have been admitted to defend small-claim cases before the justice of the peace and the *Tribunale*.[216]

II. Rights and Duties

118. Any lawyer who continuously practises the legal profession[217] has the duty to register with the *Cassa nazionale di previdenza e assistenza forense*[218] and pay contributions each year.

The *Cassa*, on the other hand, is in charge of granting pensions to lawyers (and their heirs: *pensione di reversibilità*), assist women lawyers on maternity leave and so on.

According to the new *legge professionale* of 2012 (*see* paragraph 113), moreover, a lawyer has the duty to stipulate an insurance against professional liability as well as an insurance for himself and his collaborators to cover any damage deriving from an accident they might suffer while performing their professional activities within or outside their office. These rather controversial duties only became effective in November 2017, following a Decree of the Ministry of Justice of 22 September 2016 establishing the essential conditions and basic requirements for such mandatory insurances.

119. A certified lawyer has the right to be paid by his or her clients and to have his or her own local Bar Association approve his or her invoices for payment.

For a very long time, in Italy, contingency fees agreement (*patto di quota lite*) were forbidden. As a matter of fact, a lawyer's fees were periodically determined by the National Bar Association, which drafted professional rates (*tariffe professionali*) which varied according to the value and the complexity of the case and the activities performed therein by the lawyer.

After normative reforms in 2006[219] and a modification of the forensic deontological code,[220] however, it became possible for a lawyer and his or her client to

214. Only lawyers who have been practicing for at least fifteen years can defend cases before the Supreme Court.
215. R. Caponi, 'Italian Civil Justice Reform 2009', *ZZPint* (2009).
216. After at least a year of pre-exam practice.
217. Above certain yearly income limits.
218. More about the *Cassa* in R. Danovi, *Corso di ordinamento forense e deontologia*, 6th edn (Milan: Giuffrè, 2000), 225 et seq.
219. With the so-called decreto Bersani on the enhancement of competition and the liberalization of commercial and professional activities.
220. The latest version of this code was approved by the *Consiglio nazionale forense* on 12 Jun. 2008.

agree on a compensation connected with the fulfilment of certain goals. The professional law of 2012 (*see* paragraph 113), however, at Article 13(4) prohibits agreements where a lawyer receives, as compensation, a share of the claim in dispute. Quite obscurely, though, the new law, at Article 13(3), also allows agreements whereby the lawyer is paid a percentage of the value of the claim. The rational of these two provisions, however, is quite clear: agreements where, at the start of the case, the lawyer is awarded a percentage of the claim, irrespective of the outcome of the dispute, are allowed; agreements where a lawyer, at the end of the case, gets a share of the claim (eventually) awarded are not.[221]

In 2012, moreover, the 'tariff system' was repealed (Article 9 of DL No. 1 of 24 January 2012) and new principles were introduced concerning lawyers' fees. As a matter of fact, decree of the Ministry of Justice No. 140 of 20 July 2012, introduced (effective as of 23 August 2012) new criteria (*parametri*) for taxing a lawyer's fees (*compensi professionali*) by a judge, filling the void created by repealing the previous tariff system. The Decree of the Ministry of Justice No. 55 of 10 March 2014 has reformed these criteria, making them more rational (and more rewarding for lawyers). The new system thus created is now also followed when legal costs are awarded against the losing party (*see* paragraph 305) at the end of judicial proceedings. As a matter of fact, the new system based on 'compensi' is much simpler than the previous one: in the past, for each single professional activity of a lawyer (from serving a document to visiting the court's offices, from attending a hearing to examining a court's order) a tariff existed. Today, on the other hand, compensation refers to whole phases of the proceedings (basically, a preliminary stage where the lawyer prepares for the case, an introductory phase, where the lawyer files the claim or the defence, a preparatory stage, where the case is prepared for the decision, a decision phase, where the lawyer files his final briefs, and an enforcement phase). The new criteria set by the Ministry of Justice provide for different groups, depending on the value of the dispute. Within each group, an average compensation is given for each phase of the case: such average compensation may be reduced or raised depending on various factors, like the quantity of activities performed, the complexity of the dispute, the results obtained. A lawyer's compensation may be raised (up to 40%) when the case is settled, which can be seen as an attempt to avoid a lawyer considering the continuation of the dispute as some sort of professional 'investment'. On the other hand, the judge may reduce a lawyer's fees when she considers that abusive conducts have been performed in order to hinder the speedy dispatching of the case or when a lawyer was involved in vexatious litigation (*see* paragraph 180). As a general rule, moreover, the criteria set by the Ministry of Justice are deemed not to be binding: in other words, the judge may always reduce or raise the compensation levels provided therein according to the specific circumstances of the dispute. The criteria for determining a lawyer's fees have lately been updated and clarified by a decree of the Ministry of Justice, No. 55 of 10 March 2014.

Recently, the lawmaker also tried to make a lawyer's compensation more transparent and foreseeable for the client. As a matter of fact, the old tariff system made it very hard to predict the global final amount of a lawyer's fees and a conflict of interest was thought to exist between the lawyer and the client. In January 2012,

221. R. Danovi, *supra*, 94.

therefore, new legislation was enacted which basically made it compulsory for a lawyer to give the client, at the start of a case, a written estimate of the costs of his professional services. This duty was very much criticized by lawyers and at first the new *legge professionale* of December 2012 toned it down. As a matter of fact, under the original version of Article 13(5) of the *legge professionale*, the lawyer was supposed to give a written estimate of the foreseeable costs of his services only upon the client's request. This provision, however, was modified by Law No. 124 of 4 August 2017, which made the written estimate to the client mandatory again. In other words, since August 2017, at the start of their professional relation, a lawyer is required to inform the client about the foreseeable amount of the related expenses and professional remuneration. Not to provide such a written estimate may be sanctioned as a violation of a legal ethics provision.

A lawyer also has the right to take part in the 'political' activities of the Bar Association both at the national and at the local level (e.g., to elect or be elected as a member of the directive bodies of the Association).

120. The exercise of the legal profession is absolutely incompatible with:

- any commercial activity, under both one's own and somebody else's name. In particular, a lawyer may not be part of a company as an unlimitedly liable associate. On the other hand, he or she can act as head or president or delegate of a limited liability company;
- being a subordinate (private or public) employee;[222] university or high school part-time professors and lawyers working for the legal offices of public entities, however, are exempted;
- performing any other profession (e.g., public notary, priest, journalist, mediator).

Other relative incompatibilities exist, *inter alia*,[223] for:

- judges of the Constitutional Court;
- members of the CSM;
- honorary judges (insomuch as a lawyer who is appointed as an honorary judge cannot defend cases pending before his or her own office or in another level of the procedure after it was decided by his or her office; *see also* paragraph 102).

In cases of incompatibility or when one of the enlistment requisites ceases to exist, the lawyer will be cancelled from the professional list.

121. Legal ethics set rules a lawyer must comply with both in his or her professional and his or her personal life. The basic source of these provisions are the

222. After Law No. 339 of 25 Nov. 2003, it is no longer possible for a lawyer to serve as a part-time public employee: *see* E. Sacchettini, 'Nel termine dei trentasei mesi di moratoria le incongruenze del regime transitorio', GD 48 (2003): 128.
223. For a complete list of relative incompatibilities, *see* R. Danovi, *supra*, 70 et seq.

Forensic Professional Law (*see supra*, paragraph 113) and the Forensic Deontological Code,[224] as revised by the National Forensic Council on 12 June 2008.

It is the task of the Bar Association to enforce deontological rules and promote disciplinary actions against lawyers.

The main duties of a lawyer can be summarized as follows:

- the duty to behave fairly, with dignity and decorum (also as concerns one's personal life when the lawyer's behaviour becomes, so to speak, open to the general public);
- the duty to act loyally and correctly in his or her professional practice;[225]
- the duty to behave loyally vis-à-vis his or her own client,[226] the classic example being the elimination of evidence or omitting to perform certain procedural activities in a timely fashion; whenever a conflict of interests exists with his or her own client, the lawyer should abstain from the case.[227] Even if the lawyer may give up his or her client's defence when serious reasons for doing so exist, he or she must give timely notice, releasing all the information required for the proper prosecution of the case;
- the duty of confidence and secrecy. For its intrinsic nature, a lawyer's activity is deeply rooted in confidence. A lawyer acknowledges many confidential facts of and about his or her clients and he or she must not abuse or misuse such knowledge. It must be stressed that the violation of professional confidentiality is a criminal felony. The lawyer may never be compelled to violate his or her duty of confidence and secrecy;
- the duty of independence: a lawyer must defend his or her client's case in good faith and in the client's best interest, but always from an autonomous standpoint;
- the duty of the defence;
- the duty of competence: a lawyer should never assist in a case he or she is not professionally prepared to take care of;
- the duty of professional updating: this duty is linked with the duty of competence, insomuch as it is the lawyer's duty to always keep in touch with the developments in the law and in the case law;
- no absolute duty to tell the truth exists for Italian lawyers. As a general rule, in judicial proceedings, there is no obligation for the lawyer to tell the truth. Within specific contexts, however, when the alleged facts are the basis on which a judicial order is sought, the lawyer is under a deontological duty to state the truth.[228] Moreover, the lawyer should never file in the proceedings documents that he or she knows are counterfeit or use evidence that he or she is aware of being false. A lawyer is also under the obligation to mention judicial decisions he or she has already been awarded with or denied or that he or she has previously applied for

224. In R. Danovi, *supra*, 381 et seq.
225. For example, he or she should not bring judicial proceedings in bad faith.
226. The violation of this duty can also be sanctioned as a criminal felony.
227. For example, a lawyer who assisted two spouses in familiar disputes should abstain from representing one of them in a dispute against the other.
228. For example, in eviction proceedings, a lawyer can never falsely say that the defendant is in default of payment.

on the same factual basis.[229] However, the lawyer may abstain from presenting the court with case law and legal opinions which negate or go against his or her own juridical allegations;
– the duty to avoid incompatibilities (*see supra*, paragraph 120);
– the prohibition of hoarding for clients: it is considered unworthy of a lawyer to hoard for clients, especially if at another lawyer's expenses;
– the prohibition against using offensive and inconvenient expressions in the course of judicial proceedings (Article 89 CPC). Even in the heat of the argument, a lawyer should never use offensive expressions against the counterpart or his or her lawyer or, of course, the judge. It must be remarked that, disciplinary sanctions aside, the judge can always order offensive expressions to be cancelled from the case file, with a pecuniary sanction on the offender (Article 89 CPC).

122. Until very recently, a lawyer was forbidden from advertising in any form his or her professional activities, to the point that even specifying one's main field of practice on the lawyer's own paper was frowned upon. DL No. 223 of 4 July 2006, implemented by Law No. 248 of 4 August 2006, however, in at attempt at liberalizing the Italian economy, allowed lawyers to release information about their practice, titles and main fields of expertise as well as their fees, in a transparent and truthful way. Moreover, DL No. 138 of 13 August 2011, implemented by Law No. 148 of 14 September 2011, stated that informative advertisement should be allowed by any means and that such information should be transparent, truthful, fair and not deceiving or disparaging. Following such principles, the new professional law of 2012 (*see* paragraph 113) allows a lawyer to advertise her professional activity, the organization and structure of her firm, her professional specializations, and scientific and professional titles. Informative advertisement may be disseminated though any means, also electronic ones: however they should be transparent, truthful, fair and not comparative with other professionals, unclear, deceitful, denigrating or suggestive. If a lawyer does not comply with these provisions, she violates legal ethics and may be sanctioned accordingly (*see* paragraphs 125 et seq.).

123. In his or her relationships with other lawyers, a lawyer must behave with colleagueship, of course, without violating the duty to defend his or her own client. No personal information about a colleague can ever be disclosed, unless it is deemed indispensable for the dispute at hand. A lawyer may never pass judgment on a colleague's professional activity or on the state of a dispute without that colleague's consent.

In the course of judicial proceedings, a lawyer is under a duty not to deposit the 'privileged' letters he or she wrote or received from another lawyer, unless they contain the terms of a settlement agreement, or they represent the evidence of having performed an obligation. A lawyer also must not talk to the judge about a case in the absence of his or her counterpart.

229. *See* Art. 14 of the Forensic Deontological Code.

124. As a general rule, in the course of judicial proceedings, a lawyer should abstain from talking to the prospect witnesses about the circumstances on which they shall be heard, in such a way as to influence their depositions.

III. Discipline

125. When a lawyer violates one or more of his or her deontological duties, he or she may be sanctioned. Until the reform of 2012 (*see* paragraph 113), a lawyer was under the jurisdiction of the local Bar Association (*Ordine*) he or she was a member of. Things changed with the new *legge professionale*: *Consigli distrettuali di disciplina* (Disciplinary District Councils) were created as autonomous bodies, separated from the local Bar Associations, with first instance disciplinary jurisdiction over lawyers. A council's decision may be appealed against a disciplinary board of the National Bar Association (*Consiglio nazionale forense*) whose decision may in turn be appealed before the *Corte di cassazione*.[230]

126. Under the new professional law of 2012, when an *esposto*[231] is filed with the *Consiglio distrettuale di disciplina* of the place where the lawyer is licensed or where the alleged violation of legal ethics took place, a preliminary phase starts where the lawyer is asked to clarify the situation. Only when the *esposto* is deemed grounded, do disciplinary proceedings start with the gathering of evidence and the discussion and the decision of the case.

127. The applicable sanctions are:

- a warning (*avvertimento*): the lawyer is warned that his conduct violated legal ethics; this sanction is awarded for light violations;
- a blame (*censura*), that is, a formal statement as to the committed fault;
- suspension from the exercise of the profession, for no less than two and no more than five years, for serious violation of legal ethics;
- expulsion (*radiazione*): a general prohibition from exercising the profession for the most serious faults; an expelled lawyer loses is professional status.

IV. Civil Liability of the Lawyer

128. In the exercise of his or her professional activities, a lawyer may also face civil liability. This is a rather controversial subject, and new trends are emerging both in the case law and in the general public attitude. Possibly as a consequence of the expansion of the civil liability boundaries vis-à-vis other professional activities (most notably, the medical profession), the public is more aware of the duties and obligations of a lawyer and, for both the right and the wrong reasons, clients are today readier to sue their former lawyers on civil liability grounds.

---

230. R. Danovi, *supra*, 112.
231. For example, from a client or a colleague.

129. Traditionally it was not easy to challenge a lawyer's civil responsibility, since a lawyer was considered to be under an obligation to perform in the best interests of the client to the best of his or her possibilities (*obbligazione di mezzi*) but not to actually achieve the results that his or her client seeks or desires (*obbligazione di risultato*). This distinction, however, in recent years has somehow blurred: as a matter of fact, the *Cassazione*, in recent rulings, has tightened the standards of professional liability for lawyers, increasing the level of care and competence a lawyer has to show in the exercise of his or her profession, as concerns the best way to satisfy his or her client's needs. As an example, when a client asks a lawyer about the chances of success of a judicial claim, the lawyer is under the obligation to give all of the necessary information to the client, so that she can take a sound decision concerning future actions. The weaknesses of a client's case should be duly pointed out, as well as any uncertainty in the application of the law in the area of interest. Procedural defects and faults are particularly troublesome, because they usually derive from lack of diligence or care on the side of the lawyer. Moreover, sanctions against abuse of process, though nominally granted against the parties, may have side-effects against the parties' lawyers, insomuch as the latter may be considered ultimately liable for such abusive conducts.

Having said this. in order to be awarded damages for professional liability, a client has the burden to prove a relation of cause and effect between the lawyer's lack of diligence or care and the negative outcome of the case: in other words, the client must show that, without the lawyer's mistake, he or she would have won (or not lost) the case,[232] which of course, some quite obvious professional mistakes aside, is not an easy thing to show.

§2. (Public) Institutions and (Private) Organizations

130. In the Italian tradition, a lawyer used to work as a sole practitioner or in (relatively small) family firms. This had social and cultural origins: lawyers usually came from well-off families, and often the practice was transmitted from one generation to another. It was also deemed unsuitable for lawyers to organize in 'commercial' structures, thereby losing the personal character of the profession, considering that the so-called *intuitus personae* is the basis on which the lawyer-client relationship is built.

For decades, an insurmountable obstacle was posed by Article 21 of Law No. 1815 of 23 November 1939, which expressly prohibited lawyers (and other professionals) from establishing, exercising or directing, under any guise, companies, institutions, agencies or entities with the function to provide counselling or professional legal advice.[233] One of the rationales of this provision was that the *intuitus*

232. For example, even if a lawyer negligently omitted to timely file an appeal against a decision, the client has to show that, had the appeal been brought, it would have likely been allowed by the Court of Appeal.

233. In deeper detail *see* M. Franzoni, 'Le società di professionisti', *Quaderni dell'avvocatura* (1993): I., 115 et seq. The author notes that this prohibition came from the Fascist intention to avoid that Jew professionals could exercise – under the 'corporate veil' – any professional activity in violation of the 'race legislation'.

personae would obviously be lost in a corporate, impersonal and commercial structure. The Law of 1939[234] only allowed lawyers to form professional associations with other lawyers (*studi associati*). In a *studio associato*, the associate lawyers usually share both the expenses and the incomes, with obvious advantages under the organizing point of view and also for establishing more competitive and dynamic firms. The *studio associato* has no legal standing or 'persona' of its own, apart from some tax and financial aspects: as a matter of fact, the client enters into a direct professional relationship with the associate lawyer(s), who is personally (and exclusively) liable for his or her activities. Some forms of association, on the other hand, are only made to share the expenses, each professional remaining independent as concerns his or her own earnings. For young lawyers, these forms of partnerships are the only way to face growing expenses and organize professionally competitive structures. Today, most legal practices in Italy are organized in *studi associati* of some kind.

Not all lawyers working in a firm, of course, are 'equal' partners: it is also quite common to have lawyers working for another lawyer, with a more or less fixed salary, not always and not necessarily proportionally connected to the value of a case or the global income of the firm.

131. The prohibition against companies among professionals was lifted only in 1999, with DL No. 526 of 21 December, implemented by DLGS No. 96 of 2 February 2001, which for the first time allowed lawyers to form companies (*società tra professionisti*).[235] In particular, lawyers could form '*società in nome collettivo*', i.e., a company model where the personal contribution of the associates prevails over capital and the associates have unlimited liability for the company's obligations. Moreover, only practising lawyers may take part in such a company. Law No. 161 of 2014 (effective as of 25 November 2014) further provided that the business name of a company between lawyers must mandatorily contain the mention that it is a '*società tra avvocati*' or 's.t.a.'

In this context, the new professional law of 2012 (*see* paragraph 113) delegated the Government to enact legislation on companies among lawyers (*società tra avvocati*).[236] Such delegation, however, expired in August 2013, without the Government having taken any normative action in this regard. The majority opinion, therefore, is that now lawyers may (still) not form '*società tra professionisti*' with other professionals (*s.t.p.*) but only *società* with other avvocati (*s.t.a.*).[237] It also has to be remarked that with Law No. 97 of 2013 the previous ban for European (non-Italian) lawyers to form a '*s.t.a.*' in Italy has been lifted, as long as at least an Italian practising lawyer is a partner of such company.

---

234. Reference can be made to the European Interest Economic Grouping (EU Regulation No. 2137/85).
235. *See* M. Stella Richter Jr., 'Società tra avvocati: prime riflessioni su costituzione, modificazione e nullità', FI (2001): V, 332 et seq.
236. *See* G. Alpa, 'Le società tra avvocati. Note preliminari', in *Le società tra i professionisti*, RTDPC, Special issue (2013): 1.
237. Some authors, however, believed that in 2012, prior legislation concerning 'società tra avvocati' was repealed, so that lawyers could only form traditional *studi associati* and not companies of any kind: R. Danovi, *supra*, 77.

A further step in this normative evolution came with the Decree of the Ministry of Justice No. 23 of 4 February 2016, effective as of 16 March 2016, providing for operating rules for professional associations. Today, as a matter of fact, individual lawyers may form multidisciplinary associations with other professionals organized in specific professional associations (*Ordini* and *Collegi*). Non-organized professionals may thus not take part in these multidisciplinary associations. Any individual lawyer may only participate in a single professional association at any time.

Finally, Law No. 124 of 4 August 2014 introduced a new Article 4*bis* in the professional law of 2012, allowing lawyers to form companies to exercise the legal profession. Any of the existing company types may be used for this purpose. At least two-thirds of the shareholders, however, must be lawyers registered in a Bar List or other professional registered in the relevant lists. Even though organized as a company, the exercise of the legal profession is always referred to professional shareholders possessing the necessary requirements for the specific activity. Companies for the exercise of the legal profession (STA: *Società tra avvocati*) are bound to respect the Code of legal ethics and are subject to the disciplinary jurisdiction of the Bar Association they belong to.

Part II. Jurisdiction

Chapter 1. Domestic Jurisdiction

§1. Domestic Conflicts of Jurisdiction

132. In Italian civil procedure, a clear distinction must be drawn between the jurisdiction (*giurisdizione*) and the competence (*competenza*) of the courts. The first notion refers to the general power granted by the law to the courts belonging to the so-called ordinary judicial order to decide determined categories of cases; the latter identifies the specific court(s) which has the power to decide an individual dispute. In other words, competence is a 'fragment' of jurisdiction, and no competence exists without jurisdiction.

Because of this clear distinction, to avoid confusion, I will use the word 'jurisdiction' only in reference to the external limits of the general power of adjudication of the Italian civil courts. All matters of distribution of the disputes among those courts (concerning subject-matter, value and venue issues) will go under the notion of competence.

133. Domestically, conflicts of jurisdiction may arise between civil and administrative courts and, in general, between the judiciary power and the executive power.

As concerns an individual's subjective juridical positions, traditionally, the Italian legal system distinguishes between subjective rights (*diritti soggettivi*) and legitimate interests (*interessi legittimi*); the latter refer to the position of the individual vis-à-vis a public administration, as concerns his or her safeguard against unfair and unjust behaviour of the executive in the exercise of its authoritative powers. With a general (and inaccurate) distinction, it can be said that disputes concerning subjective rights are brought before ordinary civil courts, while those concerning legitimate interests must be brought before the administrative courts (*see supra*, paragraph 19). Sometimes, however, exclusive administrative jurisdiction exists over specific subjective rights.

134. Conflicts of jurisdiction may also arise over disputes relating to the validity of catholic marriages, vis-à-vis the ecclesiastic courts' order. Such conflicts have now become quite common, since the *Corte di cassazione* ruled that, after the new Treaty between Italy and the Holy See of 18 February 1984, the ecclesiastic tribunals could no longer claim exclusive jurisdiction over annulment proceedings and that prior Italian proceedings could be adjudicated notwithstanding the subsequent start of an ecclesiastic dispute over the same marriage.[238]

§2. INTERNATIONAL CONFLICTS OF JURISDICTION

I. Introduction

135. Conflicts of jurisdiction in the transnational setting take place when a dispute contain a foreign element (e.g., residence of one of the parties), so that the State must preliminarily verify whether a connecting factor exists in order for the exercise of its jurisdiction over the dispute to be justified. If no connection exists, the case is usually dismissed (with an exception for the so-called *forum necessitatis*, admitted by certain Italian authors).[239]

When two or more States claim jurisdiction over the same dispute, conflicts of jurisdiction can take the form of parallel proceedings, which may in time lead to a conflict of decisions and obstacles to the free circulation abroad of the judgments rendered in the concurring states.

II. International Treaties

136. In the light of forum shopping and of the delicate policy implications behind rules on transnational jurisdiction, it is submitted that drafting multilateral Treaties, inspired on a real and substantial connection between the forum and the dispute, is the most efficient solution to deal with conflicts of transnational jurisdiction. However, such Treaties are rather hard to agree upon among the States, as the recent experience of a (shelved) draft of a worldwide Convention on jurisdiction and recognition at the Hague Conference clearly shows.[240]

A. The European Common Juridical Space

137. Italy is among the founding States of the European Communities and is now a member of the European Union. Most of the conflicts of jurisdiction arising before Italian courts concern other Member States. Not surprisingly, therefore, the conflict rules most commonly applied today are those provided for by Regulation (EU) No. 2012\1215[241] (the so-called Brussels I*bis* Regulation), on jurisdiction in

238. *Inter alia, see Cass.* 18 Apr. 1997, n. 3345, FD, 1997, 213.
239. *See* P. Biavati, *Giurisdizione civile, territorio e ordinamento aperto* (Milan: Giuffrè, 1997), 230.
240. *See* A. Von Mehren, *Drafting a Convention on International Jurisdiction and the Effects of Foreign Judgments Acceptable Worldwide: Can the Hague Conference Project Succeed?*, 49 AJCL 191 (2001); F. Juenger, *A Hague Judgments Convention?*, 24 Brook. J. Intl. L. 111 (1998); R. Brand, *The 1999 Hague Preliminary Draft Convention Text on Jurisdiction and Judgments: A View from the United States*, RDIPP 31 (2004); Pocar & Honorati, *The Hague. Preliminary Draft Convention on Jurisdiction and Judgments* (Cedam 2005).
241. *See supra*, para. 41.

civil and commercial matters.[242] In recent years, also the provisions provided for by Regulation (EU) No. 2201/03[243] (Brussels II*bis*) on jurisdiction in matrimonial and parental responsibility disputes are rather often used, since conflicts of jurisdictions in these areas of the law are becoming ever more common.

It is beyond the scope of this monograph to enter into any detail about these uniform European pieces of legislation, which are rather well known by practitioners all over the world and would deserve a monograph of their own to be fully analysed.

It should be remarked that Italian courts are ready to apply any Court of justice decisions concerning European Regulations on matters of transnational jurisdiction. In recent years, however, after the Amsterdam Treaty temporarily restricted to national courts of last resort the possibility to raise a preliminary question to the Court in Luxembourg, the Italian *Corte di Cassazione*, at times, appeared to be reluctant to refer to such course of action. As an example, reference may be made to the way the Italian Supreme Court interpreted the new provision on contractual jurisdiction set by Article 5, No. 1, *litt.* (*b*) of Regulation No. 44/01. As a matter of fact, when it came to determine how to define the notion of 'delivery of the goods' mentioned therein in relation to contracts of sale, the court initially favoured a normative approach, with reference to the principles set by the Vienna Sales Convention.[244] In doing so, the *Cassazione* never considered it necessary to apply for a preliminary question before the Court of justice and even stating[245] that such an application would have been 'superfluous'. After a couple of years, however, the Italian Supreme Court overruled its previous case law and came to adopt a factual approach to the notion of 'delivery' even before the Court of justice clarified that this was the right interpretation of the new rule. The *Cassazione*, nonetheless, even in this circumstance failed to refer the case to the European judges.[246]

242. *See* M.A. Lupoi, in: Carpi, Taruffo (eds), *Commentario breve al codice di procedura civile*, 6th edn (Padua: Cedam, 2009), 2875; L. Mari, *Il diritto processuale civile della convenzione di Bruxelles*, vol. I, *Il sistema della competenza* (Padua: Cedam, 1999).
243. *See supra*, para. 41. *See also* M. De Cristofaro, in: Bonilini, Chizzini, Confortini (eds), *Codice ipertestuale di separazione e divorzio. Commentario con banca dati di giurisprudenza e legislazione* (Turin: Utet, 2005), 895; M.A. Lupoi, *Brussels II: New Rules for Transnational Matrimonial Disputes*, in *Essays on Transnational Comparative Civil Procedure* 105 (F. Carpi & M.A. Lupoi eds., Giappichelli 2001); M.A. Lupoi, *The New Lis Pendens Provisions in the Brussels I and II Regulations*, 7 ZZPInt 149 (2002).
244. *Cass. SU* 27 Sep. 2006, n. 20887, GD, 2006, No. 43, 63; *Cass. SU* 14 May 2007, n. 10941, RDIPP, 2008, 221; *Cass. SU* 20 Jun. 2007, n. 14300, *ivi*, 511; *Cass. SU* 19 Mar. 2009, n. 6598, GCM, 2009, No. 3, 479; *Cass. SU* 17 Jul. 2008, n. 19603, *ivi*, 2008, 1158; *Cass. SU* 27 Feb. 2008, n. 5091, GC, 2010, I, 97; F. Ferrari, 'Ancora in materia di regolamento n. 44/2001(CE e del concetto di "luogo di consegna dei beni" di cui all'art. 5, n. 1, lett. b', GC (2007): I, 1411.
245. *Cass.* 20 Apr. 2007, n. 14300, *supra*, §3.4.
246. *See* M.A. Lupoi, *The New Provisions on Contractual Jurisdiction in Regulation (EU) 44/2001* in *Comparative Studies on Business Tort Litigation* 122 et seq. (R. Sturner & M. Kawano eds., Mohr Siebeck 2011).

B. Other International Treaties on Jurisdiction

138. Italy has ratified several bilateral[247] and multilateral Conventions which contain rules on transnational jurisdiction.

With no possibility to provide for an exhaustive list,[248] it is worth mentioning here the Montreal Convention of 28 May 1999 on air transport,[249] the Hague Conventions on minors,[250] the Vienna Convention of 1980 on the international sale of goods.[251]

The rules of international Treaties will as a general rule supersede domestic provisions, within the scope of application of the former.

It has to be noted however that, in the relations with the other Member States of the EU, most multi- and bilateral conventions have been superseded by the uniform European provisions, within their respective scope of application.

III. Rules Applicable in the Absence of a Treaty

139. Italian rules on international jurisdiction have been reformed by Law No. 218 of 31 May 1995 (*see supra*, paragraph 37).[252,253] Most notably, the Italian nationality of the defendant is no longer a general connecting factor as it used to be before, under Article 4 CPC, even though nationality (and the application of Italian law) still plays an important role in many specific matters.

140. General jurisdiction of the Italian courts, whatever the subject-matter of the dispute may be, exists when the defendant is either resident or domiciled in Italy.

Domicile of election, however, is no longer a connecting factor. Enterprises and companies can also be sued in Italy if they have a legal representative here.[254]

According to Article 43 CC, a person's residence is the place where he or she habitually demurs, while his or her domicile is the place where he or she has concentrated his or her interests and business.

141. As concerns special jurisdiction, within the scope of application of Regulation (UE) 1215/15 (i.e., civil and commercial matters as defined by Article 1 of

247. *See* R. Martino, *La giurisdizione italiana nelle controversie civili transnazionali* (Padua: Cedam, 2000), 189 et seq.
248. *See* F. Pocar et al., *Codice delle convenzioni di diritto internazionale privato e processuale*, 3rd edn (Milan: Giuffrè, 1999).
249. *Uniform law review*, 1999, 948; *see* Carbone, 'Criteri di collegamento giurisdizionale e clausole arbitrali nel trasporto aereo: le soluzioni della convenzione di Montreal del 1999', RDIPP (2000): 5.
250. Picone, 'La nuova convenzione dell'Aja sulla protezione dei minori', RDIPP (1996): 705.
251. S. La China, 'La convenzione di Vienna sulla vendita internazionale di diritto uniforme. Profili processuali: la giurisdizione', RTDPC (1990): 769.
252. *See* M.A. Lupoi, *Conflitti transnazionali di giurisdizioni* (Milan: Giuffrè, 2002); Lupoi, M.A., *International Jurisdiction* in *Civil Justic in Italy* 307 et seq. (M. De Cristofaro & N. Trocker eds., Jigakusha 2010).
253. *See* R. Martino, *supra.*
254. Article 3(1) of Law No. 218 of 1995.

the Regulation), Italy has opted to extend the jurisdictional provisions contained in sections 2, 3 and 4 of Title II of this Regulation to disputes against defendants domiciled in a third State.[255] In other words, Italy has effectively harmonized her domestic provisions on jurisdiction to (most) of the European rules in civil and commercial matters, in the true spirit of the common juridical space.

It is a controversial issue whether Italian courts may refer preliminary questions to the European Court of Justice (ECJ) concerning the interpretation of the Brussels I rules, in relation to disputes against defendants domiciled in a third State. From the court point of view, this might prove possible; it is however submitted that this would prove highly inconvenient vis-à-vis the 'extra-community' defendant.

142. In matters outside the scope of application of the Brussels I Regulation, special jurisdiction may also exist if the Italian rules on venue competence (*see infra*, paragraphs 161 et seq.) provide for a forum in Italy.[256]

This 'indirect' method to solve matters of jurisdiction is different from the one previously followed under the CPC, where the distinction between jurisdiction and competence was rather well marked. This 'new' solution, in the German tradition, should help solve conflicts of jurisdiction in specific areas, like enforcement of decisions or non-contentious jurisdiction. It is submitted, however, that this innovation brought by Law No. 218/95 has negative effects, because it can easily lead to the exercise of exorbitant and improper fora, as it has already happened in several reported cases.[257] This is particularly troublesome, especially in the light of the fact that the *renvoi* to the rules on territorial competence has a quite wide scope of application. Some commentators, therefore, believe that this provision should be interpreted in a 'constitutionally oriented' manner, in order not to refer to it when it would lead to the exercise of a jurisdiction lacking any real connection to the parties and the dispute.

143. Law No. 218/95 also provides for several special connecting factors for specific disputes:

- as concerns absence and presumption of death, Italian courts have jurisdiction if the national law of the interested person was Italian law; if the last residence of the person was in Italy; if the court's decision can have juridical effects in Italy (Article 22);

255. As a matter of fact, Art. 3(2) of Law No. 218 of 1995 still refers to the provisions of the Brussels Convention of 1968, but commentators agree that such reference should now be extended to the Regulation provisions which took the place of the former. *Contra*, however, *Cass.* 21 Oct. 2009,n. 22239, *ord.*, GD 2 (2010): 70.
256. G. Raiti, 'Nuovi e (troppo) ampi orizzonti aperti alla giurisdizione italiana in materia di separazione e divorzio per effetto del rinvio alle disposizioni sulla competenza territoriale', GC (1999): I, 2384.
257. For example, automatic *forum actoris* when the defendant has no known abode in Italy, as per Art. 18(2) CPC: *see Trib.* Catania 20 Dec. 1999, GM, 2000, I, 545. For other applications, *see Cass.* 9 Dec. 1996, n. 10954, RDIPP, 1997, 958 (in insolvency proceedings); *Cass.* 12 Sep. 1997, n. 9033, FI, 1998, I, 2526 (in paternity matters); *Cass.* 27 Nov. 1998, n. 12056, RDI, 1999, 526 and *Cass.* 3 Feb. 2004, n. 1994, GC, 2004, I, 900 (both in a personal separation dispute); *Trib.* Milano 27 Feb. 2002, in RDIPP, 2002, 1040 (in a divorce case).

- in matrimonial disputes (i.e., litigation concerning the annulment of a marriage, personal separations and divorces), apart from the cases under Article 3, and also when one of the spouses is an Italian citizen or the marriage was celebrated in Italy (Article 32);
- in litigation concerning filiation or personal relations between parents and children, as *per* Articles 3 and 9, and also when either a parent or the child is an Italian citizen or resides in Italy (Article 37);
- in adoption, when at least one of the adopters or the adopted is an Italian citizen or a foreigner residing in Italy or the adopted is a foreign minor abandoned in Italy; in disputes concerning personal or economic relations between the adopted and the adopters or between the adopters and their parents, as *per* Article 3 and also when the adoption is subject to Italian law (Article 40);
- as concerns the protection of incapacitated adults, whenever it is necessary to promptly and provisionally safeguard the person or his or her assets in Italy (Article 44); – in hereditary disputes, when the deceased was an Italian citizen at the time of death; if the succession was opened in Italy;[258] if the most economically consistent part of the hereditary assets is located in Italy; if the defendant is either resident or domiciled in Italy or has consented to the exercise of Italian jurisdiction, unless the claim relates to immovable assets abroad; if the claim refers to assets in Italy.

144. Unlike the former provisions of the CPC, Law No. 218/95 contains a specific provision for jurisdiction in non-contentious matters (*giurisdizione volontaria*). Article 9 states that, in addition to any other connecting factor provided for by Law No. 281/95, Italian courts also have jurisdiction in this context when the decision concerns an Italian citizen or a person who is resident in Italy or when the case refers to situations or relations to which Italian law is applicable.

145. No limits to jurisdiction exist as concerns preliminary matters (i.e., issues that must be solved before and in order to adjudicate the merits of a claim) as long as they can be incidentally decided by the court, with no res judicata effects (Article 6 Law No. 218/95).

146. Traditionally, Italian courts do not enjoy any discretion whether to exercise or dismiss the jurisdiction vested upon them by statutory provisions. Among commentators, however, there is a growing consensus about the need to check the compatibility between the connecting factors provided for by the law and the constitutional principles of due process, especially as concerns effective relief and the safeguard of the right of the defence of the parties.

147. Jurisdiction is established with reference to the state of fact and law existing at the time the proceedings are originally brought, and it does not cease to exist should those conditions change in the course of the trial (*prorogatio jurisdictionis*):

258. That is, the person was in Italy at the time of death.

for example, if the defendant was resident in Italy at the time of service of the initiating petition, Italian courts have (and maintain) jurisdiction even if, later in time, the defendant moves abroad.

On the other hand, in the light of the economy principle, a case cannot be dismissed (even if at the time the proceedings were started Italian courts lacked jurisdiction), should a connecting factor arise ex post facto, after a modification of the relevant facts or statutory provisions (e.g., the defendant was originally resident abroad, but permanently moves to Italy after the start of the proceedings) (Article 8 Law No. 218/95).

148. Article 10 of Law No. 218/95 allows Italian courts to render interim measures either when a domestic court has jurisdiction on the merits or when such measures have to be enforced in Italy.[259] No extraterritorial provisional remedy can therefore be granted if Italian courts do not have jurisdiction on the merits.

It is worth mentioning that, traditionally, lis pendens rules (*see infra*, paragraph 152) are not applied in relation to interim proceedings, where no res judicata is formed.

149. Article 4 of Law No. 218/95[260] has deeply innovated the Italian rules concerning jurisdiction by consent, especially as concerns jurisdiction clauses, whose admissibility was severely limited by the (abrogated) Article 2 CPC.

It is now possible for the parties to draft jurisdiction clauses to refer a dispute (otherwise within the jurisdiction of Italian courts) to a foreign judge, as long as it concerns rights of which the parties may freely dispose (*diritti disponibili*) and written proof of such clause can be given. A choice of foreign forum, however, is no longer binding, should the foreign court or arbitrators fail to exercise the jurisdiction vested upon them or cannot decide the case for any reason.

150. The parties, lacking any other connecting factor, may also voluntarily submit to the jurisdiction of the Italian courts. The parties' consent may be either expressed (normally in the form of a choice of the Italian forum clause of which written proof can be given) or tacit. Article 4(1) l. 218/95 clarifies that a defendant who appears before the court without preliminarily raising a defence of lack of jurisdiction effectively accepts the jurisdiction of the Italian courts. Following the rationale of the case law concerning Article 24 of the Brussels I Regulation, such objection may be raised along with other defences on procedural or substantial grounds, as long as it is clear that the former has a preliminary character vis-à-vis the latter.

151. Italian jurisdiction can never be established in disputes concerning rights in rem over immovable assets located abroad (Article 5, Law No. 218/95). On the other hand, jurisdiction can be found in contractual or in personam disputes related

259. G. Raiti, 'Competenza cautelare italiana e giudizio civile straniero dopo la legge 353/90', RDP (1993): 766.

260. *See* I. Queirolo, *Gli accordi sulla competenza giurisdizionale tra diritto comunitario e diritto interno* (Milan: Giuffrè, 2000); A. Righetti, *La deroga alla giurisdizione* (Milan: Giuffrè, 2002).

to such immovable properties – even though this could lead to conflicts of jurisdiction (and possibly, denials of recognition of the Italian judgment in the State where the *res* is located).

152. Article 7 of Law No. 218 of 1995, inspired by Article 21 of the Brussels Convention of 1968, has for the first time recognized international lis pendens (*litispendenza internazionale*) in Italy.[261]

As a matter of fact, according to the now abrogated Article 3 CPC, previous foreign proceedings were considered absolutely irrelevant if the same dispute was subsequently brought before the Italian courts.

After the reform of 1995, however, applying the *ne bis in idem* principle in the international context, in the light of the principle of automatic recognition of foreign judgments introduced by Articles 64 et seq. of Law No. 218/95, the jurisdiction of the Italian court is denied if previous proceedings between the same parties on the same subject-matter are pending abroad, and the Italian judge comes to the conclusion that the foreign judgment is likely to be recognized in Italy (*pronostico di riconoscimento*). If this is the case, Italian proceedings are not dismissed but stayed, so that, should the foreign court decline its jurisdiction or the foreign proceedings be discontinued or a decision on the merits of the claim not be rendered, the original stay can be lifted and the case adjudicated upon.

The date of seisin is determined according to Italian law as concerns proceedings in Italy (i.e., the moment when the claim is filed in court or handed to the bailiff should it be served on the defendant before its filing in court), and to foreign law as concerns proceedings pending abroad.[262]

153. No general 'lis pendens' rule in relation to connected claims in the transnational setting exists in Italy. Article 7(3) of Law No. 218/95 only states that, when a prejudicial issue falls to be decided in previously pending foreign proceedings, the Italian judge may stay his or her proceedings if he or she thinks that the foreign decision may be recognized in Italy. As a general rule, therefore, Italian proceedings will not be stayed should a related claim be pending abroad.

154. Civil proceedings pending in Italy, following the territoriality principle, as a general rule, are always governed by Italian procedural provision (*lex fori*) (Article 12 of Law No. 218/95), even when some foreign elements are present in the dispute.

Italian will always be the official language of the proceedings, and all foreign documents will normally need to be translated.[263]

It has to be observed, however, that certain European or domestic provisions expressly allow or impose on the judge the application of foreign procedural law in order to perform specific activities: for example, the enforcement of foreign

---

261. *See* M.A. Lupoi, 'Litispendenza internazionale e riconoscimento delle sentenze straniere in Italia: due normative allo specchio', RTDPC (1998): 1215.
262. Article 7(2).
263. In certain areas of Italy, where linguistic minorities are traditionally concentrated, however, special statutes allow proceedings to be held in languages other than Italian (e.g., Alto Adige, where German may be used).

rogatories concerning means to gather evidence unknown to the Italian legislation is allowed as long as those means do not violate the principles of Italian public policy.[264] Article 71(3) hands down a similar rule in relation to service in Italy of foreign decisions or documents.

264. Article 69(4) of Law No. 218 of 1995.

Chapter 2. Competence

§1. Introduction

155. Rules on competence determine which specific court has the power to decide a given dispute within the jurisdiction of the ordinary civil courts. The code of civil procedure gives out criteria to determine both the 'vertical' and the 'horizontal' distribution of civil cases between different courts.

As concerns 'vertical' competence of the Italian courts, after the elimination of the *pretore* in 1998, only two courts exist for civil proceedings at first instance, that is, the *Giudice di pace* and the *Tribunale*. Only in very rare cases does the Court of Appeal have competence at first instance (e.g., recognition of foreign judgments or foreign arbitral awards).

§2. Value and Subject-Matter Competence

156. As a general rule, at first instance, disputes are distributed between the *Giudice di pace* and the *Tribunale* according to their economic value (*competenza per valore*): after a reform in 2009, litigation for a value of up to EUR 5,000.00 is brought before the justice of the peace (Article 7 CPC); on the other hand, any dispute with a value of more than EUR 5,000.00 falls to be decided by the *Tribunale* (as well as any dispute for which a value may not be determined: *valore indeterminabile*).

As a major exception, it has to be noticed that disputes for damages deriving from road or maritime collisions, for a value of up to EUR 20,000.00, fall within the value competence of the *Giudice di pace*.

157. The value of the dispute is determined in relation to the value of the plaintiff's claim; whenever the plaintiff brings more claims together, to determine the competent court, the respective value of each claim is added to the others (Article 10 CPC). Rules are also set to determine the specific value of certain types of disputes, such as those regarding obligations, alimony, immovable goods, enforcement proceedings and the division of common property (Articles 11–17 CPC).

158. The economic value of a dispute becomes irrelevant when the law grants exclusive competence to a court over specific subject-matters (*competenza per materia*), irrespective of any value consideration.

Thus, the *giudice di pace* has exclusive subject-matter competence on the disputes listed in Article 7 CPC, concerning namely:

(a) the marking of boundaries of immovable property and legal distances between trees and hedgerows;
(b) the measuring and using of common services in condominiums;
(c) smoke, heat and noise disturbances between neighbours as *per* Article 844 CC;
(d) some minor disputes concerning pensions.

On the other hand, according to Article 9 CPC, the *Tribunale* has exclusive subject-matter competence, irrespective of value, over tax and finance disputes, personal status and matrimonial claims, *querela di falso* (*see infra*, paragraph 310), enforcement of judgments, honorific rights and disputes of no ascertainable value.

159. Irrespective of value and subject-matter, however, a court can always decide *incidenter tantum* any preliminary issue falling outside of its own competence, since, on the preliminary issue, the decision will spread no res judicata effect. Only when either the law (e.g., as concerns status issues) or the parties require an issue to be adjudicated with res judicata effects, does the court have the duty to transfer the whole case to the court of higher competence (Article 34 CPC).

160. As a general rule, a court can always decide any counter-claim raised by the defendant, related to the object of the dispute and which do not exceed its subject-matter or value competence (Article 36 CPC).

§3. Territorial Competence (Venue)

I. General Venue

161. Once the 'vertically' competent court has been identified vis-à-vis the value and the subject-matter of the case, it is necessary to determine which territorial court of that kind will provide for the actual venue for the dispute.

The code hands out criteria that determine both general and special territorial competence; in the so-called general forum (*foro generale*) any action may be brought against the defendant, irrespective of its subject-matter. Special competence grounds, on the other hand, provide for alternative cumulative fora in which the action may (*criteri facoltativi*) or has (*criteri esclusivi*) to be started, in connection with certain elements of the dispute.

The general connecting factors to determine venue are either the residence (*residenza*) or the domicile (*domicilio*) of the defendant, in compliance with the traditional principle *actor sequitur forum rei* (Article 18 CPC). *Residenza* is the place where a person habitually demurs, *domicilio* where he or she has fixed the main centre of his or her interests and business (Article 43 CC). If both the *residenza* and the *domicilio* of the defendant are unknown, an action can be brought in the place where the defendant is temporarily demurring (*dimora*). Only when the defendant does not have any known abode in Italy, may the action be brought in the forum of the plaintiff's residence (*forum actoris*).[265]

As concerns companies and legal persons, venue is found in the place where the defendant has its main or secondary seat or an agent who can represent it in court.

In multiparty disputes, all the different defendants can be sued in the *foro generale* of one of them, as long as the various claims are related to each other and a joint decision is necessary (Article 33 CPC).

265. Article 18(3) CPC.

II. Special Venue

162. Articles 20–30*bis* CPC list several connecting factors, which grant special venue with reference to the subject-matter of the dispute.

Special territorial venue is granted therein:

- In disputes over obligations of any kind, to the court of the place where the obligation in question either arose or falls to be performed (Article 20 CPC). In contractual matters, reference must be made to the provisions of the CC concerning the place where a contract is considered to be concluded (i.e., the place where the offeror knows about the acceptance of the offeree: Article 1326 CC) or where an obligation falls to be performed (Article 1182 CC). The so-called *forum solutions*, in contractual disputes, is determined according to the agreement of the parties or to the customs or to the nature of the obligation to be performed. In the absence of specific agreements between the parties, obligations to deliver specific and identified goods fall to be performed in the place the goods were located at the time the obligation arose. Pecuniary obligations must be performed at the domicile of the creditor at the time performance becomes due. This provision only applies to obligations to pay a specific and predetermined sum (e.g., the price of the goods in sale contracts), not to obligations to restore damages or to pay a lawyer's fees if they were not agreed upon in advance. Only when it is otherwise impossible to determine the place of performance, must the obligation be performed at the domicile of the debtor at the time performance becomes due.
- In tort disputes, venue is found both at the place where the tort was committed (*forum actionis*) and at the place where the damage was suffered (*forum eventi*).[266]
- Disputes concerning rights in rem on immoveable property, lease and free-loan contracts of immovable assets and businesses, the marking of boundaries between two neighbouring properties and other similar actions fall to be decided by the judge of the place where the immovable asset or the business is located.
- Disputes concerning the possession of an asset (*azioni possessorie*) and *denuncia di nuova opera e di danno temuto* (interim measure to avoid imminent damage to be caused to one's own property deriving from someone else's activities or goods) must be brought in the place where the relevant events have taken or might take place (Article 21 CPC). This special venue is considered to have an exclusive character; in other words, the general *fora* are not applicable here.
- Hereditary disputes are decided by the court of the place where the succession was opened, that is, the domicile of the defunct at the time of death (Article 22 CPC, in relation to Article 456 CC); if the succession was opened abroad, venue exists in Italy in the place where the main part of the Italian hereditary assets is located or, failing that, in the residence of at least one of the defendants.
- Disputes between associates of a company are decided by the court of the company's seat; litigation between co-owners of an asset, of the place where the main part of the common goods is located (Article 23 CPC).

266. More about this in M. De Cristofaro, *Il foro delle obbligazioni* (Turin: Giappichelli, 1999).

– Litigation related to a guardianship or to a patrimonial administration is centred in the place where guardianship or administration is exercised (Article 24 CPC).
– Special venue provisions apply when the defendant is a public administration, which by law is assisted by lawyers belonging to an ad hoc internal structure (*Avvocatura dello Stato*), with territorial offices (*distretti*) located in the main cities. Venue is therefore granted to the court of the place where the local office of the *avvocatura* is found, within whose district the ordinary competent court is otherwise located (Article 25 CPC).
– Enforcement against movable and immovable goods takes place in the court where the goods are located; enforcement against the debtor's credits takes place in the court of the residence of the debtor (Article 26 and 26*bis* CPC). The *giudice dell'esecuzione* (enforcement court) is also the venue for all forms of opposition to the enforcement (Article 27 CPC).

163. As a general rule, parties can freely agree upon the venue for their dispute, before or after litigation has arisen between them. This agreement must be in writing, and it is deemed to have exclusive effects only if it clearly specifies so. Otherwise, it only confers concurrent territorial jurisdiction to the chosen court.

Agreements on venue, however, are not allowed for the disputes listed in Article 28 CPC: litigation where the intervention of the *Pubblico Ministero* is mandatory, enforcement of decisions and opposition to enforcement, interim relief, disputes over possession of a good, chambers proceedings and any other dispute in reference to which the law specifically provides for mandatory territorial jurisdiction.

Disputes listed in Article 28 aside, it is always possible for the defendant to tacitly accept venue, simply by not timely raising the relevant objection (*see infra*, paragraph 171).

§4. Main Claims and Ancillary Claims

164. The fact that more claims are joined together in the same proceedings can affect the competence of the original court. As a general rule, territorial competence can always be derogated as a consequence of related actions being brought together (e.g., as concerns subsidiary claims: Article 31 CPC). Value and subject-matter competence create more problems, though. These problems usually arise as a consequence of the defendant bringing his or her own defences into the litigation, therefore widening the original scope of the dispute. The code tries to ensure that the parties' mutual claims and defences are decided by the same court in the same set of proceedings (*simultaneus processus*). In certain cases, this might require the whole case to be transferred to a court of higher competence. This happens, for example, when a guarantee claim is raised by the defendant, when the global value of both the main and the guarantee claims goes beyond the value competence of the original court (Article 32 CPC). A similar solution is adopted for set-offs[267] and counter-claims; here, however, at certain conditions, the original court may prefer

267. On set-off in civil proceedings *see* E. Merlin, *Compensazione e processo*, vol. I (Milan: Giuffrè, 1991) and vol. II (Milan: Giuffrè, 1994).

to adjudicate the main claim and remit only the set-off or the counter-claim to the court of higher competence (Articles 35–36 CPC).

§5. Other Issues Related to the Competence of the Court

165. In compliance with *ne bis in* idem principle, if the same action between the same parties is brought before different judges, the court second seized must dismiss the case on lis pendens grounds (*litispendenza*).[268] With a certain degree of approximation, two sets of proceedings are deemed to concern the same action when they involve the same parties and have the same object and title.[269] In Italian procedural literature and case law, however, different positions exist as concerns this 'identity' issue, as a reflection of the different notions of res judicata followed, respectively, by the doctrine and the courts. In general, courts tend to apply a wider notion of res judicata, which, for example, extends to preliminary issues to those actually decided in the dispute.

Lis pendens is traditionally considered to relate to the competence of the court, and the relevant judgment is subject to the same forms of appeal as any decision on issues of competence. The lis pendens objection can be raised, even on the court's own motion, at any state and level of the procedure. Seisin is determined in relation to the date of service of the plaintiffs' claim on the defendant or to the date when the claim is filed in court, if the originating petition takes the form of a *ricorso* (Article 39 CPC).

166. When two actions between the same parties are simultaneously pending, one taking in the whole scope of the other (*continenza*), the second action must be dismissed and joined with the previous one, if the first competent to decide both; otherwise, the first action is joined to the second.[270,271]

The cases where such situation may be found are traditionally given two rather different notions: on the one hand, academics believe that in order for *continenza* to exist, there should be a difference in the 'quantity' of each action, so that one of them is a fraction of the scope of the other (e.g., a claim concerning a single instalment vis-à-vis an action referring to the payment of the whole amount due by one of the parties). Case law, on the other hand, gives a wider meaning to *continenza*, including also cases where the scopes of the two concurring actions are actually different, but in one of them an issue falls to be decided which solves a logical and juridical necessary question for the solution of the other case (*presupposto logico necessario*),[272] for example, when the first set of proceedings was started to decide on the validity of a contract and the other for the enforcement of the same contract.

---

268. *See* A. Giussani, '*Complex Litigation*' in *Civil justic in Italy*, 161 et seq. (M. De Cristofaro & N. Trocker eds., Jigakusha 2010).
269. *See* G. Franchi, *La litispendenza* (Padua: Cedam, 1963).
270. Article 39(2) CPC.
271. *See* A. Lorenzetto Peserico, *La continenza di cause* (Padua: Cedam, 1992).
272. *Cass.* 10 Mar. 1999, No. 2077, GD, 1999, No. 17, 79.

167. Moreover, when related actions are simultaneously pending before different judges, the ancillary action is joined to the main one; in all other cases, the second dispute is joined to the previous one. This may happen when two actions require to be decided simultaneously because of certain subjective and/or objective connections between them. No joinder must be ordered, however, when the previous action has reached a more advanced stage than the second so that they would not be efficiently be prepared for Judgment together.

Joinder of related actions is considered an issue of competence, and the relevant defence may be raised, also on the judge's own motion, not later than at the *prima udienza di trattazione* (Article 183 CPC).

Chapter 3. Resolution of Jurisdiction and Competence Conflicts

168. According to the wording of Article 37 CPC, lack of jurisdiction of an ordinary civil court vis-à-vis an administrative court or a public administration can be contested by both the judge and the parties at any stage, and phase of the procedure (e.g., also in appeal). In other words, this defence is not subject to any explicit procedural preclusion. However, the *Cassazione*[273] ruled that Article 37 CPC should be read in the light of the principles of procedural economy and of the reasonable duration of the proceedings, taking into consideration the gradual loss of relevance of the issue of jurisdiction in civil proceedings, since judicial adjudication is no longer considered an expression of public sovereignty but rather as a means to satisfy the parties' rights. With these preliminary remarks, the court came to the conclusion that, under Article 37 CPC, the issue of jurisdiction may be raised at any moment during first instance proceedings, and that the first instance decision may be appealed against on lack of jurisdiction grounds. However, appeal decisions may not be further appealed before the *Cassazione* on a lack of jurisdiction defence, and that defence may not be raised before the *Cassazione* if the issue was not raised at the appeal level: as a matter of fact, in that case, the jurisdiction issue is considered to be covered by what the Supreme Court refers to as 'implicit' res judicata. It is widely believed that in this decision (and in other similar ones), the *Cassazione* has effectively exercised a 'normative' function, basically redrafting the text of Article 37 CPC. Very strong comments and opinions have been expressed against this 'invasive' case law, and it is argued that, in the future, the Italian Supreme Court should take a more traditional approach to the interpretation of procedural rules.

Moreover, a public administration can always contest before the *Corte di cassazione* the jurisdiction of a civil court in a case it is not a party of.

After a reform brought by Law No. 69 of 2009,[274] an ordinary court, when declining its own jurisdiction in a case within the jurisdiction of an administrative court (or vice versa), does no longer simply dismiss the case. As a matter of fact, today, the dismissing court will also indicate the national judge it deems having jurisdiction on the case. A Supreme Court decision on these matters is always binding for any judge and for the parties, even in another set of proceedings on the same subject-matter.

The parties, after the first decision has become res judicata, may, within three months, bring the case before the court indicated in that decision; at this point, the dispute will continue before the new judge, preserving the substantial and procedural effects of the original claim. In other words, following this *translatio iudicii*, no preclusion or procedural bar is met by the parties, preserving the function of the claim initially brought before the 'wrong' court. Evidence gathered before the first judge may still be used in the prosecution of the case before the second court, but it will be given less weight, as *argomenti di prova* only (*see* at paragraph 320). The second court, however, may still bring the case before the Supreme Court, for a binding ruling on the issue of jurisdiction.

---

273. 9 Oct. 2008, n. 24883.
274. *See* G. Trisorio Liuzzi, NLCC (2010): 1217.

With this important reform, the lawmaker has expressly acknowledged the unity of the jurisdictional system of Italian courts, establishing a mechanism for ordinary, administrative, tax and special court to communicate with each other and preserve the parties' rights, in a less formalistic way than in the past.

169. Lack of transnational jurisdiction can be found on the court's own motion, at any stage and phase of the proceedings (Article 11 Law No. 218/95) when the defendant did not file a defence (*contumacia*) or anyway if the dispute refers to rights in rem on foreign immovable assets or if the Italian jurisdiction is denied by the provisions of international Treaties.

In any other case, it is the defendant's burden to contest the court's transnational jurisdiction as his or her first preliminary defence, at any stage and phase of the proceedings, as long as he or she has not already consented to the exercise of that jurisdiction. In other words, a defendant who did not file a defence and was found in default is not precluded from raising a lack of international jurisdiction objection if he or she decides to subsequently join the proceedings (*costituzione tardiva*), as he or she would be precluded from other defences (*see infra*). However, he or she must raise this objection as his or her first defence or he or she will be considered having tacitly accepted the court's jurisdiction as *per* Article 4(1) Law No. 218/95 (*see supra*, paragraph 150).

170. It is possible to bring matters of domestic and transnational jurisdiction before the *Corte di cassazione*, until the case is decided on the merits at first instance, by means of *regolamento di giurisdizione* (Article 41 CPC). Unlike *regolamento di competenza*, this is not a form of appeal, but rather an incident in the procedure, to definitively solve the jurisdiction issue at the very beginning of the dispute.

The petition is brought to the *Cassazione* in the forms of a *ricorso*; the *Cassazione* usually decides with a nine-judge panel (*sezioni unite*); a five-judge panel (*sezione semplice*), however, may be involved if the same issue was previously adjudicated upon by *sezioni unite*.

The court's judgment determines whether ordinary civil courts have jurisdiction to decide the dispute at hand.

While waiting for the Supreme Court's decision, proceedings pending at first instance may be stayed only if the trial judge finds that the *regolamento* is not prima facia inadmissible, or the jurisdiction objection is not clearly ungrounded (Article 367 CPC).[275]

Regolamento di giurisdizione aside, first instance judgments on matters of jurisdiction can be appealed before the Court of Appeal and then to the *Corte di cassazione*.

171. Law No. 69 of 2009 has extensively reformed the rules of the CPC concerning conflicts of competence. Traditionally, an objection of lack of competence can be raised both by the defendant and the judge. After 2009, however, the former

275. This is a recent reform, to avoid abuse of the *regolamento di giurisdizione*, which previously had automatic staying effects on the proceedings on the merits.

has the burden to raise any competence-related (value, subject-matter of venue) defence in his or her very first defensive brief, which he or she also must timely file in court, at least twenty days before the first hearing. If not timely raised, this defence is definitively precluded from being raised by the defendant at a further stage of the proceedings. In order for the defendant to be aware of this procedural preclusion, in 2009, Article 163 CPC (concerning the formal requirements of the originating claim) has been reformed so that today, a plaintiff is under the burden to warn the defendant about the consequences of not raising a timely defence of lack of competence. If such warning is missing, the claim is considered to be invalid.

A peculiar requirement must be complied with when the defendant contests venue: as a matter of fact, in order for such defence to be admissible, the defendant must also single out the competent alternative court and deny competence in the forum chosen by the plaintiff under any applicable ground.[276] If the other parties agree with such indication, the case may be transferred to that other court within three months. Otherwise, the originally seized court will have to decide on the defence of lack of territorial competence, either with a preliminary decision or at the end of the proceedings.

Lack of subject-matter, value and mandatory territorial competence can also be raised by the judge of his or her own motion at the first hearing. After that time limit expires, competence is consolidated onto the seized court and it cannot be contested anymore later in the proceedings.

172. On the parties' objection, or on the judge's own motion, when lack of competence is raised, a decision must be rendered on that issue by the court, either at the preliminary stage or at the end of the proceedings, according to what the instructing judge believes more suitable for the dispute at hand. After 2009, the judge is no longer required to deliver a judgment when he or she decides to rule on the issue of competence at a preliminary stage; today, an *ordinanza* will be rendered instead. The rational of this innovation is that less procedural requirements have to be complied with when releasing an *ordinanza* rather than a *sentenza*: as a matter of fact, the decision may be rendered at the hearing, after oral argument, with a short reasoning. The court, however, also has the option of deciding on any issue of competence at the end of the proceedings, in the decision on the merits: when this is the case, the decision will be taken as a judgment.

If a court dismisses the case for lack of competence, it must also point out the alternative competent court. Unless an appeal is brought against such ruling, the burden is then on the most diligent party to transfer the case to the alternative court referred to in the first judge's decision. At this point, the latter court cannot, as a general rule, decline to decide the case on lack of competence grounds. Only when the second judge questions his or her own subject-matter or mandatory territorial competence, in order to avoid negative conflicts of competence, must he or she refer to the *Corte di cassazione* for a ruling on competence, by way of *regolamento d'ufficio di competenza*. Unlike the other forms of *regolamento di competenza* brought by the parties (*see infra*, paragraph 173), this *regolamento* presented on the court's own motion is not an appeal but an incident in the proceedings.

276. Article 38(1) CPC, as revised by Law No. 69 of 2009.

173. Orders and judgments given on issues of competence,[277] lis pendens and *continenza* (Article 39 CPC) and joinder of related actions (Article 40) can be appealed against.

If competence is the only issue on which the decision was rendered, it can only be appealed by way of *regolamento necessario di competenza*, that is, a special appeal which is brought directly to the *Corte di cassazione*, bypassing the second instance appeal judge.

If the decision was rendered on both issues of competence and other procedural or substantive matters, there is a choice between an ordinary appeal to the Court of Appeal and recourse to the *Cassazione*, by way of *regolamento facoltativo di competenza*. It can also happen that an ordinary appeal and a *regolamento* are contemporarily brought by different parties against the same decision: in such cases, the *regolamento* has to be decided first and the appeal (or the time limit to bring an appeal) is therefore stayed.

When the *Cassazione* rules upon a *regolamento di competenza*, its decision, as concerns the determination of the competent court, is binding not only in the proceedings in which the issue was raised, but also in any future dispute between the same parties on the same subject-matter, should the original one be discontinued because of the inactivity of the parties (*estinzione*). This binding authority of a procedural decision outside of the proceedings it was rendered in is an anomaly in Italian civil procedure.

If, according to the *Cassazione*, the originally seized court is competent, the case can go ahead before it; otherwise, it has to be moved to the alternative court identified by the *Cassazione*. This transfer needs a formal and timely[278] impulse by the party who has an interest to let the case proceed to judgment (*atto di riassunzione*), failing that, the case is discontinued.

277. As concerns the structure and the effects of judgments on issues of competence *see* G. Arieta, *La sentenza sulla competenza* (Padua: Cedam, 1990).

278. That is, within three months of the court's decision: Art. 50 CPC.

Part III. Actions and Claims

Chapter 1. Actions

§1. Definition

174. Traditionally, the (civil) jurisdictional function in divided into three main areas of operations: proceedings where the existence of a right is ascertained and the related remedies granted (*cognizione*), enforcement proceedings, and interim and provisional jurisdiction. In this chapter and in the following ones, the first group will be analysed.

Cognizione proceedings are brought by the plaintiff to ascertain the existence of a right and obtain any necessary order related thereto against the defendant. A civil action, therefore, is always connected to a subjective right.

The right of action, however, in Italian procedural literature, is considered to be partially abstract vis-à-vis the substantive right it refers to. In other words, the right to bring an action exists even if the substantive right the complaint is based upon does not. Therefore, the right of action consists in the plaintiff's right to obtain a decision on the merits from the judge, not necessarily to have his or her claim allowed.

Substantive rights are created and provided for by substantive statutes and do not depend on the forms of action available in the procedural system. On the contrary, there is no formal limitation to the type of action a plaintiff can bring, as long as some conditions are met.

175. Traditionally, the *cognizione* actions a plaintiff can bring are divided into three general categories, according to the kind of remedy the court is asked to provide for:

(1) declaratory actions (*azione di accertamento mero*)[279] can be brought when the existence or the limits of a substantive right are in dispute between the parties. The judgment (which may also consist of a negative declaration) establishes

279. Fabiani, 'Interesse ad agire, mero accertamento e limiti oggettivi del giudicato', RDP (1998): 545; C. Cariglia, *Profili generali delle azioni di accertamento negativo* (Turin: Giappichelli, 2013); E. Merlin, 'Azione di accertamento negativo di crediti ed oggetto del giudizio (casi e prospettive)', RDP (1997): 1064; I. Pagni, 'Note sui limiti di ammissibilità della domanda di mero accertamento', FI (2003): I, 1730.

whether such right exists or not and its contents and limits, and it does not need any further enforcement;

(2) when a right has been infringed upon, an action can be brought to order the infringing party to restore the situation *quo ante*, if possible, and otherwise to pay in kind to compensate for the damages suffered by the plaintiff (*azione di condanna*). Decisions rendered in such actions may need to be enforced against the losing party, if he or she does not voluntary comply with the order of the court;

(3) finally, a court's decision may be required in order to create, modify or extinguish a legal relationship between the parties (*azione costitutiva*) or a personal status.[280] Sometimes, the court's intervention is an *extrema ratio*, when the parties cannot agree to spontaneously intervene on their relationship themselves (e.g., to annul a contract); in other cases, there is no voluntary alternative to the judicial decision and recourse to the court is considered necessary (e.g., to obtain a divorce). Such decisions arguably produce their substantive effects only when they have become res judicata and the situation has therefore been definitively established or removed. No enforcement is, however, required, since the legal relationship is directly created, modified or extinguished by the court's decision.

§2. Admissibility

176. Traditionally, three conditions (*condizioni dell'azione*) are required to exist before a complaint can be deemed to be formally valid:

(1) As concerns standing,[281] the plaintiff must claim to be vested with the right the action is based upon (*legittimazione ad agire*); since the right of action is partially abstract *see* paragraph 174, this condition exists even if, at the end of the proceedings, the plaintiff's complaint is dismissed. This is a corollary of the *principio dispositivo*: only the owner of a right can decide if and when to go to court to have that right adjudicated upon and vindicated (Article 81 CPC).

- On the passive side, the action must be brought against the proper counterpart, the so-called *legittimato passivo*, who will suffer the substantive effects of the decision, should the plaintiff's complaint be allowed.
- Only in exceptional cases, specifically allowed by the law, may someone bring an action in his or her own name to have another person's right adjudicated upon (*legittimazione straordinaria*). An example of this is given by Article 2900 CC, which grants a creditor's standing to bring an action to vindicate a right of his or her debtor against another person, in order to take advantage of the court's decision (*azione surrogatoria*).
- In the CPC, Article 111 deals with a hypothesis of *legittimazione straordinaria*, when the right in dispute is transferred from one of the parties to another person

280. *See* A. Proto Pisani, 'Appunti sulla tutela c. d. costitutiva', RDP (1991): 60.

281. *See* L. Montesano & G. Arieta, *Trattato di diritto processuale*, vol. I, tome I (Padua: Cedam, 2001), 296 et seq.

in the course of the proceedings (*successione a titolo particolare nel diritto controverso*). When this happens, proceedings can continue between the original parties, even if one of them is no longer vested with the right in dispute but rather is a substitute (*sostituzione processuale*) for the new owner. The final decision, however, will also spread its effects on the latter, who will then have standing to bring an appeal against it even if he or she did not take part in the proceedings at first instance. On the other hand, the new 'owner of the right' may decide to join in the proceedings before the judgment is rendered. If that happens, the original party may be dismissed from the dispute, as long as all the other parties express their consent.

(2) The plaintiff must have an actual interest in bringing the proceedings (*interesse ad agire*),[282] in the sense that the court's decision must be necessary to solve a real and actual dispute. As concerns declaratory actions, such interest exists when there is a serious dispute about the existence and the content of a right; in actions for positive orders against the defendant, interest is found in the alleged infringement of the plaintiff's right; in the *azioni costitutive*, interest is considered *in re ipsa*, in the sense that such actions can be brought only when and if the substantive prerequisites for creating, modifying or extinguishing a legal relation may be shown to exist.

(3) Finally, the plaintiff's alleged right must be allowed under the existing laws (*possibilità giuridica*). Since there is no system of forms of actions, it is possible for new rights to be recognized and implemented over the years, in compliance with the evolution of the juridical sensibility of the courts, especially vis-à-vis fundamental constitutional rights.

177. The three conditions examined in the previous paragraph must exist before the merits of the complaint may be decided upon. Other prerequisites must however be present at the time the petition is filed, in order for that complaint to be decided on the merits (*presupposti processuali*).

First of all, the case must be brought before a proper and competent court. If the court lacks either jurisdiction or competence, the case will be dismissed on procedural grounds (*sentenza di rito*).

Only parties who may freely exercise their own rights can take part in the proceedings and perform the acts of the procedure (*legittimazione processuale*).

Both at the substantial and at the procedural level, there is a clear distinction between being vested with a right and having the capacity to exercise that right. In Italy, individuals under 18 years of age do not have that capacity (*capacità di agire*) and therefore lack *legittimazione processuale*. Also certain categories of adults may find themselves unable to exercise their own rights in and out of courts (e.g., legally incapacitated persons, bankrupts).

Individuals who cannot freely dispose of their rights must be represented in court by a tutor or a guardian (*rappresentanza legale*), in compliance with the rules concerning their own status.[283]

---

282. *See* L. Montesano & G. Arieta, *supra*, 298 et seq.; M. Marinelli, *La clausola generale dell'art. 100 c.p.c. Origini, metamorfosi e nuovi ruoli* (Trento, 2005).

283. Article 75(2) CPC.

Similar problems are faced by associations, corporations, public bodies and legal persons of all kind, which participate in the proceedings through their legal representatives.

Sometimes, specific authorizations[284] or deliberations[285] are necessary for guardians or legal representatives to be regularly invested with representative powers. If this is the case, the judge should verify at the start of the proceedings that all representative requirements have been complied with and, if necessary, order the party to regularize his or her position (Article 182 CPC).

Whenever it finds that a party is lacking a necessary tutor, guardian or legal representative, the court may also appoint a temporary representative. The same happens when conflict of interests exists between the party and his or her legal representative.

It is also possible for a person, otherwise able to exercise his or her own rights, to voluntarily delegate another person to take part in the proceedings in his or her name and on his or her behalf (*rappresentanza volontaria*), but not in disputes which concern personal rights (e.g., legal separation). However, pure procedural representation is not allowed, and a party's agent must combine both substantive and procedural representative powers.

Both legal and voluntary representatives take part and perform the acts of the proceedings but do not become parties and do not either suffer from the negative or take advantage of the positive effects of the decision rendered therein. Only in rather extraordinary cases (e.g., *falsus procurator*) will a representative be ordered to pay the other party legal costs.

178. Finally, it must be reminded that, in the vast majority of civil cases, the parties (or their legal or voluntary representatives) need to be assisted by a certified lawyer,[286] who will provide the legal defence and take all the necessary procedural steps in their name and on their behalf, without of course becoming a party to the proceedings or being involved in the res judicata effects of the decision. Only in cases before the *giudice di pace*, for a value of no more than EUR 1,100.00,[287] may the party litigate without a lawyer (Article 82 CPC). Moreover, lawyers may always self-defend themselves (Article 86 CPC).

The party must issue a power of attorney on his or her lawyer (*procura*), with a separate written document prepared or certified by a notary (*atto pubblico* or certified private writing). The *procura*, however, may be, and most commonly is, also released on the margins or at the bottom of certain written acts of the procedure to which the power of attorney refers, typically the original petition (*citazione*) or the defendant's first defence (*comparsa di risposta*). Here, the client's signature under the power of attorney may be certified as authentic by the lawyer himself or herself (Article 83 CPC).

284. For example, from the tutelary judge as concerns minors.

285. For example, from the collective body of whom the representative is the expression.

286. Only lawyers belonging to a special list are entitled to defend cases before the *Corte di cassazione* (*avvocati cassazionisti*): *see* para. 264.

287. The 'self-defence' value limit was raised by Art. 13 of *DL* No. 212 of 22 Dec. 2011. Previously it amounted to EUR 516,14.

Power of attorney is presumed to be released for a determined instance of the procedure only, unless the party expresses a different intention therein. However, it automatically extends its effects to any necessary enforcement activities connected to the decisions rendered in the proceedings.

179. After the lawyer has filed a defence on behalf of his or her client, he or she is entitled to perform and receive all the acts of the proceedings, unless the law expressly states that an act falls to be performed by the party himself or herself. Most notably, all the communications and notices will be performed at the lawyer's address.

The lawyer always has the prerogative to give up his or her defence when he or she has good reasons for doing so; the client, on the other hand, is free to revoke his or her power of attorney with no need to motivate his or her choice; until a new lawyer is appointed, however, this has no effect on the procedural counterpart (who, for example, can continue to serve his or her acts on the original defender) or on the court.

§3. VEXATIOUS LITIGATION

180. The code of civil procedure requires the parties and their lawyers to behave loyally and fairly in the course of the proceedings. The violation of rules of conduct by the lawyer will be reported by the judge to the local Bar Association. Moreover, the procedural behaviour of the party will be evaluated by the judge and used as a means to support the evidentiary conclusions the latter may have reached (*argomento di prova*).

More in general, the code sanctions vexatious litigation with aggravated costs. Vexatious litigation may be defined as the situation where the losing party is found to have either sued or defended himself or herself in bad faith or inexcusable lack of diligence. After the reforms of 2005–2006 and 2009, such form of abuse of process are sanctioned much more effectively than in the past.

First of all, on the counterpart's request, the court may order the losing party to pay both legal costs and damages (Article 96 CPC). In practice, this sanction is not often allowed by Italian courts, since the winning party must prove that he or she suffered some extra damages as a consequence of the dispute he or she had to bring or resist to. Case law shows that such proof is a very hard one to give.

In 2009, however, a new paragraph was added to Article 96 CPC stating that, in any case, in granting orders for costs, the judge may, even on his or her own motion, sentence the losing party to pay to the counterpart, a sum of money equitatively awarded. This new provision is much more effective than the traditional one: here, there is no need to prove that the losing party has caused any actual damage to the counterpart: the mere fact that he or she was found to have sued or resisted in bad faith is deemed enough to sentence him or her to pay for these extra costs.[288] Moreover, the law does not fix any limits to the amount of money which the judge may

---

288. A. Briguglio, 'Le novità sul processo ordinario di cognizione nell'ultima, ennesima riforma in materia di giustizia civile', GC (2009): II, 270; *Trib.* Piacenza 7 Dec. 2010, <www.ilcaso.it>.

award; in other words, the court now enjoys complete discretion in sanctioning vexatious litigation. Case law refers to this new sanction as a form of punitive award,[289] to safeguard both private and public interests.[290]

Case law shows that judges are applying this new provision rather extensively, as a reaction to clearly abusive practices,[291] that is, procedural behaviours in bad faith or with the intent to disrupt or interfere with the fast and efficient dispatching of the case.[292] As a way of example, a judge held a plaintiff to be liable for these extra costs since he had petitioned for seizure against the defendant's properties without filing a document in his possession which clearly showed that his case was unfounded. It is believed that, in the medium term, the application of the new Article 96(3) CPC may help effectively curtailing vexatious litigation in Italy. On the other hand, the advisability of granting the court such wide discretionary powers is questioned, since it may infringe upon the parties' right of action or defence when the judge adopts low standards of culpability.[293]

In rather extreme circumstances, the court may also order a party's lawyer or representative to pay for these extra damages. This will happen, for example, when the lawyer has acted without a power of attorney or has consciously tried to disrupt the course of justice.

---

289. *Trib.* Varese 23 Jan. 2010, *ord.*, <www.ilcaso.it>.
290. *Trib.* Piacenza 7 Dec. 2010, <www.ilcaso.it>.
291. *See*, e.g., *Trib.* Salerno 27 May 2010, <www.ilcaso.it> and *Trib.* Varese 23 Jan. 2010, *supra*, which refer to an abuse of the right of action.
292. For instance, many decisions mention the serious culpableness or malice of one of the parties: *see Trib.* Salerno 27 May 2010, *supra*; *Trib.* Padua 10 Nov. 2009, *ord.*, GM, 2010, 1858; *Trib.* Piacenza 7 Dec. 2010, *supra*; *Trib.* Verona 1 Jul. 2010, *ord.*, GD, 2010, No. 49–50, 24; *Trib.* Modena 22 Sep. 2010, n. 1208, <www.giuraemilia.it>.
293. *See* for instance *Trib.* Terni 17 May 2010, GM, 2010, 1834, stating that Art. 96(3) CPC may sanction also common culpability (*colpa comune*).

Chapter 2. Claims and Defences

§1. Definition and Distinctions

181. As we have seen (*see supra*, paragraph 174), there is no closed set of forms of action in Italian civil procedure, and a plaintiff can bring any complaint, as long as it is based on some rule of law. On the other hand, the maxim *iura novit curia* applies and, in theory, it would be enough for the party to give the relevant facts to the judge who will then be in charge of applying the relevant rules. In practice, in their defences, lawyers will always, at least, suggest the applicable law with reference to more or less specific case law.

182. Theoretically, there is no limit to the complaints a plaintiff can bring against the same defendant in a single action. Most often, a main complaint and some ancillary/subsidiary complaints (e.g., interests and inflation-related damages) will be brought together. It is also rather common for parties to graduate their claims, with a principal and one or more subordinated complaints, should the main one be rejected.[294] Sometimes, however, it will be impossible to cumulate complaints to which different procedural models should apply or for which different courts have exclusive subject-matter competence.

It is also possible for more plaintiffs to sue together one or more common defendants or for a single plaintiff to sue more defendants together (Article 103 CPC: *litisconsorzio facoltativo*).[295] This may take place, however, only if the various claims are connected to each other as concerns their objects or their titles (*connessione propria*) or if the joint decisions depend from the solution of identical questions of facts or law (*connessione impropria*). In other words, *litisconsorzio facoltativo* is admitted only insomuch as it enables the court to solve, in one set of proceedings, several connected disputes, under the principle of procedural economy (*see* paragraph 184).

183. There are cases where either the law or the nature of the substantive right in dispute makes it necessary for the judgment to be rendered in favour or against a plurality of parties (Article 102 CPC: *litisconsorzio necessario*).[296] Such is the case, for example, of a dispute in which a common property must be divided among more than two owners: as a matter of fact, all of the owners of the same asset are necessary parties to the proceedings, and they must sue or be sued together. In some cases, a statutory provision specifies that a certain dispute must necessarily be adjudicated between a plurality of parties.

Disputes of this kind cannot be decided in the absence of one or more proper and necessary parties; to this end, the court has a duty to order the participating parties

---

294. *See* C. Consolo, *Il cumulo condizionale di domande* (Padua: Cedam, 1985).
295. On multi-parties proceedings *see* S. Menchini, *Il processo litisconsortile*, vol. I (Milan: Giuffrè, 1993). Specifically on *litisconsorzio necessario see* G. Tarzia, *Il litisconsorzio facoltativo nel processo di primo grado* (Milan: Giuffrè, 1972).
296. *See* Frasca, 'Note sui presupposti del litisconsorzio necessario', RDP (1999): 399 et seq., 745 et seq.; Tomei, 'Alcuni appunti in tema di litisconsorzio necessario', RDP (1980): 669.

to summon the absent ones within a certain time limit. Should this order not be complied with, the action would be discontinued.

A judgment rendered in the (unnoticed or uncured) absence of a necessary party will have no legal effects as concerns both the participating parties and the absent ones (*inutiliter data*).

184. Italian proceedings are governed by an 'economy' principle (*principio di economia dei giudizi*: *see* paragraph 49), according to which it is proper and functional to try more related issues at the same time and in the same trial, to save time and money and avoid conflicting decisions. A number of provisions, therefore, exist in order to consolidate related actions pending before the same or different courts (e.g., Articles 40 and 274 CPC).

Other provisions exist to coordinate the activities of different courts when related actions are simultaneously pending. According to Article 295 CPC, for example, a court has to stay the proceedings in order to wait for another court to decide a relevant preliminary issue, when such decision will have res judicata effects also on the other dispute (e.g., an alimony dispute will be stayed while another court adjudicates upon the paternity issue).

185. It is also possible that bringing together related complaints (*see* paragraph 182) will make the preparation and the decision of the case lengthy and uneconomic. This may happen, for example, when some disputed claims would be ready to be decided on the basis of documents already collected in the court files while others claims need oral evidence to be gathered or lengthy expert investigation to be performed. In such cases, the court may order the joint claims to be severed from each other.[297]

186. To avoid conflicts of decisions and in compliance with the economy principle, a *ne bis in idem* principle governs Italian civil procedure, according to which the same action cannot be pending before different courts at the same time. A strict 'prior in time' rule applies and the second seized court must dismiss the case (*litispendenza*: Article 39 CPC).[298] When the same action has been duplicated before the same court, on the other hand, on the judge's own motion, the two proceedings are joined together (*see* paragraph 165).

187. Whenever actions are pending before different courts between the same parties and the object of one of them is 'included' in the object of the other, they will be consolidated together (*continenza di cause*) (*see* paragraph 166).

§2. Defences

188. The defendant becomes a party to the proceedings immediately and automatically upon being served with the plaintiff's petition. In order to actively take

297. Article 103(2) CPC.
298. *See* G. Franchi, *La litispendenza* (Padua: Cedam, 1963).

part in the dispute, however, he or she needs to file an answer to the plaintiff's complaint (*comparsa di risposta*) and formally present his or her defences to the court (*costituzione in giudizio*). If he or she does not do so, he or she will be held in default.

189. The most basic defensive line for a defendant is simply to deny the facts on which the plaintiff's action is based (*eccezioni improprie*). This will have the result of compelling the plaintiff to satisfy the burden of the proof and offer evidence as to the existence of those facts, which might eventually lead to a victory by default for the defendant, should the plaintiff not meet this onus. After the reform brought by Law No. 69 of 2009, however, it is no longer enough for the defendant to simply 'deny' the facts on which the plaintiff's claim is based. As a matter of fact, in compliance with the new version of Article 115(1) CPC, the defendant has a burden to specifically contest facts which he or she alleges not to be true. If such burden is not duly complied with, the judge will consider those facts uncontested (and therefore relieve the plaintiff from the burden of proving them).[299]

Today, therefore, when a defendant does not clarify his or her position vis-à-vis a certain set of facts or situations, he or she will be deemed to have accepted those facts as true. Of course, this only works in relation to rights of which a party may freely dispose of.

It is not yet clear however which standard must the defendant meet in his or her denial of the facts alleged by the plaintiff. It is felt that he or she should specifically point out the circumstances that he or she considers to be untrue, but some argue that the new provision might effectively require the defendant to present his or her own version of the relevant facts on which the plaintiff's claim is based. As an example, in a recent decision, a Court of First Instance held that in a dispute concerning the conditions of an immoveable located in Italy, it was not enough for the defendants to simply reply that they were not in the conditions to appreciate the plaintiffs' allegations since they were domiciled in France.[300]

Moreover, even when a fact is not contested by the counterpart but its existence is positively denied by the evidentiary materials gathered in the course of the proceedings, that fact will not be taken into consideration by the judge.

The principle of specific contestation is also not relevant as concerns legal qualifications of facts or evaluations which may be derived from facts. Non contestation, moreover, does not compensate for wanting legal requirements of an act: for instance, it was found that when a contract requires to be stipulated in writing, lack of the written document may not superseded by non contestation from the counterpart.[301]

Parties should contest the facts on which the other parties rely at the latest in the first written brief filed after the first hearing (*see* paragraph 199).[302]

---

299. B. Sassani, 'L'onere della contestazione', <www.judicium.it>.
300. *Trib.* Cuneo 5 Oct. 2010, GM, 2011, 1041.
301. *Trib.* Rovigo-Adria 10 Sep. 2009; *Trib.* Piacenza 2 Feb. 2010, <www.ilcaso.it>.
302. A. Briguglio, 'Le novità sul processo ordinario di cognizione nell'ultima, ennesima riforma in materia di giustizia civile', GC (2009): II, 264.

Commentators agree that non contestation of a fact is irreversible; in other words, a party may not deny a fact which previously he or she has either explicitly or implicitly admitted.

Clearly, the principle of specific contestation introduced in Article 115 CPC imposes a more active role on the side of both the parties and the lawyers, and more intense communications between them. As a matter of fact, in order to effectively reply to another party's brief, a lawyer now has to analyse its content with his or her client, who should be aware of the consequences possibly deriving from a lax response. Commentators agree that the new provision might make lawyers liable for failure to efficiently inform their clients about the factual contents of another party's brief.

190. On a more active level, the defendant can raise objections (*eccezioni*) to the plaintiff's claim, as concerns either the regularity of the proceedings (*eccezioni di rito*) or the merits (*eccezioni di merito*). In particular, to oppose the complaint brought against him or her, a defendant may bring into the proceedings new facts which are incompatible and deny the existence and\or the effects of the facts on which the plaintiff's claim is based. More specifically, since the plaintiff's action is based on those facts from which his or her subjective right allegedly derives (*fatti costitutivi*), the defendant's exceptions tend to extinguish,[303] modify or render inoperative[304] those facts. Of course, these facts (*fatti estintivi, modificativi* or *impeditivi*) are part of the defendant's burden of the proof.

191. Both procedural and substantive objections are subject to a rigid preclusion system; in other words, they have to be raised within a time limit set by the law, or they may no longer be brought.

After the reforms of 2005 (*see supra*, paragraph 37), they have to be presented to the court in a written defence (*comparsa di costituzione*) filed not later than twenty days before the first hearing (Article 167 CPC). If that time limit expires, they are definitively precluded.

An exception is made for those defences (both procedural and substantive) which may be raised ex officio at any stage in the proceedings.[305]

Moreover, some defences are subject to special time limits and preclusions (e.g., jurisdiction and competence, *see* paragraphs 168 et seq.).

192. Finally, the defendant has the option to bring an autonomous action in the proceedings, by way of counter-claim (*domanda riconvenzionale*). Here, the defendant is not simply trying to have the plaintiff's complaint dismissed, but to obtain a favourable decision from the court on an alleged right of his or her own. The objective scope of the dispute is thus widened, with all the due consequences, for example, as concerns the burden of the proof, which falls on the defendant as concerns proving the facts on which the *domanda riconvenzionale* is grounded.

303. For example, a set-off defence.
304. For example, claiming performance is not yet due.
305. For example, that a contract is null and void; that the court lacks jurisdiction (*see supra*, paras n. 169 and 168).

A counter-claim must be connected to the main claim or to the exceptions raised by the defendant before it can be admitted in the dispute (e.g., the defendant can demand performance of the contract which the plaintiff wants to void).

Counter-claims are also subject to a rigid system of preclusion, insomuch as they have to be presented in the first defence (*comparsa di risposta*), which needs to be filed in court twenty days before the first hearing.

Chapter 3. Sanctions on Procedural Irregularities

§1. Formal Requirements

193. Civil proceedings consist of a series of linked and connected acts from the original petition to the final decision. Formal validity of each act, and of the procedure at large, is of particular importance, especially since, from the violation of some formal requirements, fundamental rights of the defence of both parties may be infringed.

Article 121 CPC sets out the general principles applicable as concerns the formal requirements of the acts of the proceedings, stating that, when the law does not determine specific requirements, the acts of the procedure may be done in any form which allows them to fulfil their objective function (*principio della congruità delle forme allo scopo*).

In practice, the law sets out the formal and substantive requirements of most of the main acts of the procedure (e.g., the initiating petition, the first defence of the defendant and so on); but when no legal provision can be referred to, the freedom of forms principle may be followed.

194. Articles 131 et seq. CPC, in particular, set out the formal requirements of the judge's decisions (*provvedimenti*), which may take the form of a decree (*decreto*), order (*ordinanza*) or judgment (*sentenza*).[306]

A judgment defines the proceedings, and as such it can never be revoked by the rendering judge. A judgment may decide the whole case (*sentenza definitiva*) or just a part of it, leaving the rest to be adjudicated upon in a further judgment (*sentenza non definitiva*). A judgment, moreover, may decide a case on either procedural (*sentenza di rito*) or substantive grounds (*sentenza di merito*). It must be exhaustively reasoned (*see* paragraphs 225 et seq.).

Decreti and *ordinanze* are used by the judge to give any necessary indication or order as to the prosecution of the case and its preparation for judgment. Decrees are usually rendered ex parte and are not reasoned; *ordinanze* (much more commonly used than decrees in ordinary civil proceedings) are released after the judge has heard all the parties on a specific issue or in a hearing, with a concise reasoning. Most *ordinanze* have a purely intra-procedural content (e.g., they may dispose the admission of relevant evidence, or they may contain the judge's order to the parties to join a necessary party in the proceedings). However, since the reform of 1990, several types of *ordinanza* which anticipate (certain) effects of the judgment have been introduced in ordinary proceedings as a form of provisional remedy for the parties (*see infra*, paragraphs 239 et seq.).

Both decrees and *ordinanze* can be revoked or modified in the course of the proceedings by the same judge who released them in the first place; they may never compromise the final solution of the case and, as a general rule, they automatically lose any effect if the proceedings are discontinued.

306. Article 131(1) CPC.

195. Formal requirements for performing procedural acts are not self-important but rather a means to an end: that is, the fair and just adjudication of the dispute. In other words, not every minor irregularity or deviation from the statutory model (*irregolarità*) renders a procedural activity null and void. Only more serious procedural defects and fault (*nullità processuali*) are considered by the law.

The law usually sets out also the cases of invalidity of a procedural act (Article 156 CPC). Anyway, as a corollary of the general rule set by Article 121 CPC, even when no specific provision exists, an act is considered null and void when the indispensable formal requirements to fulfil that act's objective purpose are lacking. On the other hand, an act may never be declared null and void if it has achicvcd its objective purpose, notwithstanding any fault or error therein.

Also, in this context, the law usually does indicate when a procedural act must be considered null and void, the most notable examples being Article 164 CPC, which provides for a list of faults that make a *citazione* (the original complaint of the plaintiff) null and void, and Article 160 CPC, as concerns the invalidity of service.[307]

An objection concerning the invalidity of procedural acts can usually be raised by the parties, but never the very party from which such invalidity derives. Only most serious faults can be the object of ex officio initiatives. From this point of view, a distinction is made between those defects which may be rectified (*nullità sanabili*) and those which may not (*nullità insanabili*).[308] The former may be raised by the parties only and only in their first defence after the invalid act has been put to their notice; after this time limit expires, *nullità sanabili* are effectively cured. The latter can be raised ex officio, at any stage of the proceedings. Formal invalidities of a judgment, or *nullità insanabili* of the procedure which were not detected before the decision was rendered (and are therefore 'incorporated' into the decision itself), can be attacked at the appeal level, both in ordinary appeal and before the *Corte di cassazione.*[309] However, even these *nullità insanabili* fall to eventually be cured, should the court render judgment without paying notice to them and the relevant decision not be appealed against on procedural invalidity grounds. As a matter of fact, when a decision becomes res judicata, any formal invalidity in the proceedings is definitively cured.

196. When the court declares an act of the procedure to be null and void, as a rule, it must also order for that act (and all the subsequent dependent acts) to be renovated, if possible. In other words, usually the invalidity of an act, however serious, does not imply that the whole procedure has to be struck out: rather, the case 'goes back' to the step when the invalid act was originally performed, and all the subsequent steps have to be renewed.

197. There are cases where a procedural act may be considered not just invalid, but rather non-existent (*inesistente*). This may happen when an act has defects so

307. *See infra*, para. 208.
308. *See*, e.g., 158 CPC, which specifies that any defect related to the participation of the PM in the proceedings may not be rectified.
309. In compliance with Art. 360, n. 4 CPC (invalidities of the judgment or of the proceedings).

serious that it cannot even be considered a procedural act at all. An inexistent procedural act does not have any legal effect and cannot ever be repaired or rectified.

The code disciplines only one example of procedural inexistence, with reference to a judgment which has not been signed by the judge(s) who rendered it.[310] From this provision, the legal doctrine and the case law have enucleated a general category, which comprises several other very serious procedural invalidities, not expressly sanctioned by the code as such (e.g., a *citazione* which has not been signed by the party's lawyer[311] or service of a document performed in a location which has no connection whatsoever with the addressee).[312]

§2. Time Limits and Preclusions

198. The various activities and phases of civil proceedings are scanned by (more or less rigid) deadlines and time limits, fixed by the law or by the judge, whenever the law expressly allows him to do so.[313]

Unless otherwise stated by the law, time limits in the proceedings do not have preclusive effects (*termini ordinatori*); whenever, on the other hand, a time limit is defined as peremptory by the law, the procedural activity it refers to must absolutely be performed before such limit expires (*termine perentorio*). The main difference is that peremptory deadlines can never be shortened or prolonged (Article 153 CPC). Non-peremptory time limits, on the other hand, may be prolonged once by the judge, before they elapse (Article 154 CPC). In both cases, however, once the deadline has expired, the activity which should have been performed is definitively precluded, and the interested party, as a general rule, will not be able to perform it in the future course of the proceedings.

Article 155 CPC specifies that, when calculating time limits expressed in days or hours, the beginning day or hour should not be counted, while any festive day must be counted. On the other hand, if the deadline expires on a festive day or on a Saturday,[314] it is automatically moved on to the next working day. Whenever a provision requires a certain amount of *giorni liberi* (free days) to run between two procedural activities, neither the beginning nor the final day must be counted.

Between 1 and 31 August most procedural deadlines are suspended (*sospensione feriale dei termini*). They start to run again on 1 September. An exception to this rule is provided for labour disputes, interim or provisional measures, opposition to enforcement proceedings and some other urgent matters.

199. The reforms introduced by Law No. 353/90 have tried to make proceedings speedier and more concentrated by introducing a system of preclusions to the

310. Article 161(2) CPC. *See* C. Besso, *La sentenza civile inesistente* (Turin: Giappichelli, 1996).
311. *See Cass.* 22 Apr. 1981, n. 2383, FI, 1982, I, 1383.
312. *Cass.* 6 Jul. 1982, n. 4026, GCM, No. 7, 1982.
313. Article 152(1) CPC.
314. *See* Art. 155 CPC as revised in 2005.

procedural activities of the parties, related to a series of peremptory and subsequent time limits.[315]

Roughly speaking, in the first part of the proceedings, the parties bear the burden of proposing all of their claims, counter-claims and defences, alleging all the relevant facts; when the so-called *thema decidendum* has been thus defined, the parties present their evidentiary motions to define the *thema probandum*. It must be noted, however, that after the reforms of 2005, these two phases tend to partially overlap.

More in particular, after having been notified with the plaintiff's complaint, the defendant may bring a counter-claim only in his or her first defence (*comparsa di risposta*), which he or she must file into the court at least twenty days before the first hearing. In the same *comparsa* he or she must also declare his or her intention to join a third party in the proceedings and ask the court to postpone the date of the first hearing, in order to give the third party sufficient time to prepare his or her own defences before the new hearing.

After the reforms of 2005, moreover, twenty days before the first hearing at the latest, the defendant must also present all of his or her procedural and substantive defences which the judge may not raise on his or her own motion in his or her *comparsa di risposta*: as a matter of fact the only procedural and substantive defences which can be raised thereafter are those which the court also may examine ex officio.

In 2009, Article 38 CPC was modified, imposing on the defendant also the burden to raise in the same *comparsa di risposta* any objection to the competence of the court seized.

At the first hearing, the plaintiff may ask a third party to be joined in the proceedings if this request is a consequence of the defences of the defendant; at that hearing only, may the plaintiff also raise a counter-counterclaim (*reconventio reconventionis*) against the defendant (thus widening the objective scope of the dispute), again if such activity is made necessary in the light of the defendant's defences and counter-claims.

After the reforms of 2005, both parties have a final chance to complete, rearrange or modify their claims and defences in written briefs filed within thirty days from the first hearing and in written replies presented in court in the next thirty days (Article 183 CPC). In that second document, the parties must also present all their evidentiary requests to the court. In a third written brief, filed within eighty days of the first hearing, the parties may reply to the evidentiary requests of the counterparts and petition for 'contrary' evidence (*prova contraria*). This new 'schedule' for the parties' activities is much speedier than the one previously existing, and it surely puts lawyers under a serious defensive burden, in order to timely bring a full and effective presentation of the case to the court: as a matter of fact, when the '80 days from the first hearing' time limit expires, no more factual or evidentiary issues or requests can be filed in the proceedings, unless they refer to new circumstances or to elements which was impossible for the parties to have previous knowledge of.

---

315. Arguably, the new preclusions system failed to achieve the aim of speeding up the proceedings: *see* M.A. Lupoi, *Nowhere Fast? Shortcuts to Judgment in Recent Italian Procedural Legislation*, in *Ways of Implementation of the Right to Civil Proceedings Within a Reasonable Time* 300 (Vilnius Universitetas 2016).

In the light of the recent reforms, at the second hearing, the judge should be ready to examine and eventually admit into the proceedings the evidence requested by the parties, so that the case may enter into the evidence-gathering phase at an earlier stage than in the past (when as many as four hearings could be necessary).

Strict deadlines and limits apply at the appeal stage also (Article 345 CPC). Procedural preclusions may always be overcome and the party reinstated in his or her right to perform an otherwise precluded activity if he or she shows that he or she could not act timely for force majeure or for reasons anyway beyond his or her will and control: *rimessione in termini*.[316]

In 2009, this remedy was reformed, with the abrogation of Article 184*bis* (whose scope of application was considered to be restricted to deadlines within pending proceedings and not to time limits to bring a claim, an appeal or an opposition) and the introduction of a new general provision in Article 153(2) CPC.[317] It is now clear, therefore, that a party may be reinstated in any term he or she may have not respected for force majeure, including deadlines expiring outside of the proceedings, as in the case of time limits for bringing an appeal or an opposition against a judgment or a judicial order.

It has to be noted however that courts tend to apply rather strict standards of unculpability before allowing parties to perform an otherwise precluded procedural activity.

316. R. Caponi, 'La causa non imputabile alla parte nella disciplina della rimessione in termini nel processo civile', FI (1998): I, 2658.

317. R. Caponi, *Italian Civil Justice Reform 2009* (ZZPint 2009); S. Caporusso, NLCC (2010): 854.

Part IV. Proceedings

Chapter 1. Pretrial Proceedings

200. Ordinary civil proceedings in Italy do not have a pretrial phase. Most often, however, before bringing their case to court, the parties and their lawyers have talks and possibly meetings to explore the possibility of an out-of-court settlement. In these initial skirmishes, no discovery of the counterpart's evidence usually takes place so that the instructing phase before the judge is really the first chance each party has of accessing the counterpart's documents and information. In this regard, it must be remarked that, while in the course of the proceedings, a party, at certain conditions, may obtain the exhibition of documents from the counterpart, no such order can be released before the start of the proceedings. If the case may be, as a precautionary measure, the counterpart's documents may be seized (*see infra*, paragraph 400), but this will not grant preliminary access to those documents by the seizing party, until the dispute on the right to have them forcibly filed is solved in the course of the proceedings on the merits.

201. Before starting a dispute, however, it is possible to apply for interim provisional relief (*tutela cautelare ante causam*), for example, in order to preserve a certain factual situation or to freeze the debtor's assets until the final judgment or, in some cases, to anticipate the effects of the decision on the merits. Traditionally, when these measures were granted by the court, the applying party was under a burden to start the proceedings on the merits within thirty days, or the interim order would become ineffective: as a matter of fact, in Italian civil procedure, interim measures could not exist in isolation from ordinary proceedings where the merits of the applying party's claim fell to be ascertained. After the reforms of 2005, however, the burden to bring proceedings on the merits within a fixed time limit following the grant of interim relief has been softened as concerns certain provisional measures, and in particular those which anticipate the effects of the final judgment: now, for these orders no deadline to start proceedings on the merits is established: the latter, therefore, may be started at any time by any interested party (or even never at all), as per Article 669*octies* CPC.[318]

318. D. Borghesi, 'Tutela cautelare e strumentalità attenuata: profili sistematici e ricadute pratiche', in *Sulla riforma del processo civile. Atti dell'incontro di studio Ravenna, 19 maggio 2006* (Bologna: Bononia University Press, 2007), 67; U. Corea, 'Autonomia funzionale della tutela cautelare anticipatoria', RDP (2006): 1251; E. Dalmotto, 'Il rito cautelare "competitivo"', RTDPC (2007): 267.

It is also possible to collect evidence before starting the proceedings in which that evidence is meant to be used (*provvedimenti di istruzione preventiva*).[319] Places, persons or goods may be inspected when their condition is likely to change in the time needed for the proceedings to be started, and the causes of their present condition may be ascertained by a CTU (*accertamento tecnico preventivo*: Article 696 CPC).[320]

A special form of preventive expert report has been introduced in 2005: even when no urgent gathering of pretrial evidence is necessary, it is now possible to apply to the court for the appointment of an expert who will at first try to reconcile the parties as to the payment of a certain sum of money allegedly due because of a party's failure to comply with either contractual or extra-contractual obligations. Only when such attempt at reconciliation fails, will the expert deposit his or her report in court for use in future cognizance proceedings on the relevant claims (Article 696*bis* CPC).[321]

Moreover, witnesses can be heard in advance (*a futura memoria*) by the court when there are reasons to fear that they may not be able to attend the proper proceedings (e.g., a person who is very old or very ill).

When evidence is collected before the start of the case, it will not, however, automatically enter into the materials of the proceedings on the merits: as a matter of fact, the instructing judge will always have to evaluate the admissibility and, most of all, the relevance of that evidence in the context of the dispute before the parties may file the reports of the evidence gathered before the start of the proceedings.

202. Effective as of 21 March 2011, but with a brief 'break' between the end of 2012 and the early months of 2013, before starting proceedings in several types of disputes, Article 5 of DLGS No. 28 of 2010 imposes on the parties a mandatory preliminary attempt to mediate the case (*see* paragraphs 451 et seq.).

The idea behind the introduction of this '*condizione di procedibilità*' is that by compelling litigants to at least try to mediate their dispute before actual litigation starts, they may actually come up with a settlement, thus avoiding going to court altogether. In other words, mediation (and other forms of ADR) has been used mostly as a device to disincentive judicial litigation by introducing one more mandatory step on the road to the courthouse. The lawmaker's gamble is that less cases will actually enter the courtroom and that, as a by-product, judges will have to time to dedicate to the dispatching of cases already pending before them.

---

319. *See* C. Besso, *La prova prima del processo* (Turin: Giappichelli, 2004).

320. As revised in 2005: *see* V. Ansanelli, 'Esperti e risoluzione anticipata delle controversie civili nei nuovi artt. 696 e 696-bis c.p.c.', RTDPC (2006): 1245; N. Giallongo, 'Accertamento tecnico preventivo e tutela cautelare nell'arbitrato irrituale dopo la legge n. 80 del 2005, GI, 2006, 214; E. Picozza, 'Brevi osservazioni sulle novità in tema di istruzione preventiva', RDP (2006): 1019.

321. *See* R. Bonatti, 'Un moderno dottor Jekyll: la consulenza tecnica conciliativa', RTDPC (2007): 247; G.N. Nardo, 'La nuova funzione conciliativa dell'accertamento tecnico preventivo alla luce della recente legge n. 80/2005', <www.judicium.it>; A. Tedoldi, 'La consulenza tecnica preventiva ex art. 696 bis c. p. c.', RDP (2010): 805: M. Scalamogna, 'Alcune questioni controverse in tema di consulenza tecnica preventiva con funzione concialitiva', RTDPC (2010): 957.

In particular, this mandatory mediation attempt is required in disputes concerning rights in rem, division of common properties, wills and successions, family agreements (*patti di famiglia*), lease contracts, free-loan contracts, medical liability, libel, insurance, banking and financial contracts. From March 2012, pretrial mediation became mandatory also in relation to condominium disputes.[322]

The basic idea is that a plaintiff, before being entitled to serve his or her originating claim, should file an application with one of the mediation centres approved by the Ministry of Justice to try and mediate the case. If such preliminary mandatory mediation is not duly attempted, at the first hearing, either upon the defendant's objection or even ex officio, the judge will remand the parties to mediation, fixing the following hearing after a delay of three months. It is not clear, however, how should the judge react upon being informed, at that second hearing, that none of the parties has filed an application for mediation in the time given for that purpose. While some commentators argue that the judge should let the proceedings move forward, there are reasons to believe that the law imposes a stricter solution, that is the discontinuance of the proceedings.

The mediation institution, upon receiving the plaintiff's application, will appoint a mediator and invite the other parties to take part in the mediation proceedings. If this is case, the mediator will try to help the parties reach an agreement and conciliate their dispute. When this attempt is successful, the parties' agreement will be made enforceable by the competent *Tribunale*. If the attempt fails (or if three months pass without the parties reaching an agreement), mediation ends and the parties are free to bring their dispute before the courts.

The lawmaker clearly considered that making it mandatory to at least try to mediate a dispute before starting litigation would reduce the courts' workload. In order to achieve this important goal, it has tried to lead even reluctant litigants to participate in such attempt: as a matter of fact, Article 8(4*bis*) of DLGS No. 28 (as revised by DL No. 69/2013) expressly states that, if a party refuses to take part in the mediation proceedings without 'good reason', the judge will evaluate such behaviour as an *argomento di prova* (*see* paragraph 309) in the course of the subsequent judicial litigation. It is still too early to say whether the courts will adopt stricter or laxer standards, as concerns the notion of 'good reason' in this context.

Serious doubts were originally cast, however, on the compatibility of some of the provisions of DLGS No. 28 of 2010 with the Constitution, in particular as concerned the costs of the mediation proceedings and lawyers expressed a very strong opposition against mandatory mediation. The fate of mediation appeared to be sealed when the Constitutional Court, in its decision No. 272 of 6 December 2012, declared several provisions of DLGS No. 28 related to mandatory conciliation as unconstitutional on formal grounds, claiming that, by introducing mandatory mediation, the Government had gone beyond the boundaries set to its normative intervention by Article 60 of Law No. 69 of 2009 (the *legge delega*) (*see* paragraph 6). In the following months, in fact, the number of proceedings started before mediation

322. In relation to mandatory mediation in condominium disputes, Law No. 220 of 11 Dec. 2012, on condominium in immovable property, inserted a new Art. 71*quater* in the *Disposizioni di attuazione* of the CC, giving specific directives as to the way mediation should be conducted when a condominium is a party to a dispute.

centres dramatically dropped, clearly showing that, without an obligation to do so, Italian litigants would not voluntarily try to mediate their dispute. However, after a few months, DL No. 69 of 21 June 2013, implemented by Law No. 98 of 2013, brought mandatory mediation under the limelight again, with a revised version of this ADR device (*see* paragraph 451).

203. Article 5(3) of DLGS No. 28 of 2010 makes it clear that, when the law requires a mandatory attempt of mediation, the parties are always allowed to apply to the court for any interim measures. The new procedural requirement, therefore, does not come in the way of obtaining urgent reliefs.

Moreover, paragraph 4 of the same provision specifies that in certain types of proceedings (namely, *procedimento per decreto ingiuntivo – see* paragraphs 372 et seq. –, *procedimento per convalida di licenza o sfratto – see* paragraph 379 – *procedimento possessorio – see* paragraph 397 – and proceedings for a preemptive evaluation with a conciliative function *ex* Article 696*bis* CPC – *see* paragraph 201) the plaintiff is allowed to apply to the court without previously attempting mediation. However, in the first three proceedings, should the defendant raise an opposition against the plaintiff's claim, the parties will be remanded before the mediation institutions after the preliminary phase of the proceedings, where the judge renders a provisional decision, respectively, on the enforceability of either the *decreto ingiuntivo* or the order of eviction, or on the claim for repossession.

No mandatory attempt to mediate is required in the context of enforcement proceedings, even as concerns petitions for review (*see* paragraphs 420 et seq.), in chamber proceedings or when a civil claim is filed in criminal proceedings.

204. Since 2014, moreover, DL No. 132 introduced *negoziazione assistita* as a further preliminary mandatory procedural step in many civil cases: *see* Part XII.

Chapter 2. Proceedings in First Instance

§1. Adversary Proceedings

I. Ordinary Proceedings

205. Ordinary civil proceedings in Italy develop in a series of connected hearings before the court, with both oral and written defences. Until recently, written defences were either filed in the court's offices between one hearing and the next or directly at the hearing. With the evolution of information technology, however, new provisions have been enacted concerning the so-called *processo telematico*: from 31 December 2014 (30 June 2015 in proceedings before the *Corti d'appello*), according to DL No. 179 of 18 October 2012, implemented by Law No. 221 of 17 December 2012, in particular, it has become mandatory for lawyers to file their written defences and briefs to the *Tribunali* and *Corti d'appello* directly into the e-file of the case through certified electronic e-mail, with a rather sophisticated system of electronic safe signature: this is meant to both reduce the workload of the court's offices and facilitate the court's and the lawyers' activities.

Most of the activities of the case, moreover, are now electronically recorded and most of them are no longer material (e.g., the report of the hearings before the judge should be written by the judge or the clerk directly in an electronic format, the so-called *verbale digitale*; the court-appointed expert is supposed to file its final report as an electronic file and so forth).

This far, the new system has proved effective in organizing the so-called e-file of the case, which is easily accessible for lawyers and all persons involved in the proceedings who are registered in the system (e.g., court-appointed experts) directly from their offices. This has reduced the need for lawyers to pay visit to the court's offices because they may download most of the materials of the case directly onto their computers though the electronic console. Moreover, lawyers are now enabled to file their electronic defences until 23.59 hrs. of the day on which the relevant time limit expires (if one likes such emotional stresses or is bound by time and workload to push it until the very last minutes …). There are of course drawbacks: some lawyers have struggled to update their working methods and embrace the new e-technology applied to civil proceedings. Moreover, there is some scepticism as to the adaptability of this new 'virtual' litigation to cases where long defences are filed and several documents are brought into the case, since the judge is supposed to view all of the materials of the case only through his computer's screen. Lawyers therefore often print a complimentary copy of their defences and documents and hand it to the judge, making it easier for the latter to read and evaluate them.

There is usually no statutory time limit for the next hearing. This is therefore left to the judge's discretion, according to the type of proceedings and the judge's workload. Rather often, several months (and sometimes years) elapse from one hearing to the next. The series of hearings in which proceedings develop is not concentrated. Since proceedings are not divided into a pretrial and a trial phase in the common law sense of the expressions, at their start, the parties are not usually (fully) aware of the counterpart's defensive lines, exceptions and available evidence. Therefore, each party must be given the possibility (and the time) to reply to the other's defences and requests, within the preclusions system set by the code after the reforms brought by Law No. 353/90 and the innovations of 2005 (*see supra*, paragraph 199).

206. The code gives a detailed regulation of proceedings at first instance before the *Tribunale*.

Ad hoc provisions are added for the other special procedural models. In the following paragraphs, the 'ordinary' procedure before the *Tribunale* will be analysed.

The course of the proceedings can be roughly divided into an introductory phase (the parties bring their claims, counter-claims and exceptions), an evidence-gathering phase (the courts examines and eventually allows the parties' requests, and evidence is taken) and a decision phase (judgment is rendered).

A. *Introduction of the Claim*

1. Service

207. In ordinary civil proceedings, the plaintiff's complaint is a written document called *citazione*, which must be served on the defendant by the bailiff as the very first act of the procedure.

The *citazione* is composed of two parts: the *editio actionis*, that is, the presentation of the claim to the defendant and the judge; and the *vocatio in ius*, that is, all the necessary elements to summon the defendant before the court.

In detail, a *citazione* should contain (Article 163 CPC):[323] the indication of the court seized, the names of the parties and of their legal representatives, the facts on which the plaintiff relies and the legal basis of his or her claim (*causa petendi*), the object of the dispute (*petitum*),[324] a list of the documents filed and the evidentiary requests of the plaintiff. The plaintiff must also indicate the date of the first hearing before the court and warn the defendant about the preclusions he or she might face should he or she not file a defence at least twenty days before the date of the first hearing (*see supra*, paragraph 199). After the reforms of 2005, moreover, in the *citazione* the plaintiff should specify his or her fax number or e-mail address. Since 2010, a *citazione* should also mention the tax codes of the parties.

The *citazione* should also include the power of attorney, unless a separate certified document has been arranged for that matter (*see* paragraph 178).

The *citazione* must be served on the defendant at least ninety days before the first hearing – 150 if the defendant resides abroad – (*termine di comparizione*).[325]

---

323. *See* A. Cerino Canova, 'La domanda giudiziale e il suo contenuto', in *Commentario*, ed. Allorio (Turin, 1980), A. Proto Pisani, 'Gli elementi di identificazione della domanda', in *Commentario*, ed. Allorio (Tunn, 1980), vol. I, 1059.
324. A distinction must be made between the so-called immediate *petitum* (i.e., the judgment which the plaintiff asks in his favour of the judge) and the mediate *petitum* (i.e., the proper object of the plaintiff's claim).
325. Article 163*bis* CPC, as revised in 2005.

208. Proceedings are seized (*lis pendens*) at the moment the *citazione* is served. Traditionally, the relevant date was deemed to be that of the actual delivery of the plaintiff's complaint to the defendant. In recent years, however, case law at first and then the lawmaker made it clear that the proceedings are pending on the very day that the plaintiff hands his *citazione* to the bailiff or files the petition in the court's offices, depending on the procedural model applied.[326] In other words, it may be said that, today, in Italy substantially the same rules apply to the issue of lis pendens as those provided for by Article 32 of Regulation EU No. 1215 of 2012.

Service (i.e., delivery to the addressee of an authentic copy of a document), traditionally, is performed by the bailiff (*ufficiale giudiziario*), on the plaintiff's application, in compliance with Articles 137 et seq. CPC.[327] These rather detailed rules provide for a list of the places where service can be performed and of the persons who may receive the copy of the document in lieu of the original addressee, if the latter is not found there in person.

Service can be done in personam, handing out a copy of the *citazione*[328] to the defendant wherever the bailiff happens to find him or her, within the bailiff's own territorial jurisdiction.[329] Most often, however, the document is served on the addressee at his or her place of residence or at his or her workplace. If the defendant cannot be found in those places because of his or her temporary absence, the *citazione* can be handed to a member of his or her family or to a person working with or for him or her, or to the janitor of the building. However, when this is the case, a further message is sent by certified mail to the addressee, warning him or her about the document been delivered at his or her premises.

Service may never be performed in the hands of a minor of less than 14 years of age.[330]

If the document must be served on a legal person, service is performed at the latter's seat, handing a copy to the legal representative or to any clerk in charge of receiving notices or, failing that, to any other person working therein.[331]

If no one is available or willing to receive the document on the addressee's behalf, the bailiff leaves a notice on the defendant's door and deposits the document at the local town hall, where the defendant can later collect it. The bailiff must also send a certified letter to the addressee to inform him or her of the situation.[332]

---

326. *See Corte cost.* 26 Nov. 2002, n. 477 and Art. 149 CPC as revised in 2005. *See also* R. Caponi, 'La nuova disciplina del perfezionamento della notificazione nel processo civile (Art. 149, 3° comma, c.p.c.)', FI (2006): V, 165.
327. On service of documents in Italy *see* in general S. Merz, *Le notifiche in Italia e all'estero*, 5th edn (Padua: Cedam, 2007).
328. Or any other relevant act, according to the stage of the procedure.
329. Article 138 CPC.
330. Article 139 CPC.
331. Article 145 CPC.
332. Article 140 CPC.

Service can also be performed through the postal service (e.g., when the document must be served outside of the bailiff's jurisdiction), as a certified letter.[333] Proof of delivery is provided by a post office letter's return slip.[334]

Ad hoc rules discipline service at the domicile of election of the addressee (Article 141 CPC), to a public administration (Article 144 CPC) or to a member of the Armed Forces (Article 146 CPC).

After the reform of 2009, however, it is now possible to serve an electronic document, either to a certified e-mail address or through delivery by the bailiff of a paper copy of the document, whose original he or she will then store for the next two years: Article 137(3) CPC. Moreover, Law No. 24 of 22 February 2010 introduced Article 149*bis* in the CPC[335] and modified several provisions of the code, providing for rules on service of judicial documents by certified e-mail. The system has been further implemented by the Decree of the Ministry of Justice No. 44 of 21 February 2011, providing for the technical rules for the adoption, in civil and criminal proceedings, of information and communication technologies. DL No. 179 of 18 October 2012, implemented by Law No. 221 of 17 December 2012, further amended Article 149*bis*, providing that this mode of service may be performed by using certified electronic e-mail addresses appearing in public lists or anyway available to public administrations. This innovative method of service requires the intervention of the *Ufficiale giudiziario*.

Moreover, Law No. 53 of 1994 was modified by Law No. 183 of 12 November 2011 and No. 228 of 24 December 2012 in order to enable also lawyers to serve legal documents by certified electronic mail.[336]

When a document has to be served abroad,[337] international Conventions might apply. Within the Member States of the EU, service must now be performed in compliance with the rules of Regulation No. 1393 of 13 November 2007 (*see supra*, paragraph 41). Only when no European provision or international Treaty is applicable, can the document be served by posting a copy in the office of the court seized and mailing another copy to the addressee with a certified letter. A third copy is handed to the *Pubblico Ministero*, who will transmit it to the Ministry of Foreign Affairs, in order to have it delivered on the addressee (Article 142 CPC).

When service must be performed on a person of no known abode (*persona irreperibile*), the bailiff posts a copy of the document in the town hall of his or her last known residence (or, should that also be unknown, of the place of birth of the addressee).[338]

Under certain conditions, set by Law No. 53 of 21 January 1994, lawyers may be authorized by the local Bar Association to directly serve certain procedural acts on

---

333. The Constitutional Court intervened in order to grant actual notice of service by mail on the side of the addressee: *see Corte cost.* 23 Sep. 1998, n. 346, GD, No. 39, 1998, 22; G. Balena, 'Le notificazioni a mezzo posta dopo l'intervento della Corte costituzionale', GI (1999): 1568.
334. Article 149 CPC.
335. *See* F. Valerini, NLCC (2010), 850.
336. *See* M. Gualtieri, 'Sulle notifiche in proprio dell'avvocato tramite posta elettronica certificata', RDP (2013): 1081.
337. *See* B. Gambineri, 'In tema di notifiche all'estero', FI (1997): I, 1006.
338. Article 143 CPC as revised in 2003.

their counterparts, most commonly by mail service.[339] Basically, the lawyer keeps track of all the notices he or she has performed in a certified book, where the name and the address of the addressee are recorded, together with a brief description of the type of document served and the date when notice was sent. This 'direct' form of notice has become very popular, especially in larger and more congested courts. Moreover, DL 179\12 (*see* above) and Decree of the Ministry of Justice No. 48 of 3 April 2013 gave a regulation concerning the possibility for lawyers to also serve documents through certified e-mail.[340]

209. Every form of service allowed for by Italian law should ascertain the date when the document was served on the addressee (or however deposited in the town hall or post office if not delivered in person), the place where service was performed and the identity of the person to whom the document was delivered. As a matter of fact, the bailiff attests, in a written report at the bottom of the original document, all the information required (date and time of service, name of the addressee and of the person who received the copy on the addressee's behalf). If any of these elements is missing or absolutely uncertain, or if the document was not delivered to one of the persons indicated by the relevant statutes, service is null and void, and it should be renovated before proceedings can go ahead and the defendant held in default of appearance. Great consideration is given to the right of the defendant to be duly informed of an attempt to serve a document to him or her in his or her absence from the premises. It is a fundamental task of the judge, at the very opening of the first hearing to check that the originating claim was duly served on the defendant, when the latter has not filed a defence, and, in case of uncertainty he or she will be ready to order the plaintiff to renew such service.

If legal formalities are regularly complied with, service is deemed to be valid even if, in practice, the defendant never received or collected the document. If force majeure or other events occurred that made it impossible for the defendant to be aware of such service, there can be serious implications on the regular course of the proceedings (*see infra*, paragraph 243).

Until recently, service was considered to be '*inesistente*' (nonexistent), when the document was delivered to a person or in a place having no connection at all with the addressee (*see* paragraph 197). Such 'inesistenza' was deemed to be irreparable and in certain situations it could lead to an incurable dismissal of the claim (e.g., in appeal cases where the service of the appeal was considered to be '*inesistente*', the appeal was dismissed and the first instance decision became res judicata). The *Cassazione*, however, in its recent decisions given in full chambers (*sezioni unite*) on 20 July 2016, Nos 14916 and 14917, ruled that the place where service is performed does not represent a constitutive element of service itself. Even when such place has no connection at all with the addressee, service is non *inesistente*, but simply null and void and as such curable when it fulfils its aim (e.g., when the addressee files a defence in the case, if only for contesting that service was defective, or when

339. B. Brunelli, 'Prime riflessioni intorno alla nuova legge sulle notificazioni affidate agli avvocati', RTDPC (1994): 645.

340. *See* G.G. Poli, 'Sulle novità in tema di notifiche "in proprio" degli avvocati a mezzo Pec: riflessioni a prima lettura', FI (2013): V, 154.

the defective service is renewed). According to the Court, service is *inesistente* (and therefore incurable) only when there is no service at all, i.e., when service is performed by a person who has no power to perform such activity or when the document to be served is returned to the sender without being delivered anywhere. This appears to be a less formalistic approach and one which helps preserving the practical effects of a defective service.

2. Registration by the Court

210. The moment when the *citazione* is served has many juridical implications. On the substantive side, for example, legal interests become due and time-bars are suspended; on the procedural side, proceedings are now pending and the same action cannot be brought before a different court (*lis alibi pendens*). These two types of effects, however, are not related to the same notion of service. Procedural effects (and in general effects which concern the position of the serving plaintiff) are automatically produced on the day the *citazione* is delivered to the notification authorities. Substantial effects (and in general every deadline which relates to the receiving party's right of the defence), on the other hand, only start to run from the moment the document is actually delivered to the addressee.

After the *citazione* has been served, moreover, the plaintiff is bound to the claims he or she has made and cannot subsequently add new ones or ask for joinder of more parties within the same proceedings, unless this widening of the original scope of his or her claim(s) depends or is a consequence of the defendant's own defences and counter-claims (*see supra*, paragraph 199).

Moreover, from the day service is performed, if the right in dispute is transferred to a third person, proceedings will continue between the original parties, with the possibility of the purchaser of the right to join the proceedings. The judgment will always have res judicata effects vis-à-vis the new owner of right (*see supra*, paragraph 176).

211. After mere notice of the originating claim, however, seisin of the dispute cannot be considered definitive. As a matter of fact, within ten days of service, the plaintiff bears the burden of filing the case in the court seized, by depositing the original *citazione* (with the bailiff's service protocol at the bottom), any relevant document and the power of attorney (unless the latter was already incorporated in the *citazione*).

Registration of the case is technically called *iscrizione della causa a ruolo*: at this moment, the court's clerk gives a progressive number to the case (*numero di ruolo*), which will be used to identify it for the duration of the proceedings.

If the case is not timely filed, service of a new *citazione* is needed. It is also possible, if not unlikely, that, should the plaintiff omit to do so, the defendant himself or herself registers the case in the court, at the moment of filing his or her own defence, should he or she, for any reason, want to proceed with the dispute.

212. Following the *iscrizione a ruolo*, the court's clerk prepares a file (*fascicolo d'ufficio*), in which a copy of the *citazione* is inserted, along with the parties' own files (*fascicoli di parte*), and the written report of the incoming hearings, a copy of the judge's orders and decisions, and so on. This file is then handed to the court's president, who designates the instruction judge (*giudice istruttore*), who will also be the adjudicating judge if the case falls to be decided by a single judge (*cause monocratiche*); he or she will otherwise be the reporting judge to the three-judge panel (*cause collegiali*).

At this point, the instructing judge can either confirm the date of the first hearing indicated by the plaintiff in his or her *citazione* or postpone it, according to his or her own calendar and workload. If this is the case, a communication is made to the parties, with the indication of the new date of the hearing.

213. If the defendant wants to take active part in the proceedings, he or she has to formally manifest his or her intention to do so, filing in court (*costituzione in giudizio*) (no later than twenty days before the first hearing) a written answer (*comparsa di risposta*) to the plaintiff's *citazione*. In this document, he or she has to present all of his or her defences, objections (both procedural and on the merits) and counter-claims. Any relevant document may also be filed in the defendant's *fascicolo di parte*.

The defendant may also express his or her intention to join a third party (e.g., a co-tort feasor), at the same time requiring the court to postpone the first hearing so that, between the date when the joinder motion is served on the third party and that hearing, at least ninety days elapse (Article 269 CPC). The *Cassazione* recently ruled that, even though the relevant provisions do not expressly say so, the judge has a discretion to not admit such request to join a third party, when a sufficient connection is not found to exist between the substantial positions of the original parties and that of the third party. Judges are therefore now exercising this discretionary power in order to avoid abuse of process.

The defendant may also file his or her answer at the first hearing, but at this point he or she will be precluded from most defensive activities (i.e., bringing a counterclaim, asking for joinder of a third party, raising procedural and substantive defences which may not be raised on the court's own motion) (*see* paragraphs 190 et seq.). Basically, he or she will be entitled only to contest the facts on which the plaintiff relies, to raise defences which the judge could raise of his or her own motion and to present evidentiary requests.

If a defendant does not file a defence even at the first hearing, the judge will declare him or her in default, after checking that a valid claim was duly and timely served on him or her.

B. Progress of Proceedings

1. Preparing the Case for the Decision (*Fase Istruttoria*)

214. The 'model track' for proceedings before the *Tribunale* is a mixed system, where written defences mix with oral hearings and arguments before the court. A basic scheme is provided by the CPC which applies to every dispute, irrespective of its nature. Some options are offered according to the specificities of the single case, the main difference being between those disputes that require the gathering of evidence and those which can be decided on the available documents or in which purely legal issues are raised. Different options are also given as to the way the court can render its judgment at the end of the trial. As a matter of fact, it is believed that the Italian approach to the conduct of civil proceedings is rather rigid and leaves very little room for flexibility and discretion. The stress is on the law to analytically govern every step of the procedure. The need is felt, however, of a system where judges and parties could organize the progress of proceedings through mutual collaboration. A first step in this direction may be represented by the new Article 81*bis* that was inserted in 2009, in the implementing provisions (*disposizioni di attuazione*) of the CPC, to introduce the so-called calendar of the proceedings (*see infra*, paragraph 314). Moreover, in 2014, a new Article 183*bis* CPC was introduced, enabling the judge to switch to a simplified (summary) procedure, when the dispute is deemed to be simple (*see* next paragraph).

215. As it was pointed out (*see* paragraph 200), in ordinary proceedings there is no pretrial phase, and the date of the first hearing is chosen and indicated by the plaintiff in the *citazione*.

The defendant usually formally presents himself or herself to the court and files his or her answer twenty days before that hearing.

At the first hearing (*prima comparizione delle parti e trattazione della causa*: Article 183 CPC, as revised in 2005),[341] the judge must preliminary check that the proceedings have been regularly established against the defendant(s).

If the defendant has not presented a defence and is not present at the hearing, the very first thing the judge must do is verify whether the *citazione* was properly served on him or her. If service appears to be faulty, the court must order the plaintiff to renovate service of the *citazione* on the defendant.

Even if the *citazione* was regularly served, the court must still check whether the *citazione* itself complies with the requirements of Article 163 CPC and is therefore formally valid.

Article 164 CPC lists the grounds on which a *citazione* is considered invalid,[342] distinguishing between the errors of the *editio actionis*[343] and those of the *vocatio in ius.*[344] If any relevant defect is found, the judge orders the plaintiffs to serve a new amended *citazione* on the defendant. The effects of this new service go back to the date the original *citazione* was served on the defendant for errors pertaining to

341. *See* A. Graziosi, 'La nuova udienza di trattazione: una prima lettura', RTDPC (2006): 943.
342. G. Della Pietra, *La patologia della domanda giudiziaria* (2008).
343. The object of the dispute has not been indicated or is absolutely uncertain; the facts on which the plaintiff's claim is based have not been disclosed.
344. The identity of the parties has been omitted, the court seized has not been indicated, the date of the first hearing is missing, the defendant was not given at least ninety days to defend himself before the first hearing, the defendant was not warned as to the procedural preclusions deriving from a late defence.

the *vocatio in ius*, otherwise from the date the second service has been performed.[345] This means that, for example, in between the two notices, the plaintiff's claim could become time-barred.

Only if and when both service of the *citazione* and the *citazione* itself have been duly checked upon, and amended if the case may be, may the judge declare the absent defendant to be in default of appearance (*contumacia*).

On the other hand, when a defendant files his or her first defence in the court, all errors and faults of both the service and the *citazione* are immediately cured, since, even if faulty, these acts have successfully pursued procedural purpose. Having said this, it must be added that, for certain errors or omissions, the defendant has a right to be served a new amended *citazione*[346] or be given a delay to integrate his or her own defences,[347] before the trial can proceed.

At the first hearing, the court also orders joinder of any proper and necessary parties not served with the original claim nor joined in by the defendant, in compliance with Article 102 CPC (*litisconsorzio necessario*) and checks that the parties are regularly represented in the proceedings, giving all the necessary orders (e.g., requiring necessary authorizations to be filed in the court).

After the reforms of 2005, the parties are no longer required to personally appear before the court at the first hearing in order to be freely interrogated by the judge, who, previously, was also required to try and reconcile them, when the nature of the dispute so allowed. Nowadays, this attempt at conciliation may be performed by the judge only upon the parties' joint request (Article 185 CPC).

At the first hearing, the judge should also enquire the parties for clarifications on the facts in dispute and point out the issues which can be raised ex officio (e.g., issues of jurisdiction and competence or even substantive matters, like the validity of a contract).

For this hearing to be useful, both the parties and the judge should prepare the case throughout beforehand, for example, to be in the position to agree on some uncontested facts and on the order in which to prepare and decide any preliminary issue. In practice, this hearing is often just a formality, because the judge's excessive caseload prevents him or her from studying the details of the case before meeting the parties in court. Lawyers, on the other hand, often delegate junior colleagues, with little knowledge of the dispute, to attend hearings in their place.

At this hearing, the plaintiff may also ask the judge to be allowed to join a third party in the proceedings or bring a counter-counterclaim (*reconventio reconventionis*), if such activities are made necessary in the light of the defendant's defences and counter-claims (*see* paragraph 199). Case law makes clear that such powers may be exercised only when the plaintiff was not in the position to involve the third party in the dispute or raise the new claim without examining the answer of the

---

345. The rationale between this different treatment of the errors in the *citazione* depends on the fact that a faulty *editio actionis* makes it impossible for the defendant to comprehend exactly what is the objective content of the plaintiff's petition and the subjective right the plaintiff brings to justice.
346. When the facts of the case or the object of the dispute have been omitted, the *citazione* must be integrated accordingly.
347. When the defendant has been given insufficient time to file his defence before the hearing or if the defendant was not warned about the procedural preclusions related to a late defence.

original defendant. After the first hearing, the plaintiff is precluded from bringing any new claims or joining new parties into the dispute.

In 2014, in one more redrafting of procedural rules to try to shorten the length of civil proceedings,[348] a new Article 183*bis* was introduced in the CPC, which basically enables the judge, at the first hearing, to decide that the case is suited to be summarily dispatched, therefore switching to a summary procedural mode regulated by Articles 702*bis* et seq. CPC (*see* paragraphs 343 et seq.). This procedural switch may be applied, e.g., to simple cases, requiring little (if at all) gathering of evidence and which are thus eligible to be conducted in a deformalized summary way, in order to reach a decision faster.[349] The new procedural device, so far, appears to be scarcely used in practice, mostly because the procedural mechanisms set forth in Article 183*bis* CPC are rather unclear and because the judge is not necessarily ready, at the first hearing, to take decisions concerning the complexity of the case.

In compliance with the new Article 185*bis*, brought into the CPC by DL No. 69 of 21 June 2013, implemented by Law No. 98 of 9 August 2013, moreover, at the first hearing (but also later, until the case is ready to be decided) the judge has the prerogative to present the parties with a settlement proposal. The parties are free to evaluate and accept such proposal: if that is the case, the dispute is settled. Otherwise, the case proceeds to judgment but the judge will take into consideration the fact that the parties have unreasonably rejected his proposal when it comes to taxing the costs of the proceedings: basically, either the losing party will be fined for abuse or process under Article 96(3) CPC[350] or the winner might be awarded less than it would normally have been (*see* paragraph 305). Article 185*bis* CPC has been extensively applied,[351] especially in larger courts, like the *Tribunale* of Rome, where the judge often formulates her settlement proposals after evidence has been gathered, so that such proposals are effectively an anticipation of the final judgment.[352]

216. At the end of the first hearing, any party may require the judge to fix deadlines to file as many as three consecutive written briefs (supplemental pleadings).[353]

As we have seen (*see supra*, paragraph 199), in the first brief (to be filed within thirty days of the hearing), the parties may modify and/or clarify their claims and

348. DL 12 Sep. 2014, No. 132, converted into Law 10 Nov. 2014, No. 162.

349. M.A. Lupoi, *Nowhere Fast? Shortcuts to Judgment in Recent Italian Procedural Legislation*, in *Ways of Implementation of the Right to Civil Proceedings Within a Reasonable Time* 304 (Vilnius Universitetas 2016).

350. *Trib.* Milano 26 Jun. 2013, decree, <www.ilcaso.it>, arguing that such is the case when a litigant, using due diligence and care, was in the position to be aware that the proceedings would lead to a certain outcome; *Trib.* Roma 23 Sep. 2013, order, GD 41 (2013): 17; *Trib.* Roma 24 Oct. 2013, order, GD 45 (2013): *Ins. speciale*, XIV.

351. *Trib.* Milano 26 Jun. 2013, *supra*.

352. *Trib.* Roma 23 Sep. 2013, *supra*; *Trib.* Roma 30 Sep. 2013, order, GD (2013): n. 45, *Ins. speciale*, III; *Trib.* Bari 31 Oct. 2013, order, GD (2014): n. 2, *Inserto speciale*, XIV.

353. *See* A. Briguglio, 'Il nuovo rito ordinario di cognizione: meno udienze, più preclusioni (dalla l. n. 80/2005 alla l. n. 263/2005)', <www.judicium.it>; D. Dalfino, 'Characteristics of procedure', in *Civil justice in Italy*, *supra*, 75 et seq.

defences (but not, at this point, bring new claims or precluded defences into the proceedings).

In the second brief (within no more than sixty days after the hearing), they may reply to the counterparts' new claims and defences and bring defences which are a consequence of those new claims and defences. In the same brief, each party has the burden to present his or her own evidentiary requests and to file any relevant document.

Finally, in their third brief (within no more than eighty days after the first hearing), the parties may present evidentiary requests as a response to those presented by the counterparts (*prova contraria*).

This sequence clearly shows the inflexibility of the Italian procedural model: the number and the contents of the parties' written briefs are predetermined by statute as well as the days assigned for preparing each of these defensive documents. It is worth noting that, since these time limits are qualified and peremptory, they may not be extended. In practice, in order to bypass this rigid model, judges, when fixing the following hearing (often, several months away from the first one), will state that the deadlines for filing the written briefs will only start to run from a future date, and not from the very next day after the first hearing: for example, on 1 February, the judge may fix the next hearing on 20 September and rule that the time limit of thirty days to file the first brief will start to run from 2 May).

The time limits mentioned above are extremely important, because the parties are precluded for performing the relevant procedural activities should they not comply with them. In particular, after the time limit for filing the second brief elapses, the parties will be precluded from making any 'direct' evidentiary request. Any evidentiary gap in their defensive positions will then become unbridgeable.

217. Third persons may join or be joined in the proceedings when a sufficient connection is deemed to exist between them and the subject-matter of the dispute, in order to avoid multiple litigation and conflicting decisions and to decide in just one set of proceedings 'complex' legal relationships.

Parties may voluntarily join (*intervento volontario*) in pending proceedings:[354]

- when they claim to be vested with a right which is both autonomous and incompatible with the one in dispute between the original parties (*intervento principale*);[355] here, the joining party adopts a 'conflictual' stance vis-à-vis all of the original parties to the dispute;
- when they are vested with a right which is connected with the one in dispute between the original parties (*intervento litisconsortile*);[356] here, the joining party takes a conflictual position only vis-à-vis some of the original parties, while supporting (or being procedurally indifferent) to the remaining litigants;

354. Article 105 CPC.
355. For example, when proceedings are pending between A, claiming to be the owner of an asset, and B, who holds such asset, C can voluntary join, claiming to be the real owner of the very same good.
356. For example, another victim of the same tort in proceedings started by another person against the same tort-feasor.

– when they are vested with a right which is dependent on the one in dispute between the parties (*intervento adesivo dipendente*). This is a rather peculiar form of 'action' on the side of the joining party. As a matter of fact, Article 105(2) CPC enables this form of joinder when the third party has an 'interest' in the pending dispute. The *ratio* of this remedy is to enable a person, who would be indirectly affected by the res judicata between the original parties, to participate in proceedings where no right of his or her own is adjudicated in, to 'support' the position of the party from which his or her own right derives. For example, a sub-lessee may want to take part in proceedings where the validity of the original lease contract is debated between lessee and lesser, to avoid that, should that contract be declared null and void, also his or her sub-contract consequently be borne down.

The original parties are not in the position to avoid such joinder; in other words, there is no remedy available to quickly and effectively strike out the joining party from the proceedings.

218. Third parties may also be joined in the proceedings on the original parties' (*intervento per istanza di parte*)[357] or on the judge's own motion (*intervento per ordine del giudice*).[358]

The parties may ask to join a third party to whom the dispute is common or from whom they want to be guaranteed. The second option is rather frequently used, especially in certain types of disputes (e.g., litigation involving a defendant who has an insurance to cover his or her professional liability). The defendant must manifest his or her intention to join another party in his or her very first defence, which he or she must file at least twenty days before the first hearing. The plaintiff, on the other hand, can only ask to join third persons when such joinder depends on the contents of the defendant's own defences (*see* paragraph 199).

Ex officio joinder can be ordered anytime in the course of first instance proceedings, vis-à-vis third persons who are deemed to have a 'common' interest in the dispute. This power is not frequently used, and only when the original claim and the related evidence-gathering phase appear to potentially infringe upon the third parties substantive rights. In other words, when the judge orders to join a third party, it should not be considered as the exercise of an inquisitorial power, but rather as a safeguard for the third party, to enable him or her to be aware of the existence of proceedings whose subject-matter is connected to his or her own substantial position, as would happen, for example, when the original parties debate upon the validity of a contract, a third person is also a signatory of.

When joinder of a third party is ordered by the judge, it is the burden of the most diligent party to serve a joinder notice on such third person, within the time limit set by the judge.

If the judge's order is not complied with, the case is cancelled from the court's roll and eventually discontinued unless timely reinstated.

357. Article 106 CPC.
358. Article 107 CPC. *See* N. Trocker, *L'intervento per ordine del giudice* (Milan: Giuffrè, 1984).

219. From the moment a third person joins or is joined in the proceedings, he or she automatically becomes a regular party, with all ordinary procedural duties and rights. He or she will also be bound by the res judicata effects of the judgment.

A third party may voluntary join proceedings pending between other parties at any moment before the judgment, but he or she is precluded from performing those procedural activities which the original parties can no longer perform at the time of joinder.[359] In other words, a voluntarily joining party will be in the position to exercise full procedural powers only if he or she files his or her first defence within the time limit set for the *costituzione in giudizio* of the defendant (i.e., not later than twenty days before the first hearing).

On the other hand, parties who are joined by the other parties or by the judge always enjoy full defensive prerogatives. This means that they may perform any procedural activity, irrespective of the stage the proceedings have reached at the time they are joined. In other words, the course of the proceedings is basically rewinded to enable the joined parties to catch up with the activities so far performed therein.

220. After the reforms of 2005, when the last of the three deadlines granted by the judge at the first hearing expires (i.e., in theory, eighty days after the hearing itself), the parties should have fully presented to the judge all of their claims, defences, objections, documents and requests for the gathering of oral evidence, thus putting the judge in the position to examine and eventually allow those requests at the second hearing.

On the other hand, after the last deadline indicated in Article 183(6) CPC elapses, the subject-matter of the dispute may not be changed in any way, and only new (or previously unknown) facts or *ius superveniens* can be alleged by the parties.

221. The progress of the proceedings, at this point, depends on the nature of the dispute and on the issues to be tried.

If the case may be decided on the documentary evidence already presented by the parties or if no evidence-gathering phase is necessary since only legal issues need to be solved, the court is in the position to immediately render judgment.

The court may also decide to give judgment on some (procedural or substantive) preliminary issues, when such decision appears likely to define (at least in part) the merits of dispute.[360]

Otherwise, the evidence-gathering phase begins.

222. In Italian civil procedure, no pretrial discovery takes place so that the parties rarely are aware in advance of the evidence on which their counterpart relies or even of the documents available to him or her. There is therefore an intrinsic element of 'surprise' which the parties have to deal with in the course of the proceedings.

It is the judge who supervises the evidence-gathering phase in the course of the trial.

---

359. G. Verde, 'Le ricadute del sistema delle preclusioni sull'intervento volontario', GC (1999): I, 3472.
360. For example, a lack of jurisdiction or a time-bar objection.

Documents may be deposited and evidentiary requests advanced by the parties in compliance with the deadline fixed by the trial judge at the end the first hearing as per. Article 183(6) CPC (*see supra*, paragraph 216). No further evidentiary requests can be presented to the court after this deadline has elapsed, unless new documents or evidence are subsequently discovered or come into being.

223. Should admissible and relevant evidence need to be gathered, the core of the trial is dedicated to this activity.

When all the admitted evidence has been collected, the court is ready to decide, and the parties are invited to state their final conclusions (*precisazione delle conclusioni*).

2. Opinion by the *Pubblico Ministero*

224. The participation of the *pubblico ministero* in civil proceedings is not so frequent.

When he or she does bring a civil action or joins in already pending proceedings (*see supra*, paragraphs 95 et seq.), he or she performs certain activities, in compliance with his or her role therein. He or she does not, however, deliver an opinion to the court in the French tradition. Rather, he or she offers 'conclusions' to the court, basically proposing the claim to be allowed or denied.

C. Judgment

1. Deliberation

225. Talking about the deliberation phase before the *Tribunale*, it is necessary to distinguish between the disputes that fall to be decided by a panel of three judges (*decisione collegiale*) and those (the vast majority) in which a single judge decides.

In the case of the former, after the parties have stated their final conclusions at the last hearing before the instructing judge (*udienza di precisazione delle conclusioni*), they have sixty days to deposit their final written defences (*comparse conclusionali*), in which they resume the facts of the dispute in the light of the available evidence and suggest the factual and legal reasons for rendering judgment in their favour. Within twenty subsequent days, each party can reply in writing (*memoria di replica*) to the other's *comparsa conclusionale*. After that, the court should deliver its judgment in chambers within sixty days (Article 275 CPC).

Ordinarily, there is no longer a final public discussion hearing before the three-judge panel (*udienza collegiale*). As a matter of fact, this proved to be a cumbersome (and useless) formality which was eliminated by the reform of 1990. Nowadays, it is a prerogative of either party to demand the case to be discussed orally before the panel both at the time the final conclusions are stated and, later, within the deadline for the deposit of the *memoria di replica*. At the discussion hearing, the trial judge presents the case to the rest of the panel, and the parties expose their oral arguments; the judgment is deposited within the following sixty days. In practice, this final public hearing before the panel court is almost never requested by the parties.

The scenario depicted above was modified in 2015, by Law No. 208, in an attempt to reduce the duration of simpler cases[361]. Today, therefore, when the *giudice istruttore* deems that the case may be decided following an oral examination in compliance with Article 218*sexies* CPC (*see* paragraph 226), he will remand the file to the three-judge panel, setting a hearing for the *precisazione delle conclusion*i and the oral presentation of the parties' final defences. The panel will then deliver the judgment at the same haring, at the end of the parties' presentations.

At the decision stage, the court goes through the various preliminary issues before (if ever) considering the merits of the case. Should the three judges disagree on how to solve any single issue, majority decisions are taken. The judgment will not, however, present minority opinions. The text of the judgment is usually written by the trial judge and signed by him or her and the president of the panel.

226. When the case falls to be decided by a single judge, the law provides for different styles of deliberation.

The written mode is the one most commonly used; sixty days after the final conclusions are stated at the last hearing, the parties deposit their *comparse conclusionali* and, in the subsequent twenty days, their *memorie di replica*; finally the judge renders his or her decision (within the following thirty days).

If one of the parties so demands, the judge will fix a hearing for the oral discussion of the case. Before that hearing, the parties will deposit their *comparse conclusionali* only (but no *memorie di replica*). The decision should be deposited within thirty days of the hearing (Article 281 *quinquies* CPC) (mixed written and oral method).

As a third possibility (oral mode) (Article 281*sexies* CPC), the judge may order the case to be discussed orally at the hearing, with no written defences. When this mode is chosen, the judge will deliver the full (concise) decision at the very end of the discussion hearing. This form of deliberation is normally used to decide preliminary issues (e.g., jurisdiction or competence) or rather simple issues of fact and law. If effectively used, it can prove a very useful tool in decongesting the court's backlog and frustrating dilatory practises of the parties. In recent years, judges appear more and more ready to recur to this oral mode of deciding cases.

227. As a general rule, in adjudicating a case, the judge is required to apply the law, unless the law itself allows him or her to render an equitable decision. In other words, the judge is bound to apply the written law and cannot himself or herself create the legal solution for the case (Article 113 CPC) (*principio di legalità*).[362]

A corollary principle derive from such rule: the judge has a monopoly as concerns the selection of the applicable law and its application. The parties' allegations and qualifications, from the legal point of view, are not binding for the court (*iura novit curia*).

---

361. *See* Buffone, G., Tribunale collegiale: ammessa la discussione orale, in GD, 2016, n. 6, p. 59.
362. A. Carratta & M. Taruffo, *Poteri del giudice*, *supra*, 233 et seq.

The law leaves indeed very little room for an equitable decision:[363] apart from cases decided by the *Giudice di Pace*, for a value of less than EUR 1,100.00 (*see* at paragraph 102), under Article 114 CPC, the judge may emit an equitable decision, either at first instance or at the appeal level, only when the dispute concerns rights of which the parties may freely dispose of and all of the parties make a common application for such a decision. In practice, this provision is barely ever applied.

In this context, the notion of equity implies a decision of the single case, not governed by the legal provisions otherwise applicable, but rather by considerations of fairness, in relation to the subject-matter of the dispute, the parties and their conditions. In other words, equity should allow the judge to render a decision which is more suitable and 'just' for the case at hand than it would by a strict application of the rule of law.

When the judge is allowed by the law or by the parties to render an equitable decision, however, he or she does not enjoy an unreviewable discretion: as a matter of fact, the judge is always under the obligation to follow fundamental values (i.e., the ones set in the Constitution) and to apply the main principles governing the subject-matter he or she has to decide upon. Moreover, the course of the proceedings always needs to be governed in compliance with statutory provisions and may not be regulated 'equitably'.

2. Different Kinds of Judgments

228. Several types of judgments may be given, depending on their content and their role within the dispute they are rendered in.

First of all, it is possible to distinguish between procedural and substantive judgments, depending on whether they decide on issues of procedure only (*sentenze di rito*) or enter into the merits of the substantive right (*sentenze di merito*). The main difference is that procedural judgments do not become substantive res judicata, and they spread no binding effects outside the proceedings they are rendered in.

Judgments on the merits can be roughly divided into three main categories: (*1*) decisions that simply ascertain the existence and the scope of a substantive right (*sentenze di accertamento mero*); (*2*) decisions that contain orders to the losing party to pay a sum of money, perform an action, restrain from doing something, deliver a good and so on (*sentenze di condanna*); and (*3*) decisions that create, modify or extinguish a legal relationship between the parties or a personal status (*sentenze costitutive*).

Sentenze di condanna can also take the form of a 'generic order' (*condanna generica*), when the court simply ascertains the existence of a party's liability and the generic duty to restore the damages deriving from it, while leaving the determination of the exact amount or performance due (*quantum*) to a later decision of the same or another court.

---

363. R. Martino, 'Poteri equitativi del giudice e giudizio di impugnazione', in *La giurisdizione nell'esperienza giurisprudenziale contemporanea*, *supra*, 245 et seq.

A '*condanna*' can also be 'for the future' (*condanna in futuro*), when payment or performance shall become due in a future date or upon the taking place of a conditional requirement.[364]

Finally, in certain cases, it is possible for the judge to release a *condanna con riserva*, which is based on an incomplete ascertainment of the relevant facts and which can therefore be annulled by a subsequent judgment.[365]

229. A distinction should also be made between final and interlocutory decisions.

An interlocutory decision (*sentenza non definitiva*) is a judgment which only decides on part(s) of a more complex dispute, leaving the rest to a following decision. In other words, interlocutory decisions never end the proceedings in which they are rendered; therefore, special appeal provisions apply.

An interlocutory decision is usually rendered in two sets of cases. On the one hand, the trial judge can always consider the case ready for judgment on some procedural and/or substantive preliminary issue. If the decision on the preliminary issues determines the whole dispute before the court seized (e.g., the contract on which payment was requested is held to be null and void; the action is dismissed for lack of jurisdiction or competence, and so on), the judgment is final. But if the preliminary issue is decided in a way which is not incompatible with the prosecution of the proceedings,[366] an interlocutory decision is handed out and proceedings are brought back before the instructing judge. On the other hand, at the decision stage, the court can always find that the case is not ready for judgment (in part or wholly) and reopen the instructing phase for further evidence gathering, possibly rendering an interlocutory decisions on those parts of the parties' claims which are ready to be decided.[367]

Interlocutory judgments can be appealed against at the moment they are given. Or, the parties may express their intention to appeal them later, together with the final decision (*riserva d'appello*). This intention, however, has to be timely disclosed to the court, before the term for bringing the appeal elapses.

3. Formal Aspects of the Judgment

230. Article 132 CPC lists the formal requirements of a judgment. Recently, the lawmaker has tried to reduce such requirements, in order to make the deliberation phase faster.

---

364. For example, when a deadline fixed by the court, the parties or the law elapses. This happens, e.g., in eviction proceedings when the lease contract has not yet reached its final term or in divorce judgments, as concerns the monthly payment of alimony.

365. Article 35 CPC constitutes a typical example of *condanna con riserva*, in relation to set-offs, whenever the judge chooses to limit his decision to the main claim and remit the set-off defence to a court of higher value competence: *see* G. Scarselli, *La condanna con riserva* (Milan: Giuffrè, 1989).

366. For example, part of the plaintiff's claim is time-barred while the rest is not.

367. For example, the defendant's responsibility is ascertained but further evidence is needed as concerns the amount of damages. For a recent judicial decision, *see Cass. SU* 8 Oct. 1999, No. 711, GD, no. 44, 1999, 60.

First of all, the judgment must bear the caption 'Italian Republic' and the mention that the decision is given in the name of the Italian people (*in nome del popolo italiano*). The rendering court, the parties and their lawyers must then be identified. The parties' conclusions and (if that is the case) those of the *pubblico ministero* are then mentioned. After 2009, a concise report of the progress of the proceedings is no longer required.

At the core of the judgment is the court's reasoning (*motivazione*),[368] that is, the concise exposition of the facts of the case and of the legal reasons on which the decision is grounded. In 2009, Article 118 of the implementing provisions of the CPC has been modified, in order to make the reasoning of the judgment 'lighter'. It is now possible for the Italian judge to solve the legal points in dispute simply by referring to existing precedents. This provision of course does not create a stare decisis system, but rather it enables the judge to quickly deal with 'serial' cases. Of course, the risk exists that by availing themselves of this prerogative, judges may become less ready to examine the specific peculiarities of the case and distinguish them from previously decided ones.

Interestingly, judges are expressly prohibited from quoting academic writing in their reasoning. What judges therefore usually do is to generically refer to the 'best doctrine', without mentioning any specific writer or book. It is felt that this prohibition is quite anacronistic.

At the end of the judgment, the court delivers its proper order (the so-called *dispositivo*) which may be more or less complex, depending on the claims and defences adjudicated upon.

The judgment's draft is then signed and dated by the court and handed out to the court's clerk. Before it can be available to the public, it must however be copied by the court's offices. This can take a few days, but also several months in some overworked or under-staffed courts. When this is finally done, the judgment is considered published (*pubblicazione della sentenza*). From this moment, the six-month limit for bringing an appeal starts to run (*see* paragraph 233).

4. Notice and Service

231. After the judgment has become public, its *dispositivo* is communicated to the parties by the clerk of the court.

It has to be remarked that judicial decisions are subject to taxation (usually, a percentage of the value of the decision itself), with such exceptions as divorce, legal separation and labour decisions. The parties are not allowed to get an authentic copy of the judgment before paying such taxes (exception: when that copy is necessary to lodge an appeal or to start enforcement proceedings).

After registering the decision at the local tax agency, the winning party is in the position to serve a copy of the judgment on the losing one, so that the thirty days limit to bring an appeal starts to run. Such service, however, is never mandatory.

368. Monaci, 'L'esperienza della motivazione nelle sentenze civili', RTDPC (1999): 253.

5. Res Judicata

232. In Italian civil procedure, procedural res judicata (*cosa giudicata formale*) is clearly distinguished from substantive res judicata (*cosa giudicata sostanziale*), the latter being a legal and logical consequence of the former.[369][370]

233. Procedural res judicata can be defined as the situation where no 'ordinary' appeal may be raised against a judgment anymore. Appeals are qualified as 'ordinary' when they are the 'normal' remedy to attack a judgment before a superior (or a 'different') court than the one which rendered it.

The basic idea behind the notion of 'ordinary' appeals is that they have to be raised within a statutory deadline. When that deadline elapses, ordinary appeals may no longer be raised, and the judgment becomes res judicata in the procedural sense of the expression.

Appeal, *regolamento di competenza*, petition to the *Corte di cassazione* and *revocazione*, in cases 3 and 4 of Article 395 CPC, are qualified as ordinary appeals in the Italian legal system.

The law establishes two different deadlines for bringing an ordinary appeal. The so-called short time limit runs for thirty days, from the moment the decision is notified by one party to the other. The time limit is longer (sixty days) for a petition to the *Cassazione*. Interestingly, when a judgment is notified, the short time limit to bring an appeal starts to run for both the party who receives the notice and the one who requests it. In other words, when a party's claims have not been fully allowed, he or she might be reluctant to notify the decision to the counterpart, in order not to also compel himself or herself to rush and file an appeal against the parts of the decisions he or she is unsatisfied with. On the other hand, the 'losing' party might want to notify the judgment, to avoid it being appealed by the (partially) winning counterpart and come out with an even worse outcome at the appeal level.

The 'long' time limit is considered if the decision is not served from one party on the other. As a matter of fact, all ordinary appeals may be brought within six months[371] of the day of publication of the judgment in the court's offices (*see supra*, paragraph 230).

A special rule is provided for *regolamento di competenza*, which may be brought within thirty days of the date the clerk of court communicates to the parties that the judgment has been published.

After these deadlines have expired, only extraordinary appeals can be raised (*see infra*).

Procedural res judicata forbids every Italian court from deciding again a dispute or an issue previously decided upon by another court (*ne bis in idem*). As such, every judgment, irrespective of its procedural or substantive content, is subject to becoming procedural res judicata.

369. A. Giussani, 'Effects of Judgments – Res Judicata', in *Civil Justice in Italy*, *supra*, 123 et seq.
370. In general, on res judicata in civil proceedings, *see* S. Menchini, *Il giudicato civile* (Turin: Utet, 1988).
371. This shortened deadline was introduced in 2009; before then, it was a year.

234. Substantive res judicata, on the other hand, concerns the binding effects of the court's assessment of the rights on which the parties' claims were based.

To have substantive res judicata effects, a judgment must previously become procedural res judicata.

Not all judgments, however, can acquire substantive binding effects. In particular, procedural decisions usually do not have any effect at all outside of the proceedings in which they were rendered.[372] An exception is made for *Cassazione* rulings on competence, which are binding for any future dispute between the same parties if the original proceedings are discontinued.[373]

Only judgments on the merits of the case (*sentenze di merito*) can spread their effects outside of the proceedings in which they were rendered, onto the substantive relationships between the parties.

235. According to Article 2909 CC, the court's assessment of the right in dispute has binding effects on the parties and their proxies (*eredi* and *aventi causa*) only (i.e., the heirs of the original parties or the new owner of the right adjudicated upon).

However, it cannot be said that the substantive res judicata effects of a decision are always and necessarily confined to the parties and their legal successors;[374] also some third persons can suffer from the indirect or extended effects of res judicata, for example, when a person's right depends upon the existence of a right or a legal relationship between other parties.[375] To prevent the reflection of the negative effects of res judicata upon their own rights, these third persons have the possibility to voluntarily join in the proceedings while they are still pending (*intervento adesivo dipendente*), in order to support the position of the party from which their rights depend (*see* paragraph 217). At certain conditions, third parties can also bring extraordinary appeals against a decision (*see infra*, paragraphs 280 et seq.).

It is also possible to talk about the extension of the res judicata effects to certain individuals who were not parties to the dispute (e.g., *sostituzione processuale* in compliance with Article 111 CPC, *see supra*, paragraph 176).

236. The implications of substantial res judicata are that the court's ascertainment of the legal relationship is binding for the parties, and the same issue cannot be adjudicated upon *ex novo* in further proceedings. As a matter of fact, the judgment sets down the 'legal truth' of the parties' relationship and such 'truth' cannot be further contested, not even by raising exceptions and facts that could have been raised before the first court but were not (*il giudicato copre il dedotto ed il deducibile*). Of course, res judicata concerns the past: new circumstances and events may

372. For example, a trial court decision on jurisdiction does not bind the same or another court in future disputes between the same parties having the same subject-matter.
373. *See infra*, para. 317.
374. On these issues *see* F. Carpi, *L'efficacia 'ultra partes' della sentenza civile* (Milan: Giuffrè, 1974); E. Allorio, *La cosa giudicata rispetto ai terzi* (Milan: Giuffrè, 1935).
375. As would be the case vis-à-vis the parties to a lease contract and to a sub-lease contract respectively.

always change the legal relationship between the parties, notwithstanding a previous res judicata.[376]

The res judicata ascertainment of a right has implications also as concerns any dependant right and action, insomuch as the former cannot be relitigated in any future action concerning related disputes. For instance, if the validity of a contract has been ascertained in previous proceedings, it will be impossible for the debtor, in a subsequent dispute for the enforcement of such contract, to raise the invalidity issue again. The reverse is not necessarily true, however. It is a matter of some controversy whether a decision on the effects also extends to the validity of the legal relationship from which those effects derive. On the one hand, case law tends to adopt a laxer view, according to which res judicata can extend to issues and questions which were not actually in dispute between the parties but which are logically and juridically implied in the judgment,[377] going as far as admitting implicit res judicata on those issues which are the logical and juridical antecedent of the matters actually adjudicated upon. The doctrine, however, relying on Article 34 CPC (*see* paragraph 159), which allows the judge to decide *incidenter tantum* issues which are specifically in dispute between the parties, tends to adopt a stricter notion of res judicata, that never goes beyond the scope of the matters and issues actually disputed between the parties.[378]

Res judicata effects, on the other hand, do not extend to the so-called obiter dicta, that is, to those statements a court makes on related issues to the ones which fall to be adjudicated, but which do not change the results of the dispute at hand.

6. Interpretation and Rectification of Judgments

237. The normal way to amend erroneous or faulty judgments is through the appeal system. If a judgment is not timely appealed against, it becomes res judicata and it cannot be modified anymore, defective as it might be (with the exception of extraordinary appeals, *see infra*, paragraphs 272 et seq.).

However, when the judgment contains simple material mistakes (e.g., misspelled names, arithmetic errors, mistaken dates and so on), it is possible to make a motion to the same court that rendered the judgment to have it rectified. Since this is not an appeal, there are no fixed time limits to file such motion.

According to Article 288 CPC, if all the parties agree on the rectification, the court simply corrects the judgment by decree. Otherwise, the parties have to appear before the court. The order which amends the mistake(s) will then be annotated on the original copy of the judgment.

---

376. More details in R. Caponi, *L'efficacia del giudicato civile nel tempo* (Milan: Giuffrè, 1991).
377. For example, the validity of a contract in an action for performance.
378. A. Attardi, 'In tema di limiti oggettivi della cosa giudicata', RTDPC (1990): 475; C. Consolo, 'Oggetto del giudicato e principio dispositivo – I – Dei limiti oggettivi e del giudicato costitutivo', RTDPC (1991): 215; A. Proto Pisani, 'Appunti sul giudicato civile e sui suoi limiti oggettivi', RDP (1990): 386; S. Satta, 'Accertamento incidentale', in *Enciclopedia del diritto* (Milan: Giuffrè, 1958), 243.

7. Penalty in Case of Non-compliance

238. In Italy there is no proper doctrine of contempt of the court. There is no general automatic sanction for debtors who do not voluntarily comply with a court order.

At certain conditions, however fraudulent non-compliance with a court decision can be punished as criminal felony (Article 650 CP).

In recent years, several sectorial new provisions have introduced as remedies to try and coerce a reluctant debtor to 'voluntarily' comply with an order given by the judge. By way of example, mention may be made of Article 140(7) of DLGS No. 206 of 6 September 2005 (the so-called Consumer Code) which states that, in decisions aimed at safeguarding the collective interests of consumers, the judge may establish a deadline for complying with any order given therein and also fix a pecuniary penalty (from EUR 516.00 to EUR 1,032.00), for each repeated failure to comply or for each day of non-compliance, according to the seriousness of the situation.

A similar fine was introduced by Article 6 of DLGS No. 231 of 9 October 2002, No. 231, on combating late payment in commercial transactions.

Finally, in 2009, Article 614*bis* has been brought in the code of civil procedure, introducing a general *astreinte* (i.e., a measure of indirect coercion).[379] Upon the party's application,[380] when releasing an order for non-pecuniary performance,[381] the judge may determine a sum of money according to the circumstances of the case which the party receiving the order will be bound to pay should he or she fail or be late to comply with it, unless such remedy appears to be manifestly unfair. In case of failure to comply or repeated infringement, the creditor will thus have a title to enforce against the debtor's asset. It will then be the burden of the debtor to raise an opposition against the enforcement, should he or she contest failure to comply with the judge's order. The distribution of the burden of the proof will shift from the creditor to the debtor, depending on whether repeated violation or failure to comply is alleged.[382]

This remedy tries to ensure indirect coercion to comply with a judicial order, making it more convenient for the obliged party to comply with the order rather than not.[383] This new remedy has still a limited scope of application (e.g., it cannot be obtained to enforce an order to deliver an asset or release an immoveable property

379. C. Asprella, 'L'attuazione degli obblighi di fare infungibile e di non fare', GM (2011): 117; Lombardi, 'Il nuovo art. 614-bis c. p. c.: l'astreinte quale misura accessoria ai provvedimenti cautelari ex art. 700 c. p. c.', GM (2010): 401; E. Merlin, 'Prime note sul sistema delle misure coercitive pecuniarie per l'attuazione degli obblighi infungibili nella l. 69/2009', RDP (2009): 1548; R. Caponi, 'Italian Civil Justice Reform 2009', *supra*; G. Miccolis, NLCC (2010), 1047; F. Ferrari, N. Bocharova, 'The astreinte in the Italian and Russian administrative (judicial) and civil proceedings', Russ. law jour. 3 (2015): 10 et seq.

380. *See* Tribunale Terni 4 Aug. 2009.

381. This specification of the object of her order was introduced in 2105 (DL No. 83).

382. M. Bove, 'La misura coercitiva di cui all'art. 614-bis c. p. c.', <www.judicium.it>, 8; E. Merlin, *supra*, 1552.

383. M. Bove, *supra*, 1.

nor in the context of labour relationships),[384] but it is now being used rather effectively, for example, in the context of interim provisions or provisional orders.[385]

It is submitted that the parties may even voluntarily include an *astreinte* in the context of a judicial settlement.

8. Provisional Orders

239. Given the severe crisis of the Italian judicial system and the length of ordinary proceedings, sometimes the possibility to obtain a provisional decision is the only form of justice a party can get within a reasonable delay.

A distinction must be made between those orders which may be provisionally given by the court, at some given conditions, to anticipate (in part or in whole) the effects of the final decision and proper interim relief. The main practical difference between these two types of remedies is that provisional orders, as an exception to the ordinary rule concerning the court's orders, maintain their effects even if the proceedings in which they were rendered are discontinued without a final decision; moreover, their release does not require showing any urgency. Interim relief, on the other hand, as a general rule (but *see* paragraph 383) cannot exist without pending proceedings on the merits. Moreover, interim relief usually requires showing the existence of some urgent reasons for the judge's intervention.

Between 1990 and 1995, some new kinds of provisional orders have been introduced in civil ordinary proceedings as a means to decongesting the courts, on the assumption that, once a provisional order of payment is given, the parties lose much of their interest in the litigation (the creditor has obtained what he or she wanted, the debtor has incurred in what he or she was trying to avoid), with a high chance they will, in one way or the other, abandon or discontinue the dispute.

240. The provisional orders which may be applied for in ordinary proceedings are:[386]

- an order to pay sums which are not contested by the counterpart (*ordinanza per il pagamento di somme non contestate*) (Article 186*bis* CPC):[387] when both parties are actively participating in the proceedings, on one of the parties' motion, if the other party does not contest that part of the sum claimed is due, the court can order payment of that uncontested sum. Such order can be enforced against the debtor (*titolo esecutivo*). It cannot become res judicata, however, and it may be revoked or modified by the judge during the course of the dispute or in the final

---

384. *See* E. Silvestri, *The Devil Is in the Details: Remarks on Italian Enforcement Procedures*, in *Enforcement and Enforceability. Tradition and Reform* 213 (C.H. Van Rhee & A. Uzekac eds, Intersentia 2010).
385. *Trib.* Terni 4 Sep. 2009, *ord.*, FI, 2009, No. 9, *Anticip. e novità*, 9; *Trib.* Cagliari 19 Oct. 2009, GM, 2010, 394; *Trib.* Verona 9 Mar. 2010, *ord.*, GM, 2010, 1857.
386. Cf. A. Didone, *Le ordinanze anticipatorie di condanna* (Milan: Giuffrè, 1998).
387. Lapertosa, 'La tutela sommaria anticipatoria (Art. 186*bis*, 186*ter* c.p.c.)', RDP (1997): 767.

judgment; should the proceedings be discontinued, it will keep its enforcing force;[388]

- an order to pay a sum of money or to deliver a specified good or quantity of goods (*ordinanza-ingiunzione*) (Article 186*ter* CPC):[389] this order can be given when the creditor has some documentary evidence of his or her credit, and it can always be revoked or modified by the judgment on the merits. It is automatically enforceable against the debtor only if he or she lacks any written counter-evidence. If the debtor is in default, the order must be served on him or her so that he or she can bring a defence in the proceedings within twenty days of service. Only if the default debtor does not timely present his or her defence or if such defence is not based on some written counter-evidence does the order of payment become enforceable against the debtor;
- an order on the evidence gathered at the end of the instructing phase (*ordinanza post-istruttoria*) (Article 186*quater* CPC):[390] This is a special remedy, which was introduced in 1995 with a particular consideration for those proceedings which were not subject to the reform of 1990 (*vecchio rito*) and in which, therefore, there was still a long delay between the last hearing before the instruction judge and the discussion hearing before the three-judge panel (sometimes, more than one year could pass before this last – and usually useless – hearing). Article 186*quater* CPC was therefore introduced to allow the court, on one of the parties' motion, to order to the counterpart to pay a sum of money, deliver a good or release an immovable property. This provisional order is peculiar insomuch as it can only be given at the end of the evidence-gathering phase and therefore it is not a summary decision as the two other orders for payment examined *supra*. It follows that, even if, in theory, such orders may be revoked or modified by the final judgment, in practice, they are usually confirmed for the simple reason that the evidentiary materials on which the order is given are the same on which the court renders its concluding decision. In other words, this order effectively anticipates the judgment, with much lighter formal tasks for the court, in particular as concerns its reasoning, which can be rather concise. To make this remedy more attractive to the creditor litigants, in 2005, Article 186*quater* CPC was revised so that now the provisional order will automatically acquire the full effects of a judgment if the debtor does not declare his or her wish that the judgment be given by the court, within thirty days of the order being communicated to the parties. This means that, failing such a timely declaration from the debtor, the order will become directly appealable just like an ordinary judgment and, as such, it will eventually acquire full res judicata effects. The same will happen if the proceedings are discontinued before the final judgment is delivered.

388. A. Ronco, 'Ordinanze per il pagamento di somme ed estinzione del processo', GI (1996): IV, 325.
389. R. Conte, *L'ordinanza di ingiunzione nel processo civile* (Padua: Cedam, 2003).
390. F. Santangeli, *L'ordinanza successiva alla chiusura dell'istruzione* (Milano: Giuffrè, 2001).

§2. Default Proceedings

241. When a party does not formally present his or her first defence before the court, he or she is held in default and proceedings continue in his or her absence.

Unlikely as it might be, even the plaintiff might be in default of appearance, if he or she does not register the case in court after serving his or her petition on the defendant. Such registration might then be performed by the defendant, who could even make the dispute proceed to judgment in the plaintiff's absence (Article 290).

Most commonly, it is the defendant who chooses to not take part in the proceedings, which therefore continue in his or her absence. The system, however, in compliance with the right of the defence, ensures that such absence is really a voluntary choice and not simply the consequence of the defendant not being aware of the starting of proceedings against him or her. To this end, at the first hearing (*see supra*, paragraph 214), the instructing judge checks that a valid *citazione* has been served on the defendant in compliance with the existing rules. If faults are found either in the *citazione* or in its service, the *citazione* has to be served again on the defendant with the necessary amendments. Only when this has been properly performed, can the judge declare the defendant in default and let the proceedings continue (Article 291 CPC).

242. A defendant in default does not suffer any automatic negative effect: even in his or her absence, the plaintiff has to satisfy his or her own burden of the proof as to the existence of the facts on which his or her claim is based. As a matter of fact, in the Italian tradition, a defendant who does not file his or her defence is considered as tacitly contesting the claim (*ficta contestatio*), therefore putting on the plaintiff possibly an even heavier evidentiary burden, since he or she may not take advantages of the other party admitting or not contesting some of the facts on which his or her claim is grounded.[391]

On the other hand, the defendant does not have an absolute right to be informed about the evolution of the proceedings. Only some very important acts and events must be formally put to the attention of the party in default, in order not to infringe on his or her right of the defence.

Article 292 CPC lists the documents and acts which must be served on the party in default in order for the proceedings to be valid:

- the instructing judge's order which admits the formal interrogation or the oath of the party in default;
- written briefs of the parties containing new claims or counter-claims;
- any judgment rendered in the proceedings; and
- communications concerning the filing of new private writings of the party in default (*scritture private*).

391. *See* A. Raganati, 'Il processo contumaciale tra eccessivo garantismo e principio di autoresponsabilità', <www.judicium.it>.

243. The party in default has the right to join in the proceedings at any time before the final hearing of the instructing phase by filing a defence in court. However, he or she cannot perform any procedural activity which is precluded to the other parties at the time of his or her joinder. Only when the party which files a late defence (*costituzione tardiva*) shows that the original *citazione* or its service was invalid, can he or she be reinstated in his or her right to a full defence (*rimessione in termini*) (Article 294 CPC).[392]

A party in default which proves that he or she was not regularly served with a valid petition may bring an appeal against a judgment which would otherwise be covered by procedural res judicata.[393]

Of course, the defaulting party's objections as to the regularity of the starting phase of the proceedings can be raised at any appeal level.

392. *See* F. De Santis, *La rimessione in termini nel processo civile* (Turin: Giappichelli, 1997).
393. Article 327(2) CPC.

Chapter 3. Review Proceedings

§1. Introduction

244. Before analysing the different kinds of review proceedings, it is necessary to make some introductory remarks on the appeals system in Italy.[394]

Review proceedings are distinguished between ordinary and extraordinary remedies, depending on their relation with procedural res judicata (*see* paragraph 233).

Ordinary remedies – that is, appeal (*appello*), petition to the *Corte di cassazione* (*ricorso per Cassazione*), *regolamento di competenza* and *revocazione ordinaria* – can only be brought within a fixed time limit, before the judgment becomes res judicata. Conversely, a judgment can never become res judicata until the time limits to raise ordinary appeals have expired. Extraordinary remedies – *revocazione straordinaria* and *opposizione di terzo* – on the other hand, may be brought against judgments which have already become res judicata.

245. A petition for review of a judgment must always be reasoned; in other words, the applicant has the burden to point out the reasons why a given judgment, from his or her point of view, is 'defective' and should therefore be revoked or modified. Should those reasons lack or be too generic, the petition is not admissible. Most review proceedings can only be brought on certain grounds, specifically listed in the relevant rules (*impugnazioni a critica vincolata*). The reasons for review must then fall into at least one of these grounds. Ordinary appeal (*appello*), on the other hand, does not need meeting specific grounds and can also be based on the general injustice suffered by the losing party (*impugnazione a critica libera*).

246. In Italy, no leave to appeal is ever necessary: as a matter of fact, appeals are automatic, as long as certain conditions are complied with (*condizioni dell'impugnazione*).

First of all, only the parties to the lower-instance proceedings can raise an appeal against the decision rendered therein (*legittimazione ad impugnare*). Of course, the party may be physically different (e.g., the original plaintiff died, and his or her heirs took his or her place), but the centre of substantive interests must be the same.

As a general rule, all the parties to the lower-instance proceedings must take part in the review proceedings.[395] Depending on the nature of the substantive right in dispute and on the peculiarities of the procedure, sometimes their presence is necessary (*cause inscindibili* and *cause* which are dependent from each other)[396] so that, should an unsummoned party not be joined in the review proceedings by the most diligent party, within the deadline fixed by the court, the appeal cannot proceed to judgment (*inammissibilità*) and no further review of the same kind can be requested, even if the deadline to bring it has not fully expired yet.

---

394. *See* M. De Cristofaro, 'Appeals', in *Civil Justice in Italy*, *supra*, 226 et seq.
395. *See* T. Carnacini, *Il litisconsorzio nelle fasi di gravame* (Padua: Cedam, 1937).
396. Article 331 CPC.

When, on the other hand, the parties' positions can be severed from each other with no risk of irreconcilable judgments (as concerns the possibility to simultaneously enforce the relevant decisions), after the time for the unsummoned parties to bring an appeal has expired, the appeal proceedings can continue even if some of the original parties are not present therein (*cause scindibili*).[397]

247. There must also be an interest in the review of the decision (*interesse ad impugnare*),[398] and therefore only the losing party can apply for it to revert the outcome of such a decision; of course, more than one party can end up dissatisfied by a judgment, for example, when the plaintiff obtains less than he or she demanded and the defendant has to pay more than he or she expected. In such cases, both parties can raise an appeal against the same decision.

Moreover, there may be cases when a party's interest in the review of the decision is not an actual one, for example, as would be the case of a defendant whose objection to the court's jurisdiction was dismissed, when the plaintiff's claim was any way denied on the merits. Such defendant would have an interest in appealing the court's decision on the jurisdictional issue only if the plaintiff's appeal on the merits is allowed. Conditional appeals (*impugnazioni condizionate*) are thus allowed, enabling a party to appeal a decision on grounds which have to be examined only if the appeal judge will find the main petition for review well grounded.

To prevent conflicting decisions and to save time and money, all appeals against the same decision must be brought together in the same proceedings, by way of *impugnazione incidentale* (i.e., the review petition brought by the party sued in appeal by another party).

If autonomous appeals (*impugnazioni principal*) are simultaneously brought against the same decision, the relevant proceedings must be joined together.

248. Finally, one must consider whether a specific decision can be appealed against as a matter of law (*possibilità di impugnare*).

Of course, a certain hierarchy of review proceedings has to be respected (*appello* – usually – comes before a petition before the *Cassazione*) and, as a general rule, only proper judgments (*sentenze*) can be reviewed, insomuch as *decreti* and *ordinanze* (*see supra*, paragraph 194) usually have provisional effects and are superseded by the final judgment rendered in the same proceedings.

However, at least according to the case law, substance prevails over forms and even decisions which mistakenly have the contents of a *sentenza*, and the form of either a decree or an *ordinanza* can be appealed against as if they were a *sentenza*.

Moreover, according to Article 111 of the Constitution, every decision which permanently infringes subjective rights in violation of the law and which cannot otherwise be reviewed may be brought before the *Cassazione* by means of an extraordinary petition (*ricorso straordinario*).

249. The starting of review proceedings does not automatically prevent or stay the enforcement of the decision appealed against. A special petition has to be filed

397. Article 332 CPC.

398. *See* L. Salvaneschi, *L'interesse ad impugnare* (Milan: Giuffrè, 1990).

to obtain the so-called *sospensiva* (stay) of the provisional enforcing authority of the decision. If an appeal is allowed, however, all the parts of the decision which are a consequence of the part which was thus annulled are struck out also; the same happens to all the acts which have been performed in compliance with the part of the judgment which was struck out or anyway reviewed (e.g., the enforcement proceedings of a first instance decision which was annulled by the Court of Appeal).

§2. APPEAL

250. Appeal (*appello*) grants a general review of judgments rendered at first instance. Sometimes, the possibility to bring an appeal against a decision is expressly denied by the law. Article 360(3) CPC also allows the parties (now even before the first instance judgment is released)[399] to agree on skipping the appeal phase and go directly before the *Corte di cassazione* (*ricorso per saltum*).

An appeal allows a review of the first judgment on both legal and factual grounds, as well as on the reasons given by the first court and on the general injustice of the outcome of the lower proceedings. Traditionally, Italian law provided (almost) no limits to the possibility to appeal against a first instance decision: as a matter of fact, until the reform of 1990, appeal proceedings were even granted greater relevance in Italian civil litigation, so that one could come to the conclusion that proceedings before the first judge were only a preliminary step to bring the case before the second instance court, with very wide possibilities to bring new factual or evidentiary elements into the case (*novum iudicium*). After 1990, however, first instance proceedings were given greater importance and appeal proceedings were qualified and disciplined as revisions of the first decision (*revisio prioris instantiae*). Access to the second tier of jurisdiction still remains virtually unlimited, though, and this, in time, has led to a situation where appeal proceedings are the ones which last longer of all in the context of the Italian judicial system, and the Courts of Appeal are struggling to handle an ever-increasing backlog. In many Courts, the average length of an appeal case is today between three to four years.

In order to try and improve the situation, DL No. 83 of 22 June 2012, implemented by Law No. 134 of 7 August 2012, introduced a very important reform as concerns access to the appeal level in Italian civil litigation. A new Article 348*bis* has been introduced in the code of civil procedure providing for a 'filter' to the second instance tier of jurisdiction (*filtro in appello*).[400] According to the new provision, as a matter of fact, an appeal is considered to be inadmissible if, at the first hearing, the court finds that the appeal has 'no reasonable chance of success'. This filter, however, does not apply to appeals where the PM is a necessary party (*see* paragraph 97) not to appeals in summary proceedings (*see* paragraphs 343 et seq.). The new provision has been criticized for giving too wide a discretionary power to

399. Article 366(3) CPC as revised in 2006.

400. *See* Bove, M., La pronuncia di inammissibilità dell'appello ai sensi degli articoli 348 bis e 348 ter c. p. c., in Riv. dir. proc., 2013, 389; Lupoi, M.A., Nowhere fast? Shortcuts to judgment in recent Italian procedural legislation, in Ways of implementation of the right to civil proceedings within a reasonable time, Vilnius: Vilnius Universitetas, 2016, p. 305.

the appeal judges who could easily dispose of unwanted cases by simply saying that they have no prospect of success. In practice, so far, this has not proved to be the case. So far, however, practice appears to show that when appeal courts apply Article 348*bis* CPC, their decisions are always very considerate and extensive. When it is used, the new filter proves to be an effective remedy to dispose of prima facie ungrounded appeals[401] but it surely failed to eliminate the backlog at the appeal level.[402]

It is generally said that when an appeal is raised, the whole dispute is brought before the higher judge (*principio devolutivo*). In practice, however, in the light of the adversary principle, the party who brings the appeal has the burden to specifically point out which of his or her claims, defences and issues which were not allowed by the first instance court he or she wishes the appeal court to re-examine.[403] Claims and defences that were rejected by the first court and which are not raised again at the appeal stage are considered moot and covered by res judicata (*acquiescenza*: Article 346 CPC).

251. After the reform of Law No. 353/90, the appeal stage has acquired a new role: no longer a *novum iudicium*, rather a mere review of the original petition, where the appeal court revises the first instance proceedings and decision with very little possibility for the parties to introduce new claims, defences and evidence.

As a matter of fact, according to Article 345 CPC, no new claims are admissible at the appeal stage, that is, the subject matter of the dispute may not be wider than the one which was decided at first instance.[404] Only ancillary claims relating to interests and damages suffered after the first judgment can be brought *ex novo*.

New defences and exceptions are forbidden too (in compliance with the preclusions system at first instance), with the exception of those defences that can be raised ex officio by the court.

As concerns 'evidence', until 2012, under Article 345 CPC only new evidence which the court deemed to be indispensable to decide the case or in relation to which the party showed that it was impossible for him or her to apply for admission at an earlier stage could be allowed at the appeal stage.[405] In 2009, Article 345(3) CPC was partially modified, in order to make it clear that these restrictions also applied to the filing of new documents.[406] In 2012, the provisions of Article 345

---

401. *See* R. Martino & A. Panzarola (eds) *Commentario alle riforme del processo civile dalla semplificazione dei riti al decreto sviluppo*, (Turin: Giappichelli, 2013); M. Bove, 'La pronuncia di inammissibilità dell'appello ai sensi degli articoli 348 bis e 348 ter c. p. c.', RDP (2013): 389; R. Poli, 'Il nuovo giudizio di appello', RDP (2013): 120; G. Verde, 'Diritto di difesa e nuova disciplina delle impugnazioni', RTDPC (2013): 507.
402. *See* M.A. Lupoi, *Nowhere Fast? Shortcuts to Judgment in Recent Italian Procedural Legislation*, in *Ways of Implementation of the Right to Civil Proceedings Within a Reasonable Time* 305 (Vilnius Universitetas 2016).
403. With specific reference to evidentiary requests not allowed at first instance *see Cass.* 26 Oct. 2000, n. 14135, GC, 2000, I, 3117.
404. *See* A. Bonsignori, 'Il divieto di domande e di eccezioni nuove in appello', RTDPC (1998): 65.
405. For example, the availability of a new eyewitness is discovered after the first instance judgment was released.
406. *See* A. Briguglio, 'Le novità sul processo ordinario di cognizione nell'ultima, ennesima riforma in materia di giustizia civile', GC (2009): II, 262.

CPC were made stricter still by repealing the possibility to bring new 'indispensable' evidence.[407] Today, therefore only new evidence (including new documents) which the party proves to have been unable to bring at first instance on force majeure grounds are allowed in appeal proceedings. In other words, the lawmaker has redrafted the appeal stage as a 'closed door' re-examination of the case decided at first instance (the *revisio prioris instance* notion brought to its extreme implications), clearly in an attempt at discouraging appeals. An exception is provided for summary proceedings (*see* paragraphs 343 et seq.). However, it is always possible for a party to challenge the counterpart to take an oath (*giuramento decisorio*).

252. A justice of the peace's decisions may be appealed before the *Tribunale* and a *Tribunale*'s judgments before the Court of Appeal.

Territorial appeal competence depends on the judiciary circuit to which the first instance court belongs to.

The Court of Appeal sits during the whole instructing phase and decides the case as a panel of three judges. However, in an attempt to optimize the use of judicial resources in appeal proceedings, Article 350(1) CPC was modified in 2011: today it is therefore possible for the President of the panel of the Court of Appeal to appoint a single judge to assist should evidence need to be gathered or renewed (an unlikely event, as a matter of fact …).

In the *Tribunale*, instead, appeals are always decided by a single judge.

253. Unless specifically ruled otherwise, appeal proceedings follow the same provisions applicable to first instance proceedings before the *Tribunale* (Article 359 CPC).

The petition is brought by way of a *citazione*, served on the defendant and then filed into the court for registration of the case, with a copy of the appealed judgment. The *citazione* should originally contain the same elements required at first instance by Article 163 CPC, plus a concise exposition of the facts of the case and the proceedings at first instance, with the specific reasons for the appeal.[408] In 2012, however, stricter formal requirements were introduced for the appeal petition, allegedly in order to fasten the activities of the second instance judge in dispatching the case. Basically, according to the revised version of Article 342 CPC, an appeal petition must now clearly point out the parts of the decision which the party wishes to appeal and state the modifications which are applied for as concerns the factual investigation of the first instance judge. Moreover, the petition must state the circumstances from which the alleged violation of the law derives and their relevance in relation to the decision appealed against. In other words, according to these new requirements, the appeal judge should be in the position to decide the case by simply reading the petition (and the other party's reply) with no need to read any further materials. Many commentators have stated that the lawmaker has thus

407. *See* M. Fornaciari, 'Ancora una riforma dell'art. 360 n. 5 c. p. c.: basta, per favore, basta!', <www.judicium.it>, 1; A. Tedoldi, 'I motivi specifici e le nuove prove in appello dopo la novella "iconoclasta" del 2012', RDP. (2013): 145.

408. *See* Rascio, 'Ancora sui motivi di appello: il requisito della specificità e le conseguenze della violazione dell'art. 342 c.p.c. nella giurisprudenza della Suprema Corte', FI (2000): I, 218.

implemented the principle of self-sufficiency of the appeal petition.[409] Arguably, the new formal requirements are also likely to function as an effective tool to dispose of weak or poorly written petitions: as a matter of fact, when the requirements set by Article 342 CPC are not met, the claim is considered to be inadmissible and the appeal is disposed of without any further investigation as to the merits of the case.[410]

Not later than twenty days before the first hearing, may the defendant file his or her first defence (*comparsa di risposta*) containing any appeal he or she might be entitled to raise against the same judgment (*appello incidentale*, *see supra*, paragraph 247).

No third parties can join or be joined in appeal proceedings, with the exception of those third parties who could appeal the judgment by means of an *opposizione di terzo* (Article 344 CPC).

If the review petition is not timely filed in the court after service, the appeal is dismissed (*improcedibilità dell'appello*: Article 348 CPC) and the first instance decision becomes res judicata. The appeal is also dismissed if the plaintiff does not appear before the court at the first two hearings. Before the appeal can proceed to judgment, the court must verify whether all the necessary parties are present or have been served with the appeal petition or if the start of the appeal has been communicated to the unnecessary parties, as *per* Articles 331–332 CPC (*see supra*, paragraph 246).

254. Usually, the most important part of the preliminary stage of appeal proceedings is the court's decision whether to stay the provisional enforcing authority of the first instance decision (*sospensione della provvisoria esecutorietà della sentenza*). On the party's motion, the court decides on such petition during the first hearing.[411] Enforceability of the first instance decision will be stayed (*in toto* or in part) only if serious and well-grounded reasons for doing so are shown by the appellant (*gravi e fondati motivi*). After being revised in 2005, Article 283 CPC now makes it clear that, in order to reach his or her decision, the court may consider whether any party might become insolvent. Appeal judges appear to be rather strict when deciding on such a petition. In general, they will be reluctant to enter into the merits of the appeal and rather examine the urgency side of the matter (*periculum in mora*). When the amount of money the applicant would be expected to pay under the first instance decision is not substantial, a petition for *sospensiva* will most likely be denied.

In order to discourage petitions for a *sospensiva* (which require the Court to make an early evaluation of the case, using precious time and resources), Article 27 of Law No. 183 of 12 November 2011 has added a paragraph to Article 283 CPC, stating that when such a petition is declared inadmissible or manifestly unfounded, the judge may sentence the applying party to pay a sanction of between EUR 250 and

---

409. M. Fornaciari, *supra*, 1; R. Russo, 'Dialoghi sulle impugnazioni civili al tempo della spending review', <www.judicium.it>, 2.

410. *See* A. Tedoldi, *supra*, 145.

411. In urgent cases, the party can apply for a preliminary hearing before the date set in the *citazione* for the first hearing proper.

EUR 10,000. Such order, however, may be revoked by the final decision of the court on the merits of the appeal.

At the first hearing, moreover, the court is supposed to decide whether the case satisfies the 'reasonable chance of success' set by Article 348*bis* CPC (*see* paragraph 250). This decision is based on a summary evaluation of the appeal, as concerns both the procedural aspects and its merits. If the test is passed, the case goes through the filter and moves to the next step of the proceedings. If, on the other hand, the appeal is deemed to be inadmissible, the Court releases an order to close proceedings before her. Article 348*ter* CPC specifies that such decision should be briefly reasoned, even by referring to factual elements reported in one or more of the briefs of the proceedings or to concurring precedents. At this point, the petitioner may appeal (not the Court's order) but the decision of the first instance judge directly before the Court of Cassation (this is due to the fact that under Article 111(7) of the Constitution, a party has an absolute right to appeal before the Supreme Court against any decision having binding effects on her rights, when no other remedy is available: *see* paragraphs 80, 253).

255. An evidence-gathering phase can take place at the appeal level also;[412] in the light of the 'no new evidence' rule of Article 345 CPC (*see supra*, paragraph 251); however, it is allegedly infrequent for new oral evidence to be admitted and gathered by the appeal court. Also, evidence gathered at first instance can be renewed or collected again. In practice, however, an appeal petition is usually decided on a re-evaluation of the same evidence collected at first instance.

256. At the end of the evidence-gathering phase (or immediately, if no new evidence is admissible or necessary), the court invites the parties to present their final requests (*precisazione delle conclusioni*), and final defences (*comparsa conclusionale* and *memoria di replica*) are filed by the parties before the court's decision: in other words, like at first instance, the final judgment is usually rendered out of court, after an exchange of written defences by the parties. In 2011, however, to try and accelerate the course of the proceedings in simpler cases, the lawmaker extended to the appeal stage the possibility for the judge, after gathering any available evidence or immediately at the first hearing, to invite the parties to discuss the case orally and then to render his decision at that very same hearing (Articles 351 and 352 CPC). Arguably, this new simplified procedural mechanism to decide an appeal is hardly ever used in practice.

Only before the Court of Appeal may the parties apply for a final oral discussion before the panel (which, in practice, is rather infrequent).[413]

257. The appeal decision can dismiss the review petition, thereby confirming the first instance judgment, or allow the application and wholly or partially modify the decision appealed against.

---

412. *See* G. Ruffini, *La prova nel giudizio civile di appello* (Padua: Cedam, 1997).
413. Article 352(2) CPC.

As at first instance, the legal costs of the winning party are usually taxed on the losing party; if the appeal is allowed, the court can modify the first court decision on legal costs at first instance.

As a general rule, the appeal judge, in allowing the review petition, always decides the case on the merits *ex novo*, correcting the legal or factual mistakes contained in the first instance decision. This is true even when rather serious procedural faults occurred before the lower court; it is submitted that, in practice, this can result in an infringement of the right of defence of a party.[414]

Only in rather exceptional (and mandatory)[415] cases must the appeal judge allow the appeal, annul the first instance decision and then send the case back to the lower court for a de novo trial. This happens when the first court mistakenly dismissed the case on lack of jurisdiction grounds, service of the original *citazione* on the defendant was null and void, some necessary party was not joined in the proceedings as *per* Article 102 CPC or was erroneously driven out of the dispute, the judgment was not signed by the rendering judge(s) as *per* Article 161(2) CPC (*sentenza inesistente*), the case was stricken out in violation of Article 308 CPC.

§3. Petition to the *Corte Di Cassazione*

258. The right to bring a petition before the *Corte di cassazione* is sanctioned by Article 111 of the Italian Constitution.[416] Thereby, before any new system based on leave to appeal to the *Cassazione* may be introduced in Italy, the Constitution will have to be changed. In civil matters, even within the limited jurisdiction of our *Cassazione*, tens of thousands of petitions are filed each year into the court, which now renders more than 30,000 judgments yearly. This situation is of course rather unsatisfactory: the court is severely overloaded, even though in recent years it appears to have been able to reduce its backlog;[417] a delay of at least two or three years separates the petition from the judgment; also, inconsistency of the decisions rendered by the various sections of the *Corte* (or sometimes by different panels of the same section) is rather frequent, thus impairing the fundamental function of the

414. For example, according to *Cass.* 13 Mar. 1997, n. 2251, GD 17 (1997): 29, when, on appeal, it is found that the *citazione* at first instance in default proceedings was invalid, the case must be decided *ex novo* by the Court of Appeal, without a remittal to the Court of First Instance.

415. *See* Toffoli, 'Sulla possibilità, e i limiti dell'applicazione in via analogica delle disposizioni degli artt, 353 e 354 c.p.c. in tema di rinvio della causa al primo giudice da parte del giudice d'appello', FI (1996): I, 1302.

416. G. Campeis & A. De Pauli, *Il giudizio di Cassazione. Le novità della riforma* (Ipsoa, 2006); G. Monteleone, 'Il nuovo volto della Cassazione civile', RDP (2006): 943; F. Morozzo Della Rocca, 'Le modificazioni in materia di processo di Cassazione tra nomofilachia e razionaliz-zazione dell'esistente', *Corr. giuridico* (2006): 449; R. Poli, 'Il giudizio di cassazione dopo la riforma', RDP (2007): 9; B. Sassani, 'Il nuovo giudizio di cassazione', RDP (2006): 217; M. Taruffo, 'Una riforma della Cassazione civile?', RTDPC (2006): 755.

417. R. Caponi, *The Performance of the Italian Civil Justice System: An Empirical Assessment*, ILJ 22 (2016); R. Caponi, *European Minimum Standards for Courts. Independence, Specialization, Efficiency. A Glance from Italy*, in *Festschrift fur Professor Nikolaos K. Klamaris* 156 (Sakkoulas Publications 2016). Some fear, however, that this reduction in the courts' backlog may be a consequence of the current economic crisis rather than of an improved judicial context: *see* G. Fonderico, 'Giustizia, quell rischio che i risultati positive siano legati alla crisi', GD 8 (2016): 10.

court of granting the uniform interpretation of the law. In order to try and reduce the court's backlog and to emphasize its role as the main point of reference in relation to the correct interpretation of the rule of law, proceedings before the *Cassazione* have been extensively revised in 2006 and in 2009.

259. Before the *Cassazione*, it is possible to petition for the review of either Court of Appeal judgments or unappealable decisions; however, Article 111(7) of the Constitution makes it possible to appeal before the Supreme Court every decision which infringes on subjective rights in violation of the law and which is subject to no other form of superior review (*ricorso straordinario*). It is also possible for the parties to agree on bypassing the Court of Appeal, directly appealing a first instance judgment before the *Cassazione* (petition *per saltum*: Article 360 CPC).

260. Being concerned just with the juridical aspects of the case (*giudizio di legittimità*) and not with the reconstruction and interpretation of the relevant facts, whenever a review petition is allowed, the *Cassazione* only deals with the annulment of the judgment appealed against (*giudizio rescindente*), and the case is then remanded back to a court belonging to the same order of the court which rendered the quashed judgment (*giudice di rinvio*)[418] to render a fresh decision on the merits (*giudizio rescissorio*).

When the very serious procedural mistakes listed in Articles 353–354 CPC (*see supra*, paragraph 257) are found at the *Cassazione* level with reference to the proceedings at first instance, however, the case is exceptionally remanded to the first instance court (*rinvio improprio*).

In certain cases, however, even when the appeal is allowed, no remittal to an inferior court takes place: this can happen either when the whole proceedings are struck out or when the *Cassazione* itself exceptionally substitutes the judgment appealed against with a new decision on the merits (*see infra*, paragraph 262).

261. Until recently, the *Cassazione* decided with an order in chambers, with no public discussion hearing, only in a limited number of cases under Article 375 CPC. As a matter of fact, in the light of the present formulation of our Constitution, which makes any restriction to the general right to bring a petition before the *Cassazione* unconstitutional, the decision in chambers has always been seen as a tool to speed up the proceedings and reduce the court's backlog. Article 375 CPC, therefore, over time went through several reforms,[419] the latest of which, in 2016, basically (and controversially)[420] made a decision in chambers the general procedural option when

418. On the nature of remittal proceedings *see Cass.* 18 Jun. 94, No. 5901, FI, 1995, I, 1277. *See also* E. Ricci, *Il giudizio civile di rinvio* (Milan: Giuffrè, 1967); R. Provinciali, *Il giudizio di rinvio* (Padua: Cedam, 1936).
419. Law No. 89 of 24 Mar. 2001 and DLGS No. 40 of 2006. *See* A. Briguglio, 'La pronuncia in camera di consiglio della Corte di Cassazione (riflessioni sul nuovo Art. 375 c.p.c.)', RDP (2001): 1006.
420. *See*, e.g., the critical remarks of B. Sassani, 'Da Corte a Ufficio Smaltimento: ascesa e declino della "Suprema"', <www.judicium.it>.

a single section of the Court is in charge of deciding the case.[421] An exception is made by the reformulated Article 375 CPC when a public hearing appears appropriate in light of the particular relevance of the issue at hand or when the case successfully goes through an inadmissibility exception by the so-called *sezione filtro* (*see* paragraph 268). Also the full chambers of the Court may decide a case in chambers when they declare a *ricorso* or a *controricorso* inadmissible or when they decide upon a *regolamento di competenza* or a *regolamento di giurisdizione*.

262. Article 360 CPC lists the five grounds on which a petition to the *Cassazione* must be based; they are traditionally divided into procedural and legal grounds. The former concern the formal validity and regularity of the proceedings and the judgment; the latter refer to the proper and sound application and interpretation of the rules of law to the dispute at hand by the lower courts.

Article 360 Nos 1–2 CPC grant appeal to the *Cassazione* respectively on jurisdiction and competence grounds. Here, the role of the *Cassazione* is to point out the competent court; should the petition be allowed, the case will be remitted, on one of the parties' motion, to the court indicated by the *Cassazione*. If such remittal is not timely, the proceedings are discontinued; the Supreme Court's decision on matters of competence, however, is binding on any trial court if the same case is eventually started anew by the parties.

A petition to the *Cassazione* can also be based on the violation or mistaken interpretation by the lower court of either the law or the national labour contracts (Article 360, No. 3 CPC). Here, the court performs its main function as concerns the uniform interpretation of the rule of law and of the contractual agreements of the parties in matters of labour law.

The court's role is to review the judgment in the light of the rules and the relevant case law; when an appeal is allowed, since the court, as a general rule, cannot decide upon the merits of the case, it enumerates a legal principle (*principio di diritto*) which must then be applied to the facts of the case by the court of lower instance to which the case is remitted. After the reform of 2006, the court also hands out legal principles in any other case where it has decided upon a particularly important juridical issue: Article 384(1) CPC.

Only when no new evidence on the facts needs (or may) be gathered, can the *Cassazione* decide the merits of the case, applying its own legal principle to the facts as already ascertained at the trial level (Article 384 CPC).[422]

The *Cassazione* can also review a decision as concerns the formal regularity of the proceedings and of the judgment (Article 360, No. 4 CPC); if an appeal on this ground is allowed, unless the procedural fault is so serious that the proceedings have to be dismissed with no decision on the merits,[423] the case is remitted to a lower

421. DL 31 Aug. 2016, n. 168, converted into Law 25 Oct. 2016, No. 197. *See* A. Panzarola, 'La difesa scritta ed orale in Cassazione dopo il Protocollo d'intesa Mascherin-Santacroce e la legge 25 ottobre n. 197', GPC (2016): 1061.

422. *See* M. Bove, 'Sul potere della Corte di Cassazione di decidere nel merito della causa', RDP (1994): 707; M. De Cristofaro, 'La Cassazione sostitutiva nel merito. Prospettive applicative', RTDPC (1999): 279.

423. For example: the judgment was not signed by the rendering judge (Art. 161 CPC).

court, which will then renovate all the faulty procedural steps, so that a new judgment is rendered in compliance with the procedural indications of the *Cassazione*.

The last ground of appeal to the *Cassazione* has traditionally been very often referred to by the litigants and it surely is rather controversial. According to the original text of Article 360, No. 5, the *Corte* could review a judgment when the lower court's reasoning was either inconsistent or insufficient or if the judgment was not reasoned at all. As a matter of fact, the *Cassazione* could be called upon to review the legal reasoning of the lower court, checking that the reasons for the decision were clearly, consistently and sufficiently stated. This implied that the court had to examine the merits of the dispute, with the risk of going beyond its institutional role.[424]

The reform of 2006, to avoid a too extensive interference of the court with the lower court's activities, first revised Article 360, No. 5 CPC, so that the error in the reasoning of the judgment appealed against should concern a fact that was both in dispute and fundamental for the decision of the case.

This specification however was deemed to be insufficient in order to avoid an extensive use of this ground of appeal to bring proceedings before the Court of Cassation. In 2012, therefore, the lawmaker redrafted the provision of Article 360, No. 5 CPC, which now allows an appeal before the Cassazione only for failure to examine a fact which was decisive for the resolution of the case and which was in dispute among the parties.[425] Apparently, then, it is no longer possible to attack a decision alleging that it is insufficiently or inconsistently reasoned. Commentators have expressed rather hard critics against this reform,[426] which is considered to be too restrictive and possibly unnecessary. However, it is submitted[427] that since both Article 111(6) Const. and Article 132 CPC require a decision to be reasoned; they implicitly refer to a reasoning which is both complete and consistent, in order not to be only a formality, devoid of real contents. If this is the case, then, a decision which is poorly or inconsistently reasoned can still be appealed against before the Supreme Court, if not under No. 5 of Article 360 CPC, under its No. 4 (procedural defects: *see* above).

Another new restriction to an appeal under Article 360 No. 5 CPC derives from the so-called *doppia conforme* in relation to the ascertainment of facts by the merit judges: when the appeal decision confirms the facts as investigated by the first judge, then it is no longer possible to bring an appeal before the Supreme Court on

424. *See* P. Nappi, 'Legittimità e merito nel giudizio di Cassazione: il controllo della motivazione', GC (2001): II, 49.

425. *See* L. Piccinini, 'I motivi di ricorso in cassazione dopo la modifica dell'art. 360, n. 5 c. p. c.', RDP (2013): 407.

426. *See* C. Consolo, 'Lusso o necessità nelle impugnazioni delle sentenze', <www.judicium.it>; M. Bove, 'Giudizio di fatto e sindacato della Corte di cassazione: riflessioni sul "nuovo" art. 360, n. 5, c. p. c.', GPC (2012): 677; R. Caponi, 'Norme processuali 'elastiche' e sindacato in Cassazione (dopo la modifica dell'art. 360, 1° comma, n. 5, c. p. c.)', FI (2013): V, 149; M. Fornaciari, 'L'inammissibilità del ricorso per cassazione ex art. 360-bis c. p. c.', RTDPC (2013): 645.

427. M. Fornaciari, 'Ancora una riforma dell'art. 360 n. 5 c. p. c.: basta, per favore, basta!', <www.judicium.it>, 4–5.

grounds related to the reasoning of the decision. Also this new restriction, brought forth in 2012, has been harshly criticized.[428]

When the reasoning of the appealed judgment is found faulty, the judgment is quashed, and the case is remitted to a lower court to render a new judgment with a fresh reasoning, following the guidelines of the *Cassazione*. Only when the reasoning of the judgment is faulty, but the actual decision is correct (it is indeed possible to reach the right legal outcome for the wrong juridical reasons), can the *Cassazione* directly correct the reasoning of the decision with no remittal of the case to a lower court.

263. Article 363 CPC, as revised in 2006, enables also the *Procuratore Generale* of the *Cassazione*, in the interest of justice, to demand the review of a decision which the parties have not timely appealed against or which is not appealable, in order to enable the court to state the legal principle the lower court should have followed.

Even after the revisions of 2006, this quite peculiar form of review keeps on being hard if at all used.

In order to stress the role of the *Cassazione* as the main interpreter of the rule of law, Article 363 now also allows the court to state a legal principle in relation to petitions which it has declared inadmissible.

In both cases, the court's judgment has no effect on the lower court's decision (which is still binding for the original parties).

264. The petition to the *Cassazione* takes the form of a *ricorso* which is first served on the defendant[429] and then filed in the court, within twenty days of the date of service.

In the *ricorso*, some very important formal requirements must be complied with. First of all, a special and specific power of attorney (*procura speciale*) must be released by the party to a lawyer with a special licence to defend cases before the Cassazione (*avvocato cassazionista*).[430] The *ricorso* should also mention the parties, the judgment appealed against, a concise summary of the proceedings and of the facts of the case, the specific reasons for appeal.

In the reform of 2006, a new formal requirement was introduced: when the review petition was based on Nos 1–4 of Article 360, the *ricorso* should also contain specific legal questions (*quesito di diritto*) to enable the court to state corresponding legal principles (*principio di diritto*). Allegedly, this new requirement was

---

428. T. Galletto, '"Doppio filtro" in appello, "doppia conforme" e danni collaterali', <www.judicium.it>, 11; G. Impagniatiello, 'Crescita del Paese e funzionalità delle impugnazioni civili: note a prima lettura del d. l. 83/2012', <www.judicium.it>, 6.

429. Within sixty days of service of the judgment or six months of its publication when no service took place.

430. So far, in order to become *cassazionista*, an Italian lawyer just had to wait: after twelve years of continuing practice, as a matter of fact, he would be licensed to stand before the Supreme Court. The new *legge professionale* of 2012 (*see* para. 113), however changed this situation. Since 2012 it is possible to become *cassazionisti* either by taking a special exam after five years of practice or by attending with honours the *Scuola superiore dell'avvocatura* (i.e., a centre of higher education for lawyers), after eight years of practice.

meant to put an emphasis on the role of the *Cassazione* as a court strictly concerned with the interpretation of the rule of law. However, it also worked as an effective workload-reducing factor for the court, since, according to Article 366*bis* CPC, whenever the legal question was omitted or not properly formulated, the petition was struck out. The case law of the *Cassazione* showed that the court was ready to give a very strict and formalistic notion of *quesito di diritto*, therefore making a large number of petitions inadmissible on purely procedural grounds. This position was unsatisfactory and in 2009, Article 366*bis* CPC was quickly repealed. No formulation of legal questions in the *ricorso* is therefore required now.

Law No. 69 of 2009, however, introduced a new form of 'filter' for petitions to the Supreme Court (*filtro in Cassazione*),[431] in order to try and make access to the *Cassazione* harder for prima facie frivolous or unfounded appeals, thus reducing the court's workload. According to the new Article 360*bis* CPC, a *ricorso* will be deemed inadmissible if the decision appealed against has solved the relevant legal issues in compliance with the case law of the *Cassazione*, and the claimant does not show good reason to revert those precedents, or if the complaint concerning the violation of fair trial principles appears to be manifestly unfounded.

Reference to the application of the *Cassazione* precedents by the lower courts should not be interpreted as a form of stare decisis. Rather, the new provision tries both to encourage lower courts to follow the Supreme Court case law, therefore making the outcome of decisions more predictable and to compel the petitioner to consider the advisability of filing a *ricorso* against a decision which most likely will be confirmed by the Supreme Court. However, if good reasons are shown, the *Cassazione* may always decide to reverse its own case law and follow a new interpretative track.

After the reform of 2006, the *ricorso* must analytically point out the procedural acts, the documents and the contracts it is based upon; also, if this requirement is not complied with, the *ricorso* is struck out.

Within twenty days of service, the *ricorso* must be filed in the court in Rome. Article 369 CPC specifies which documents should be filed with the *ricorso*, the most important being a certified copy of the judgment appealed against, the special power of attorney, in case it was not already attached to the *ricorso* served on the defendant, the documents and the contracts on which the petition is grounded. The petitioner (*ricorrente*) must also ask the clerks of the court which rendered the decision appealed against to transmit the court's file of the case to the *Cassazione*; a copy of this request must be filed with the *ricorso* in the court.

265. Within twenty days of the deadline for filing the *ricorso* in the court, the petitioner's counterpart (*resistente*) may serve his or her own defence on the *ricorrente*, in the form of a *controricorso*.[432] In the *controricorso*, the *resistente* replies to the petitioner's allegations, exposing his or her reasons for denying the review

431. A. Briguglio, 'Chi ha paura del "filtro"?', <www.judicium.it>; G. Ianniruberto & U. Morcavallo, *Il nuovo giudizio di Cassazione* (Milan: Giuffrè, 2010), 137 et seq.

432. Failing that, he will not be able to deposit further written defences, but only to appear at the oral hearing before the court: Art. 370 CPC.

petition. Should he or she have partially lost the case at the lower instance, he or she may also bring an incidental appeal.[433]

Also the *controricorso* must be filed in the court within twenty days of service.

266. Since the *Cassazione* does not decide the merits of the case, no evidence-gathering phase can ever take place before it, and no new document can be deposited by the parties, with the exception of those documents which concern the formal validity of the judgment and the admissibility of either the *ricorso* or the *controricorso* (Article 372 CPC).

267. An appeal to the *Cassazione* does not automatically stay the enforcement of the lower-instance decision; however, such stay can be allowed, on the party's petition and if a serious and irreparable harm is held to exist by the court which rendered the judgment appealed against.

268. After a *ricorso* has been filed, the first President of the Court may assign the case to the full division (*sezioni unite*) of the court, in order to solve important new legal issues or to solve contrasts between the case law of different sections of the court itself (*see* at paragraph 88).

If this is not the case, after the reform brought by Law No. 69 of 2009 (which introduced the new 'filter' for the petitions to the *Cassazione*: *see* paragraph 264), the first President of the Court assigns the case to a special section (the so-called *sezione filtro*), which is in charge of checking whether the grounds exist for disposing of the petition in chambers, for the reasons stated in Article 375(1), Nos 1 and 5.[434] This section is composed by five judges coming from all the other sections of the court (Article 67*bis* of the *Ordinamento giudiziario*).[435]

Basically, at this stage, the special division verifies if the petition is manifestly grounded or ungrounded. If this is the case, one of the members of the panel (*consigliere relatore*) writes an opinion stating the reasons for disposing of the case in chambers, which is then communicated to the parties. The latter may at this point file a written brief before a hearing in chambers takes place. The final decision is then taken with an *ordinanza*.

If the case is not decided in chambers on the grounds mentioned above, the First President then assigns it to a single section of the court. One of the members of the panel is appointed as reporting judge (*consigliere relatore*). If the section fixes a public hearing, the relevant date is then communicated to the parties, which can file a written defence not later than five days in advance. A *resistente* who has not timely served his or her *controricorso* is precluded from filing such final defence.

At the public hearing, the reporting judge presents the relevant facts, the contents of the decision appealed against and a summary of the parties' defences. It is then

433. To which, the *ricorrente* can reply by serving a *controricorso* on the counterpart.

434. Article 376 CPC was modified in 2016: now, when, upon a summary examination of the *ricorso*, the *sezione filtro* does not find these reasons to apply, the President sends, without any formality, the case to a single section of the Court.

435. *See* F.S. Damiani, NLCC (2010), 981 et seq.

the turn of the *Pubblico Ministero* to expose his or her conclusions,[436] after which the parties' lawyers finally present their oral arguments before the panel. No replies are admitted.[437] After the discussion of the case, the panel renders its decision in chambers. The judgment is then handed to the court's clerk who will publish and communicate it to the parties. It may take several months after the hearing before the judgment is available to the public.

If the case falls to be decided in chambers (as it is the rule today for the single sections of the Court), on the other hand, the new Article 380*bis* (1) CPC, introduced in 2016, provides that the parties' lawyers and the *Pubblico Ministero* are informed of the date when the case will be decided.[438] The *Pubblico Ministero* may then file his written conclusions at least twenty days before that date. The lawyers may file their briefs within ten days beforehand. When a case is decided in chambers, the PM and the lawyers are not admitted to appear before the Court. Since 2016, in other words, when a case is decided in chambers, there is no meeting between the Court and the (public and private) parties, who have no chance to have their defences heard orally. Arguably, public discussion before the Court was indeed a mere formality, since the case was decided upon an examination of the written defences. Many commentators, however, believe that these new provisions effectively turn the *Cassazione* into a sort of decisions-factory. The role of the lawyers is also mortified.

269. As it has been observed earlier, if the petition is allowed, the case will normally be remitted to a lower court for the prosecution of the proceedings in the light of the court's determinations. Only in special cases (Article 384 CPC, *see supra*, paragraph 262), will the court allow the appeal and decide on the merits, with no further prosecution of the case. In other cases, when serious procedural mistakes have occurred at the lower instance, the court may strike out the case with no decision at all on the substance of the case.[439]

If the case is remanded, the lower court will have the power to decide on any restitutory claim depending on the enforcement of the judgment quashed by the Supreme Court; if the appeal is allowed, but no remittal takes place, those claims are presented to the same court which rendered the quashed decision (Article 389 CPC).

If the petition is denied, the *Cassazione* will normally tax on the *ricorrente* the legal costs incurred by his or her counterpart; when a remittal is required, the court will leave any decision on legal costs to the lower instance court; when the appeal is allowed and the court decides the merits of the case, it will also take a decision concerning the costs of the dispute.

---

436. Article 379 CPC was modified in 2016: beforehand, the *Pubblico Ministero* got to speak after the parties' lawyers.

437. Article 379(3) as reformed in 2016.

438. *See* C. Graziosi, 'La Cassazione "incamerata": brevi note pratiche', <www.judicium.it>. According to *Cass.* 10 Jan. 2017, n. 395, these new procedural rules are compatible with the fair trial principles set by the Constitution.

439. Article 382 CPC: absolute lack of jurisdiction; the original claim could not be filed or the case brought on.

270. A *Cassazione* decision, as a general rule, is not subject to any form of further appeal. However, simple material or arithmetic mistakes in the judgment can be corrected with a petition to the court.

Moreover, when the court decision is vitiated by a factual mistake as per Article 395, No. 4 CPC (*see infra*, paragraph 276), it can be appealed by means of *revocazione*.

According to Article 391*ter* CPC (introduced in 2006), in those cases where the court may exceptionally decide a case on the merits (*see supra*, paragraph 262), its judgment may also be attacked by way of *revocazione* (Article 395, Nos 1, 2, 3, 6 CPC) (*see infra*, paragraphs 276–277) or *opposizione di terzo* (*see infra*, paragraphs 279 et seq.).

§4. Other Review Petitions

I. *Regolamento di Competenza*

271. *See supra*, paragraph 173.

II. Extraordinary Appeals

272. Extraordinary review petitions can exceptionally be brought against a decision which is technically covered by procedural res judicata (*giudicato formale*). Being an exception to the *ne bis in idem* principle, these appeals are based on a closed set of specific grounds to offer a remedy for situations where the notion of a just judgment is at stake.

On the one hand, one must consider the *revocazione*, which is a remedy for the parties of the original proceedings to have a judgment modified whenever it is discovered that the court's decision was vitiated by a misrepresentation of the facts of the dispute. On the other, *opposizione di terzo* is an extraordinary appeal which can be brought by third persons, whenever their substantive position is someway hampered by the decision rendered between the original parties.

A distinction must also be made between those extraordinary review petitions which are not subject to any preclusive deadline (*opposizione di terzo ordinaria*) and those whose final deadline is related to a future (and uncertain) event (*opposizione revocatoria; revocazione straordinaria*).

A. Revocazione

273. As a matter of fact, *revocazione*[440] is a 'mixed' type of appeal.

Article 395 CPC lists six grounds of *revocazione*; two of them refer to the so-called *revocazione ordinaria*, which can be brought only before the ordinary time

440. *See* E. Fazzalari, 'Revocazione (diritto processuale civile)', in *Enciclopedia del diritto*, vol. XL (Milan: Giuffrè, 1989), 293.

limits to bring an appeal have expired; the other four refer to the *revocazione straordinaria*, which can be raised against decisions otherwise covered by res judicata.

The 'ordinary' grounds are based on faults which emerge from the very text of the judgment; the 'extraordinary' ones consist of 'hidden' faults, which must be discovered before they can be used as a tool to quash the decision to which they refer. Accordingly, the thirty days' time limit to bring *revocazione straordinaria* only starts to run from the day the relevant 'hidden' fault is ascertained.

274. Not being based on a procedural or substantive mistake of the rendering court, a petition for *revocazione* can be brought before the same court which delivered the judgment (Article 398 CPC).

The first act of the proceedings is a *citazione*, which must present, in particular, the specific grounds on which the petition is based, all the necessary evidence and, for *revocazione straordinaria*, the date on which the 'hidden' fault was discovered. A special and specific power of attorney is required.

275. Only judgments rendered by a Court of Appeal or which are not subject to any form of appeal can be reviewed by means of *revocazione*; of course, *revocazione straordinaria* can also be brought against first instance judgments which, at the time, were not appealed against.

276. Revocazione ordinaria can be proposed:

- against a decision that is based on a factual mistake of the court, which can be ascertained in the light of the acts of the proceedings and of the documents deposited therein. According to Article 395 No. 4 CPC, such mistakes consist in the judge finding true a fact which is indisputably false or vice versa, as long as the (in)existence of such a fact was not in dispute between the parties. Here, the court's mistake is simply based on an incorrect reading of the documents and the acts of the case. It is not a material mistake, but it is not a legal or logical mistake either;
- when the decision conflicts with another decision previously rendered between the same parties which has become res judicata, as long as the res judicata defence was not raised in the proceedings.[441] Here, two conflicting judgments are rendered between the same parties on the same subject matter and the second must give way to the first, in compliance with the *ne bis in idem* principle. Since this is a case of *revocazione ordinaria*, the provision at hand seems to imply that, if no petition for *revocazione* is timely raised and the second judgment becomes res judicata too, it is destined to prevail over the previous one.

277. Revocazione straordinaria, on the other hand, can be petitioned for when:

- the decision is vitiated by the malicious behaviour of a party against the other (*dolo*) (Article 395, No. 1 CPC);

441. Article 393(5) CPC.

- the judgment is based on evidence which was subsequently ascertained or admitted as being false (Article 395, No. 2 CPC);
- new decisive documents are discovered after the decision is rendered. It has to be added, however, that only those 'late discoveries' which depend on external events (force majeure) or on the counterpart's malicious behaviour can be considered here (Article 395, No. 3 CPC);
- the decision is vitiated by the malicious behaviour of the judge (Article 395, No. 6 CPC).

278. If the petition for *revocazione* is allowed, the judgment is quashed and a new judgment is rendered, after a fresh evidence-gathering phase if the case may be.

The courts also decide upon any consequent restitutory claims. The *revocazione* decision cannot be subject to any further petition for *revocazione*, but it is otherwise subject to the appeals decisions of that kind are normally subject to.[442]

B. Opposizione di Terzo

279. *Opposizione di terzo*[443] allows third persons to attack judgments rendered in proceedings to which they did not participate.

Two different forms of opposition are provided for by Article 404 CPC, *opposizione ordinaria* and *revocatoria* respectively.

280. *Opposizione ordinaria* can be brought by any third party whose rights are allegedly infringed by a judgment rendered between other parties which has become res judicata or which has provisional enforcing authority.

Two categories of third parties may make use of this extraordinary remedy:

(1) necessary and proper parties who were not joined in the proceedings in compliance with Article 102 CPC (*litisconsorti necessary pretermessi*); and
(2) third parties who claim to be vested with a right which is autonomous and incompatible with the right adjudicated upon by the judgment, the most classic example being someone who alleges to be the real owner of a good, when the judgment concerned a property claim between two other persons. Here, the third party would not be bound by the judgment between the other parties and such judgment could not lawfully be enforced against him or her; however, the judgment creates uncertainty as concerns the legal relationships at hand, and the third persons could suffer de facto from the enforcement of the decision.[444] When such conflicts arise, the third person could join the proceedings between the original parties to vindicate his or her own right (*intervento principale*, *see*

442. For example, if a first instance decision is revoked, the *revocazione* judgment can be appealed and then brought before the *Cassazione*.
443. *See* Nicoletti, 'Opposizione di terzo', in *Enciclopedia del diritto* (Milan: Giuffrè, 1980), 478.
444. For example, the judgment creditor seizes the good in the hands of the judgment debtor and subsequently disposes of it.

supra, paragraph 217); or he or she could start fresh proceedings against one or both the other parties to have his or her right adjudicated against them; finally, he or she could bring *opposizione ordinaria di terzo* before the court which rendered the judgment to prevent any enforcement of the decision, and have the infringing judgment revoked and substituted for a new judgment.

281. On the other hand, *opposizione di terzo revocatoria*[445] can be brought by the creditors and the persons who have acquired the adjudicated right from one of the parties of the original proceedings (*aventi causa*), whenever a judgment was the effect of malicious conduct on the sides of the parties.

Ordinarily, third persons (creditors and *aventi causa*) would suffer from the negative effects of a decision rendered against their debtor or the person who ceded his or her right to them (*dante causa*). Even if they were not parties to the proceedings in which the decision was released, such extension of the res judicata effects on them depends upon the very nature of the adjudicated right. Only when the original parties colluded between them in order to fraud their creditors or *aventi causa*, can the latter attack the decision, just like it would be possible for them to attack a contract concluded to fraudulently subtract certain assets from the debtor's estate.

282. The proceedings follow the rules normally applied in the court before which the *opposizione* is brought, that is, the same court which rendered the decision appealed against.

445. Article 404(2) CPC.

Part V. Incidents

283. In the course of civil proceedings, incidents can happen, which can roughly be divided into two categories: on the one hand, it is necessary to consider events which take place before the instructing judge; on the other hand, events which open an interlocutory phase before another judge or court. To the former category, stay, interruption and discontinuance of the proceedings belong; to the latter, several types of interlocutory applications.

Chapter 1. Stay of the Proceedings (*Sospensione del Processo*)

284. Proceedings are stayed in any situation in which the court finds itself in a temporary impossibility to proceed or decide the case.

The code refers to *sospensione* of the proceedings in Articles 295 et seq. CPC, which deal with voluntary and mandatory stay.

As to the former, the possibility for the parties to jointly ask the court to stay the proceedings for no longer than four months (usually when an out-of-court settlement has to be negotiated) is not very often used in practice.[446]

Much more important from both a practical and a theoretical standpoint is the so-called mandatory stay (*sospensione necessaria*) declared by the judge when he or she or another court must decide another action, whose outcome will have binding effects on the proceedings. In other words, to avoid conflicting decisions,[447] whenever, in the course of the proceedings, the need arises to decide a preliminary issue which falls to be adjudicated in already pending parallel proceedings, the action is stayed until a final decision in the other dispute is rendered. This stay lasts until the prejudicial issue has been decided with a res judicata judgment.

The prejudicial issue may be pending before a civil, a criminal or an administrative court.

Article 7(3) of Law No. 218 of 1995 now allows the court to stay the proceedings also when a (previously brought) prejudicial dispute is pending abroad.

285. When an action is stayed, only urgent acts can be performed. The action, however, is still pending, and no deadline or time limit can expire during the stay.

The stayed proceedings do not restart automatically after the prejudicial issue has been adjudicated: on the contrary, it is normally the parties' burden to file a petition into the court, requiring a hearing to be fixed. If this is not complied with, the case is discontinued.

286. The judge's decision to stay the case may be reviewed by the *Cassazione* by way of *regolamento necessario di competenza*[448] (*see supra*, paragraph 173).

If such an appeal is not timely brought, the *Cassazione* ruled that it is then not possible for the parties to apply for the stay to be lifted before the prejudicial proceedings have been defined.[449]

---

446. Article 296 CPC.

447. *See* A. Attardi, 'Conf litto di decisioni e sospensione necessaria del processo', GI (1987), IV, 417; M.G. Canella, 'La sospensione del processo civile nella giurisprudenza della Cassazione dopo le modifiche dell'art. 295 c.p.c.', RTDPC (1998): 1441; D. Volpino, 'L'economia della sospensione necessaria per pregiudizialità civile tra celerità dei giudizi ed uniformità delle decisioni', RTDPC (2004): 1459.

448. *See Cass.* 8 Nov. 1997, n. 11035, FI 1998, I, 3640.

449. *Cass. SU* 1 Oct. 2003, n. 14670, *ord.*, GI, 2004, 727.

Chapter 2. Interruption of the Proceedings

287. Interruzione del processo (interruption of the proceedings) (Articles 299 et seq. CPC) has similar effects to those of a stay (no acts of the procedure may be performed while the case is interrupted), but different causes: as a matter of fact, proceedings have to be temporarily interrupted whenever a peculiar sudden event infringes on the parties' right of the defence.[450]

288. Proceedings are interrupted when a party dies or loses his or her legal capacity; here, interruption is automatic if the relevant event takes place before the party had a chance to file his or her first defence (*costituzione*); it requires a formal declaration by the party's lawyer when it recurs after the party's *costituzione* in the proceedings. Special provisions are given for the party in default.[451] In these cases, it is necessary to allow the party's heirs or guardian to join in the proceedings in his or her place or in his or her behalf.

Proceedings are also automatically interrupted when the party's lawyer dies or is suspended or stricken off the professional list to give the party the chance (and the time) to instruct a new lawyer.

289. For interrupted proceedings to restart:

(a) the party's heirs or guardian must voluntarily file a defence (*prosecuzione del giudizio*); or
(b) the counterpart must file a petition to the court to fix a new hearing, with subsequent notice on the original party's heirs or guardian (*riassunzione*).[452]

Both *prosecuzione* and *riassunzione* of interrupted proceedings must take place within three months of the interruption. Otherwise the dispute is discontinued.

450. *See* C. Punzi, *L'interruzione del processo* (Milan: Giuffrè, 1963); G.P. Califano, *L'interruzione del processo civile. Gli artt. 299 ss. c.p.c.* (Naples, 2004); D. Culot, *L'interruzione del processo civile* (Milan: Giuffrè, 2006).
451. Article 300(4) CPC.
452. A. Saletti, *La riassunzione del processo civile* (Milan: Giuffrè, 1981).

Chapter 3. Discontinuance of the Proceedings

290. Proceedings may be discontinued for several different reasons.[453] First of all, the parties may reach a settlement in court, thereby putting an end to the litigation. Their agreement is written down and signed in the report of the hearing, and such report will be an executive title for the enforcement of the obligations assumed therein.

The parties may also voluntarily abandon the proceedings (*rinuncia agli atti*). For such a withdrawal to be effective, however, the agreement of all the parties who would have an interest in the prosecution of the case is required: unilateral withdrawal is not usually allowed, unless, of course, the counterpart is in default.

The intention to abandon the proceedings (and the other party's acceptance) must be manifested directly by the party (also through an agent) at the hearing or in a written document served on the counterpart(s). Unless otherwise agreed upon, the abandoning party must pay the counterpart's legal costs.

Finally, discontinuance of the proceedings may be the effect of the parties' inactivity (*estinzione del processo per inattività*). Civil proceedings are governed by the *principio dispositivo*, according to which it is the parties' burden not only to start the proceedings but also to make them proceed to judgment.

Thus, if, after service of the originating claim, no party registers the case into the court, the proceedings will never, so to speak, be ignited ex officio.

Also, it is the parties' burden to attend the hearings before the judge. If both parties do not appear at a hearing, the court will fix a subsequent hearing. If no one attends this second hearing too, the case will be cancelled from the court's roll (*cancellazione della causa del ruolo*).[454]

The same will happen as a consequence of the parties' non-compliance with the court's order to serve joinder on a third person[455] or to renovate service of the *citazione* on the defendant when the original service was vitiated.[456]

In all these cases, and anytime a dispute is cancelled from a court's roll, the parties have the possibility to take it on again (*riassunzione*) by filing a petition to the court within three months of its cancellation from the roll. After three months, the case is discontinued.

291. Whenever the parties do not comply with one of the (very important) orders of the court listed in Article 307(3) CPC,[457] the case is withdrawn from the court's record, and immediate discontinuance follows, with no possibility to take the case on again within three months.[458]

292. Article 307(4) CPC used to be rather problematic: as a matter of fact, this provision stated that discontinuance of a case operated as of right, but that

---

453. Articles 306 et seq. CPC.
454. Massari, 'Cancellazione della causa dal ruolo', in *Novissimo digesto italiano*, vol. II (Tunn: Utet, 1957).
455. Article 291 CPC.
456. *See* para. 215.
457. For example, the order to join necessary third parties – *litisconscorzio necessario*, Art. 102 CPC.
458. Article 270 CPC.

proceedings would go ahead unless any interested party raised that issue before any other defence. In other words, discontinuance could not be raised ex officio and could, so to speak, be cured, if proceedings followed their course without the parties timely opposing it.

In 2009, this paragraph of Article 307 was redrafted and today, discontinuance of the proceedings not only operates as of right, but it may also be declared on the judge's own motion with an *ordinanza* of the instructing judge or with a judgment of the three-judge panel. The new rule makes it clear that the parties no longer have a monopoly as concerns the discontinuance of the case. Its wording also leads to believe that the court may raise such an objection at any stage in the further course of the proceedings, possibly years after the event which gave rise to such discontinuance. In other words, the new solution to the problem appears to be rather uneconomic.

293. A case may be discontinued either with a judgment or by the instructing judge with an *ordinanza*; against such order, the parties may raise an opposition (*reclamo*) to the *collegio* (i.e., the three-judge panel).[459]

294. When a case is discontinued, for whatever reason, no decision on the merits is rendered, so that the original claim is not covered by res judicata. To avoid any doubt, Article 310(1) CPC states that discontinuance of a case does not extinguish the action; In other words, the same claim might be brought again to justice in the future with no preclusive effect.

295. Discontinuance carries away most acts of the procedure, which lose any juridical effect. According to Article 310 CPC, only non-final judgments on the merits rendered in the course of the proceedings and decisions by the *Cassazione* on issues of competence survive. This means that any future action will have to be started before the court which the *Cassazione* indicated as competent in its decision.[460]

It must be observed, however, that also orders granted by the instructing judge in compliance with Article 186*bis*, *ter* and *quater* CPC (*see supra*, paragraphs 239 et seq.) survive the discontinuance of the case in which they were disposed.

Moreover, after the reforms of 2005, also interim measures which put forward the effects of the decision on the merits remain in force even after proceedings are discontinued (*see* paragraphs 382 et seq.).

Evidence gathered in discontinued proceedings must be gathered *ex novo* in fresh proceedings; otherwise, it can only play a minor role as simple *argomenti di prova* (*see infra*, paragraph 320).

---

459. Interestingly, this is the last surviving case of the so-called *reclamo al collegio*, according to which, before the reforms of the 1990s, all the orders of the instructing judge might be immediately opposed to the *collegio*, in charge of the final decision.

460. This is the only case where a procedural judgment (*sentenza di rito*) has binding effects outside of the proceedings in which it was rendered (*efficacia ultrattiva*).

296. It is worth noting that discontinuance of an action is a rather frequent event in Italian civil proceedings. As a matter of fact, mostly for tax reasons,[461] when the parties settle their dispute, they prefer to reach out-of-court settlements, thereby instructing their lawyers not to attend the hearings before the court any longer, which, in time, leads to the discontinuance of the case.

461. Taxes must usually be paid to register judicial settlements.

Chapter 4. Interlocutory Applications

297. In the course of the proceedings, sub-proceedings over specific issues may have to take place in front of a different court, before the main dispute can proceed to judgment.

§1. Reference to the ECJ for a Preliminary Ruling

298. Whenever issues concerning the interpretation of European law are raised in the proceedings, the court may (and sometimes must, in compliance with the rules of the EC Treaties) refer to the ECJ for a preliminary ruling.[462] The national proceedings are stayed[463] until the ECJ delivers its judgment, which the referring court is bound to follow.

§2. Reference to the Constitutional Court

299. In a similar vein, whenever the incompatibility with the Constitution of a legal provision is raised in the course of civil proceedings[464] or of an arbitration,[465] and the judge deems such issue (*questione di legittimità costituzionale*) both relevant[466] and not prima facie ungrounded, reference is made to the Constitutional Court to review the matter at hand, and the case is stayed.

The Constitutional Court may allow or deny the constitutional question: in the former case, the provision at hand is said to be unconstitutional and the court's decision is published on the official journal of the republic (*Gazzetta Ufficiale*): from the day after such publication, the unconstitutional provision ceases to have legal effects,[467] and it will not be applicable to any pending dispute. When a question is denied, it does not necessarily imply that the relevant provision is constitutional: the same or a similar question may indeed be raised again with no preclusive and no res judicata effects.

In practice, the court often releases interpretative and manipulative decisions. As a matter of fact, a given normative provision can be interpreted in two or more different ways and not necessarily all of them are (un)constitutional. In such cases,

462. *See* A. Briguglio, *Pregiudiziale comunitaria e processo civile* (Padua: Cedam, 1996); G. Raiti, *La collaborazione giudiziaria nell'esperienza del rinvio pregiudiziale comunitario* (Milan: Giuffrè, 2003).

463. Unlike a stay disposed according to Art. 295 CPC (*see supra*), where two sets of proceedings exist, here (and in the other cases which follow in the text) the parenthesis before the ECJ is considered to be part of the original procedure, and the expression *sospensione impropria* (improper stay) is used to stress this structural difference.

464. By the parties, the PM or ex officio.

465. *See Corte Cost.* 28 Nov. 2001, n. 376, GC, 2001, I, 2883 and now, after the reform of 2006, Art. 819*bis*(1), n. 3.

466. That is, the case cannot be decided without solving the constitutionality issue.

467. *See* Cuocolo, *Principi di diritto costituzionale*, 2nd edn (Milan: Giuffrè, 1999), 804.

what the court does is giving a constitutionally oriented interpretation of a provision, by either allowing or denying the constitutional question posed by the referring judge. The compatibility of these para-normative decisions with the distribution of powers within the State has been questioned, since the court has sometimes effectively created new rules out of existing provisions.

§3. *Querela di Falso* (Summons Challenging a Document)

300. *See infra*, paragraph 310.

§4. Challenge of Judges

301. *See supra*, paragraph 69.

Part VI. Legal Aid and Legal Costs

Chapter 1. Legal Aid

302. Granting a party the right of access to justice is but an empty statement if, in practice, it is too expensive for him or her to defend his or her own rights in court.

In Italy, like in many other countries, to hire a lawyer's services proves very costly; also expert witnesses may be rather expensive and court taxes have to be paid. In other words, without some form of financial subsidy, it might be practically impossible for not well-off parties to bring proceedings or to oppose another party's claim.

The drafters of the Constitution were aware of this situation: Article 24(3), therefore, disposes that it is the State's task to grant financial aid for the less well-off to bring and resist an action before a court. This noble statement, however, has not been efficiently implemented in practice by the lawmaker, especially in the civil field. In particular, for many decades, the provisions of RD No. 3282 of 30 December 1923 proved rather ineffective in granting legal aid to destitute parties in civil proceedings.[468]

303. To improve on this situation, Law No. 134 of 29 March 2001 was drafted, providing for a new set of rules on legal aid in civil, administrative and non-contentious jurisdiction proceedings, which integrated the provisions of Law No. 217 of 30 July 1990, originally on legal aid in the criminal field. These provisions have now been included in the new mini-code on the costs of justice (DPR No. 115 of 30 May 2002, Articles 74 et seq.).[469]

Persons with a gross family[470] income of (as of today) no more than EUR 11.528,41 per year may apply to have their legal costs be paid by the State, when their claims are not prima facie ungrounded (*non manifestamente infondati*). The petition, containing an exposition of its factual and legal grounds,[471] is presented to the Bar Association of the place where proceedings are already pending or where

468. *See* F. Carpi, '*Legal Aid in Italy and Europe*', in *Essays on Transnational and Comparative Civil Procedure*, 3–12 (Carpi, Lupoi ed., (Giappichelli 2001).

469. *See* G. Scarselli, *Il nuovo patrocinio a spese dello Stato nei processi civili ed amministrativi* (Padua: Cedam, 2003).

470. There are cases, however, where only the personal income of the party is considered: e.g., in relation to disputes in which a conflict of interests exists between the person claiming legal aid and the other members of her family.

471. This will usually require the petitioner to instruct a lawyer – before knowing whether he will be granted legal aid, which is a contradiction in terms of sorts.

the competent forum is located. Should the application be denied, it is possible to present it again to the competent judge, who will decide upon it *ex novo*.

If the application is allowed, the State will take care of all the legal costs incurred by the party, in particular as concerns the lawyer's fees and those of any party or CTU. Neither the lawyer nor the experts may require the party to pay them anything on top of the fees taxed in their favour by the judge and which the State will pay. To do otherwise, would amount to a serious deontological offence on the part of the lawyer.

However, the party is bound to choose his or her lawyer only among those included in a special list, kept by the local Bar Associations. On the other hand, after Law No. 35 of 24 February 2005, the party may choose a lawyer included in the list of a different Bar Association than the one of the competent territorial court.[472]

The State's financial assistance will be provided to the beneficiary party through all the different instances of the case, unless the petitioner's claim is rejected at first instance. The assisted party will not pay taxes for his or her procedural acts, but any legal costs taxed by the court on his or her counterpart will be paid to the State.

Admission to legal aid may be revoked if, in the course of the proceedings, the necessary requirements cease to exist (e.g., the party's yearly income goes beyond the fixed limit) or if the judge concludes that the beneficiary party sued or resisted suit in bad faith or vexatiously.

These provisions are complemented by those of DLGS No. 116 of 2005, granting legal aid in transnational disputes,[473] on similar grounds as those provided for domestic cases.

The main drawback of legal aid in Italy, of course, is represented by the income limit, which is too low and effectively cuts off from legal aid most families with limited resources but not absolutely destitute.

Initially, the new system seemed to be working rather efficiently. Today, however, due to a general shortage of funding for legal aid, it may even take years before lawyers are duly paid for their services. Moreover, when a lawyer is engaged under the *patrocinio a spese dello Stato* scheme, he or she will be entitled, by law, to only a fraction of the ordinary fees accorded by the applicable tariffs. Originally, as a matter of fact, a lawyer's compensation was statutorily halved. To make matters worse, Law No. 147 of 2013 reduced such compensation of a third of the average one, according to the applicable standards (*see* paragraph 119). After this drastic reduction, many say that legal aid in Italy has effectively been repealed. Even more than before, therefore, skilled and experienced lawyers will tend to refuse to take clients on a legal aid scheme. Destitute parties, thus, will be compelled to refer to less experienced or less busy lawyers, ready to take on any case, even if badly and belatedly paid, and possibly not efficient or competent enough.

472. *See* E. Sacchettini, 'Richiesti solo due anni di anzianità per l'accesso agli elenchi degli Ordini', GD 11 (2006): 20.

473. *See* E. Sacchettini, 'Gratuito patrocinio per le cause transfrontaliere', GD 46 (2003): 64.

Chapter 2. Legal Costs

304. Access to justice has a cost.[474] As a matter of fact, in most disputes, in Italy, taxes have to be paid both at the beginning (at the moment the case is registered in court: *contributo unificato*)[475] and at the end of the dispute (to register the court's judgment: *tassa di registro*). While the tax for registering the case in court is represented by stamps which have to be attached to the file by the court's clerk, the tax for registration of the judgment is paid in specific offices of the Finance Ministry (*Agenzia delle entrate*).

The cost of both the *contributo unificato* and the *tassa di registro* varies according to the economic value of the dispute. From 2011 onwards, as a consequence of the economic crisis, the cost of *Contributo unificato* has been progressively and significantly raised, arguably restricting access to justice for less well-off claimants, thus raising issues of unconstitutionality. *Contributo unificato*, moreover, is now due also for disputes previously exempted (e.g., labour and divorce proceedings). The idea that court fees are now effectively used as a means to discourage litigation is reinforced when one considers that, after Law No. 183 of 12 November 2011, *contributo unificato* for appeal cases is raised by 50% and doubled for appeals before the Court of cassation. Moreover, court fees now also have to be paid by a defendant who brings a counter-claim in the proceedings or declares the will to join a third party in the dispute. Payment of 'contributo unificato' is now also used as a sanction for procedural irregularities (e.g., when a lawyer fails to write down his tax code or certified e-mail address in a claim or defence). Moreover, from 30 January 2013, when an appeal (or petition for review of a judicial decision of any kind) is declared inadmissible or totally denied, the appellant is required to pay *contributo unificato* again, as both a sanction and a deterrent from bringing an ungrounded appeal.

The main costs of civil proceedings, however, are represented by lawyers' fees. Also CTUs (and, of course, the experts directly appointed by the parties) charge the parties for their professional activity.[476]

305. The general rule is that every party advances his or her own expenses at the time the relevant procedural actions are taken.[477] At the end of the proceedings, however, the losing party ordinarily is ordered to pay for the winning party's legal costs (*le spese seguono la soccombenza*), according to the sound determination of the court, in compliance with existing professional fees.[478] The losing party will also normally pay the costs of any party-appointed expert or CTU.

When there is a plurality of losing parties, each is taxed by the court proportionally to his or her interest in the case; but if the losers have a common interest, they

474. More details in G. Scarselli, *Le spese giudiziali civili* (Milan: Giuffrè, 1998).
475. Provisions on *contributo unificato* can now be found in Arts 9 et seq. of *DPR* No. 115 of 2002.
476. The expert hands his bill to the judge, who taxes it on one or all of the parties, in compliance with specific court tariffs.
477. Article 8 *DPR* No. 115 of 2002.
478. Article 91 CPC.

can also be individually sentenced to pay the whole costs (the paying party will then have the right to demand payment *pro quota* from the other co-debtors).

Whenever both parties end up losing (i.e., some of their respective claims or defences are not allowed (*soccombenza reciproca*), or the dispute concerns absolute new issues or there was a change in the case law concerning the main questions at hand); however, the court may decide to compensate the legal costs between them,[479] or to tax on one party only a portion of the costs of the other.[480]

In an attempt to encourage parties to reach an amicable agreement in the course of the proceedings, Article 91(1) was redrafted in 2009:[481] the new formulation specifies that, if the judge allows the claim in an amount which is not more than the one which was proposed by the other party in an attempt to settle the dispute and which the winning party refused without good reason, the latter will have to pay the costs which the former sustained after making such proposal. In other words, when an offer to settle is made during the procedure, the parties have to balance that offer against the plausible outcome of the dispute, in order not to risk sustaining part of the costs of his or her adversary. Refusing a reasonable settlement proposal might also be considered an abuse of process and sanctioned accordingly under Article 96(3) CPC (*see* paragraph 180).

The proposal may come up from either of the parties. Defendants, in particular, are encouraged by the new provisions to balance their chances in the proceedings and eventually present a reasonable settlement offer before the case goes on to the deliberation phase. The judge may present the parties with settlement proposals too, under Article 185*bis* CPC (*see* paragraph 215). Proposals may also be formulated by a mediator, in the course of mediation proceedings, in compliance with Article 11(1) of DLGS No. 28 of 2010 (*see* paragraph 458).[482]

The provision examined here also raises some procedural doubts, however. For instance, the law does not clarify the requirements the mentioned 'proposal' should comply with. Commentators agree on the fact that such proposal should be in written form, that is it should be formally brought to the attention of the judge. For instance, it may be formulated by the party in the course of a hearing or written down in one of the briefs filed in court. Possibly, even a proposal made by the party before the start of litigation could be taken into consideration, for example, when it was sent in a written communication to the would-be plaintiff.

It is also possible for the parties' lawyers to ask the court to tax legal costs directly in their favour, so that they may directly enforce that part of the judgment against the debtor in their own name.[483]

If a party sued or contested the suit in bad faith or vexatiously, he or she can also be sentenced to pay damages on top of the winning party's legal costs (Article 96 CPC): *see also* at paragraph 180.

479. In other words, each party will pay for her own lawyer and experts.

480. Article 92 CPC, as revised in 2014: the new formulation of the rule should reduce the discretionality of the judge to compensate the costs of the case between the parties.

481. *See* A. Doronzo, NLCC (2011), 767 et seq.

482. M. Palmieri & G. Angelone, 'Il regolamento delle spese processuali dopo le riforme del codice di procedura civile', GM (2013): II, 683.

483. Article 93 CPC.

Part VII. Evidence

Chapter 1. Burden of Proof

306. According to Article 2697 CC, it is the burden of the party who brings a claim to prove the existence of the facts on which that claim is founded (*fatti costitutivi*); on the other hand, the party who resists a claim has to prove the facts on which his or her defences are based, that is, facts which extinguish (*fatti estintivi*)[484,485,486] or modify (*fatti modificativi*)[487] the facts the plaintiff's claim is based upon or which anyway prevent that claim from being presently allowed (*fatti impeditivi*).[488]

In the Italian procedural system, the judge is always under a duty to adjudicate the claim, with no possibility to simply dismiss the case with no decision on the merits for lack of evidence (the so-called *non liquet*). Whenever the existence of a fact is in dispute, it is therefore necessary for the interested party to bring evidence to show that that fact effectively came into being. From this standpoint, it can be said that the plaintiff bears the primary burden of proof, in the sense that his or her petition will be rejected if he or she fails to prove the relevant facts, and the decision will have res judicata effects on the non-existence of the plaintiff's alleged right. In other words, the defendant must meet his or her burden of proof only when the facts on which the plaintiff's claim is based are not in dispute or have been effectively proved.

When a party fails to satisfy his or her burden of the proof, he or she will not be in a position to sustain his or her claims and defences, and this will normally imply his or her losing the case. Establishing which party had the burden to prove a given fact is therefore fundamental whenever, at the decision stage, the court comes to the conclusion that no proof was given of that very fact.

307. Of course, facts and circumstances whose existence is not contested by the counterparts do not need to be proved.[489]

---

484. On evidence in civil proceedings, *see* in general L.P. Comoglio, *Le prove civili*, 3rd edn (Turin: Utet, 2010).
485. *See* C. Besso, *Evidence: The Framework*, in *Civil Justice in Italy*, *supra*, 95 et seq.
486. For example, the claim is time barred.
487. For example, the content of the obligation on which the petition is based was modified after the contract was originally concluded.
488. For example, the deadline for payment of a debt has not yet expired.
489. *See* A. Carratta, *Il principio della non contestazione nel processo civile* (Milan: Giuffrè, 1995).

This principle is traditionally applied in Italian civil procedure, but until recently it was interpreted in a rather narrow way. As a matter of fact, mere silence failed to be considered as an implicit admission of the facts on which the other party relied and even rather generic denials were deemed sufficient to consider a fact as 'contested' in this context.

Moreover, a party in default of appearance always was (and still is) considered as implicitly contesting the plaintiff's claim.

Over the years, however, case law tried to introduce stricter standards,[490] and finally Law No. 69 of 2009 redrafted Article 115 CPC,[491] making it clear that when a defendant does not specifically deny the facts on which the plaintiff rely, the judge will consider those facts as not contested (*see* at paragraph 189).[492]

The burden of proof can also be inverted, switching it from one party to the other. This can happen either through a contractual agreement between the parties (with a number of restrictions, however, especially as concerns those rights which cannot be freely disposed of: *diritti indisponibili*); or, more often, through a mechanism called *presunzione legale*, where a legal provision predetermines that, from a given known fact, the existence of some other unknown fact may be inferred.[493]

Such mechanism can usually be superseded by contrary evidence from the party which suffers the effects of the legal presumption (*presunzioni relative*); in other words, here the ordinary burden of the proof is switched from the plaintiff to the defendant;[494] in other instances, the law allows no contrary evidence (*presunzioni assolute*): here the burden of proof is by all rights bypassed.

490. *See Cass. SU* 23 Jan. 2002, n. 761.
491. Del Core, 'Il principio di non contestazione è diventato legge: prime riflessioni su alcuni punti ancora controversi', GC (2009): II, 275; A. Tedoldi, 'La non contestazione nel nuovo art. 115 c. p. c.', RDP (2011): 76.
492. B. Sassani, 'L'onere della contestazione', <www.judicium.it>.
493. For example, whenever two cars collide in a car crash, the liability is presumed to be distributed 50/50 among the two drivers.
494. In the example *supra*, one the drivers proved that the other is wholly liable for the crash.

Chapter 2. Admissibility of Evidence

308. The legal treatment of evidence in the Italian civil judicial system is mainly split between the CC and the code of civil procedure; the former contains the substantive rules pertaining to the admissibility and the effects of the various means of presenting evidence, the latter hands out the procedural rules which regulate their admission in the course of the proceedings.[495]

309. In Italian proceedings, no pretrial discovery phase exists (*see* paragraph 199). As a rule, each party will be aware of the evidence available to the counterpart only in the course of the proceedings.

Not all evidence, however, comes into being during the trial. As a matter of fact, a distinction has to be made between those means to obtain evidence which are formed outside (and normally before) the proceedings (*prove precostituite*) and those which are formed during and on the occasion of the trial.

The former (typically, documents) are introduced in the proceedings simply by filing them in the court (within the preclusive time limit set by Article 183(6) CPC); the latter have to be requested by the parties, and the court must approve their taking in the light of two different standards: from the legal point of view, the requested evidence must satisfy the legal requirements set by the CC (*ammissibilità*). From a factual point standpoint, moreover, evidence must refer to the facts of the dispute and be relevant to the court's decision (*rilevanza*). In order to be approved by the judge, *prove costituende* must be both admissible and relevant.

The court's decision concerning the admissibility and the relevance of evidence (which the judge usually renders after the first hearing and the filing of the parties' briefs: Article 183 CPC) is not binding on the court itself at the decision stage, and it is always possible for the judge to reopen the evidence-gathering phase (*rimessione in istruttoria*) to admit means of evidence that were originally discarded, as long as the interested party insists on their taking.

As concerns the effects of evidence on the court's decision, a further distinction must be made between those means of evidence which bind the court to the facts ascertained therein (*prove legali*) and the ones which may be freely evaluated by the judge (*prove liberamente valutabili*).[496] In theory, our system privileges the latter, and Article 116(1) CPC sets out a general principle according to which the judge decides the case upon its free appreciation of the evidence, unless the law disposes otherwise.[497] In practice, however, binding means of evidence play a stronger role than freely appreciable ones.

In evaluating evidence, the judge can refer to the balance of probability and the law of average. He or she must, however, always clarify the reasons why, for example, he or she considered one witness more trustworthy than another.

Moreover, Article 116(2) CPC allows the judge to take into consideration also some elements which do not have an evidentiary value in itself but which may be used to uphold the court's evaluation of proper evidence. Such elements are referred

495. *See* C. Besso, *supra*, 94.
496. A. Carratta, 'Prova e convincimento del giudice nel processo civile', RDP (2003): 27.
497. *See* M. Taruffo, *supra*, 519 et seq.

to as *argomenti di prova* and may be found in several statutory provisions. In general, the judge will appreciate as an *argomento di prova* the parties' behaviour, their failure to comply with any of his or her orders and so forth. The basic idea is that the judge's decision may not be based on *argomenti di prova* alone, but *argomenti di prova* may be mentioned to support a decision and the evaluation of available evidence made therein.

Unless very serious logical mistakes are committed, the free evaluation of evidence by the trial courts can never be interfered with by the *Cassazione*, which does not enter into the merits of the lower courts' discretionary appreciations of the relevant facts.

310. Among *prove legali*, the most important role is played by documents: *atti pubblici* and *scritture private*.

Atti pubblici (authentic instruments under the seal of a public officer) (Articles 2699 et seq. CC) are formed by notary public or other public officials, who bear witness to the truthfulness of certain elements of the document (e.g., date, place of stipulation, identities of the parties in a contract). Whenever a party alleges that those elements have been falsely stated or otherwise counterfeited, an incident must take place before a three-judge panel of the *Tribunale*, to ascertain whether the document is 'genuine' (*querela di falso*). Before such incident can proceed, however, the court must ask the party who presented the document whether he or she still wants to rely on it for his or her case. When a negative answer is given, the document is simply kept out of the file. Otherwise, the *querela* is brought to the three-judge panel of the *Tribunale*, where evidence is gathered to ascertain whether the forgery claim is grounded or not. During the course of these sub-proceedings, the proceedings on the merits are stayed. If the petition is allowed, annotations are made on the document, and the relevant judgment has *erga omnes* effects in relation to the ascertained forgery.

An *atto pubblico*, however, never has binding evidentiary effects as concerns the inner truth of the statements made by the parties before the public official or their real intentions, so that no *querela di falso* is necessary to contest the relevant part of an *atto pubblico* in these concerns.

Scritture private (private writings) on the other hand, are documents written or signed by the counterpart; they are relevant on the assumption that underwriting a document is a way to express acceptance of its contents. Here, however, evidentiary binding effects only concern the party's signature, when it has been either accepted by the party herself as her own or certified as authentic by a public notary or verified through an incident in the proceedings, so that the party may not subsequently deny having written or signed the document.

Whenever a *scrittura privata* is filed in the proceedings by a party, the counterpart has the chance, as his or her first subsequent defence, to disown his or her signature therein,[498] as long as that signature was not certified as authentic by a

498. Exception: a party in default who files a late defence may always, as her first defence, disown *scritture private* produced against her earlier in the proceedings.

notary.[499] If the filing party still wants to rely on the document, a verification incident in the proceedings takes place (*giudizio di verificazione*).[500] The court ordinarily appoints a graphology expert who ascertains whether the signature was forged or is authentic.

311. Other binding means of obtaining evidence are the confession and the oath. Both are declarations made by the parties of the dispute; the former concerns facts which negatively affect the confessing party's case, and it can be either spontaneous or provoked, either outside of or in the course of the proceedings.

The so-called judicial confession (*confessione giudiziale*) is normally provoked by means of a formal interrogatory of the party (*interrogatorio formale*). This interrogatory is performed by the judge, who asks the party questions which were previously written by the counterpart. The latter basically aims at making the deponent admit facts that would be detrimental for his or her procedural position. In answering these questions, however, the party is not under an obligation to tell the truth; so there are no sanctions for making untruthful statements in this context. If and when a party admits one or more facts on which she or he is being interrogated about, such admission will be considered a 'confession', and it will be binding on the judge as concerns the existence of the admitted facts. If the party appears before the judge and refuses to be interrogated or fails to attend without good reason the hearing where his or her interrogatory has been planned, the judge may consider as admitted the facts on which the party had to be interrogated about.

Formal interrogatory (and confession) is never admitted in relation to rights of which the parties may not freely dispose of.

On the other hand, an oath (*giuramento*) concerns facts which are favourable to the party who renders it. There are two main forms of oath: *decisorio* – which is rendered upon the challenge of the counterpart – or *suppletorio* – upon the court's own motion.

If the challenged party takes the oath,[501] he or she wins on the relevant point of the case; if he or she refuses, he or she loses.

In practice, *giuramento* is very rarely used as a means to obtaining evidence in contemporary civil proceedings in Italy.

312. Witness testimony is a widely used means to gather evidence even though the depositions of witnesses are often considered rather unreliable by judges.

As a rule, in Italy, a party (or a person who would be entitled to join or be joined in the proceedings because of an immediate interest of him or her own in the case) is prohibited from deposing as a witness in a dispute he or she is personally involved in.

---

499. In that case, *querela di falso* may be brought.

500. *See* V. Denti, *La verificazione delle prove documentali* (Turin: Utet, 1957).

501. It is also possible for her to refer the oath on the challenging party, in other words, to counter-challenge her to take the oath.

Only 'third' persons (i.e., persons who are not – and could not become – parties to the dispute at hand) may be called – by the parties or, in certain instances, by the judge – to testify.[502]

A witness may only be called to depose on facts he or she has first-hand knowledge of. Moreover, he or she may not express value judgments or opinions as to the facts he or she has been called to depose about.

A witness' deposition is freely evaluated by the judge, taking into consideration any existing relationship between the witness and the parties, and the general accuracy of the testimony.

The CC sets many limits to the admissibility of witness testimony in relation to contracts,[503] in particular as concerns those contracts which require to be made in writing in order either to exist (*ad substantiam*)[504] or to be proved (*ad probationem*). Limitations are set also as concerns witness deposition concerning oral additional clauses allegedly approved by the parties at the time they stipulated a written contract.

Other important limits are set in the particular discipline of certain substantive situations and relations: for example, it is ordinarily impossible for the party to prove through witness testimony that a contract has been simulated between them. Recently, Law No. 124 of 4 August 2017 introduced specific limits to witness testimony in car accidents disputes, in order to avoid frauds.

502. In general, on the subjective limits to witness testimony *see* L. Dittrich, *I limiti soggettivi della prova testimoniale* (Milan: Giuffrè, 2000).
503. Article 2721 CC et seq.
504. Here, witness testimony is admitted only when the original written contract was lost or destroyed.

Chapter 3. Administration of Evidence

§1. Introduction

313. The adversary principle (*principio dispositivo*) is a fundamental guideline of the evidence-gathering phase. According to Article 115 CPC, unless otherwise allowed by the law, the judge is under an obligation to decide the case upon the evidence which the parties themselves have handed out, under the burden of the proof principle.

From this point of view, there is an absolute prohibition for the judge to refer to his or her own direct knowledge of the relevant facts (*divieto di scienza privata*), with an exception for those facts generally known by the majority of the community the judge belongs to (*fatto notorio*).[505]

It has to be observed, however, that the adversary principle is not as absolute in this context as it is in relation to the allegations of the facts of the dispute. Some inquisitorial powers were already provided in the original version of the 1942 CPC: the judge can thus ex officio dispose an informal interrogation of the parties in order to clarify the facts of the case, order an inspection or ask for information to a public administration. Moreover, the court, at certain conditions, may require a party to take an oath (*giuramento suppletorio*; *see supra*, paragraph 311).

After the reform of 1998, the judge's inquisitorial powers in the course of ordinary civil proceedings have been expanded. Whenever a case falls to be decided by a single judge of the *Tribunale*, Article 281*ter* CPC now allows the judge to dispose ex officio the hearing as witnesses of those persons to which the parties made references to, when they appear to know the truth. While this provision is not likely to be extensively used in practice, it is very interesting, insomuch as it is the only rule in the code to refer to the 'ascertainment of the truth' as an aim of civil proceedings.

314. The admission of oral evidence is requested by the parties within the time limit set by Article 183 CPC (*see supra*, paragraph 199).

The circumstances on which formal interrogatory, oath and witness depositions should be rendered must be formulated by the parties as specific chapters with the indication of the persons whose testimony is required. As a matter of fact, Italian law is rather formal and strict under this point of view, and it may severely restrict the parties' capabilities of ascertaining the truth.

After 2009, under the new Article 81*bis* of the implementing provisions of the CPC,[506] the judge, at the time of deciding which evidentiary requests of the parties may be allowed, is called upon to draft a schedule of the proceedings (*calendario del processo*), basically fixing a series of subsequent hearings dedicated to evidence-gathering. In the lawmaker intentions, this is meant to render this phase shorter than before, when the judge used to fix any following hearing at the end of the previous one. Under this new system, the judge should be able to concentrate the hearings

505. For example, historic facts or the local inflation rate.
506. I. Pagni, NLCC (2010), 1167.

where evidence is collected, therefore making proceedings shorter. Judges, however, do not seem particularly fond of this new provision, because it requires some planning on their part, which might be incompatible with future emergencies and new cases requiring urgent judicial intervention. The terms established under the calendar, moreover, may always be modified, even on the judge's own motion when there are good reasons for doing so, which makes the whole notion of scheduling the course of the evidence-gathering phase more promotional than useful in practice. In 2011,[507] however Article 81*bis disp.att.* CPC has been modified, in order to make it more effective. The calendar of the proceedings now has to schedule also the final hearing before the instructing judge, within a reasonable delay. Moreover, failure to comply with the terms of the calendar or the part of the judge, the CTU and the parties may lead to disciplinary sanctions.

The judge will examine the parties' requests and admit those means of evidence that he or she deems both admissible and relevant for the decision of the case.

Oral evidence is always taken by the judge at the presence of the parties. However, if the party who requested the evidence is not present at the hearing where the latter should be taken, such evidence will be lost, unless the counterpart insists on its taking.

More hearings may be necessary to go through all the admitted evidence requests. A written report is made of all the oral depositions of both the parties and the witnesses, and the judge can make written remarks as to the behaviour of either the parties or the witnesses at the hearing.

If evidence must be gathered outside the tribunal district, the judge can hand out such task to the local judge (Article 203 CPC: *prova delegata*).

§2. Forced Production of Evidence

315. In Italian civil proceedings, there is no general right of access of a party to the counterpart's documents, files and materials, and no fishing expeditions in the other party's documents are admitted.

Within certain limits, however, the judge, on the other party's motion, can order one of the parties or a third person to present in court specific documents that he or she deems necessary for his or her decision.

Special provisions are set out to prevent any unnecessary damages to third parties and to dispose the acquisition of certified copies of business documents (Article 210 CPC).[508]

When a party's right to obtain the presentation of a document is contested (e.g., the counterpart alleges that such document is confidential), it is possible to seize and store it, to avoid such evidence from being maliciously disposed of or made anyway unavailable, while the court decides upon the exhibition request (*sequestro giudiziario di prove*: *see infra*, paragraph 400).

---

507. Article 1 *ter* of DL No. 138 of 13 Aug. 2011.

508. *See* D. Turroni, 'Produzione e acquisizione del documento nel processo civile', RTDPC (2011): 175 et seq.

§3. Deposition by Witnesses

316. Until recently, the law requested witnesses to always make an oral deposition before the judge. No written statements or affidavits could be handed down in lieu of the oral testimony.

In 2009, however, Article 257*bis* was inserted in the CPC, introducing the so-called written testimony (*testimonianza scritta*).[509] The drafting of this new provision was rather controversial and, in the end, the final text allows a witness to answer in writing to the party's answers only under rather exceptional circumstances. First, all of the parties must agree on such written deposition. Moreover, the judge has a discretion not to allow it, taking into consideration all the relevant circumstances. If both these conditions are met, a form will be mailed to the witness who should then fill and sign it and then send it back to the court's offices. Failure to comply on the side of the witness will be sanctioned with a fine. After reading the written answers of the witness, the judge may always decide to summon the witness before him or her, to be interrogated in person. This new mode of collecting testimony has proved very unpopular and is rarely used.

Another innovation brought forth in 2009, however, appears to be more successful: as a matter of fact, Article 257(7)*bis* CPC makes it possible for the judge to allow the parties to collect written depositions in order to confirm expense documents filed in the proceedings (e.g., an invoice for the sale of a good or for performance of a service to the party).[510]

Since there is no pretrial phase, the hearing is normally the first chance for the party to hear the other party's witnesses.

On the other hand, the relation between the party, his or her lawyers and his or her witness is very delicate indeed. While the witness can be incriminated for perjury if he or she renders a false deposition before the judge (*see infra*, paragraph 319), for a lawyer it is deemed inappropriate, from a deontological point of view, to have contacts with a witness before a hearing to unduly influence the contents of the latter's deposition (*see supra*, paragraph 124). To unduly influence a witness, moreover, is a criminal felony.

317. The instructing judge is the only one who can interact with the witness at the hearing, posing him or her the questions set out by the parties and admitted by the court and asking for any clarification or detail. The lawyers and the *Pubblico Ministero* should communicate with the witnesses only through the instructing judge.[511]

No cross-examination is admitted in the common law sense: a party may only require the judge to have the counterpart's witness answer some of his or her questions too, ask clarifications from the witness at the hearing and have witnesses of his or her own answer on the same circumstances on which the counterpart's

509. *See* F. Corsini, 'La prova testimoniale assunta in forma scritta', RDP (2010): 856; Palmieri & Angelono, 'La testimonianza scritta nel processo civile', <www.judicium.it>; E. Picozza, 'La prova per testimoni, tra deposizione orale e testimonianza scritta, a seguito della riforma del 2009', RDP (2010): 869; R. Caponi, 'Italian Civil Justice Reform 2009', *supra*.

510. *See* C.M. Cea, NLCC (2010): 879.

511. Article 253(2) CPC.

witnesses deposed (*testi a riprova*). Whenever different testimonies conflict with each other, the witnesses may be summoned together before the court to give clarifications.[512]

318. At the hearing, the witnesses enter the courtroom one by one (only the parties may be present at a witness' deposition) and solemnly declare to tell the truth.[513] The witness discloses to the judge his or her name, date of birth, residence, occupation and any relation with the parties.

319. Whenever a witness refuses to testify or if it appears likely that a witness did not tell the truth in his or her deposition, the instructing judge may report him or her to the *Pubblico Ministero*, and criminal proceedings may be initiated. It is, however, possible for professionals, priests and other persons specified by the law (e.g., mediators, in compliance with DLGS No. 28 of 2010) to abstain from rendering a deposition in court as witnesses whenever, in doing so, they would break a duty of confidentiality.

§4. Deposition by the Parties Themselves

320. The parties can never testify as witnesses. They may be freely interrogated (*interrogatorio libero*) during the course of the proceedings by the judge on his or her own motion (Article 117 CPC) or upon the joint requests of all of the parties (185 CPC). In the former case, the interrogatory is a means for the judge to receive clarifications on the facts of the case directly from the interested parties. In the latter, the interrogatory should be a means to lead the parties to reconcile and settle the case.

The parties' statements in the course of an *interrogatorio libero* can never be used against them.[514] They can only be used as simple *argomenti di prova*, that is, as arguments devoid of evidentiary value *ex se*, which simply corroborate evidence otherwise gathered. In practice, however, if a party, in the course of his or her 'free' interrogation, makes factual admissions against himself or herself, he or she will likely be considered by the court as not contesting those facts, which therefore will not need to be proved by the counterpart.

A party may request the other to be formally interrogated by the judge, to make his or her confess as to the existence of certain factual circumstances (*see supra*, paragraph 311).

Each party may also challenge the other to take an oath as to the truth of certain factual allegations in his or her own favour (*see supra*, paragraph 311).

512. Article 254 CPC.
513. Article 251 CPC, which required the witness to take an oath to God has been declared unconstitutional by *Corte Cost.* 4 May 1995, n. 149.
514. *See* Bernasconi, 'Sulla efficacia probatoria delle dichiarazioni rese dalle parti in sede di interrogatorio libero', RDP (1996): 619.

§5. Expert Evidence

321. In Italy, technical or scientific issues are not proved through witness testimony: as a matter of fact, a witness deposes about objective facts, declarations and actions which he or she himself or herself performed or said or saw others perform or say, not to expose his or her personal opinions about any issues (however authoritative his or her knowledge on the subject might be).

Whenever technical or scientific issues need to be solved that the judge is not in the position to ascertain himself or herself, therefore, an expert is appointed by the court to deal with them.[515]

322. Expert evidence is not considered evidence in the strict sense of the word. It may be disposed on the court's own motion and, unlike other evidentiary requests, it can be required by the parties at any time during the instructing phase.

323. Expert evidence is very commonly employed in Italian proceedings. In some types of dispute, it might even be the only admissible or relevant way to ascertain the facts of the case.[516]

Experts (*consulenti tecnici d'ufficio*: CTU) are usually chosen by the judge out of specific lists, according to the nature of the issue to ascertain.

A CTU may be challenged by the parties for the same reasons as a judge, and he or she can abstain from accepting the court's assignment on the same grounds as a judge (*see supra*, paragraphs 69 et seq.).

324. When expert evidence is admitted, the judge invites the prospect expert to appear before him or her and swear to faithfully perform the task for which he or she is appointed. At this point, the judge, more or less analytically, formulates one or more questions to guide the expert's enquiries.[517] The expert is then given a time limit to complete his or her activities, but prorogations can be granted when necessary.

The parties may appoint their own experts (*consulenti tecnici di parte*: CTP), who have the right to participate in the *CTU*'s activities and expose their opinions to him or her.

325. The CTU has very wide investigating powers; *inter alia*, he or she may try to reconcile the parties and reach a settlement to end the litigation. At the end of his or her enquiry, he or she writes down a report (*perizia*) of his or her activities, detailing the results he or she has reached and the specific answers to the court's questions, taking into consideration the *CTP*s' observations and remarks, as Article 195 CPC, reformed in 2009, now specifically requires.

---

515. *See* E. Protettì, M.T. Protettì, *La consulenza tecnica nel processo civile*, 3rd edn (Milan: Giuffrè, 1999); M. Taruffo, 'La prova scientifica nel processo civile', RTDPC (2005): 1079.

516. For example, to ascertain the physical damages suffered by the plaintiff in a car collision.

517. For example, ascertain the value of an immovable asset and the possibility to divide it in two autonomous fractions in proceedings to divide common properties.

The expert can also be summoned by the court to render oral or written clarifications about his or her report.

In rather exceptional circumstances, the whole enquiry may be renovated with a new expert if the case may be.

326. The expert's report is not binding on the judge, who will, however, very rarely move away from the expert's conclusions. In practice, therefore, an expert's report will be most often outcome determinative.

In this light, it is important to stress that a *CTU* must be both independent and impartial in the exercise of his or her functions.

§6. Inspection by the Judge

327. The judge may ex officio dispose the inspection of places, goods and persons,[518] taking care to safeguard, in the latter case, the dignity of the person to be inspected.

Such inspection may be taken by the judge himself or herself, with the assistance of a CTU as the case may be (*see supra*), or through a rogatory to the judge of the place where the inspection should take place.

During the inspection, the judge may hear witnesses and give any necessary order.[519]

In practice, in civil proceedings the judge most often delegates the inspection to an expert, who will then write a report to him or her.

518. Article 258 CPC.
519. For example, at given conditions, he may order access into third persons' properties (Art. 262 CPC).

Part VIII. Particular Proceedings

328. The Italian civil procedural system is characterized by a growing number of particular or special proceedings which deal with specific disputes more efficiently and in a speedier way than ordinary proceedings.

As a matter of fact, in order to reduce the number of special proceedings regulated outside of the codes, DLGS No. 150 of 2011 was enacted. Basically, as many as twenty-eight special proceedings were collected in a single price of legislation and regulated under one of the 'models' (labour, summary and ordinary proceedings) (*see* paragraph 30).

Some special procedures regulate proper cognition proceedings as an alternative (or an integration) to the model of the proceedings at first instance before the *Tribunale*.

Other special proceedings do not aim at granting the full ascertainment of the right in dispute but, rather, to provide the plaintiff with an enforcement order within a short delay.

Finally, interim measures are in a league of their own, halfway between cognition and enforcement proceedings.

Even if special and particular proceedings share some common guidelines, they are all individually characterized by some specific features so that it is appropriate to examine at least the most important of them in some detail.

Chapter 1. Particular Cognition Proceedings

§1. Labour Proceedings

329. The so-called *rito del lavoro*[520] was introduced in 1973 as part of a comprehensive reform of labour law. Given the peculiar nature of labour disputes, the lawmakers tried to closely follow the three principles of orality, concentration and immediacy, aiming at creating fast, efficient and fair proceedings. Even if the structural problems of civil justice have hampered labour disputes too, especially in the past decade, the *rito del lavoro* is still an example, so very much so that it was recently extended to lease contracts[521] (*rito locatizio*)[522] and (briefly) to road accidents disputes (*see supra*, paragraph 38).

330. The cases to which *rito del lavoro* applies are listed in Article 409 CPC: most notably, not only traditional subordinate private and public labour relations, but also (commercial) agencies and other relations based on continuous and coordinated personal activities (*rapporti para-subordinati*) are included.

331. Since 1998,[523] labour disputes were the only procedural model in Italy in which some sort of pretrial phase existed. As a matter of fact, at that time, to try and reduce the courts' backlog, the original text of the CPC was modified, imposing on the plaintiff, before judicial proceedings could be started,[524] to preliminarily try to reach a settlement with the counterpart, before special conciliation Commissions (*commissioni di conciliazione*) instituted within the local offices of the Ministry of Labour, composed by representatives of both the workers and the employees.[525]

To that end, the plaintiff had to file a petition to the Commission to summon the parties and try to settle them. If no summon was arranged within the next sixty days, the plaintiff was in the position to freely start judicial proceedings. If the parties settled their dispute before the Commission, a report was written and signed by them. If no agreement was reached, the parties could decide to refer their dispute to arbitration, if the applicable national collective labour contracts so allowed.

It is worth noting that this pretrial compulsory conciliation phase was subsequently adopted in several other types of disputes to try and reduce the courts' backlog.[526] The success rates of this 'forced' conciliation, however, was never particularly exciting.

520. F.P. Luiso, *Il processo del lavoro* (Turin: Utet); *Il processo del lavoro*, Borghesi ed., in: Carinci (dir.), *Diritto del lavoro*, vol. VI (Turin: Utet, 2005); G. Gioia, 'Labor process and labor alternative dispute resolution in the Italian system', Comp. Lab. & Pol'y J 34 (2012–2013): 813.
521. Law No. 353 of 1990.
522. Article 447*bis* CPC.
523. DLGS No. 80 of 1998.
524. The action cannot otherwise proceed to judgment (*improcedibilità*).
525. Articles 410 et seq. CPC; *see* A. Nascosi, *Il tentativo obbligatorio di conciliazione stragiudiziale nelle controversie di lavoro* (Milan: Giuffrè, 2007).
526. For example, *see* Art. 10 of Law No. 192 of 18 Jun. 1998, on sub-supply contracts.

This may explain why, in 2010, Law No. 183 (the so-called *Collegato lavoro*: *see* paragraph 37) reformed the pretrial phase, rewriting Article 410 CPC and basically going back to the situation which existed before the reform of 1998. Today, therefore, a preliminary attempt to settle the dispute is no longer mandatory, but facultative only.[527]

332. If the conciliation attempt is not tried or fails, the plaintiff may file a petition into the *Tribunale* of the place where the labour contract came into being or where the workplace is located or where the agent has his or her domicile. As a matter of fact, *Tribunali* enjoy subject-matter competence over labour disputes. Moreover, territorial competence in this area of the legal disputes is mandatory, and no contractual choice of forum clause is allowed.

To grant concentration and immediacy, the general idea is that the case should be decided in just one hearing. To this end, both parties must fully prepare and present their case before appearing in front of the court, with very strict preclusions: as a matter of fact, both the plaintiff and the defendant must expose and articulate in their respective first defences (*ricorso* and *memoria difensiva*) all of the relevant facts, documents, claims, defences and evidentiary requests they wish to rely on.

The initial petition takes the form of a *ricorso*, which, unlike a *citazione*, does not mark out the date of the first hearing and is not immediately served on the defendant: on the contrary, a *ricorso* is first filed in court in order to enable the judge to set the date of the first hearing before him or her by decree.

The *ricorso* and the judge's decree are then served on the defendant, who has a burden to file his or her defence ten days before the hearing fixed by the judge.

In the course of the proceedings, the parties' have very narrow possibilities to introduce new requests or defences and, in order for them to do so, the judge's authorization is previously required.

The hearing before the judge is the focal point of the proceedings, with oral defences being preferred to written arguments. At the hearing, both parties must attend in person so that the judge may freely interrogate and try to reconcile them.

If possible, oral evidence is gathered immediately after the parties' requests are allowed. Otherwise, future hearings can be fixed.

As concerns the gathering of evidence, it must be remarked that labour proceedings have a strong inquisitorial character: as a matter of fact, the judge has the power to admit, on his or her motion, any evidence, even beyond the limits set by the CC for the admissibility of the means to gather evidence. The judge may also request information to the trade unions and the employers' associations and inspect the workplace, interrogating the workers he or she finds therein, in order to gather information about the dispute at hand.

After evidence has been collected, the parties present their final oral defences[528] to the judge, who renders his or her decision at the end of the discussion, by reading the so-called *dispositivo*, that is, the authoritative part of the judgment, as well as

527. *See* A. Nascosi, 'Un ritorno al passato: il collegato lavoro ripristina la facoltatività del tentativo di conciliazione per le controversie di lavoro', RTDPC (2011): 215 et seq.; G. Gioia, *supra*, 829 et seq., with a list of ADR which may be used in labour disputes.

528. If necessary, written briefs can be authorized.

the factual and legal reasons for his or her judgment. After a reform of Article 429 CPC in 2008, it is now possible for the judge, after oral discussion of the case, to just read the *dispositivo* of the judgment and then hand down the full reasons for judgment in the following sixty days, only when the dispute is particularly complex.

If the *dispositivo* orders the employee to pay a sum of money to the worker, the latter has the possibility to immediately start enforcement proceedings, even before the whole judgment is available. In order to stop such enforcement, therefore, the employee must file an unreasoned appeal, alleging that he or she will otherwise face irreparable damage (*appello con riserva dei motivi*). Full reasons to appeal will have to be filed after the complete judgment has been released.

Apart from the main labour proceedings described above, also special labour proceedings exist to deal with specific situations. It is worth noting here a very recent type of proceedings introduced to deal with the unfair dismissal of an employee by Law No. 92 of 2012.[529] The structure of these proceedings is rather peculiar: they start with a preliminary summary phase which ends with a provisional decision as to whether the worker was unfairly dismissed or not. Such decision may then be opposed before the same *Tribunale* which rendered it, and the subsequent decision may be reviewed by way of *reclamo* before the Court of Appeal.

§2. Proceedings Before the *Giudice Di Pace*

333. Some special provisions are provided to grant speedy proceedings to the disputes falling within the small-claims competence of the justice of the peace.[530]

The general idea is to have less formal procedures, with a stress on the conciliation prerogatives of the justice of the peace,[531] with limited possibilities for the parties to appear before the judge without a lawyer (*see* paragraph 178).[532]

It is even possible (if unlikely …) to bring an oral petition directly to the judge, which will then be written down in a report that the plaintiff will serve in the defendant.[533]

Both parties can present their first formal defences to the court on the very day of the first hearing, with no procedural preclusions.

At the first hearing, the justice of the peace tries to reconcile the parties; if no settlement is reached, the parties present their evidentiary requests and deposit their documents. An oral discussion follows the evidence-gathering phase, and a judgment is deposited after fifteen days. It must be remarked that, under Article 113

529. *See* C. Consolo, 'Vere o presunte novità, sostanziali e processuali, sui licenziamenti individuali', CG (2012): 729; D. Dalfino, 'Il nuovo procedimento in materia di impugnativa del licenziamento nel d.d.l. Fornero', GPC (2012): 759; F.P. Luiso, 'La disciplina processuale speciale della legge n. 92 del 2012 nell'ambito del processo civile: modelli di riferimento ed inquadramento sistematico', <www.judicium.it>.

530. *See* Consolo & Tommaseo (eds), 'Istituzione del giudice di pace', NLCC (1995): 628.

531. The parties may even voluntarily appear before the justice of the peace to try to settle disputes which would fall outside the value and subject-matter competence of the judge (Art. 322 CPC).

532. In disputes with a value of less than EUR 516.

533. Article 316 CPC.

CPC,[534] in disputes with a value of less than EUR 1,100.00 the justice of the peace renders equitable decisions with no strict application of existing legal rules.[535]

334. After the revision of Article 339(3) CPC in 2006, every judgment of the justice of the peace can be appealed before the *Tribunale* and subsequently to the *Corte di Cassazione*.

If the judge rendered an equitable decision (*see* paragraph 333), however, the latter may be appealed only on certain specific grounds (i.e., the violation of procedural, community or constitutional provisions or when the basic principles of the relevant areas of the law have not been duly followed).

§3. Separation and Divorce Proceedings

335. No uniform procedure for all family matters disputes exists. Moreover, subject-matter competence for parental responsibility is split between *Tribunali ordinari* and *Tribunali per i minorenni*, and the boundaries of such division are not always easy to determine. For a long time, the institution of a *Tribunale della Famiglia*, for the solution and adjudication of every family dispute, has been debated and pleaded for but so far no statute has been enacted to bring a much-needed solution to this issue.[536]

Remedies in this area of the law can be provided in several different forms, mostly through proceedings in chambers.[537] In particular, this model of special proceedings is applied to all disputes concerning minors before the *Tribunale per i minorenni* and to disputes before the *Tribunale ordinario* concerning parental responsibility over minors born out of wedlock (*famiglie di fatto*). When unmarried parents litigate over parental responsibility, therefore, proceedings are started with a *ricorso*, a hearing before a three-judge panel of the *Tribunale* is arranged and the other party is summoned to appear. When evidence needs being gathered, the *Tribunale* takes all of the necessary steps in a deformalized way, then the case is decided with a decree, which may be appealed against before the *Corte d'appello*.

A more analytical procedural regulation is provided for legal separations and divorce disputes.

A legal separation or a divorce may be either based on an agreement between the parties or contentious. When the parties succeed in reaching an amicable solution for their matrimonial dispute they have the possibility, since 2014, to either file a joint petition in the court (*separazione consensuale* or *divorzio a domanda congiunta*) or avoid going to court and formalize their agreement with a *negoziazione assistita* (assisted negotiation) (*see* Part XII) or even by a simple declaration before the major (*separazione* or *divorzio in proprio*). When such agreement cannot be

534. *See* A. Carratta & M. Taruffo, *supra*, 233 et seq.

535. Monnini, 'Art. 113, c. 2: dall'equità del g conciliatore all'equità del giudice di pace', FI (1998): I, 3170; however, *see supra*, para. 101.

536. *See*, recently, F. Danovi, 'Il riparto delle competenze tra giudice minorile e giudice ordinario: il Tribunale unico della famiglia', DF (2011): 257.

537. For more details on proceedings concerning minors, *see* L. Querzola, *Il processo minore in dimensione europea* (Bologna: Bononia University Press, 2010).

reached, in order to become separated or divorced the parties have no alternative to litigating their case in court (*separazione* or *divorzio giudiziale*), with the mandatory intervention of the *Pubblico Ministero*.

The regulation of separation before a court is laid down in the code of civil procedure (Articles 706 et seq.),[538] while the rules governing a judicial divorce declaration are contained in the special provisions of Law No. 898 of 1970, as subsequently modified by Law No. 74 of 1987. Both regulations have been extensively revised by the reforms of 2005–2006 (*see supra*, paragraph 37).[539] Basically, however, the same procedural model applies to both contentious separation and divorce. Assisted negotiations in matrimonial matters and agreements before the major, on the other hand, are regulated, respectively by Articles 6 and 12 of DL No. 132 of 2014 (*see* paragraphs 469 et seq.).

336. Consensual and contentious separation share a common procedural phase before the President of the *Tribunale*, but contested separations require subsequent full cognition proceedings to decide on every issue in dispute (responsibility for the breakup of the family, parental responsibility, alimony and so on). One of the fundamental distinctions between these two forms of separation is that, in contested proceedings, only certain claims may be adjudicated upon (i.e., those claims strictly connected with the separation, like the issue of liability in the matrimonial crisis, parental responsibility, alimony, the use of the family house and so on), while other claims between the parties (most notably, disputes concerning common properties and other money claims not related to the dissolution of marriage) are usually deemed not to be admissible in this procedural context. In consensual separations, on the other hand, the parties enjoy wide freedom as concerns the content of the agreements between them. As a matter of fact, it is most common for the parties to dispose in these proceedings of their common properties (most notably, real property) and define all sorts of disputes or issues between them.

337. Contested separation proceedings start with a *ricorso* filed in the *Tribunale* of the place of the last common residence of the parties.[540] If the spouses did not have a (last) common residence in Italy, then the case must be filed in the residence or domicile of the defendant. If the latter is not resident or domiciled in Italy, the plaintiff is allowed to sue in the forum of his or her own residence or domicile. If even the plaintiff is neither resident nor domiciled in Italy, any *Tribunale* of the Republic will have competence.

---

538. *See* E. Vullo, 'Procedimenti in materia di famiglia e di stato delle persone', in *Commentario del Codice di Procedura Civile*, ed. S. Chiarloni, tome I (Bologna: Zanichelli, 2011), 1 et seq.

539. *See* G. Balena, 'Giudizio di separazione personale dei coniugi', FI (2006): V, 66; F. Cipriani, 'Processi di separazione e di divorzio', FI (2005): V, 140; Corder, 'Giudizio contenzioso di separazione e di divorzio, Giudizio di primo grado', in *Separazione, divorzio, annullamento*, ed. Sicchiero (Bologna: Zanichelli, 2005), 479; F. Danovi, 'Le nuove norme sui procedimenti di separazione e di divorzio', RDP (2005): 849; A. Graziosi, 'Osservazioni sulla riforma dei processi di separazione e di divorzio', RTDPC (2005): 1113; F. Tommaseo, 'La disciplina pro-cessuale della separazione e del divorzio dopo le riforme del 2005 (e del 2006)', FD (2006): 7.

540. M.A. Lupoi, 'La riforma dei procedimenti della crisi matrimoniale: profili sistematici e fase introduttiva', RTDPC (2006): 955.

In this procedural model, the parties do not need to articulate all of their respective claims and defences in their first briefs. This means that the originating petition may even be rather brief and not very detailed. As a matter of fact, the scope of the first hearing before the President of the *Tribunale* is to try and conciliate the parties, so that the latter are encouraged not to say too much at the start of the case, in order not to make the dispute harsher. Upon filing the *ricorso*, a hearing is fixed before the President of the *Tribunale* by decree. *Ricorso* and decree are then served on the defendant, who may file an answer within a deadline set by the President, before the hearing. Both parties are supposed to attach their latest tax documents to their first briefs.

At the presidential hearing, the parties are heard by the President, separately at first, then together. The President tries to settle their dispute but if such attempt fails (as it normally does), he or she will render an order containing provisional and urgent dispositions (*provvedimenti provvisori ed urgenti*) which are meant to govern the personal and patrimonial relations between the spouses and (eventually) their children in the course of the proceedings.[541] The law indeed presumes that, in this kind of disputes, a provisional regulation of the parties' relations always has to be granted, before the final judgment is released, with no need for a *periculum in mora* to be shown in the case at hand: in other words, in this area of the law, an intrinsic urgency is found to exist, so that the parties do not need to show to the President that, unless his order is granted, they or their children will suffer some irreparable harm.

The nature of these provisional measures is controversial. Undoubtedly, they have a 'precautionary' function, in so far as they aim at giving immediate protection to some very sensible situations. On the other hand, the academics are divided between those who believe that these provisional measures should be considered as proper precautionary measures (*provvedimenti cautelari*)[542] and those who think that they have a different nature,[543] mostly related to their enforceability. There are of course some procedural implications deriving from the different qualification that may be given to the President's provisional measures. In particular, if one believes that they are proper precautionary measures, they are governed by the rules of precautionary proceedings (*rito cautelare uniforme*) (*see* paragraphs 386 et seq.). Arguably, however, they are not proper precautionary measures: as a matter of fact, the President's order is given even when no *periculum in mora* is shown, so one of the necessary conditions of precautionary proceedings is missing; moreover, when minors are involved, the President's urgent measures may be granted even ex officio[544] and the President has a wide discretion in the type and the content of measures he may grant,[545] even without a strict instrumental connection with the final decision. It is

541. For example, the authorization to the spouses not to live together anymore, measures concerning minors, alimony and so forth. *See* M.A. Lupoi, *Interim Measures in Italian Family Proceedings*, in *Provisional Measures in Italian and Greek Procedural Law* 43 (K. Makridou & G. Diamantopoulos eds, Sakkoulas Publications 2016).

542. *See*, e.g., recently *Trib.* Reggio Emilia, 27 Apr. 2012, <www.ilcaso.it>.

543. *See Trib.* Udine, 21 May 2009, *ord.*

544. *Cass.*, 9 Jun. 1990, n. 5636.

545. *Cass.*, 11 Oct. 1978, n. 4519.

preferable, therefore, to consider these measures as summary decisions aimed at providing immediate enforcement to the parties' rights.

The President's decision is mostly based on the documents that the parties have filed with their initial defences and on the parties' answers to the President's questions at the hearing. It is therefore a decision based on a summary and incomplete evaluation of the facts of the case. When the need arises, however, it is possible, for the President in the course of this preliminary phase to collect some evidence: for example, when some dangerous situation is considered to exist, the President may hear the children before granting his decision about the latter's relations with both parents; or, when the 'official' income and assets of the parties are prima facie unrealistic, he may order the Tax Police to do some investigations about them. Such investigations, however, are not commonly used in practice at this early stage of the proceedings.

The *ordinanza presidenziale* does not bind the court's final decision but is provisionally enforceable. After the reform of 2006, moreover, it may be reviewed by way of *reclamo* to the Court of Appeal, using proceedings in chambers (*see* paragraph 206).[546] The deadline to bring this *reclamo* is ten days since the order is served from one party on the other.

The Court's review of the case after a *reclamo* is filed shares the same nature as the President's decision: in other words, the Court is called to grant a summary examination of the President's order, on the same evidence that was under the President's scrutiny. Many Courts of Appeal will not allow new evidence to be brought before the court, not even new documents. The rationale is that the *reclamo* should not be considered as an occasion to have the Court review the President's exercise of discretion: on the contrary, Courts of Appeal allow a *reclamo* only when some major and self-evident faults are found in the first instance decision in relation to either the facts or the law.

The order of the President may also be modified or revoked by the instructing judge, in the course of the proceedings, even if no new circumstances are alleged: in other words, the single judge in charge of preparing the case to be decided may modify the President's order even on the grounds of a different exercise of judicial discretion. This however is not very common in practice and most often a single judge will confirm the President's order, unless some new factual or legal grounds are brought to his attention.

A rather obscure area concerns the coordination between *reclamo* to the Court of Appeal against the President's order (*see* above) and the power of review granted to the single judge by Article 709 CPC. As a matter of fact, the law does not clarify whether the single judge may review a President's order which has been confirmed by the Court of Appeal, when no new circumstances are alleged. Not surprisingly, some very diverse case law has been released in the past decade on this issue and practically any conceivable solution has been explored in practice. Indeed, different

546. M.A. Lupoi, 'Aspetti processuali della normativa sull'affidamento condiviso', RTDPC (2006): 1063; M.A. Lupoi, *Interim Measures in Italian Family Proceedings*, in *Provisional Measures in Italian and Greek Procedural Law* 47 (K. Makridou & G. Diamantopoulos eds, Sakkoulas Publications 2016).

courts apply different approaches and the same case may be treated in rather different ways depending on the venue where the issue arises.

The law does not specify whether also the instructing judge's *interim* order may be reviewed by the Court of Appeal as the President's order may, This statutory 'silence' has been interpreted in rather different ways: some argue that, even if no remedies against this provisional measure are expressly provided for, it should be possible however to either apply Article 708 CPC by analogy (and thus make use of *reclamo* to the Court of Appeal)[547] or *reclamo* to the three-judge panel of the Court of First Instance under Article 669*terdecies* CPC. This second solution, in particular, is favoured by those who believe that *interim* orders granted by the single judge in the course of matrimonial proceedings have a proper precautionary nature and should be procedurally treated as such.[548] The first solution (*reclamo* to the Court of Appeal) has been denied by every Court of Appeal where such a *reclamo* has been lodged, so it cannot be considered a viable proposition.[549] The second option was initially faced with some case law approval but over the years the number of first instance courts which considers a *reclamo* against a single judge's order to be inadmissible is steadily growing and may now be considered the vast majority.[550] The (indeed debatable) rationale for this approach is that the single judge's order does not have a proper precautionary nature[551] and that Article 708 CPC is an exceptional rule, which may not be interpreted in an extensive way, to embrace situations not expressly considered therein.[552]

After the presidential hearing, the case moves onto the tracks of ordinary proceedings before the instructing judge of the *Tribunale*. The reform of 2005 has clarified certain unclear aspects of the way proceedings move from one phase to the next: in particular, the President's order now also fixes peremptory deadlines for both parties to complete their defences and requests and the date of the next hearing before the instructing judge. Only at this point, do both parties face the traditional preclusions for the presentation of their respective claims and objections. The first hearing before the instructing judge is by all accounts regulated by Article 183 CPC (*see supra*, paragraphs 199, 215 et seq.). Some special provisions, however, apply.

First of all, according to the new Article 336*bis* CC, introduced by DLGS 154/2013 (*see* paragraph 38), in any proceedings where decisions concerning a minor are granted, the judge is required to hear children above 12 years of age, and even

---

547. *Trib*. Genoa, 2 Apr. 2006, *ord*., FI (2006): I, 2213; *Trib*. Reggio Emilia, 6 Nov. 2006, *ord*., FI (2007): I, 973; *Trib*. Rome, 7 Jul. 2006, *decr*., DF (2007): 210.

548. *See*, e.g., *Trib*. Foggia, 2 May 2006, FI (2006): I, 2213; *App*. Catania, 14 Nov. 2007, *ord*., <*www.famigliaeminori.it*>; *App*. Naples, 5 Mar. 2007, *ord*., FI. (2007): I, 1916.

549. *See*, e.g., *App*. Bari, 16 Jun. 2006, FI (2006): I, 3242; *App*. Bari, 29 Aug. 2007, *decr*., FI (2008): I, 3334; *App*. Firenze, 11 Jul. 2006, *ord*., <*www.judicium.it*>.

550. *Trib*. Foggia, 2 May 2006, *ord*., FI (2006): I, 2213;; *Trib*. Reggio Emilia, 6 Sep. 2012, <*www.ilcaso.it*>; *Trib*. Milan, 13 Jun. 2013, <www.ilcaso.it>.

551. *Trib*. Udine, 21 Apr. 2009, *ord*.; *Trib*. Padova, 7 Apr. 2011, *ord*.; *Trib*. Modena, 28 Oct. 2011, *ord*.; *Trib*. Milan, 13 Jun. 2013, <www.ilcaso.it>.

552. *See* M.A. Lupoi, *Interim Measures in Italian Family Proceedings*, in *Provisional Measures in Italian and Greek Procedural Law* 51 (K. Makridou & G. Diamantopoulos eds, Sakkoulas Publications 2016).

younger if they appear to him or her mature enough (*ascolto del minore*).[553] With reference to previous legislation (now repealed by DLGS No. 154/2013), the Supreme Court[554] ruled that it was mandatory for the judge to hear a minor in any dispute in which he or she is involved and that, should the judge fail to do so, the whole proceedings would be invalid. The new Article 336*bis* CC, however, while still requiring, as a rule, that a minor be heard in proceedings in which he is involved, provides for two exceptions: namely when such hearing is against the best interest of the child or manifestly unnecessary. Some therefore argue that the new legislation has rendered a minor's hearing by the judge a discretionary and not mandatory activity.

DLGS No. 154/2013 has also brought new provisions concerning how to perform this activity. As a matter of fact, in the past, the law did not clarify this important point and heterogeneous practices started to develop in different courts. Some judges, e.g., heard the minor directly, others preferred to delegate such task to an expert or to the Social Services. Doubts also were raised as concerned a lawyer's right to attend such hearings: the majority of courts seemed to give a negative answer. In order to grant the parties' right of the defence, however, some courts enabled lawyers to present a list of questions they would have liked the judge to ask the minor.[555] The new Article 336*bis* CC, however, has changed this state of the matter, making it clear that a minor should be heard directly by the judge, possibly assisted by an expert or other auxiliaries. The so-called assisted hearing has therefore been allowed. Apparently, on the other hand, it will no longer be possible to delegate such hearing to other professionals.[556] Moreover, the new provision specifies that parents, lawyers, PM and the child's special minder may assist at the hearing, but only upon the judge's authorization (or, even without such authorization, from a different room, e.g., through a one-way mirror); they are also allowed to propose to the judge questions and matters on which to hear the minor's opinion. Before starting to listen to the minor, the judge should inform her about the nature of the proceedings she is involved in and about the effects and consequences her declarations may have. The minor's declarations are then written down in a report. Audio or video recording is also allowed.

The opinions expressed by a minor before the judge are not considered evidence. As a matter of fact, hearing the minor is functional to understanding her, in order to take her point of view into consideration before granting a judicial decision which will be relevant for her life and well-being. The Supreme Court has stated that, after the recent reforms in this area of the law, a minor can no longer be considered as a witness,[557] because he needs to be considered a 'substantial' party to the proceedings.[558] It should be remarked, anyway, that the court is never bound by the

553. *See*, recently, P. Di Marzio, 'L'audizione del minore nei procedimenti civili', DF (2011): 366 et seq.
554. *Cass. SU* 21 Oct. 2009, n. 22238, FD, 2010, 67; *Trib.* Varese 10 Feb. 2010, *ord.*, <www.altalex.com>.
555. *Trib.* Varese 10 Feb. 2010, *supra.*
556. *See* G. Savi, 'L'atto processuale dell'ascolto ed i diritti del figlio minore', DF (2013): 1351.
557. *App.* Catania 12 Dec. 2013, <www.ilcaso.it>.
558. *Trib.* Milan 11 Dec. 2013, order, <www.ilcaso.it>.

opinions expressed by the minor, though it must give reasons to not take them into consideration.[559]

In proceedings concerning minors, moreover, the courts enjoy extensive inquisitorial powers.[560] Since it is their task to take care of the best interests of the child, they may release any relevant order irrespective of the parties' requests. They may also collect any evidence of their own motion. In particular, according to Article 336*ter* CC, the judge may order the Tax Police to investigate about the incomes and the possessions of both parents, when their tax documents appear insufficient to give a clear picture of their economic and patrimonial positions.

Before deciding the case, moreover, the judge also has the prerogative to suggest the parties to try to settle their dispute before a family mediator (*see* at paragraph 450).

In the early phases of the proceedings, either party may apply for a 'partial' decision concerning only the separation (*sentenza non definitiva*). When this is the case, the court will render a judgment where only such issue is adjudicated, leaving all the other issues in dispute (particularly, any responsibility issue) to be decided at the end of the proceedings.[561] This course of action is very popular: as a matter of fact, the three-year time limit which has to elapse before a separated couple may apply for a divorce starts to run from the day the parties appear at the hearing before the President of the *Tribunale*. The judgment on their separation, however, must also have become res judicata before divorce may be applied for. With this 'partial' judgment, therefore, the parties are enabled to file a petition for divorce while separation proceedings may still be pending. Only immediate appeal is allowed against these partial decisions.

The final judgment will substitute any provisional order given in the course of the proceedings with retroactive effect, unless specified otherwise. Such judgment may be appealed before the Court of Appeal, which decides in chambers. The appeal is brought with a *ricorso*, which should be filed in court within the ordinary deadline (*see* at paragraph 233). The court then fixes a hearing in chambers, where the case is argued orally. Usually, very little evidence-gathering activities take place at the appeal level. The court's judgment may be further appealed before the Supreme Court.

Even after a separation decision has become res judicata, however, the parties have the right to apply to have it revoked or modified if new circumstances arise: in this area of the law, as a matter of fact, judgments are always rendered *allo stato degli atti*, that is, in the light of the existing situation, and are liable to be subsequently 'adapted' to the modifications in the relationship and in the conditions of the parties.[562] When the legal requirements are met, the interested party files a *ricorso* in the competent *Tribunale*, which will then fix a hearing before a three-judge panel. The other party of course has the right to defend himself or herself, and

559. *Cass*. 17 May 2012, n. 7773, GD 1 (2013): 63.
560. These powers have even been extended by the recent reform on joint custody (Law No. 54 of 2006).
561. *See Cass. SU* 3 Dec. 2001, n. 15248, FD, 2002, 11.
562. Article 710 CPC provides special chambers proceedings to modify the original conditions of a separation. Similar modifications are admitted in divorce proceedings (e.g., as concerns alimony: *see Cass*. 28 Jan. 2000, n. 958, GD. 13 (2000): 69).

even to apply for a modification of the same decision (of course for different reasons). The court decides in chambers, releasing a final decree which will then be subject to a special form of appeal (*reclamo*). The main difference vis-à-vis ordinary appeal is that *reclamo* should be brought within only ten days of the moment the decree is served from one party onto the other. Should the decree not be notified, the ordinary 'long' time limit (i.e., six months since the day the decision was published) applies.

338. A consensual separation is much faster (and usually cheaper) than a contested one. Of course, the parties must have reached an agreement as to the personal and patrimonial conditions of their separation. As it was pointed out above (*see* at paragraph 336), the parties, in this context, are free to solve any kind of dispute between them, even in relation to claims not directly connected with the separation itself. However, the *Tribunale* will check whether the parties' agreement is in compliance with mandatory provisions and public policy, in particular as concerns the position of any minor involved.

From the procedural point of view, the parties file a *ricorso* in the *Tribunale* of the place where at least one of them resides. They may be assisted by the same lawyer or by a different lawyer for each of them.

The *ricorso* will present the agreements reached by the parties, in order for the *Tribunale* to examine them.

A presidential hearing is fixed and, after a ritual attempt of the President to reconcile the spouses, the parties are asked to confirm the conditions they have agreed upon in the *ricorso*. At this point, a three-judge panel of the *Tribunale* will review such conditions in chambers, verifying, in particular, that the best interests of any minor is safeguarded therein and, if that is the case, the separation is ratified with a decree (*decreto di omologa*).

If the *Tribunale* believes that some of the parties' conditions cannot be thus ratified, it may not ex officio change the content of the parties' agreement. On the contrary, the latter are required to review their conditions and propose new solutions to the court. If the parties do not comply with this invitation, their agreement will not be certified.

It is by now recognized that the parties may want to fake a separation, in order to take advantage of some of the legal effects connecter thereto. In particular, sometimes, consensual separations are used as a veil to justify transfers of property from one spouse to the other, in order to avoid enforcement on that property from creditors of the transferring spouse. Case law therefore enables creditors to attack consensual separation agreements, in order to have them revoked as concerns transfers of property which may be detrimental to their interests.

339. In Italy, as a rule, divorce may be applied for only after the spouses have been legally separated (since 2015) for at least six months, running from the day they appeared before the *Presidente* of the *Tribunale* (*see* paragraphs 337 et seq.) (twelve months in case of a contentious separation). Other grounds for divorce (listed in Article 3 of Law No. 898 of 1970), like the non-consummation of the marriage, are more rarely invoked.

Also in this context there is a distinction between contested divorce proceedings (*divorzio giudiziale*) and divorce upon a joint petition (*divorzio congiunto*). Until recently, a judgment was considered to be always necessary (*sentenza costitutiva*) for two spouses to divorce. Since 2014, however, spouses may decide to divorce by way of *negoziazione assistita* (*see* Part XII), with no need to appear before the court.

340. When the parties agree as to the conditions of the divorce, they may sign and file in the *Tribunale* of the place of residence or domicile of either of them a joint petition. A hearing is fixed before a three-judge panel, where the parties are supposed to confirm the conditions they have agreed upon. The *Tribunale* reviews those conditions and then releases a judgment if it finds that they comply with the public policy, mandatory provisions and the best interests of any minor involved. If such a review leads to a negative outcome, the proceedings are automatically converted to the contentious model (*see* below).

341. Contested divorces proceedings, on the other hand, follow the same steps of contested separation proceedings. As a matter of fact, after 2006, separation and divorce are governed by provisions having basically the very same content. Also here, therefore, there is a preliminary phase before the President of the *Tribunale*, which is mainly focused on an attempt to settle the dispute and in granting provision remedies.

Here, however, different rules on venue apply, since the Constitutional Court declared Article 4 of Law No. 898 of 1970 incompatible with the Constitution insomuch as it granted territorial competence on the court of the place of last common residence of the parties.[563] The residual connecting factors therefore apply (*see supra* at paragraph 337).

The subsequent phase before the instructing judge follows the same procedural rules which govern separation disputes (*see* paragraph 337).

Divorce can be pronounced with a partial judgment (*sentenza non definitiva*), leaving all the other contested issues to the further course of the proceedings case. This way, the parties are freed from the conjugal tie before the end of the whole proceedings, enabling them, for example, to immediately remarry while the case is still actually pending.

The dispute is always decided by a three-judge panel with a *sentenza* which is then appealable before the Court of Appeal. Chambers proceedings take place at the appeal level, like in separation appeals (*see* paragraph 337).

Like in the case of a separation, also the provisions regulating the former spouse's personal and economic relationships may be modified should the situation change after the divorce judgment has been rendered. Article 9 of Law No. 898 of 1970 provides for the same proceedings in chambers examined in the context of separation (*see* paragraph 337).

---

563. *Corte cost.* 23 May 2008, 169, FI, 2008, I, 2081 basically held that such connecting factor was unreasonable.

342. Law No. 54 of 2006 introduced an interesting procedural device under Article 709*ter* CPC.[564]

This new provision applies in separation and divorce proceedings as well as in proceedings concerning minors born out of wedlock. The remedies provided therein may be applied for either in the course of pending proceedings or through an autonomous petition.

In the first place, parents may file a claim in the court to let the judge solve a conflict which has arisen between them in relation to a minor (e.g., a dispute concerning the kind of school the child should be sent to).

They may also ask for the court to modify the existing provisions governing their relations with their children, in case of non-compliance with existing judicial orders and when a serious threat is posed to the well-being of the minors. Here, the judge may not only modify the existing provisions (e.g., turn from joint custody to exclusive custody over the child): he or she also has the power to inflict sanctions on the parent who failed to comply or which posed threats to the well-being of the minor.

Four different types of sanctions may be issued in this context:

(1) a formal warning;
(2) damages for the child;
(3) damages for the other parent;
(4) a fine.

Part of the case law believes that with these sanctions, the lawmaker has introduced a form of punitive damages in the Italian legal order,[565] but the majority of commentators deny this solution.

So far, case law is showing that the remedies of Article 709*ter* CPC may indeed be very effective, in particular as a form of indirect coercion to comply with a judicial order.

§4. *PROCESSO SOMMARIO DI COGNIZIONE* (SUMMARY PROCEEDINGS)

343. Law No. 69 of 2009 brought a new procedural model into the Italian legal order.[566] As a matter of fact, Articles 702*bis* et seq. were inserted in the CPC, introducing the *procedimento sommario di cognizione*, a notion which may roughly be translated as summary proceedings.

In Italian civil procedure, the term 'summary' may have various meanings and implications. Roughly speaking, the judge's ascertainment is 'summary' when it is not exhaustive, or it is based on a lower standard of persuasion (e.g.,: the likelihood of the existence of a right) or on certain types of evidence only. In this context,

---

564. *See* M.A. Lupoi, M.A., *supra*, 53.
565. *See Trib.* Messina 5 Apr. 2007, *decr.*, FI, 2008, I, 1689; *Trib.* Vicenza 15 Apr. 2010, FD, (2010): 705.
566. R. Caponi, *Italian Civil Justice Reform 2009*, *supra*; Guaglione, NLCC (2010), 1118; M.A. Lupoi, 'Sommario (ma non troppo)', RTDPC (2010): 1225; M.A. Lupoi, *Nowhere Fast? Shortcuts to Judgment in Recent Italian Procedural Legislation*, in *Ways of Implementation of the Right to Civil Proceedings Within a Reasonable Time* 303 (Vilnius Universitetas 2016).

however, the lawmaker has used the term 'summary' with another connotation. It is widely believed that the new summary proceedings are functional equivalents of ordinary ascertainment proceedings: as a matter of fact, the judge's final decision is given the same authority and effects of an ordinary judgment. This means that the word 'summary' here does not refer to an investigation which is not complete or exhaustive as to the existence of the relevant facts, but rather to a simple and fast evidence-gathering phase, for cases which may be decided on the basis of the relevant documents or of just a limited amount of oral evidence.[567] In other words, these new proceedings are destined to be used in simple cases,[568] where the facts are not contested or may be easily ascertained.[569] In these simple cases, the lawmaker has introduced proceedings which aim at being fast and effective. As a matter of fact, the first published decisions appear to have been granted in just a few months, therefore within a delay which is not even comparable to that of ordinary proceedings. For this reason, many commentators promote the use of this procedural model, even though court's practices sometimes express suspicions, if not open hostility towards it.

344. Summary proceedings are an alternative to ordinary cognition proceedings.[570] In other words, the plaintiff is free to choose among these two procedural models.

However, if a plaintiff chooses to file a petition for summary proceedings, he or she cannot be sure that the judge will uphold such choice. As a matter of fact, at the first hearing, the judge will review the case and the parties' defence, and decide whether to move the case to the tracks of ordinary proceedings or to keep it as a *procedimento sommario*. The defendant, on the other hand, might want to induce the judge to move to the ordinary track, by bringing new claims, defences and evidentiary requests to make the case more complex.[571]

345. Summary proceedings are admissible only for disputes within the competence of the *Tribunale* at first instance, where the case falls to be decided by a single judge. Summary proceedings may not therefore be tried before either the *Giudice di pace*[572] or the Court of Appeal.[573]

---

567. *Trib.* Varese 18 Nov. 2009, *ord.*; R. Caponi, in G. Balena, R. Caponi, A. Chizzini, S. Menchini, *La riforma della giustizia civile* (Turin: Giappichelli, 2010), 206.
568. *Trib.* Varese 18 Nov. 2009, *ord.*; M. Bove, 'Il procedimento sommario di cognizione di cui agli articoli 702-bis ss. c. p. c.', <www.judicium.it>, 6.
569. *Trib.* Varese 18 Nov. 2009, *ord.*; B. Capponi, 'Note sul procedimento sommario di cognizione (Art. 702-bis e segg. c. p. c.)', <www.judicium.it>, 3.
570. A. Briguglio, 'Le novità sul processo ordinario di cognizione nell'ultima, ennesima riforma in materia di giustizia civile', GC (2009): II, 260; L. Dittrich, 'Il nuovo procedimento sommario di cognizione', RDP (2009): 1582.
571. *See* R. Caponi, in G. Balena, R. Caponi, A. Chizzini, S. Menchini, *supra*, 198.
572. *Trib.* Modena 18 Jan. 2010, *ord.*; L. Dittrich, *supra*, 1585.
573. *Trib.* Modena 18 Jan. 2010, *ord.*

Any type of claim within this scope of application may be tried with summary proceedings.[574] Moreover, it must be possible to decide the case through a summary evidence-gathering phase (i.e., through simple and fast evidentiary activities, performed in an informal setting, without strict application of the legal rules).[575]

It is up to the judge at the first hearing to decide on how to let the case proceed. There are neither fixed guidelines nor clear-cut standards for the judge's decision. Ideally, in order to be 'simple', the evidence-gathering phase should be confined to just one hearing,[576] but even a series of hearing is considered to be compatible with this procedural model, as well as the need to gather oral or expert evidence.[577] When complex and articulated evidence-gathering must take place, the case should be moved to the ordinary track.

In these summary proceedings, the court enjoys important discretionary powers, and the rules may be applied in rather flexible ways. In order to try and provide some operative guidelines, some *Tribunali* have even released Protocols to govern their own local practices.

346. The originating petition takes the form of a *ricorso*, whose content is substantially the same of an ordinary *citazione* (*see* at paragraphs 214 et seq.), the only missing element being the date of the hearing, which will be fixed by the judge, after the case is filed in the court.

The plaintiff is not compelled to specify his or her evidentiary requests, but it will be in his or her interest to show the judge that the case is apt for a summary evidence-gathering phase.

The parties need legal counselling also for this type of proceedings. The *ricorso* is filed in court, and the President appoints a judge who will fix a hearing by decree. Unfortunately, in many courts, judges tend to fix such hearing with a very long delay, therefore making this remedy much less effective than it could.

347. The *ricorso* and the judge's decree are then served on the defendant at least forty days before the hearing. The defendant must file a full defence ten days before the hearing at the latest, presenting all of his or her defences, requests and counterclaims, including an application to join a third person he or she wants to be guaranteed by. The more complex the defendant's answer, the more likely the case to be moved on the ordinary track.

574. F.P. Luiso, 'Il procedimento sommario di cognizione' <www.judicium.it>, 1; S. Menchini, 'L'ultima 'idea' del legislatore per accelerare i tempi della tutela dichiarativa dei diritti: il processo sommario di cognizione', *Corriere giuridico* (2009): 1026; *Trib.* Modena 18 Jan. 2010, *ord.*; M. Bove, 'Il procedimento sommario di cognizione di cui agli articoli 702-bis ss. c. p. c.', <www.judicium.it>, 1; L. Dittrich, *supra*, 1586.

575. F.P. Luiso, *supra*.

576. R. Giordano, 'Il procedimento sommario di cognizione', GM (2009); *Trib.* Taranto 2 Mar. 2010, *ord.*, <www.ilcaso.it>.

577. G.F. Ricci, *La riforma del processo civile. Legge 18 giugno 2009, n. 69* (Turin: Giappichelli, 2009), 110; *Trib.* Taranto 2 Mar. 2010, *ord.*, <www.ilcaso.it>; *Trib.* Brescia 10 Feb. 2010, *ord.*, <www.ilcaso.it>.

348. At the first hearing, the judge will check the admissibility of summary proceedings, the regularity of service of the originating petition and his or her own competence (Article 702*ter* CPC).

If he or she finds that he or she has no competence over the dispute, the case is struck out.

The most important decision, however, at this stage, concerns the track the proceedings will take: as it was pointed out earlier, if the judge comes to the conclusion that no evidence needs to be gathered or that a fast and informal evidence-gathering place may be enough to ascertain the relevant facts, then the case will go on as summary proceedings. Otherwise, the ordinary track will be taken, and the judge will fix a hearing to perform the activities listed in Article 183 CPC (*see* at paragraph 215). Once the ordinary track is taken, it is not possible to bring the case back on the summary one: so to speak, the change of track is irreversible.[578] The relevant decision, moreover, may not be appealed against. In other words, the judge enjoys an uncontrolled discretion in deciding which track to follow. Rather often, summary cases are moved to the ordinary track simply because the judges' backlog is so congested that they are not in the position to devote to summary proceedings the immediate attention they deserve. On the other hand, it is always possible to switch from summary to ordinary proceedings even after the first hearing, should the judge find out that, evidence-wise, the case requires deeper investigations than it was evident at first.

When the case proceeds on the summary track, any relevant and admissible evidence is collected irrespective of formalities under the judge's direction. The notion of informal evidence-gathering must not be taken to mean that the burden of the proof is superseded or that a lower evidentiary standard needs be reached in order to allow the claim on the alleged facts. Rather, the judge will be in the position not to strictly follow the rules of the code concerning the way evidence is gathered in the course of the proceedings. For example, some commentators believe that, in this context, witnesses may be heard with no need to previously set out the questions they will be asked.[579]

These activities may be completed in just one hearing as well as in a limited and compact series of hearings. When all the evidence has been collected, the case is immediately ready to be decided.

349. In this procedural model, concentration and orality govern the operations of both the parties and the judge. This means that as soon as the evidence is collected, the judge may require the parties to orally discuss the case.

When oral arguments have been heard, the decision is taken in the forms of an *ordinanza*, possibly directly at the very same hearing. In practice, the judge may also give the party the possibilities to file a written brief and reserve his or her decision outside of the hearing.[580]

The *ordinanza* which is granted at the end of summary proceedings at first instance is in reality the functional equivalent of a full judgment. As a matter of fact,

578. S. Menchini, *supra*, 1030.
579. G.F. Ricci, *supra*, 110; L. Dittrich, *supra*, 1595; *Trib.* Varese 18 Nov. 2009, *ord.*
580. L. Dittrich, *supra*, 1596.

it may be appealed against like it was a judgment, before the Court of Appeal. Curiously, the lawmaker introduced here a peculiar time limit to bring such appeal, that is thirty days running from the day the *ordinanza* was communicated to the parties. No 'long' time limit is provided for: clearly, the lawmaker (for no apparent reason ...) was concerned about granting fast res judicata effects to this summary decision.

The *ordinanza* has provisional enforcement effects, and it may be used to register a mortgage on the debtor's immoveable properties. If it is not timely appealed, it will become res judicata, and it will enjoy the same authority granted by Article 2909 CC to judgments (*see* paragraphs 232 et seq.).

350. An appeal against a summary *ordinanza* basically follows the ordinary rules for proceedings before the Court of Appeal (*see* paragraphs 253 et seq.). No new claims are allowed, but there is a laxer approach here as concerns new evidence. As a matter of fact, in the original version of Article 702*quater* CPC, the three-judge panel could examine any relevant new evidence, not only indispensable one, like in ordinary appeal (*see* paragraph 251). The lawmaker, apparently, envisaged a more active evidence-gathering role of the appeal judge in this context, as a consequence of the 'summary' ascertainment of the relevant facts performed by the judge of first instance. This approach underwent a revision in the 2012: as ordinary appeals were reshaped as 'closed doors' re-examination of the case (*see* paragraph 251), appeals against summary orders are still treated differently, because of the very nature of summary proceedings at first instance. As a matter of fact, today, in this context, only new 'indispensable' evidence is allowed: in other words, the door to new evidence has not been completely closed (as in ordinary appeals) but rather left slightly ajar.

At the end of appeal proceedings, a judgment will be granted, which will be subject to further appeal before the Supreme Court according to the ordinary provisions.

§5. Chambers Proceedings

351. The drafters of the CPC, originally, introduced the so-called chambers proceedings in relation to that particular form of jurisdictional activity called *giurisdizione volontaria* (non-contentious jurisdiction),[581], [582] where the judge is called by the law not to adjudicate disputes on subjective rights between litigating parties but rather to govern private law relationship characterized by strong public interests.

The very nature of this type of judicial function is rather controversial. Some authors believe that it has a true jurisdictional character and is indeed part of the judicial jurisdiction of the courts;[583] others assume that it has prevailing administrative implications, and refer to it as a form of judicial administration of interests,

581. *See* C. Merlo, *Disposizioni comuni ai procedimenti in camera di consiglio,* in *Art. 737–795* (Bologna: Zanichelli, 2017), 1 et seq.
582. *See* E. Fazzalari, *La giurisdizione volontaria* (Padua: Cedam, 1953).
583. *See* V. Denti, 'La giurisdizione volontaria rivisitata', RTDPC (1987): 325.

where the judge's role is to administer such situations with impartiality, in the interests of the law.

352. Giurisdizione volontaria is characterized by the absence of a dispute between two or more parties in the ordinary sense of the expression. Sometimes, the judge is called upon by the law to render a decision concerning just the applicant.

Indeed, the words *volontaria giurisdizione* are never used in the rules under examination here: their content, however, clearly shows that they were originally meant to govern proceedings where no subjective rights were at stake. As a matter of fact, the whole notion of chambers proceedings implies a procedural model where the court decides in a private hearing, unbound by the rigid formalities of ordinary contentious proceedings.

353. Many heterogeneous proceedings fall within the notion of non-contentious jurisdiction, and it is impossible to mention them all here. Suffice to say, therefore, that they can be found in corporation and business law, commercial law, juvenile law, matters of personal capacity,[584] family law (e.g., the administration of the family assets of two spouses)[585] and so on.

The role of the judge's decision in this heterogeneous context may vary: for example, the law may require the judge to grant or deny authorizations (e.g., concerning deeds to be performed in the interests of minors or incapacitated persons) or to appoint administrators or minders.

Sometimes, the judge's decision is a fundamental part of the formative progress of a substantive right (e.g., the judge's authorization to sell the assets of a minor is an integral component of the contract of sale). In other cases, the judge's decision itself produces substantive effects.[586]

354. A peculiarity of *giurisdizione volontaria* decisions is that they never become substantial res judicata and even after the decline to file a *reclamo* against them is expired, they can always be modified or revoked but the rights previously contractually acquired in good faith by third parties are left untouched (Article 742 CPC).[587]

355. After the entry into force of the CPC, chambers proceedings became very popular with the lawmaker, which started to make extensive reference to this procedural model anytime it felt the need to subject certain types of disputes to a flexible and fast adjudicating track.

Decade after decade, reform after reform, chambers proceedings today are no longer confined to *giurisdizione volontaria*, but are used in a wide variety of contentious disputes. Just as an example, most proceedings concerning minors or

584. Articles 732 et seq. CPC.
585. Articles 735–736 CPC.
586. *See* F.P. Luiso, *Diritto processuale civile*, vol. IV (Milan: Giuffrè, 2009), 283 et seq.
587. *See* A. Chizzini, *La revoca dei provvedimenti di volontaria giurisdizione* (Padua: Cedam, 1994).

appeals in separation and divorce proceedings are decided in chambers. This situation has some quite problematic implications. As we shall see shortly, the rules governing chambers proceedings in the code are very scant and leave a lot of discretion to the court, especially as concerns the evidence-gathering phase. Many commentators, therefore, firmly believe that this procedural model is unfit to be used to adjudicate disputes over subjective rights, since they do not comply with the fair trial principles set by Article 111 of the Constitution.[588] Over the years, however, the Constitutional Court has repeatedly rejected petitions to have these provisions declared unconstitutional when applied to adjudicate over rights. What the Constitutional Court has only been ready to say is that, within proceedings in chambers, the fundamental procedural rights should always be guaranteed, therefore granting that the parties' right of the defence should always be respected, especially as concerns the parties' right to bring evidence before the court and to enjoy sufficient time to prepare and present their respective defences, even within the flexible procedural environment set by the applicable provisions.

356. Articles 737 et seq. CPC provide for common rules for every type of dispute to which chambers proceedings apply.[589] Additional specific rules are set by the provisions regulating most particular procedures. These general rules, however, are very sparse and do not present a complete procedural regulation.

As a general rule, chamber proceedings begin with a *ricorso* filed in the court and end with a reasoned decree, unless specific provisions dispose otherwise.[590]

357. Ordinarily, the case is heard by a panel of three judges of the *Tribunale*. Even if the code does not expressly say so, there is no doubt as to the necessity that, when the proceedings concern other people apart from the applicant, then the originating *ricorso* should be notified to each one of them.

Any interested party should also be given the chance and the time to present his or her defences and answers to the petition, in an appropriate and effective way. As a matter of fact, the code does not provide for fixed time limits or deadlines, so that it is up to the judge to ensure that the parties may effectively enjoy their day in court in the given case.

358. Article 738 CPC is very meagre as concerns the discipline of the evidence-gathering phase. As a matter of fact, this provision only states that 'the judge can take on information'. Apparently, the judge is allowed wide inquisitorial powers to gather any evidence he or she may deem relevant. In practice, when chambers proceedings are used to adjudicate disputes over subjective rights, the ordinary rules governing the burden of the proof and admissible evidence apply. Investigating powers are granted to the court in *volontaria giurisdizione* cases and in some other

588. L.P. Comoglio, 'Difesa e contraddittorio nei procedimenti in camera di consiglio', RDP (1997): 719; A. Proto Pisani, 'Procedura camerale e tutela degli interessi dei minori', FI (1996): V, 65.
589. *See* M.G. Civinini, *I procedimenti in camera di consiglio*, II Volumes (Turin: Utet, 1994); Maltese, 'I procedimenti in Camera di consiglio: profili generali', RDC (1997): 565.
590. Article 737 CPC.

disputes, for example, those concerning minors of incapacitated persons. In practice, chambers proceedings are often decided on the basis of documentary evidence; oral evidence is admitted only when indispensable. Chamber proceedings may be decided in just one of a few hearings. The ordinary rules concerning the decision phase are not respected: most often, the parties are expected to present their oral argument before the court. Sometimes, the filing of written briefs will be allowed.

359. The decree rendered by the *Tribunale* can be appealed within ten days of service by way of *reclamo* before the Court of Appeal, which will also be decided in chambers. The appeal procedure follows the same deformalized steps followed at first instance: a *ricorso* containing the grounds for appeal is filed with the court, a hearing in chambers is fixed, the petition is served on the resistant, who has the prerogative to file an answer and possibly a counter-*reclamo*. Usually, the case is decided after just a hearing, with no or little gathering of new information. The court also rules by decree.

360. Unless otherwise specified, a decree given in chambers only becomes enforceable when the time limit to bring the *reclamo* has expired, unless urgent reasons to grant provisional enforcement are shown (Article 741 CPC). As it was already pointed out, the judge's decisions, as a general rule, may always be revoked and modified even after the time to bring a reclamo has expired. This rule, however, only concerns *volontaria giurisdizione* decisions and not decisions where the court adjudicated proper disputed concerning substantive rights of the parties involved.

§6. Class Actions

361. Some forms of proceedings for the protection of collective or super-individual interests have existed in Italy for a few years now, with rather limited scopes of application and without a clear reform project[591] (e.g., in labour law, concerning the repression of anti-union conducts, actions for environmental protection and measures against the use of vexatious clauses in consumer contracts under Article 140 of the Consumer Code).

In recent years, however, the need was felt to introduce a new general collective remedy to safeguard situations where individual action could not be effective or where there are several subjects potentially involved in a juridical relationship. The CPC, of course, regulates proceedings where more than two parties are involved or where third parties join or are joined in. Such ordinary rules, however, may not handle in an efficient way proceedings where tens, if not hundreds or thousands, of parties are involved.

After long scientific discussions and political debate, a brand new 'action for collective redress' was introduced by Law No. 244 of 24 December 2007 in Article

591. M. Taruffo, 'La tutela collettiva nell'ordinamento italiano: lineamenti generali', RTDPC (2011): 103 et seq.; E. Silvestri, *Class Actions in Italy: Great Expectations, Big Disappointment*, in *Multi-party Redress Mechanisms in Europe: Squaking Mice?*, 198 et seq. (V. Harsagy & C.H. van Rhee eds, Intersentia 2014).

140*bis* of the Consumer Code.[592] This original remedy basically gave Associations and Committees, included in a special registry held by the Government, standing to bring collective proceedings for the protection of consumers' rights. The original version of Article 140*bis* was supposed to enter into force a few months after the approval of Law No. 244. However, mounting political and economic opposition to the new remedy led to an initial postponement of its entry into force. As a matter of fact, big firms, banks and insurance companies were particularly worried about the consequences that this collective redress could have on their business. In the end, the original version of Article 140*bis* never entered into force. Under a new Government, a completely new version of Article 140*bis* was drafted and introduced in the Consumer Code by Law No. 99 of 23 July 2009.[593]

The new provision finally entered into force on 1 January 2010 (to be further amended by Law No. 27 of 2012):[594] the remedy provided for therein is no longer an action for collective redress, governed by Associations and Committees, but a class action in the proper sense, which may be promoted by individual consumers. This new declaratory relief aims at protecting homogeneous individual rights of consumers and users as well as collective interests, as an alternative and non mandatory procedural device which may be used by individual members of the class, even through Associations or Committees he or she may be part of, in order to ascertain liabilities and obtain a judicial award for damages suffered and repayments. It is believed that the new provision does not create new rights but only provides a new remedy to protect existing rights and claims.

362. More specifically, Article 140*bis* applies to:

- contractual rights of a number of consumers and users who find themselves in a homogeneous situation vis-à-vis the same enterprise, including claims arising out of mass contracts and contracts based on standards terms and conditions drafted by one of the parties only;
- homogeneous claims arising from the purchase of a specified product, vis-à-vis the same producer, even when no direct contractual relation exists;

592. *See* R. Caponi, *The Collective Redress Action in the Italian Legal System*, ZZPInt (2009); G. Costantino, 'La tutela collettiva risarcitoria. Note a prima lettura dell'art. 140-bis del codice del consumo (2008)', in *Riflessioni sulla giustizia (in)civile (1995–2010)* (Turin: Giappichelli, 2011), 729; E. Silvestri, *supra*, 197.

593. *See* M. Bove, 'La trattazione nel processo di classe', <www.judicium.it>; R. Caponi, 'Italian "Class action" suits in the field of consumer protection: 2016 update', <https://papers.ssrn.com/sol3/papers.cfm?abstract_id=2796611>; G. Costantino, 'La tutela collettiva risarcitoria 2009: la tela di Penelope', FI (2009): V, 388 et seq.; G. Costantino, 'L'azione di classe ai sensi dell'art. 140-bis del codice del consumo. La sentenza di accoglimento. Il giudizio preventivo di ammissibilità', in *Riflessioni sulla giustizia (in)civile (1995–2010)* (Turin: Giappichelli, 2011), 743; Donzelli, L'azione di classe tra pronunce giurisprudenziali e recenti riforme legislative, Corr. giur. 13, 110; Giussani, L'azione di classe: aspetti processuali, Riv. trim. dir. proc. civ., 13, 341; Giussani, L'azione di classe: un primo bilancio, Riv. dir. proc. 12, 1177; S. Menchini, 'I primi provvedimenti relativi all'azione di classe dell'art. 140-bis cod. consumo', <www.judicium.it>, S. Menchini & A. Motto, *Art. 140 bis*, www.judicium.it; C. Punzi, 'L'azione di classe' a tutela dei consumatori e degli utenti', RDP (2010): 253 et seq.

594. R. Caponi, *supra*, 2.

– identical rights to restore damages deriving to the same consumers and users from unfair business practices and anti-competition behaviours.[595]

In other words, in the Italian class action, only individual rights having a homogeneous nature for all the members of a class of consumers or users may be protected, leaving collective or super-individual interests outside of the scope of application of Article 140*bis*. It is submitted that the expression 'homogeneous' should not be given a strict meaning in this context: in the lawmaker's intentions, as a matter of fact, what needs to be 'identical' is the source of the individual rights vested on the members of the class and the nature of the damages suffered by them.

363. In order for a class action to start, an individual consumer, eventually supported by an Association or a Committee, needs to file an application to the competent *Tribunale* to certify such action and open it to the other members of the class. Interestingly, in comparison with the original text of Article 140*bis*, the role of Associations has completely changed: in the former text, only certain certified and registered Associations had standing to represent a collectivity of consumers; under the new provisions, on the other hand, Associations may just act as procedural representatives of the consumer plaintiff. The latter, moreover, may also be supported by unregistered committees, possibly created especially with the intention to promote the class action at hand.

Only the proposing plaintiff becomes a party of the proceedings in the proper sense of the terms. Individual members of the class who join are not considered parties and do not enjoy procedural powers, nor may they appeal the final decision; however, once they have joined in, they are bound by the outcome of the proceedings.

364. The petition to have a class action certified must be brought before the ordinary *Tribunale* of the capital of the region where the seat of the defendant enterprise is located. In other words, for these rather peculiar actions, there is regional territorial competence: the rationale being that smaller *Tribunali* might not be in the position to handle such large cases. An exception is made for Italian smaller (and possibly less industrialized) regions: as a matter of fact, Valle d'Aosta cases go to the *Tribunale* of Turin, those of Trentino-Alto Adige and Friuli-Venezia Giulia to the *Tribunale* of Venice, those of Marche, Umbria, Abruzzo and Molise to the *Tribunale* of Rome and those of Basilicata and Calabria to the *Tribunale* of Naples.

The *Tribunale* always tries and decides the case with a panel of three judges.

365. The claim is proposed with a *citazione* (*see* at paragraph 217), which must be served not only on the defendant enterprise but also on the *pubblico ministero* (*see* at paragraphs 95 et seq.), who may take part in the preliminary phase of these proceedings, until the court decides whether to certify the class action or not.

---

595. *See* R. Caponi, *supra*, 3.

366. As a matter of fact, the proceedings are divided in two stages. At the first hearing, the court is called upon to decide on the issue of certification. If an affirmative decision is taken, the case goes on as a certified class action. Otherwise, the claim is dismissed. In other words, in the certification stage, the court verifies the 'seriousness' of the grounds on which the plaintiff wishes to propose his or her class action as well as the adequacy of the plaintiff to represent the whole class.

Paragraph 6 of Article 140*bis* sets the factors which the court is requested to check at this stage, whether:

– the claim is manifestly ungrounded;
– there is a conflict of interests between the plaintiff and the class;
– the individual rights are not homogeneous;
– the plaintiff is not in the position to adequately protect the interest of the class.

In other words, in this preliminary stage, the court must check both that the proposed class action is not prima facie groundless[596] and that the proposing plaintiff may appropriately represent the whole class of suitors. The appropriateness of the plaintiff might refer both to the existence of conflicting interests with other members of the class and to the 'strength' of the Association, committee and law firm supporting him or her.

Of course, the court must also check whether the claim is brought effectively by a consumer or a user. The notion of consumer is given by Article 3, letter (*c*) of the Consumer Code as the person who acts for a purpose which can be regarded as being outside his or her trade or profession. On the other hand, according to the same provision, a producer is the physical or legal person who acts for a purpose within his or her trade, commerce, art or profession or an intermediary of such person.

At the end of the preliminary hearing, the court decides with an order whether the claim may be certified as a class action. Such order may be appealed against (*reclamo*) before the Court of Appeal within thirty days of the day it was either communicated or notified to the parties.

367. If the claim is dismissed, the court awards costs against the losing plaintiff and may even order its decision to be properly advertised to let it be known to the general public.

If, on the other hand, the class action is certified, the court will establish the terms and conditions to advertise its decision to put the members of the class to timely join. Moreover, the order will define the nature of the individual rights which will be adjudicated upon in the class action, setting the standards which will be used to determine whether joining members will be accepted or not in the action.

A deadline (within 180 days of the time the decision is advertised to the public) is also fixed for class members to join in.

As it was mentioned above, in this model of class action, only the promoting plaintiff is considered a party to the proceedings. To join, members do not need to

596. *See* A. Giussani, 'La prima "uscita" della class action all'italiana soffocata da meccanismi preclusivi penalizzanti', GD 27 (2010): 16; *App.* Turin 27 Oct. 2010, *ord.*, GD 47 (2010): 60.

instruct lawyers, and they may also delegate the plaintiff to file their applications to join the class. By joining, they are not empowered to perform any procedural activity, but they will be bound by the court's final decision. On the other hand, no other party may join the action in the traditional sense of the term (*see* at paragraph 217).

As a matter of fact, the Italian class action is based on an opt-in system.[597] By joining the class action, members waive their right to bring individual claims for the case cause of action. Only joining members will be bound by the decision, while subjects vested with the same rights will be in the position to promote individual claims even if the class action is finally rejected. However, after the time limit for joining as member of the original class action has expired, no further class action may be proposed concerning the same factual situation vis-à-vis the same producer. Any subsequent class action, as a matter of fact, will be merged with the one previously filed.

Moreover, any waiver of settlement between the parties will bind only joining class member who expressly gave their consent to them. In other words, agreements in the course of the proceedings require another opt-in from the members of the class.

368. In the order which certifies the class action, the *Tribunale* also plans the course of the proceedings, taking into consideration the adversary principle and a fair, efficient and expeditious administration of the action. In particular, the schedule of the evidence-gathering phase is set and any other procedural issue is ruled upon, without any unnecessary formalities.

If the claim is finally allowed, the *Tribunale*, in its judgment, either directly awards the sums which are due to the members of the class or sets a homogeneous standard for awarding such sums.

The decision becomes enforceable 180 days after its publication. If sums are paid within this time limit, no accessory of other sum has to be paid on top of the amount awarded by the court.

The judgment may be appealed against, and the producer may apply for a stay of the enforceability of the decision. In deciding whether to grant such a stay, the Court of Appeal has to consider the global amount awarded against the producer, the number of claimants and the hardship in recovering the sum paid, should the appeal be allowed.

So far, only a few claims have been brought to have a class action certified[598] and even less have been certified and allowed,[599] leading commentators to say that the situation in Italy concerning collective redress is rather disappointing.[600]

597. R. Caponi, *supra*, 8.
598. *See Trib.* Turin 27 May 2010, *ord.*
599. *Trib.* Milan 20 Dec. 2010, *ord.*; *Trib.* Naples 18 Feb. 2013, n. 2195, GD 12 (2013): 16; *Trib.* Rome 4 Mar. 2013 (GM) (2013): 2326.
600. *See* E. Silvestri, *supra*, 205; R. Caponi, *supra*, 9.

Chapter 2. Other Particular Proceedings

§1. INTRODUCTION

369. Several other particular proceedings are provided for in the code of civil procedure for rather specific disputes and situations, which is impossible to examine here in full. Some of them, however, deserve at least a short mention.

Special procedures are provided for in matter of capacity and personal status. First of all, a specific procedure is provided to ascertain that somebody is absent or to be presumed dead. Of course, proceedings of this kind are not used very often any longer. As a matter of fact, in the past, they were mostly referred to in relation to soldiers who went missing in action during a war or to emigrants whose tracks had been lost to parents and relatives. A declaration of absence is a precondition to declare that somebody has to be presumed dead.

In this procedural model, a *ricorso* is filed in the court, and evidence is gathered. In the case of absent persons, the court may provisionally put the heirs into possession of the absentee's assets.

As concerns presumed death, the starting of the proceedings must be advertised in the State's official journal (*Gazzetta ufficiale*) and two other newspapers, with a public invitation to supply information about the missing person. Also the judgment that declares that a person is to be presumed death must be published in the *Gazzetta ufficiale* and two newspapers.

370. Mention can also be made to interdiction and incapacity proceedings and to proceedings which aim at appointing an administrator for someone who is unable to take care of his or her own business (*amministratore di sostegno*).[601] This last remedy is very popular in Italy today. As a matter of fact, interdiction tends to be used only in the most extreme of cases. For most types of physical or mental disabilities, the less invasive and more respectful of the person's dignity *amministrazione di sostegno* is preferred.

These proceedings are begun by way of *ricorso* to the *Tribunale* of the place where the interested person resides. At the start of the proceedings, the court can appoint a provisional guardian.

The *pubblico ministero* must always take part in the procedure, and the final decision may be revoked in compliance with the CC rules on interdiction, incapacity and *amministratore di sostegno*.

Other provisions are set for the procedures related to the opening of inheritances[602] and for redeeming mortgages.[603]

371. Procedures for dividing common properties and assets are also rather relevant.[604] Proceedings must be brought by or against all the common owners of the

601. *See* E. Vullo, *Procedimenti in materia di famiglia e di stato delle persone*, *supra*, 452 et seq.
602. Articles 747 et seq. CPC.
603. Articles 792 et seq. CPC.
604. Articles 784 et seq. CPC.

assets to be divided (*litisconsorzio necessario*), so that, should any necessary party not be summoned, Article 102 CPC applies.

If the right to divide the assets is not in dispute, the judge decides upon it with an order (*ordinanza*); otherwise, ordinary ascertainment proceedings take place.

In order to divide common properties, it is usually necessary to sell the assets[605] (and then divide the proceeds *pro quota* among the co-owners). The judge may delegate such activities to a notary, and the rules on judicial sales of seized goods apply. In order to ascertain the value of the assets, an expert is usually appointed, who delivers a written report.

After the assets have been sold, the judge (or the notary) prepares a plan to distribute the collected money between the parties (*progetto di divisione*). Any dispute concerning this plan is solved with a judgment. If no dispute arises, the judge renders the plan operative with an order.

DL No. 69 of 21 June 2013, implemented by Law No. 98 of 9 August 2013, introduced a new Article 791*bis* CPC which allows the filing of a joint petition to divide a common property. The peculiarity of this new procedure is that it starts before a judge but it is then assigned to and governed by a court-appointed notary public or lawyer, under judicial supervision. The scope of application and the procedural mechanisms of this new device are somehow obscure and so far no case law about it is reported. Arguably it will not be extensively used.[606]

§2. Particular Summary Proceedings

I. Summary Proceedings with Documentary Evidence (*Decreto Ingiuntivo*)

372. The unreasonable length of civil proceedings is notorious.[607] It takes years before a judgment is granted, and this of course is rather frustrating for the party looking for a remedy. The lawmaker therefore tries to provide certain special tools and proceedings to offer certain categories of plaintiff faster tracks to obtain a decision which may then be used as an enforcement title (*see* paragraph 407). In particular, some special summary proceedings exist which aim at giving a more efficient and effective alternative to ordinary proceedings in the protection of certain rights. Arguably, the most often used of them is the procedure to obtain an order for payment (*procedimento per decreto ingiuntivo*).

This procedural model presents several peculiarities: first of all, it is structured in two separate phases: only the first of them is always present, while the second is merely possible. In the first phase, moreover, the judge issues an order for payment on a debtor on the basis of a summary investigation of documentary evidence coming from just the applying creditor. In other words, the order for payment is issued ex parte (*inaudita altera parte*). The adversary principle, however, is not violated,

605. An alternative would be for one of the co-owners to buy the other co-owners' portions or for the portions to be physically separated.

606. *See* G. Finocchiaro, 'Divisione a domanda congiunta passa al notaio', GD 28 (2013): 84.

607. *See* B. Capponi, *Il procedimento di ingiunzione* (Bologna: Zanichelli, 2005); G. Arieta, 'Le tutele sommarie. I procedimenti per decreto ingiuntivo e per convalida di sfratto. I procedimenti possessori', in *Trattato di diritto processuale civile*, 2nd edn, vol. X (Padua: Cedam, 2011), 31 et seq.

since the debtor always has the chance to attack the order for payment by starting ordinary proceedings before the judge which issued the order itself.

373. The so-called *procedimento monitorio* is governed by Articles 633 et seq. CPC. Such remedy may be used to order a debtor either to pay a sum of money of a specific amount or to deliver a specified quantity of goods or a specific moveable goods.

Until recently, this remedy could not be obtained if the payment order had to be served abroad:[608] this outdated limitation, however, has finally been removed by *DLGS* No. 231 of 9 October 2002.

A fundamental requirement that needs to be complied with in this procedural model is a documentary evidence (*prova scritta*) which the creditor must file in order to prove his or her claim is prima facie well-grounded. The mere existence of this *prova scritta* justifies the release of the judge's order for payment ex parte. On the other hand, if no documentary evidence is available, the creditor may not rely on this remedy. From this point of view, in Italy, creditors may find convenient to apply Regulation No. 1896 of 2006 on the so-called European order for payment, which only requires the applicant to 'describe' any evidence he or she might be able to use, should the debtor oppose the claim.

Article 634 CPC gives a very broad definition of documentary evidence in this context.[609] In general, it can be said that a larger range of documents may be used here to support the creditor's claim than in ordinary proceedings. To this regard, it must be considered that, in the ex parte phase of the proceedings, the creditor is not required to give full evidence as to the actual existence of his or her credit. As a matter of fact, a lower evidentiary standard is applied at this point. This procedural advantage for the creditor, however, will last until the debtor raises a formal opposition to the order for payment: when this happens, the ordinary burden of the proof and evidentiary standards will apply.

In practice, the creditor may rely on documents of various origin and reliability level. Of course, documents signed or released by the debtor himself or herself have a stronger strength. However, also documents formed by a third person[610] or by the creditor himself or herself can be used here. In particular, as concerns commercial and professional[611] credits, the creditor may rely on an invoice he or she has himself or herself released to the debtor, as long as his or her business books are regularly kept and a certified extract of those books are filed with the application.

Interestingly, this procedure may also be used by solicitors, public notaries and other professionals belonging to certified Associations in order to obtain payment of their fees. For these categories of professionals, the CPC expressly states that the creditors may rely on the invoices they have formed themselves, following applicable tariffs established by statute. The relevant Associations, then, has to certify

608. *See* P. Biavati, 'L'art. 633, ultimo comma, c.p.c. è duro a morire', RTDPC (2000): 637.
609. *See* Conte, 'La prova nel procedimento per decreto ingiuntivo e nell'istanza di ingiunzione *ex* Art. 186*ter*', RDP (1999): 468.
610. *See Trib.* Perugia 5 Feb. 1996, GM, 1996, 908.
611. *See* Art. 634 (2) as revised by Art. 15 of Law No. 81 of 22 May 2017.

that the sums of money so requested are in compliance with such professional tariffs. For example, a lawyer will submit his or her own invoices to the Bar Association he or she is registered with to have it 'opinata' (certified). Such certification only concerns the correspondence between the professional activities which the lawyer claims to have performed and the values set by the tariffs for such activities. In other words, there is no control, at this stage, as to the 'merits' of the lawyer's performance. After the repealing of professional tariffs in 2012 (*see* paragraph 119), however, some claim that this provision of the code has tacitly been repealed and that a lawyer now, in order to obtain an injunction for payment, should file a written contract with his client.[612] The new professional law of 2012 (*see* paragraph 113) however, at Article 29, litt. (*l*), lists, among the prerogative and duties of the local Bar Association, the task to express opinions about a lawyer's compensation, which leads to believe that Article 633(1) No. 3 CPC is still in force though it must be read as referring not to the repealed tariff system but on the new 'compensation' standards set by the Ministry of Justice in 2012 and in 2014 (*see* paragraph 119).

374. The main special feature of these proceedings is that the first (and most often only) part of the procedure is ex parte. The creditor files a *ricorso* into the competent court (ordinary rules on matter, value and territorial competence apply). The judge then examines the documents (*prova scritta*) attached to the petition and, if the conditions set by the code appear to have been complied with, he or she immediately orders, with a *decreto ingiuntivo* (payment order), the debtor to pay or deliver to the creditor the sum or the goods requested, plus the legal costs of the ex parte proceedings.

The order is then served, together with the original *ricorso*, on the debtor, who now has the choice to either pay the sum or deliver the asset(s) to the creditor within forty days of service or to contest the order, by bringing opposition proceedings before the same court which delivered it, also within forty days of service. In other words, the adversary principle may be implemented after the order has been released, but the burden to re-establish the ordinary course of the proceedings is on the debtor, that is, on the party which would normally be involved in the proceedings as the defendant. Moreover, for the debtor, it is not enough to merely state that he or she opposes the order released against him or her: on the contrary, specific reasons must be given. This 'inversion' of the ordinary procedural roles is supposed to reduce the percentage of payment orders being opposed and to limit such oppositions to just the more 'serious' ones. From this point of view, the rules of the CPC we are examining here make life for a debtor much harder than under Regulation No. 1896 of 2006, which enable the debtor to just send back to the court a form where he or she has stated that he or she opposes the order for payment, with no need to give any reason for it. This might explain why, so far, the European order for payment is not applied for very often in Italy.

612. *See*, e.g., *Trib.* Varese 11 Oct. 2012, decree, www.altalex.com.

375. If no opposition is timely raised, the proceedings end: the order becomes enforceable and can no longer be revoked. As a matter of fact, the claim of the creditor is arguably covered by res judicata in any subsequent proceedings.[613]

The rationale behind this procedure is that, usually, the credit is not contested by the debtor, who only does not or cannot pay, so that, in the vast majority of cases, no opposition against the payment order is raised and the proceedings stop at ex parte phase with obvious advantages in terms of reduced time, costs and congestion of the courts.

376. Usually, the order can only be enforced after the forty days delay, to raise the opposition, has expired.[614]

The law, however, provides for situations where the payment order may be issued as immediately enforceable, even while the time limit to eventually raise an opposition is still running. In this way, the creditor is entitled to start enforcement proceedings even while an opposition is pending. Such enforceability of the order, however, is merely provisional (*provvisoria esecutorietà*), since it may still be revoked in the course or at the end of opposition proceedings (should they ever be started).

According to Article 642 CPC, the court must declare a payment order to be immediately enforceable (*provvisoriamente esecutivo*) when the documentary evidence on which the creditor relies is particularly cogent (a check, a promissory note or a notary deed).

A discretionary power to grant immediate enforcement of the order also exists when the risk of a serious damage is alleged and shown by the creditor or when the creditor files a document written or signed by the debtor which shows a prima facie case as to the claim being well-grounded:[615] For example, an e-mail or a fax where the debtor asks the creditor to pay his or her debt in instalments rather than as a lump sum.

377. Opposition proceedings substantially are ordinary ascertainment proceedings, in which the existence of the creditor's claim has to be verified (along with any eventual counter-claim raised by the debtor). However, since the ordinary roles are reversed here, the substantial debtor plays the role of the plaintiff (*opponente*) and the substantial creditor that of the defendant (*opposto*).

This inversion of procedural roles, however, does not go as far as to invert the ordinary burden of the proof, which still primarily rests on the creditor who must prove the existence of his or her claim.

It should be reminded here that in ex parte phase of the proceedings, the creditor is entitled to rely on a wider range of documentary evidence than it would be considered proper evidence in ordinary proceedings. At this stage, therefore, the creditor might find himself or herself in the position to have to support the documents filed with the originating petition with proper evidence (either written or oral):[616]

613. *See Cass.* 11 Jun. 1998, n. 5801, GC, 1999, I, 189.

614. Such time limit, however, may be reduced by court's decree upon the creditor's application.

615. Article 642(2) CPC as revised in 2005.

616. *See* Arts 2709 et seq. CC.

failing to do so might lead to his or her claim being found ungrounded and the payment order revoked.

On the other hand, if the debtor does not deny the existence of the original credit, but argues that the creditor may no longer claim it (e.g., because of a time-bar), the burden of the proof switches on the opponent, in compliance with the ordinary rules.

378. Raising an opposition is not usually enough for the plaintiff debtor to avoid interim compliance with the court's order. As a matter of fact, at the first hearing, the court will (discretionally) grant a provisional *exequatur* to the ex parte order, unless the opposition is based on some documentary evidence as well, or if serious reasons are shown to not make the order provisionally enforceable. In other words, before bringing an opposition, a debtor always has to balance his or her chances of avoiding such a provisional *exequatur* from being issued. Article 648(1) CPC has recently been revised,[617] and now the judge's provisional *exequatur* may also concern a non-contested fraction of the original claim (*esecuzione provvisoria parziale*).

If the order was originally granted the provisional status of enforcement title (*see supra*, paragraph 376), at the beginning of opposition proceedings, the debtor may apply for that enforceability to be stayed, always relying on some documentary evidence or strong reasons to do so.

The court decides on the opposition with a judgment which can either confirm or revoke the order and which shall be subject to all the ordinary forms of appeals. The judge's decision may also allow the creditor's claim for a smaller amount than originally granted: when this is the case, the order for payment is anyway always revoked. Interestingly, if this happens after enforcement proceedings have been started against the debtor upon the order's provisional enforceability, the enforcement procedure will not be struck out, but it will maintain its effects only in relation to the claim as determined in the final judgment. For example, this might imply that the creditor will have to restitute part of the money he or she was originally awarded after the selling of the debtor's assets.

II. Eviction Proceedings (*Convalida di Licenza o Sfratto*)

379. In relation to lease contracts, special proceedings exist to provide the lessor with an order to the lessee to release an immovable property, with as little expenses and delay as possible.[618]

Eviction proceedings can be started:

(a) when the contract has expired and the tenant will not voluntarily release the estate;
(b) when the tenant is in default of payment of the rent; or

617. By DLGS No. 231 of 2002; *see* M. Zoppellari, 'Le norme processuali contenute nel d. lgs. 9 ottobre 2002, n. 231 ed il nuovo Art. 648 c.p.c.', <www.judicium.it>.

618. *See* R. Frasca, *Il procedimento per convalida di sfratto* (Turin: Utet, 2001); G. Arieta, *supra*, 295 et seq.

(c) when the contract has not yet expired but the lessor wants to obtain an eviction order for the time the lease ends (*condanna in futuro*).

380. These proceedings begin with a *citazione* served by the lessor on the tenant, fixing a hearing before the *Tribunale* of the place where the estate is located.

If the tenant does not appear at the hearing or if he or she appears but does not raise an opposition, an eviction order is immediately granted (*ordinanza di convalida di licenza o di sfratto*), fixing the date when the tenant must release the property.[619]

381. If an opposition is raised by the tenant,[620] cognition proceedings start to solve the dispute and decide the merits of the case.

To grant a speedy decision, Article 447*bis* CPC provides for the application of special procedural rules (*rito locatizio*), loosely based on those applied to labour proceedings (*see supra*, paragraphs 329 et seq.). The final judgment is subject to the ordinary appeals.

Unless the opposition is based on some documentary evidence, however, at the first hearing the judge will provisionally order the release of the estate (in order to discourage patently unfounded oppositions).

§3. Interim Relief Measures (*Provvedimenti Cautelari*)

382. Whenever the length of ordinary cognition proceedings endangers the party's chances to enforce the judgment against his or her counterpart or to obtain an effective safeguard and restoration of his or her rights, interim measures can be granted by the court to prevent the parties' rights from being irreparably harmed in the course of the proceedings on the merits.[621]

In the context of contemporary civil proceedings, interim relief is considered an integral component of the right of action to grant the efficient adjudication of a party's claim.

Interim measures can have either conservative or anticipatory effects. Attachment of the debtor's properties is a typical conservatory measure (*sequestro conservativo*), in the sense that it freezes the debtor's assets so that, should the alleged creditor win the case, the latter shall have the chance to enforce the judgment on the attached goods. On the other hand, the so-called urgent measures (*provvedimenti d'urgenza*) typically have anticipatory effects, since, in compliance with Article 700

619. For a tenant in default of payment, it is always possible to pay the rent due in a time limit fixed by the court.

620. For example, contesting to be in default or arguing that the expiration date of the contract is different than the one indicated by the lessor.

621. *See* C. Rasia, *Provisional Remedies in Italian Law System*, in *Provisional Measures in Italian and Greek Procedural Law* 13 (K. Makridou & G. Diamantopoulos eds, Sakkoulas Publications 2016); M.A. Lupoi, *Nowhere Fast? Shortcuts to Judgment in Recent Italian Procedural Legislation*, in *Ways of Implementation of the Right to Civil Proceedings Within a Reasonable Time* 301 (Vilnius Universitetas 2016).

CPC, the court can order any interim measure which it deems necessary to provisionally assure the effects of the judgment on the merits. In any case, interim measures should never have irreparable effects.

383. In Italy, interim measures (*provvedimenti cautelari*) have traditionally been characterized by a strict link of instrumentality vis-à-vis ordinary proceedings on the merits of the petitioner's right; in other words, no interim remedy could exist without pending (or soon to be pending) ordinary proceedings.

The reform of 2005, however, provided that urgent measures ordered in compliance with Article 700 CPC and any other interim measure having anticipatory effects (*see supra*, paragraph 382) are now less strictly connected to the proceedings on the merits, both when they are rendered before the start of those proceedings, and when the latter are eventually discontinued (*see infra*, paragraph 389).

In any case, the law makes it clear that interim measures, whichever their effects may be, are always liable to be either confirmed or revoked by a judgment on the merits: therefore, they can always have provisional effects only and never become binding, under the res judicata doctrine.[622]

384. Two conditions must exist before interim remedy can be granted:

(1) the applicant must show a prima facie case as to the existence of his or her right (*fumus boni iuris*), that is, a good arguable case that his or her right is likely to exist on the basis of summary evidence;
(2) the plaintiff must also prove that a serious damage will be caused to his or her right should the measure not be granted by the court (*periculum in mora*).

At this stage, since the order must be allowed or denied with haste, the court is not in a position to open an ordinary evidence-gathering phase on the substance of the applicant's claim. Therefore, the court takes a summary decision, usually on the face of documents exhibited by the parties or on some information from third parties.[623]

385. It is possible to apply for interim relief either before the start (*ante causam*) or in the course of the proceedings on the merits, but should the latter not be timely started or end without a decision on the substance, the interim measure will lose any effect. An exception, however, as we have seen, is now made for orders given under Article 700 CPC and for any measure having anticipatory effects, which no longer require proceedings on the merits to be started within a fixed deadline when they are rendered *ante causam* and which always survive the discontinuation of the proceedings on the merits.

Any interim measure, however, is immediately struck out if proceedings on the merits end with a judgment denying the claim of the party who applied for it.

622. *See* Art. 669*octies*(6) and (8) CPC.

623. *See* Lombardo, 'Natura e caratteri dell'istruzione probatoria nel processo cautelare', RDP (2001): 464.

386. Law No. 353 of 1990 introduced a set of comprehensive common rules for all interim measures contained in the code of civil procedure and in the other statutes (Articles 669*bis* et seq. CPC: the so-called *rito cautelare uniforme*).[624] As a matter of fact, this is arguably the most successful part of the whole reform of 1990.

In Articles 669*bis* et seq. CPC, the basic characteristics of interim remedies are highlighted, in particular their instrumental nature vis-à-vis proceedings on the merits, the provisional nature of the court's orders and the summariness of the court's ascertainment of the relevant facts.

From the procedural point of view, proceedings for interim measures are incidents of the proceedings on the merits.

387. The petition for interim relief takes the form of a *ricorso* filed in the competent court, that is, the same court as that which decides on the merits of the dispute (exception: justices of the peace can never grant interim measures, and reference is then made to the *Tribunale*). Moreover, Italian judges can always grant provisional remedies which have to be enforced within the national territory, even when a foreign court has jurisdiction on the merits of the case.

If the case falls to be decided by way of *arbitrato rituale* or *irrituale* (*see infra*, paragraphs 432 et seq.), interim measures can be granted by the court that would otherwise have competence to decide the merits of the case.[625] The only exception to this general rule is provided by Article 35(5) of DLGS 5/2003, which enables the parties to grant to the arbitrators (in an arbitration over a company dispute) the power to stay any shareholders' deliberation appealed before them.[626]

388. The originating *ricorso*[627] is filed in the court first; apart from the usual elements any judicial petition must contain, if the *ricorso* is filed before the start of proceedings on the merits, it must also contain a concise exposition of the facts of the case and of the claim on which the future action on the merits shall be based. Failing that, the petition will be stricken out.

After the *ricorso* is filed, the president of the court appoints a judge (*giudice designato*) to examine the petition; the latter will fix a hearing for the parties to appear before him or her. The judge's decree and the *ricorso* are then served on the defendant, who will have the chance to deposit a written defence, exposing his or her own reasons to the court.

At the hearing, only summary information should be gathered by the court but it is not unusual for the judge to appoint an expert to investigate a situation.[628]

---

624. *See* G. Finocchiaro, 'Sul nuovo procedimento cautelare', RDP (1995): 855.
625. *See* A. Carlevaris, *La tutela cautelare nell'arbitrato internazionale* (Padua: Cedam, 2006), 251 et seq.
626. M. Maffuccini, 'Provvedimenti cautelari ed arbitrato: appunti sull'art. 35, 5° comma, D. Lgs. 17 febbraio 2003, n. 5', GI (2004): 2215.
627. L. Querzola, 'Il contenuto del ricorso cautelare: brevi spunti tratti dalla giurisprudenza successiva alla riforma', RTDPC (2000): 647.
628. For example, when the measure refers to some working construction which has to be stopped for safety reasons.

The decision (which allows or denies the remedy sought by the applicant) takes the form of an *ordinanza*, that is, a provisional decision which cannot become res judicata and which should contain a concise reasoning.

389. If an interim measure is allowed when no proceedings on the substance of the claim are pending, the applicant is under a burden to start those proceedings within a sixty day time limit.[629] If he or she does not timely comply with such requirement, the measure will become ineffective. No time limit, however, is any longer set for urgent measures taken under Article 700 CPC and for other orders having anticipatory effects.

390. In exceptional cases, when the plaintiff shows that the defendant's appearance before the judge could render the measure ineffective,[630] the petition can be allowed ex parte, with a decree which can be enforced even without the counterpart being aware of its existence.

Subsequently, the *ricorso* and the decree are served on the defendant and a hearing will take place. At the end of the discussion, the judge will confirm, modify or revoke his or her earlier decree with an *ordinanza*.

391. If the plaintiff's *ricorso* is not allowed on competence grounds, he or she is free to start fresh proceedings again, even before the same court; if, on the other hand, the petition has been found ungrounded, it can be filed again only on new grounds, facts and reasons.

392. Orders granting or denying interim relief can be appealed within fifteen days of their communication to the parties[631] by means of *reclamo* to a three-judge panel, normally within the same court.[632] The panel can confirm, modify or revoke the order, with another order which is not subject to a further appeal to a superior judge.

393. When factual or legal circumstances change after the interim measure has been granted and *reclamo* may no longer be presented, a petition may be filed to the trial judge to have the original order either modified or revoked (Article 669*decies* CPC).

394. Interim orders concerning the delivery of goods, the release of an asset or (non) performance of an action are enforced under the supervision of the rendering judge; those concerning sums of money are enforced in compliance with the rules on attachment of the debtor's assets.[633]

---

629. Volpe, 'Il passaggio dal procedimento cautelare *ante causam* al giudizio di merito', FI (1995): I, 2621; M.A. Lupoi, *supra*, c01.
630. For example, a request to freeze the defendant's bank accounts.
631. *See* Art. 669*terdecies*(1) CPC as revised in 2005.
632. Bianchi, 'Individuazione del giudice del reclamo contro il provvedimento cautelare emanato dal tribunale in composizione collegiale', RDP (1996): 874.
633. Article 669*duodecies* CPC; *see* E. Vullo, *L'attuazione dei provvedimenti cautelari* (Turin: Giappichelli, 2001).

395. An interim measure may become ineffective for a number of reasons,[634] most notably when the instrumentality link between the provisional measure having conservative effects and the dispute on the merits is broken, that is, if proceedings on the merits are not timely started or are subsequently discontinued, or if a judgment is rendered which denies the petitioner's claim. This last case also concerns orders having anticipatory effects.

396. While some particular interim measures are disciplined in laws and statutes outside the code,[635] the code of civil procedure lists several 'general' interim remedies, as well as some 'specific' ones.

Among general interim measures, it is worth mentioning seizures (*sequestri*) (*see infra*, paragraphs 398 et seq.) and *provvedimenti d'urgenza* (urgent measures) (Article 700 CPC),[636] that is, orders which can be released when no other typical interim remedy can be invoked to anticipate the effects of the final judgment, as long as some imminent and irreparable harm to the petitioner's right is shown.

397. More specific measures are provided to safeguard rights in rem from dangerous new workings in a neighbour's property (*denunce di nuova opera*)[637] or some feared damage from a neighbour's property[638] (*denunce di danno temuto*).[639]

Also, when someone has been forcefully or surreptitiously deprived of possession of a good, an application can be filed to restore the situation (*provvedimenti possessori*).[640]

The provisions contained in the code of civil procedure are rather scanty, and they make reference to the CC rules, which deal with property and actions for the safeguard of property and other rights in rem, as concerns the conditions and cases when such remedies may be invoked.

In particular, proceedings for the safeguard of possession of a good have been revised in 2005.[641] Article 703 CPC now makes it clear that this form of relief may be applied for by filing a *ricorso* in the competent court. At the end of summary proceedings, an order will be released, which will then be subject to a *reclamo* according to Article 669*terdecies* CPC (*see supra*, paragraph 392). At this point, proceedings on the merits will be started only if any interested party so requires by filing an application in court within sixty days from the communication of the interim order. Otherwise, the latter will maintain its validity, notwithstanding the lack of proceedings on the merits.

634. *See* Art. 669*novies* CPC.
635. For example, as concerns patents and copyright disputes or bankruptcy.
636. *See* E.A. Dini, G. Mammone, *I provvedimenti d'urgenza*, 7th edn (Milan: Giuffrè, 1997).
637. For example, a house built on land which is liable to slide down on the neighbouring property.
638. For example, a sick tree which threatens to fall to the ground.
639. Articles 688 et seq. CPC.
640. Articles 703 et seq. CPC. *See* G. Arieta, *supra*, 409 et seq.
641. G. Della Pietra, 'L'imparzialità del giudice civile nel riflesso del novellato procedimento possessorio', RTDPC (2007): 461; P.G. Demarchi, *Il nuovo rito civile. II. Il giudizio di cassazione e i provvedimenti speciali* (Milan: Giuffrè, 2006); V. Proto, 'La riforma del procedimento possessorio', GC (2007): II, 83.

Part IX. Seizure for Security and Enforcement of Judgments

Chapter 1. Seizure for Security

398. Seizure for security is one of the interim measures provided for by the Italian code of civil procedure.[642] Three forms of seizure are provided therein.

399. A special type of seizure (*sequestro liberatorio*, Articles 687 et seq.) concerns sums of money which the debtor requires to be posted under the custody of the court if the obligation to pay or the ways the obligation falls to be performed are in dispute, when the debtor does not want to suffer from the additional penalties of being in default of payment provided for by the CC (*mora del debitore*).[643]

400. Sequestro giudiziario (judiciary seizure) can be granted:

(a) in litigation concerning property rights or possession of an asset, when it is appropriate to seize the asset in dispute to guard and manage it, care of a keeper appointed by the court (Article 670, No. 1 CPC); this kind of seizure is instrumental to the fruitful enforcement of the final decision on the *rem* (*esecuzione in forma specifica, see infra* paragraph 418);[644] or
(b) in the course of the evidence-gathering phase, to seize documents which a party demands the other party to deposit in court, when such right of exhibition is contested, to prevent those documents from being (maliciously or not) destroyed or anyway lost (Article 670, No. 2 CPC).

401. Proper seizure for security is provided for by Articles 671 et seq. CPC (*sequestro conservativo*). Whenever it is feared that a debtor might fraudulently dispose of his or her assets against his or her creditors, the court, on the party's application, may seize the debtor's asset, to secure the fruitful enforcement of the future judgment against the debtor (*esecuzione in forma generica*).

642. *See* M. Cantillo & F. Santangeli, *Il sequestro nel processo civile* (Milan: Giuffrè, 2003); F. Verde, *Il sequestro nel diritto processuale civile*, 3rd edn (Padua: Cedam, 2006).
643. G.N. Nardo, 'Il sequestro speciale c.d. liberatorio', in *Studi in memoria di Angelo Bonsignori* (Milan: Giuffrè, 2004), tome I, 461.
644. Cfr R. Caponi, *Il sequestro giudiziario di beni nel processo civile. Profilo storico-sistematico* (Milan: Giuffrè, 2000).

The difference with *sequestro giudiziario* is that, here, there is no correspondence of the object of the main action with the assets being seized, which are considered only in relation to their monetary value, as a form of preventive attachment (*pignoramento anticipato*).

As a matter of fact, if the final judgment allows the petitioner's claim, seizure automatically turns into attachment, and the seized goods can be sold directly.[645]

402. Seizure proceedings follow the common rules on interim relief seen *supra* paragraphs 382 et seq.

A seizure order, if granted, must be enforced as per Articles 677 et seq. CPC within thirty days, or it will become ineffective.[646]

403. When *sequestro giudiziario* is allowed, a guardian is appointed by the court to manage and guard the seized goods (Article 676 CPC).

404. When perishable goods are seized, the court, on a party's motion, may order the goods to be sold, and the sale price is seized instead (Article 685 CPC).

645. *See* M. Vellani, *La conversione del sequestro conservativo in pignoramento* (Milan: Giuffrè, 1955).
646. B. Brunelli, 'Note sull'esecuzione del sequestro', RTDPC (1997), 119.

Chapter 2. Enforcement of Judgments

§1. Enforcement of Domestic Judgments

I. Proceedings

405. Civil enforcement in Italy is administered and controlled both by the courts and by civil servants performing as enforcing officers (*Ufficiali giudiziari*), at the local level:[647] every *Tribunale* has a *Giudice dell'esecuzione* (enforcement judge) who presides over the various stages of the enforcement proceedings.

On the other hand, the *Ufficiali giudiziari*, perform some very important tasks, taking care of the seizure activities as concerns enforcement of money credits and of the other functions necessary to enforce specific performance of judicial orders (e.g., when a tenant has to be evicted from a flat or a movable good returned to its owner). To become an *Ufficiale giudiziario*, a law degree is required and a State exam has to be passed.

In recent years, however, it is possible for the *Giudice dell'esecuzione* to delegate certain activities (in particular, as regards the selling of attached assets) to professionals outside of the judicial apparatus (mainly notaries public, but also lawyers and accountants). Certain investigating powers have also been given directly to the creditors.

The code of civil procedure contains the main rules for the basic forms of civil enforcement. Specific regulations, moreover, are provided for in the CC (e.g., as concerns attachment of shareholding)[648] and in other pieces of legislation (e.g., as concerns enforcement against public administrative bodies, which is subject to several limitations). Arguably, the Italian law on enforcement is too detailed and overly complicated to be effective and manageable.[649]

Apart from very limited forms of self-protection of legal rights accorded by legislation (e.g., the possibility to have assets taken into pawn sold with no need for prior judicial proceedings), no private enforcement of civil claims is allowed. Some agencies, recovering credits for public bodies or entities, however, enjoy special enforcing powers (e.g., they may order a debtor's debtor to directly pay them the money due to the former with no need for a specific judicial order).

Traditionally, enforcement of civil claims in Italy has been particularly problematic. Over time, the enforcement system originally drafted in 1940 had become inadequate to satisfy the creditor's rights timely and effectively, also taking into consideration the many costs that the applying creditor must anticipate, often with no real chance to be paid back by the debtor. Moreover, in Italy, there are no effective civil or criminal sanctions for a debtor who does not pay his or her creditors, and experience shows that it is very easy indeed to elude seizure or attachment proceedings.

---

647. E. Silvestri, '*The Devil is in the Details: Remarks on Italian Enforcement Procedures*', in *Enforcement and enforceability. Tradition and reform*, 209 (C.H. Van Rhee & A. Uzelac eds., Intersentia 2010).
648. *See* M.P. Gasperini, *Pignoramento e sequestro di partecipazioni sociali* (Turin: Utet, 2007).
649. *See* E. Silvestri, *supra*, 207 et seq.

To try and improve on this quite dramatic situation, in the years 2005–2006, the rules of the CPC concerning the enforcement of domestic judgments (and of enforcement orders in general) have been extensively revised and innovated,[650] with mixed results. The rules on enforcement proceedings have subsequently been subject to restyling on several occasions, more or less on a yearly basis, in a continuous struggle to make them more efficient and effective.[651]

One of the main outcomes of this wave of reforms is that enforcement proceedings are now heavily influenced by e-technology and digitalization. For example, all of the creditor's claims and requests to the *Giudice dell'esecuzione* are now electronically filed, through the console which has been created in the context of the so-called *processo civile telematico*. Most activities related to the selling of the attached assets are now also performed online. Moreover, DL No. 59 of 2016, converted into Law No. 119 of 2016,[652] at Article 3, established an electronic register of enforcement proceedings over immoveable assets as well as insolvency proceedings in general. This register will be accessible by the Bank of Italy which is enabled to use the information found therein in relation to its surveillance functions.

406. Enforcement proceedings are brought, upon a creditor's petition, when a debtor does not voluntary complies with an obligation carried in an enforceable title.

The enforcement system is centred on the activities of the bailiff, while the judge normally plays a quasi-administrative role, supervising the procedure.

In this area of civil procedure, the adversary system is somewhat toned down: after all, one of the parties, that is the debtor, is by definition in a passive position vis-à-vis the creditor's prima facie right to have his or her credit coercibly enforced: the enforcing mechanisms will proceed step after step, as long as the necessary impulses are given by the creditor, with no possibility for the debtor, as a general rule, to escape them. The debtor, however, is always granted the right to assist in the enforcement activities, and to check that procedural requirements and all of the legally prescribed formalities are complied with therein.

As a matter of fact, to bring the proceedings to a stop, on either procedural or substantial grounds, the debtor is required to bring formal oppositions to the judge and open incidental cognition phases.

There is no theoretical limit to the number of enforcement procedures a debtor may be subject to, as long as his or her creditors' claims have not been satisfied.

407. The point of departure of enforcement is the so-called *titolo esecutivo* (enforcement title or enforcement instrument), that is, a document which refers to a

---

650. G.L. Barreca, 'Principali novità della riforma dell'espropriazione forzata in generale', GM (2007): 603; G. Campeis & A. De Pauli, *Le esecuzioni civili*, 4th edn (Padua: Cedam, 2007); F. Carpi, 'Alcune osservazioni sulla riforma dell'esecuzione per espropriazione forzata', RTDPC (2006): 215; A. Saletti, 'Le (ultime?) novità in tema di esecuzione forzata', RDP (2006): 193; A. Briguglio & B. Capponi, *Commentario alle riforme del processo civile, II, Processo di esecuzione* (Padua: Cedam, 2007).

651. *See*, e.g., DL No. 132 of 2014, converted into Law No. 162 of 2014.

652. *See* R. Giordano, *Esecuzioni civili: le novità del 'decreto banche'* (Milan: Giuffrè, 2016); C. Barbieri, G. Campagna, *La nuova esecuzione forzata: opposizione, sospensione, estinzione dopo la l. 30 giugno 2016, n. 119* (Bologna: Zanichelli, 2017).

credit whose existence has been ascertained (*certo*), for a determined amount or quantity of either money or other goods (*liquido*), whose payment time limit has already expired (*esigibile*).

Article 474 CPC contains a list of the documents and acts which our system considers enforcing titles. Traditionally, a distinction is made between those titles which are formed in the course or at the end of judicial proceedings (*titoli giudiziali*) and titles which are formed without the intervention of a court (*titoli stragiudiziali*). The latter, of course, present a lesser degree of certainty as concerns the existence of the credit contained therein, and this is relevant at the opposition stage (*see infra*, paragraph 420).

As a general rule, judicial decisions are considered to be enforceable title: therefore, not only judgments but also decrees (*decreti*) and orders (*ordinanze*) may be used to enforce a civil claim as long as the law so provides. Judicial orders enjoy special consideration in this context, on the assumption that a judge has considered the substance of the claim before releasing his or her decision. Among judicial titles, one must consider judgments containing an order to pay a sum of money, deliver a good or perform an action (*sentenze di condanna*), as well as any other judicial order which has enforcing authority according to the relevant procedural rules. Many provisional, summary and interim enforceable decisions are provided for by either the code or special provisions.

To be enforced, a judicial decision does not need to be res judicata. However, if the enforcing authority of a judgment is stayed at the appeal level, no enforcement proceedings can take place and, if already started, they must be stayed too.

According to Article 474 CPC, however, also some documents issued outside of judicial proceedings (*titoli esecutivi stragiudiziali*) may be used to enforce the claim contained therein. Such is the case of bills of exchange, promissory notes, checks and other credit instruments having enforcing authority as of right and (from 2005) also private writings where the debtor's signature has been verified by a public notary (*scrittura private autenticata*): Article 474(2), No. 2. According to Article 474(2), No. 3 CPC, moreover, authentic instruments made by a notary or a public servant are considered enforcement orders as concerns any obligation to pay a sum of money, to deliver a good or to release an immovable property established therein.[653]

As a general rule, non-judicial titles may only be used to enforce money claims; only authentic instruments may be employed to enforce orders to deliver an asset or release an immoveable property.

Before the start of enforcement proceedings, the law requires the creditor to serve an authentic copy of the enforcement title on the debtor with a valid *exequatur* clause (*formula esecutiva*) in case of judicial orders and authentic instruments (Article 475 CPC).

Subsequently, a formal notice must be served on the defendant, requesting him or her to pay or perform his or her obligation within ten days (*precetto*: Article 480

653. *See* I. Andolina, 'Il titolo esecutivo dopo le recenti riforme del processo civile italiano', *Riv. esec. forz.* (2006): 14; R. Oriani, 'Titolo esecutivo, opposizioni, sospensione dell'esecuzione', FI (2005): V, 104.

CPC). Only when this deadline has elapsed with no payment of performance from the debtor, may the creditor start actual enforcement proceedings.

408. Two different forms of enforcement are provided for in the Italian legal system: on the one hand, generic enforcement (*esecuzione per espropriazione*) concerns money claims, and it involves the debtor's assets, which are bound by law to provide security for the debtor's obligations (Article 2740 CC). When a debtor does not voluntarily pay any amount of money, he or she owes to a creditor, his or her assets may be attached and then coercibly sold to use the money thus obtain to (indirectly) satisfy the creditor's claim, up to the value of his or her credit, plus interests and expenses. Inevitably, the vast majority of civil enforcement proceedings concern money claims.

On the other hand, specific enforcement (*esecuzione in forma specifica*) relates to orders to deliver specific movable assets (*esecuzione per consegna*), release determined immovable property (*esecuzione per rilascio*), perform a specific fungible obligation or enforce a judicial prohibition to act (*esecuzione degli obblighi di fare o di non fare*). The latter form of enforcement may be brought only if a judicial order exists which identifies and determines the relevant actions to be performed or prohibition to be enforced.[654]

409. The *Tribunale* has subject-matter and value competence in matters of enforcement. The territorial court is normally located in the place where the debtor's assets are found.

410. To start any enforcement procedure, the creditor must hold an enforcement order (*titolo esecutivo*). As a matter of fact, an enforceable title contains all the objective and subjective elements which the enforcing authorities need to verify in order to:

(a) identify both the creditor and the debtor;
(b) determine the credit, its nature and its source;
(c) verify that the credit is 'liquido, certo ed esigibile', that is, it refers to a specific and determined sum of money or a specific asset or obligation, and that it is not subject (any longer) to a term or a condition.

Upon presentation of a title providing documentary evidence of the existence of a civil claim of a creditor against a debtor, the *Ufficiale giudiziario* is bound to perform his or her enforcing activities with no further investigation of the merits of such claim.

411. In generic enforcement, the procedure begins with the attachment (*pignoramento*) of the debtor's assets, which the creditor has to request within ninety days of serving the *precetto* on the debtor (*see* paragraph 407).

---

654. On the other hand, *esecuzione per consegna o rilascio* may now also be based on an authentic instrument: *see* para. 407.

Attachment falls to be performed by the *Ufficiale giudiziario*, who enjoys special authoritative powers, with the collaboration of the creditor.

Different rules are provided for, depending on the whether the creditor wants to attach moveable (*espropriazione mobiliare*) or immovable (*espropriazione immobiliare*) assets or credits of the debtor vis-à-vis a third person (*espropriazione presso terzi*). These rules have been widely reformed in 2005/2006, hoping to make attachment more efficient and effective.

Attachment, basically, consists in the *Ufficiale giudiziario*'s singling out certain assets of the debtor and in his or her injunction to the latter not to take them away from the security of the creditor's claims.[655] In other words, attached goods are effectively legally segregated from the rest of the debtor's estate, and they can no longer be freely disposed of by him or her. Any contract or transaction between the debtor and a third person relating to such goods is legally valid, but it is ineffective vis-à-vis the attaching creditor. The new owner of the asset may prevail over the attaching creditor only if he or she acquired possession of a moveable good 'in good faith' (i.e., without knowledge of it being attached) or an immovable property when the relevant sale was registered on the public records of immovable properties on a prior date than the attachment. Should the enforcement proceedings be discontinued, however, the creditor would lose any right over the previously attached assets which the debtor sold or gave to another person.

As a general rule, the creditor is free to file several attachment petitions against the debtor's estate; however, the debtor may require the judge to limit enforcement only to some assets when their value proves to be enough to satisfy the creditor's claim.

Moreover, not every asset may be attached: as a matter of fact, some goods (e.g., the debtor's bed or wedding ring, his or her letters, the dining table)[656] or credits[657] are legally secured (in whole or at least in part) from attachment in order to safeguard the debtor's right to live and work and to preserve his or her more personal belongings.

Of course, in order to single out the debtor's assets, the creditor must be in the position to know of their existence.

It is generally acknowledged that one of the main problems of civil enforcement in Italy lies in the difficulties of finding out whether and where the debtor has assets which may be attached.

Traditionally, in Italy no effective ways of discovering such information existed, and this contributed to making enforcement proceedings very frustrating.

---

655. The general rules concerning all types of attachment have been completely revised in 2005–2006: *see* the new Art. 492 CPC: *see also* Miccolis, 'Pignoramento, ricerca dei beni da pignorare, estensione del pignoramento', FI (2005): V, 111; A. Saletti, 'Le novità in materia di pignoramento e di ricerca dei beni da espropriare', <www.judicium.it>; S. Ziino, 'Le innovazioni in tema di pignoramento e di distribuzione del ricavato', <www.judicium.it>.

656. Some other goods (mostly related to agricultural activities) may only be attached at certain times of the year: Arts 515–516 CPC.

657. To avoid the debtor being left completely destitute and unable to support himself or herself and his or her family, certain limits are set to the possibility of attaching a debtor's credits (Art. 545 CPC): e.g., alimony credits, as a general rule, may never be attached; the debtor's salary may be attached up to a fifth of its amount and so forth.

It is relatively easy to discover whether a person is a shareholder in a company or whether he or she performs commercial activities or holds a position within a corporation: the records of the Chamber of Commerce provide with such information, which is easily and cheaply available to the general public. Finding out whether a debtor is the owner of immovable properties or registered moveable assets is also relatively easy, since specific records may be looked up.

Discovering the debtor's occupation, employee or salary, on the other hand, is somehow more complicated and requires more comprehensive (and sometimes costly) investigations.

Information on bank accounts, financial investments, savings and so forth is usually the hardest to obtain for the general public.

Of course, whenever possible, a creditor should try and obtain, if not security, at least information about the debtor's financial and working conditions at the start of the relationship with a debtor. When a contract has been agreed upon, on the other hand, the debtor will generally be unwilling to voluntarily disclose any information about his or her estate, and no efficient system formerly existed in Italy to coerce such a disclosure.

To try and improve on this unsatisfactory situation, the reforms of 2005–2006 introduced some devices that should enable the creditor to gain information about the debtor's assets. According to the 'new' Article 492(4) CPC, for example, when insufficient goods are attached (or whenever the delay to sell the attached goods appears to be exceedingly long), the bailiff orders the debtor to disclose information about the existence and location of any other attachable asset. Failure to comply with such an order or rendering false declarations are treated (and punished) as criminal offences.

Moreover, information about the debtor's assets may also be obtained by the *Ufficiale giudiziario*, upon the creditor's application, through an expert appointed to examine the debtor's commercial records: Article 494(7) CPC.

Since these devices proved to be not effective, the lawmaker made new attempts at enabling the creditor to discover information about the debtor's assets. In particular, in 2014, Article 492*bis* was introduced in the CPC in order to regulate the e-search of the debtor's goods. Under this new provision (which was also implemented by the new Articles 155*bis* to 155*sexies* disp. att. CPC and later modified by DL No. 83 of 2015, converted into Law No. 132 of 2015), the creditor may file an application to the President of the *Tribunale* in order for an e-search of the debtor's assets to be performed. When such a search is authorized, either the *ufficiale giudiziario* or the creditor himself (after a reform of Article 155*quinquies* disp. att. CPC in 2015) are enabled to enquire for information to the *archivio dei rapporti finanziari* (the financial transactions archive). Through this channel, data may be acquired, e.g., concerning the debtor's employer or bank relations. This new e-search may be effective but it may also be rather time-consuming, since it takes at least a few weeks for the relevant information to be provided.

412. The code of civil procedure originally allowed creditors to freely join in an enforcement procedure begun by another creditor,[658] even if they did not hold an enforceable title, as long as they could claim a credit which was certain for a specific amount and due (*see retro*, paragraph 407).

This situation had proved to be very problematic, since it made enforcement procedures longer, and it often leads to disputes among the competing creditors: as a matter of fact, the more creditors join in a procedure, the less money each of them will eventually receive after the sale of the attached goods.

The reforms of 2005–2006,[659] therefore, completely revised Article 499 CPC, so that now, in order to join in already pending enforcement proceedings, as a general rule, a creditor must hold an enforcement title in compliance with Article 474 CPC (*see supra*, paragraph 407).

There are exceptions to this general rule, however: for example, creditors whose claim is documented in their records in compliance with Article 2214 cc. In other words, business or commercial claimants are generally allowed to join in pending enforcement proceedings.

However, creditors who do not hold an enforcement order may still be precluded from taking part in the distribution phase of the proceedings: as a matter of fact, in the initial steps of the procedure, the debtor must be convened before the judge to admit or deny any claim not supported by a title. When such a claim is denied, the self-proclaimed creditor is under the burden to start judicial proceedings wherein to obtain an enforceable order against the debtor. In the meantime, the portion of money obtained from the sale of the attached goods he or she would be entitled to is 'frozen'. However, such 'freezing' of the proceeds will only last for three years: when such time limit elapses, the creditor will forfeit his or her right to take part in the distribution. Since Italian civil proceedings are known to be quite long lasting, it might happen often that in the three years assigned to the creditor, the latter will not be in the position to acquire an enforcement title for his or her credit.[660]

As a general rule, in order for a creditor to take part on an equal footing as the other participating creditors in the distribution of the money recovered from the sale of the attached goods, joinder in the enforcement proceedings must be timely.[661] The law provides for specific deadlines, and if a creditor joins in the procedure after the relevant time limit has expired, he or she can only be awarded whatever (if anything) is left after all the other creditors have been satisfied.

Moreover, not necessarily will creditors, who are timely admitted to the enforcement procedure, have the right to take part on an equal footing in the distribution of the money made out of the judicial sale of the attached goods. As a matter of fact, creditors with a lien (e.g., a mortgage) have priority over the so-called *chirografari*

---

658. *See* V. Andrioli, *Il concorso dei creditori nell'esecuzione singolare* (Rome: Soc. ed. del Foro italiano, 1937).

659. B. Capponi, 'L'intervento dei creditori dopo le tre riforme della XIV legislatura', <www.judicium.it>; A. Tedoldi, 'L'oggetto della domanda di intervento e delle controversie sul riparto nella nuova disciplina dell'espropriazione forzata', RDP (2006): 1297; P. Liccardo, 'I nuovi modelli decisionali della vendita coattiva nelle leggi 14 maggio 2005, n. 80 e 28 dicembre 2005, n. 263 (disciplina dell'esecuzione forzata e qualità della legge)', <www.judicium.it>.

660. *See* E. Silvestri, *supra*, 210.

661. Different deadlines for joining are set for every form of attachment.

creditors (i.e., creditors with no lien). The CC also provides for a graded list of the different liens. In practice, when one or more creditors with a lien (*creditori privilegiati*) participate in an enforcement procedure, the *chirografari* creditors most often are not awarded any sum or a simple fraction of their original claim.

Should conflicts arise between creditors taking part in the same enforcement procedure (e.g., concerning the amount of the credits, the interest rates, the position in the liens list and so forth), the judge is called upon to solve them, not through ordinary proceedings but after a summary examination, at the end of which an ordinanza is granted. Against such *ordinanza*, it is possible to bring an *opposizione agli atti esecutivi* (*see* at paragraph 421). Arguably, this ordinanza does not have res judicata effects outside of the procedure it was rendered in.[662]

In the light of the new provisions introduced in the code in 2005/2006, it is possible to say that the *par condicio creditorum* principle has been severely limited by the Italian lawmaker, which adopted a 'first come first served' attitude to the enforcement of money orders. Such new approach will arguably reduce the length of enforcement proceedings but, as a downside, it will also bring forth more cognizance proceedings for creditors who need to acquire an enforceable title and, eventually, more legal costs on the debtor.

413. Since 31 March 2015, immediately after the debtor's assets are attached, the creditor must electronically file his claim into the competent court (*iscrizione a ruolo telematica*). If the relevant deadline is not respected, the attachment becomes ineffective.[663]

Moreover, within forty-five days of the date attachment is performed,[664] the creditor must file a petition to the court asking the attached goods to be sold. If such time limit is not complied with, the whole procedure must be stricken out.

Articles 501 et seq. CPC set out the common rules for sale under execution. Moreover, specific rules are given for each of the three forms of generic enforcement. To make this fundamental part of enforcement proceedings more efficient and speedier, the relevant provisions have been extensively revised in 2005–2006, in particular as concerns the sale of immoveable goods.[665] The latter type of judicial sale is obviously the one most complex, long and costly (Articles 567 et seq. CPC).

With no possibility to enter here into the tiny details and formalities of the code provisions on judicial sale of attached assets, it is worth mentioning that the assets can either be sold at a judicial auction to the best bidder or (now preferably)[666]

---

662. C. Marino, *The Wane of Res Judicata in the Italian Enforcement Proceedings*, ZZPInt 31 (2008).
663. This filing must take place within fifteen days when moveable and immoveable assets are attached and thirty days when the attachment concerns vehicles or credits.
664. Article 497 CPC as revised by DL No. 83 of 2015, converted into Law No. 132 of 2015. Beforehand, the deadline to file the 'istanza di vendita' was ninety days.
665. R. Fontana, 'Custodia e vendita nell'espropriazione immobiliare', FI, 2005, V, 122; F. De Santis, 'Il "programma" della vendita forzata immobiliare dopo le riforme: dalla frammentazione delle fasi all'unitarietà della procedura liquidativa', <www.judicium.it>.
666. As a matter of fact, the law-maker, in recent pieces of legislation made the selling of seized assets through a system of judicial auctions the exception to the rule: with reference to DL No. 132 of 2014, A. Tedoldi, *Le novità in materia di esecuzione forzata nel d. l. 12/2014*, CG (2015): 402 refers to the de facto abrogation of the liquidation procedure based on judicial auction (*vendita forzata con incanto*). *See also* R. Giordano, *supra*, 22.

through a court-appointed commission agent, who will try to sell the asset at the best possible price by private negotiations. Moreover, in recent years, new provisions have been introduced in the code of civil procedure which enable the judge to delegate the sale of attached immoveable assets to public notaries and, since 2006, also to lawyers and accountants to fasten the proceedings and reduce the backlog of the enforcement judges.[667] In this system of judicial sales, when an asset is unsold with a certain starting price, further attempts to sell it are organized at a reduced price. However, in 2014, a new Article 164*bis* disp. att. CPC was introduced, enabling the enforcement judge to order the early closing of the enforcement proceedings when it appears that a reasonable satisfaction of the creditors' claims is impossible to obtain, also in the light of the costs required to continue the proceedings. In other words, it is now possible for the judge, after several failed attempts to sell an attached asset at ever decreasing starting prices, to simply declare that the procedure is over (which means that the creditors' claim remains unsatisfied and the asset is returned to the debtor …).[668]

The reforms of 2005–2006 also introduced several devices that, in the mind of the lawmaker, should render the sale of attached goods more rewarding and transparent: for example, specific websites have been created to make the assets on sale accessible to a wider audience with information about future auctions and sales; in relation to immovable properties, the court-appointed guardian has been given wider powers to evict the debtor within a short time;[669] a potential buyer is entitled to obtain credit from a bank in order to finance his or her purchase and so on.

Article 4 of Law No. 24 of 22 February 2010 has introduced urgent measures for the digitization of judicial services. As concerns us here, such measures include the reform of Articles 530 and 569 CPC, regulating the sale of seized property. The system has then been implemented by subsequent legislation, like DL No. 83 of 2015, converted into Law No. 132 of 2015, which reformed Article 490 CPC which introduced the 'portal for the public auctions' (*portale delle vendite pubbliche*) in order to make judicial sales open to a larger public.

The judge may now decide that the deposits, the bids, the auction and the payment of the price be performed through electronic means. Also Article 533 CPC has been modified, making it possible, now, for the persons interested in buying any attached assets to view them online before the actual sale takes place. More specific rules are handed down in new articles in the so-called *disposizioni di attuazione* of the *CPC*: in particular, Article 162*ter* requires that such auctions, to be further regulated by the Ministry of Justice, should respect and safeguard the principles of competition, transparency, simplification, effectiveness, safety, accuracy and regularity of the telematic procedures. Moreover, Article 169*quarter* allows the price to be paid with a credit, debit or prepaid card or other electronic means of payment.

It is submitted that the new rules on enforcement over immoveable assets, if properly applied, should indeed make the proceedings more efficient and speedier. As a

667. *See* E. Fabiani, *La delega delle operazioni di vendita in sede di espropriazione forzata immobiliare* (Padua: Cedam, 2007).
668. For an application of this new provision *see Trib.* Belluno, 12 Jan. 2016, <www.ilcaso.it>.
669. A. Saletti, 'La custodia dei beni pignorati nell'espropriazione immobiliare', <www.judicium.it>.

matter of fact, in many *Tribunali*, in recent years, the duration of these proceedings (and the backlog of the court) have been drastically reduced.

Whatever is gained from selling the attached goods, detracted the fees for the persons involved in the sale and the other costs of the procedure, is distributed among the creditors, following the list of liens, down to the *chirografari* creditors.

Under certain conditions, it is also possible for the creditor to request the court to be paid in kind, with the assignation of the attached goods.

414. Rules on the attachment of moveable assets are found in Articles 513 et seq. CPC.

Upon the creditor's request, the bailiff grants access to the debtor's house or workplace[670] and attaches the goods he or she finds there, up to the value indicated by the creditor in the notice to pay (*precetto*), he or she has previously served on the debtor.[671]

A written report is made of the *Ufficiale giudiziario*'s operations with the indication of an approximate value of the attached goods,[672] and guardian is appointed by the bailiff.

To safeguard the debtor's right to live and work, and to preserve his or her more personal belongings, some goods can never be attached (Article 514 CPC), for example, the bed, the wedding ring, the work tools, the letters, the dining table and so forth. Some other goods (mostly related to agricultural activities) can only be attached at certain times of the year (Articles 515–516).

Sale of the attached assets is disposed in compliance with Articles 529 et seq. CPC.

Special provisions are granted for the attachment of motor vehicles and trailers under Article 521*bis* CPC, introduced in 2014 by DL No. 132 and modified in 2015 by DL No. 83.[673] Basically, an attachment petition is served on the owner of the vehicle, who is then burdened to deliver the vehicle to the local *Istituto vendite giudiziarie* (IVG) (i.e., the Institution charged with the sale of attached assets) within ten days, in order to enable the IVG to sell it. If that deadline is not respected, should the police find the attached vehicle, it will confiscate its circulation papers (*carta di circolazione*) and property documents and deliver the vehicle itself to the nearest IVG.[674] Arguably, this is a rather efficient tool to enforce pecuniary claims.

415. Articles 543 et seq. CPC regulate enforcement procedures over the debtor's credits or the debtor's goods in possession of a third person (*pignoramento presso terzi*). These procedures, which often concern the debtor's salary or bank

670. On the days and hours specifically stated in Art. 519 CPC, unless a specific authorization is released by the court.
671. L.P. Comoglio, 'La ricerca dei beni da pignorare', <www.judicium.it>.
672. Article 518 CPC has been revised in 2006, to enable the bailiff to be assisted by a professional appraiser.
673. *See* C. Cariglia, 'La nuova disciplina del pignoramento e della custodia degli autoveicoli', NLCC (2015): 436; P. Gobio Casali, 'Pignoramento di autoveicoli ex art. 521 bis c. p. c.: problemi applicativi', <www.judicium.it>.
674. For applications of this new provision *see Trib.* Padova, 25 Aug. 2015, *ord.*, <www.ilcaso.it>; *Trib.* Mantova, 25 May 2015, *ord.*, *ibidem.*

accounts, are usually very efficient for the satisfaction of medium-sized claims if updated information is available to the creditor. The collaboration of the third person (the so-called *debitor debitoris*) is required to ascertain whether the credit really exists and its specific amount or if the debtor's goods really are in the third person's hands.[675] Also, the latter must be warned that an enforcement is pending and that he or she should not pay the debt or hand back the goods without the court's permission.[676] To these ends, the creditor serves on both the debtor and the third person a written document (*atto di pignoramento*), which fulfils the legal effects of both an attachment and a petition to appear in court.

Traditionally, the third person was invited to appear before the *Tribunale*, at a hearing fixed by the creditor to render a declaration on his or her debt or on the debtor's goods in his or her possession. After the reform of 2005/2006, however, such appearance in court was considered necessary only when the debtor's salary was attached, but in 2014 also this exception was eliminated. Today, therefore, the debtor's debtor is always invited by the creditor to mail him a written declaration about any existing debts towards the debtor or any debtor's assets in his possession, within ten days of receiving the creditor's *atto di pignoramento* (Article 547 CPC).[677]

Since 2014, the venue for these proceedings is the place where the debtor resides or is domiciled (Article 26*bis* CPC).[678]

If the debtor's debtor sends a written statement confirming the existence of a debt towards the creditor's debtor, the court orders him or her to pay the creditor up to the amount indicated in the *precetto*, plus the costs of the procedure (or up to the value of his or her debt, whichever is less). The debtor's goods in his or her possession are sold and the corresponding amount is distributed among the creditors.

If, on the other hand, at the hearing, the creditor declares having received no reply from the debtor's debtor, a new hearing is arranged of which the debtor's debtor is notified. At that point, if the debtor's debtor does not appear at this second hearing or appears but refuses to render his declaration, the attached credit is considered uncontested if it is sufficiently identified.

When, on the other hand, the debtor's debtor declaration is contested or when it is impossible to identify the credit in issue without his collaboration, according to Article 549 CPC, as revised in 2015, the creditor may either let the procedure end or ask the judge to ascertain whether the credit really exists and its amount (*accertamento dell'obbligo del terzo*). According to the revised text of Article 549 CPC, this ascertainment is made by the *Giudice dell'esecuzione* himself, who renders an order having only infra-enforcement effects (in other words, no res judicata is produced at the end of the proceedings).

It must be added that to avoid the debtor from being left completely destitute and unable to support himself or herself and his or her family, certain limits are set to

675. Who also should declare whether the credit/goods have been previously attached or seized by other creditors.

676. R. Munhoz de Mello, 'La nuova disciplina degli obblighi del terzo debitore ex art. 546 c.p.c.', RDP (2007): 133.

677. *See* M. Bove, 'La nuova disciplina in materia di espropriazione del credito (d. l. n. 132/14 conv. in l. n. 162/14)', NLCC (2015): 1.

678. For an in-depth analysis of this new provision, *see* A. Saletti, 'Competenza e giurisdizione nell'espropriazione di crediti', <www.judicium.it>.

the possibility of attaching a debtor's credits (Article 545 CPC): for example, alimony credits, as a general rule, may never be attached; the debtor's work wage may be attached up to a fifth of its amount and so forth. Moreover, in 2015, DL No. 83 of 2015, converted into Law No. 132 of 2015, modified Article 545 CPC in order to introduce limits to the possibility to attach pensions (which may not be attached for a fraction corresponding to the social security check[679] increased by half its value, while the exceeding part may be attached up to a fifth of its amount) and sums deposited in a bank account and deriving from the payment of salaries or wages (which may not attached for a value of three times the social security check when they are in the bank account before the latter is attached).[680] As a matter of fact, before this recent innovation, whenever certain 'protected' credits were deposited in a bank account, they became part of the general assets of the debtor and his creditors therefore could attach them with no limits. Nowadays, then, these credits maintain at least partially their privileged status. Arguably, however, these provisions might prove hard to apply in practice, e.g., when both protected and unprotected credits are deposited in the same bank account.

416. Enforcement against the debtor's immovable properties (*espropriazione immobiliare*) requires the creditor to identify, in a written document which is served on the debtor, the specific assets he or she wants to attach. Such attached document must also be registered in the public records of immovable properties to make it known to the public at large, so that attachment can prevail over any subsequent purchaser of the same immovable properties.

Today, in some Italian courts especially allowed to test these new procedures, it is also possible to perform an electronic filing of attachment proceedings in relation to real property.[681] Sending the electronic request to attach the debtor's real property to the court's offices, however, does not (yet) completely substitute the required 'paperwork', since the creditor is also required to deliver a 'traditional' written request to the bailiff. At the moment, then, the only real advantage of this '*pignoramento elettronico*' is that, when the bailiff brings the relevant documents to the court, after service has been performed on the debtor, all of the case data will already be present in the court's file, thus reducing the processing time.

Enforcement of real property is the procedural model where the judicial sale of the attached goods is more complex, longer and costly (Articles 567 et seq. CPC). Before the asset can be sold, however, all mortgage creditors must be served a notice informing them about the start of the procedure so that they may decide to file an application to join in; if they do not, they lose their mortgage, since the good will be sold free of any lien.

---

679. For 2017, the social security check has an ordinary value of EUR 44,800.

680. L. Penasa, 'Le nuove limitazioni poste alla pignorabilità delle somme di denaro depositate presso i conti correnti bancari o postali delle rappresentanze diplomatiche e consolari straniere', NLCC (2015): 459; G. Vallone, 'L'impignorabilità di stipendi e pensioni versati su conto corrente: note a prima lettura del D. L. del 27 giugno 2015, n. 83', <www.judicium.it>; D. Borghesi, 'La l. 132/2015 interviene ancora sul pignoramento di crediti (con particolare riferimento a quelli di lavoro e previdenziali)', <www. judicium.it>.

681. *See* Salemme, 'L'impiego dell'informatica nelle esecuzioni immobiliari', RTDPC (2010): 1333.

417. Specific rules are set for enforcement on the multiparties property (Articles 599 et seq. CPC).[682] Here, the court must primarily verify whether it is possible to physically separate the debtor's portion from the rest of the asset. If this is not the case, then the whole asset is sold, and the owners who are not subject to enforcement will receive the monetary value of their proprietary portions. It is also possible to enforce a claim vis-à-vis third persons in lieu of the original debtor (*espropriazione contro il terzo proprietario*), when such person has given either one of his or her assets as a collateral warranty for the debtor's debt or has fraudulently bought a good from the debtor to keep it away from the latter's creditors, and the relevant transaction has been judicially revoked.

When these conditions are met, the original title against the debtor can be directly enforced against the third person as if he or she were the debtor.

418. Specific enforcement for delivery of a movable good (Articles 605 et seq. CPC) or release of an immovable property (Articles 608 et seq. CPC) requires the title and the *precetto* to be served on the debtor. In the *precetto*, the good to be delivered or the immoveable to be released must be specifically identified.

To enforce a delivery order, the *Ufficiale giudiziario*, upon the creditor's application, goes to the place where the movable property is (or is supposed to be) located, seizes it and hands it over to the creditor.

Releasing immovable property is usually a more complicated matter since, if the debtor does not voluntarily comply, the judicial order must be enforced by the *Ufficiale giudiziario*, eventually with the assistance of the police, in compliance with regulations on eviction of people in densely populated urban areas, if the case may be. The situation has improved a little over the last years, but it can still take several months (if not years ...) to evict a tenant from one's own apartment.

419. The court plays a more active role in the specific enforcement of obligations to perform or not perform an action (Articles 612 et seq. CPC). After service of the title and of the *precetto*, the creditor files a petition to have the *Tribunale* determine the manner to enforce the judgment.

The court then hears the parties involved and issues an order, stating the person who must perform in lieu of the debtor or remove the consequences of the debtor's activities, under the supervision of the *Ufficiale giudiziario*.

II. Judicial Review

420. Since enforcement requires a title (*titolo esecutivo*) which ascertains or documents the existence of the claim to be enforced, the debtor usually plays a passive role in the procedure. Most notably, he or she cannot bring the enforcement procedure to an end without first removing the *titolo esecutivo*. Thus he or she can do only by raising an *opposizione all'esecuzione*, that is an opposition alleging that

682. *See* A. Cardino, *Comunione dei beni ed espropriazione forzata* (Turin: Utet, 2011).

the creditor does not have a right to bring enforcement against him or her (Articles 615 et seq. CPC).[683]

There are a number of grounds on which an *opposizione all'esecuzione* can be based. For example, the debtor may contest the creditor's standing or he or she may allege that he or she is not the person mentioned in the title (e.g., an identity mix up), that a valid title is lacking, that the credit is not yet due and so on. The main (and more troublesome) ground of opposition, however, relates to the alleged inexistence of the credit to which the title refers. This type opposition (*opposizione di merito*) is not always admissible: for example, when the title is a judgment which has become res judicata, no defence can be raised which would violate the *ne bis in idem* principle and only facts which have allegedly taken place after the decision has become res judicata can be considered therein. When a decision is not yet res judicata, no opposition is admissible either, because the only way to eliminate the title is by bringing (and winning) an appeal against it. As a matter of fact, it is for the appeal court only to stay the enforceability of the decision pending the appeal. *Opposizione all'esecuzione* on the merits of the creditor's claim, however, is always permitted against non-judicial titles (*see* paragraph 407), which are privately formed and where the apparent existence of the claim only depends on specific formal requirement.[684] In 2016, in order to avoid dilatory tactics by the debtors, Article 615 CPC was modified by DL No. 59. Nowadays, in enforcement proceedings that lead to the liquidation of the debtor's assets (*espropriazione*), an opposition is only admissible if it is brought before the sale of the seized assets is ordered by the judge. In this respect, Article 492 CPC was also modified: when an asset is attached, today, the debtor has the right to be informed about this new deadline in order to be in the position to raise a timely opposition against the creditor's action.[685]

Different procedural rules and venue provisions are applied, depending on whether the enforcement has already started or not (e.g., generic enforcement starts when attachment has been performed by the *Ufficiale giudiziario*). The substance, however, is the same in both cases: ordinary cognizance proceedings are brought which run alongside the enforcement procedure and where the court has to determine whether the creditor has a valid title to enforce against the debtor or not.

At the first hearing before the judge, a decision is taken whether to stay the enforcement proceedings. When the enforcement has not yet started, the enforcing authority of the title may be stayed. In both cases, the debtor must show serious reasons to do so.[686] Basically, the opposing debtor must show that his or her opposition is prima facie well-grounded and he or she will suffer some serious damage should enforcement not be stayed. In 2015, Article 615 CPC was modified by DL No. 83: now, when only part of the creditor's claim is contested, the judge may stay the enforcing authority of the title exclusively in relation to the contested part. The single judge's decision on the application for a stay of the enforcement procedure,

683. The reforms of 2005–2006 have brought some innovations in this field: *see* A. Saletti, 'Simmetrie ed asimmetrie nel sistema delle opposizioni esecutive', RDP (2007): 885.
684. For example, a party can claim that the check enforced against him or her was forged, stolen, and so on.
685. *See* R. Giordano, *Esecuzioni civili: le novità del 'decreto banche'*, (Milan: Giuffrè, 2016), 19.
686. *See* S. Recchioni, 'I nuovi artt. 616 e 624 c.p.c. fra strumentalità cautelare "attenuata" ed estinzione del "pignoramento"', RDP (2006): 643.

after 2006, may be reviewed by a three-judge panel of the *Tribunale* by way of *reclamo* (Article 624 CPC).[687]

Following this preliminary step, the case goes on as an ordinary cognition proceeding, by registering the case in court within the deadline set by the enforcement judge. Interestingly, after the reform of 2006, if the enforcement procedure is stayed at this stage and the case is not registered to continue within the time limit set by the judge, the enforcement procedure is struck out. In other words, after the preliminary stage where the stay is granted, it is up to the creditor to take the required procedural steps to let the case go on for a decision on the merits. The creditor, therefore, has to balance his or her chances in the light of the summary decision rendered the judge on the application to stay the case. It is argued that many ungrounded enforcement actions may be struck out this way with no need to wait for the decision on the merits of the opposition procedure.[688]

If the opposition does indeed proceed to judgment, the court will decide therein whether the creditor has a right to enforce against the debtor or not. Article 616, as revised in 2006, stated that the court's decision on the debtor's *opposizione all'esecuzione* could not be appealed before the Court of Appeal, but only before the *Cassazione*, by way of *ricorso straordinario*, in compliance with Article 111 of the Constitution. This rather problematic innovation, however, was repealed in 2009, and now first instance decisions are subject to ordinary appeal again.

421. The debtor also has a right to contest the formal validity of the enforcement procedure against him or her. *Opposizione agli atti esecutivi* (Articles 617 et seq. CPC) can, as a matter of fact, be raised within twenty days to contest any procedural error or fault in the proceedings, before the enforcement court.

This opposition will not necessarily disrupt the whole procedure, but it might force the creditor to renew some steps of it.

The court's decision may not be appealed before the Court of Appeal, but only before the *Cassazione*, by way of *ricorso straordinario*, in compliance with Article 111 of the Constitution.

422. Finally, it must be mentioned that also third persons, whose rights in rem on the attached property have been infringed, may bring an opposition (*opposizione di terzo all'esecuzione*, Articles 619 et seq. CPC).[689] This typically happens when a third party alleges that he or she is the real owner of the goods which have been attached in the place where the debtor lives. Most commonly, the person who raises such opposition is a relative of the debtor; therefore, courts tend to be very careful not to allow fraudulent claims.

---

687. *See* E. Astuni, 'Il nuovo reclamo sulla sospensione cautelare dell'esecuzione e il suo ambito di applicazione', GM (2007): 1660; G. Giusti, 'La disciplina della sospensione del processo esecutivo nella contemporanea proposizione della opposizione a precetto delle opposizione alla esecuzione', GM (2007): 2232; R. Oriani, 'La sospensione dell'esecuzione (sul combinato disposto degli artt. 615 e 624 c.p.c.)', <www.judicium.it>.
688. *See also* C. Marino, *supra*, 30.
689. *See* C. Punzi, *La tutela del tezo nel processo esecutivo* (Milan, Giuffrè, 1971).

All in all, the third party's task is not an easy one: he or she cannot usually prove his or her right in rem through testimony witnesses (Article 621 CPC) and normally cogent documentary evidence is required.

§2. Recognition and Enforcement of Foreign Judgments

I. Rules Applicable in the Absence of a Treaty

423. Traditionally, a foreign judicial decision will not be given any effect in another sovereign State per se.[690] As a matter of fact, it is up for a State (State *ad quem*) to unilaterally decide whether to grant any value to a decision rendered in a foreign State (State *a quo*) and, if so, under which conditions and requirements. Today, however, for comity reasons and also out of practical and economical considerations, it would be most unusual for a legal order to deny any juridical relevance to the decisions of a foreign sovereign State; surely, this has not been the case in Italy for a very long time.

Originally, in Italy, recognition and enforcement of foreign judgments were dealt with in a section of the CPC.[691] The initial approach of the Italian lawmaker was rather restrictive and nationalistic. As concerns us here, this attitude led to very strict recognition and enforcement requirements. Moreover, as a general rule, a foreign decision was granted no legal value in Italy until it had been 'incorporated' into the Italian judicial system by a national decision rendered at the end of a special set of proceedings called '*procedimento di delibazione*'.

The Court of Appeal, upon the party's request for recognition and/or *exequatur*, would check whether the foreign decision complied with a list of requirements listed in Article 796 CPC and only after a positive review of these criteria would an Italian judgment be rendered to 'enhance' the validity in our country of the decision rendered abroad.

As a whole, this system showed a very protective attitude towards national defendants: as a matter of fact, if the foreign judgment was rendered in default of appearance of the Italian defendant, the latter always had the prerogative to ask the Court of Appeal to review the merits of the foreign decision when the *exequatur* of the foreign decision was applied for.

Moreover, as a general rule, an Italian judgment or proceedings brought in Italy, before the foreign decision became res judicata, would always preempt recognition of a foreign judgment between the same parties on the same (or a related) subject-matter.

Over the years, the original rules of the code of civil procedure on recognition and enforcement of foreign decisions had become seriously outdated and somehow

690. O. Lopes Pegna, *I procedimenti relativi all'efficacia delle decisioni straniere in Italia* (Padua: Cedam, 2009); E. D'Alessandro, *Il riconoscimento delle sentenze straniere* (Turin: Giappichelli, 2007).

691. *See* Biamonti, '*Italy*', in *International execution against judgments debtors*, vol. II (Sweet and Maxwell: ed. Salzburg).

embarrassing in the context of the European judicial space created by the Brussels Convention of 1968.

As a matter of fact, a gap too wide existed between the treatment of Community decisions vis-à-vis the treatment of third States ones. In 1995, a long-awaited reform was finally approved by Parliament. Law No. 218 of 31 May 1995, strongly influenced by the spirit of the Brussels Convention of 1968, completely reformed the Italian system of private and procedural international law, with a strong emphasis, as concerns us here, with international comity, cooperation with foreign legal orders and respect for foreign juridical values.

The provisions of Law No. 218, however, will only be applied if no European or conventional rules are applicable (*see infra*).

Like in most other countries, also in Italy a foreign decision may be considered both for its adjudicative contents and for the need to enforce the 'orders' contained therein. From the first standpoint (recognition), Italy is prepared, under certain conditions, to recognize the 'res judicata' authority of a foreign decision, in order to implement the *ne bis in idem* principle which, in this context, forbids relitigation of a subject-matter already adjudicated upon abroad and which requires a court to decide dependant claims in compliance with the decision on a preliminary question rendered abroad.

From the second point of view (enforcement), again, under certain conditions, Italy will enforce foreign judicial orders just like they were national decisions, in the application of the Italian rules on civil enforcement.

For what is relevant here, the reform of 1995 brought forth a completely new approach to the circulation of foreign decisions in Italy.

As a matter of fact, Articles 796 et seq. of the code of civil procedure were repealed and substituted for by Articles 64 et seq. of the 1995 Act, which entered into force on 12 December 1996.

These new provisions, at least from a policy standpoint, radically revolutionized the existing system of recognition and enforcement in Italy.

According to Article 64, in particular, as a general rule, foreign judgments are now automatically recognized in Italy with no need to bring special recognition proceedings;[692] in other words, foreign res judicata is now granted automatic effects in Italy (e.g., in pending litigation, concerning related disputes to the one adjudicated upon abroad).

However, the principle of automatic recognition is not an absolute one. As a matter of fact, recognition is automatic only in so far as it is not contested by the other parties or if the judgment is spontaneously complied with. Should the recognition of a foreign decision be disputed or anyway denied, however, any interested party will have to bring judicial proceedings, in order to make the court verify whether such decision complies with the conditions and requirements set forth by Article 64 of Law No. 218.

On the other hand, judicial proceedings are always required when a foreign decision needs to be enforced in Italy (*exequatur*).

---

692. F. Carpi, 'Dal riconoscimento delle decisioni all'esecuzione automatica', RDP (2005): 1127; F. Carpi, 'Il riconoscimento e l'efficacia delle sentenze straniere' RDP (1997): 981; M.G. Civinini, *Il riconoscimento delle sentenze straniere* (Milan: Giuffrè, 2001).

It is easy to see that the obvious point of reference of the Italian lawmaker in Law No. 218 was the Brussels Convention of 1968. In other words, the 1995 Act basically extended the principle of automatic recognition also to third States decisions. However, as it will be pointed out in the following pages, certain safeguards were kept even if they have been eliminated in the relations with other EU Member States.

424. Article 64 of the 1995 Act concerns foreign decisions in general, irrespective of the nature of the right adjudicated upon abroad. In addition, special provisions have also been introduced by the 1995 Act concerning the recognition of judgments on personal status and related rights (e.g., legal separation and divorce) (Article 65) and decisions rendered in non-contentious jurisdiction (the so-called *giurisdizione volontaria*) (Article 66).

In practice, as concerns the 'general' conditions for recognition of the decision in Italy set by Article 64, has not very much changed vis-à-vis the old regime of Article 797 CPC.

A judgment is subject to recognition or enforcement in Italy only insomuch as it may be qualified as 'foreign'. In other words, it must have been rendered by a non-Italian judicial body, outside of the Italian borders.

It should be noted however that, exceptionally, also decisions rendered by a foreign court within the Italian Republic may also be recognized, in compliance with specific Conventions.

As a matter of fact, according to Italian law, judgments of the Ecclesiastic Courts which declare Catholic marriages to be null and void (*sentenze ecclesiastiche di nullità matrimoniale*) are considered to be 'foreign' even though they are rendered on the Italian soil. Such judgments are therefore subject to special recognition proceedings before they may produce any legal effect in Italy.

Interestingly, from the statistic standpoint, petitions brought for the recognition of these ecclesiastic judgments outnumber those for the recognition of decisions rendered in other civil and commercial matters. It is beyond the scope of this book, however, to further analyse the recognition of these decisions.

Though similar in principle to the system created by the Brussels Convention of 1968 (and now perfected by regulation EU No. 1215 of 2012), the provisions introduced by Law No. 218 of 1995 have a much narrower scope of application than those of their European 'equivalent'.

As a matter of fact, within the European space of justice, any decision rendered by a judge, irrespective of its qualification, is allowed to circulate freely among the Member States.

On the other hand, as concerns third States, not every foreign decision is liable to be recognized or enforced in Italy in compliance with the Private international law Act 1995.

First of all, only proper judgments (or decisions which, given the same circumstances, would be rendered as judgments in Italy) can be recognized. No interim, provisional or summary decisions are therefore recognizable and/or enforceable in Italy (a major difference as compared to the 'Brussels' system).

Article 64 of the 1995 Act does indeed refer only to proper judgments (*sentenze*) (i.e., as a general rule, decisions rendered at the end of judicial proceedings). More specifically, according to the relevant case law, the term 'sentenze' must be interpreted as referring to any foreign decision which, at the same conditions, would be defined as a judgment in Italy.

Basically, all kinds of interim and protective measures, summary decisions and orders of payment rendered outside of 'ordinary' civil proceedings will not be recognized in Italy since those decisions, according to Italian procedural law, do not qualify as 'sentenze'. This issue of qualification effectively reduces the number of foreign decisions which may be recognized and enforced in Italy.

Another important limit must also be considered. In contrast with the principles applied within the European space of justice, as concerns third States, it is not enough for the foreign judgment to be provisionally enforceable in the State where it was rendered. According to Article 64, lett. (*d*) of the 1995 Act, such judgment must be 'passato in giudicato'; in other words, it must be not subject to any (further) form of ordinary appellate review or opposition, so that it has become res judicata.

The rationale for this provision is to ensure certainty and finality in the implementation of foreign judgments in Italy. A consequence of such provision, however, is that, by definition, foreign decisions having an interim or provisional nature will never be granted recognition or enforcement in Italy, and this may severely curtail the efficiency of judicial protection of rights in the transnational context.

As it has already been remarked, the 1995 Act introduced in our legal system the principle of automatic recognition of foreign judgments. This means that, as a general rule, the parties, the judge and any subject involved (e.g., the keepers of personal registers) will act in compliance with the foreign decision, with no need for any preliminary judicial proceedings to be brought in Italy.

The principle of automatic recognition, however, is not an absolute one. Judicial review of decisions rendered abroad, as a matter of fact, will be necessary should recognition be contested or the decision not voluntarily complied with. The first situation will occur when some other party contests the recognition of the decision either outside of judicial proceedings or in the course of proceedings pending in Italy where the res judicata effects of a foreign judgment are under scrutiny or fall to be relevant for any related or connected decision to be taken by the Italian judge. For example, when the winning party in foreign proceedings brings an action in Italy claiming that a sum of money is due to him or her as a consequence of a decision rendered abroad, the defendant may raise a defence that the latter does not meet the requirements for recognition in Italy set by Article 64 of Law No. 218 of 1995 (*see* below). When such a situation arises, according to Article 67(3) of the 1995 Act, it is possible for an Italian court to decide on the recognition issue *'incidenter tantum'*, that is, with no binding res judicata effects outside of the proceedings in which such issue was examined. Such a form of recognition is called 'riconoscimento incidentale'.

However, should either the law or the (one of the) parties require a binding decision on the possibility to recognize the foreign judgment in Italy, the interested party will have the burden to bring recognition proceedings before the competent Court of Appeal. If that is the case, pending recognition proceedings, the dispute on the merits will ordinarily be stayed to wait for the Court of Appeal decision and subsequently decide accordingly.

On the other hand, lack of compliance with the foreign judgment refers to the situation where a person, in charge of some legally prescribed activity connected with the decision rendered abroad, abstains from performing such activity, claiming that the foreign judgment does not meet the requirement for recognition set by the Italian legislation. As a way of example, reference may be made to the public servants in charge of updating land or real property registers or personal status databases. When such lack of compliance is met with, any person interested in the recognition of a foreign decision may bring a petition for recognition before the competent Court of Appeal.

A foreign judgment is enforced in Italy when a creditor files a petition to have the order contained in that decision forcibly executed against the debtor in our country, through attachment, garnishment or other available forms of enforcement remedies. When these procedural activities have to take place, a judicial order for enforcement (the so-called *exequatur*) has to be previously applied for. In other words, as concerns decisions coming from a non-EU State, enforcement in Italy is never automatic, and special proceedings always have to be started before the Court of Appeal having competent jurisdiction.

Only judgments expressing an order to a debtor may be enforced in Italy. On the other hand, enforcement is not limited to money judgments but it also extends to non-money judgments, which, for example, impose on a party specific performance of an action (or the elimination of the effects on an unlawful behaviour) or the surrender or releasing of property.

When the court grants the *exequatur*, the enforcement title required by Article 474 CPC (*see* at paragraph 407) is composed of both the foreign decision and the Italian judgment granting enforcement.

In order to start enforcement proceedings in Italy, moreover, it is not necessary for the Italian decision to become final: as a matter of fact, any Court of Appeal decision can provisionally be enforced pending further appeal to the *Corte di cassazione*.

425. After the reform of 1995, proceedings for the recognition and enforcement of foreign decisions in Italy are no longer considered to have a constitutive nature. In other words, the Italian legal order no longer implements or 'completes' judgments rendered abroad, so to speak, by 'incorporation' in a municipal decision. This also implies that the right adjudicated upon in the foreign proceedings 'exists' previously and independently of the Italian recognition/*exequatur* decision, which only checks on the existence of some formal requirements in the decision rendered abroad. As a matter of fact, the function of recognition proceedings in Italy is nowadays merely to verify that foreign decisions comply with the requirements set by Law No. 218 of 1995, without (re)entering into the merits of the case.

This has several procedural and substantial consequences. First of all, the foreign decision is effective in Italy as soon as it becomes final in the rendering State, and the Italian recognition decision has automatic retroactive effects to the date the petition was filed. Second, recognition and enforcement proceedings have a very narrow scope (i.e., the investigation on the requirements set by Article 64 of the 1995 Act): no new claim, counter-claim or defence may be introduced, and the foreign decision may not be interpreted or manipulated in any way by the Italian judge (e.g., it is inadmissible to ask for interests to be added to the capital sum of money awarded in the judgment rendered abroad).

Moreover, there is no time-bar for bringing of recognition or enforcement proceedings of a foreign decision in Italy. However, the debtor may refer to any applicable statute of limitation to bring an opposition to the actual enforcement in Italy of the foreign decision.

Last but not least, no review of the merits of the foreign judgment is allowed in Italy in the context of recognition/enforcement proceedings. The privilege granted by the code of civil procedure to Italian defendants which did not appear before the foreign court has been eliminated by the 1995 Act.

The Italian *Corte di cassazione*, however, has stated that the nature of the rights adjudicated abroad is not completely irrelevant in the context of recognition/ enforcement proceedings, since the Italian and the foreign decisions are to be considered as a whole when it comes to the latter's enforcement in Italy.[693] As a consequence, the Supreme Court came to the conclusion that the *Pubblico Ministero* (i.e., the investigating judge acting on behalf of the State to safeguard public interests in civil proceedings) must necessarily take part in recognition proceedings of a decision rendered on a subject-matter where, under Italian law, the *Pubblico ministero* should necessarily intervene in such proceedings.[694]

Italian academic writings express contrasting views as to the effects which should be granted in Italy to a foreign decision granted recognition in our country. On the one hand, some authors believe that the foreign judgment should be granted the same effects, that is, enjoys in the State where it was rendered, within the framework of the Italian principles on the objective and subjective limits of res judicata; according to others, on the other hand, the procedural effects of foreign judgments should be regulated by Italian law, while substantial effects (including the scope of res judicata) should be left to the law of the rendering State.[695] As concerns enforcement, however, only remedies available according to Italian law may be obtained in Italy after the *exequatur* to the foreign decision has been granted.

Recognition and enforcement proceedings may be brought in Italy, in the first place, when the defendant is domiciled there.[696] Moreover, the *Corte di cassazione* has recently (and rather controversially) stated that such proceedings may be brought in Italy even though, at the time the originating petition is served, the debtor has no assets here.[697] In other words, *exequatur* may be applied for even though no

693. *Cass.* 6 Jun. 2003, n. 9085.

694. With reference to proceedings concerning the recognition of a foreign divorce judgment, *Cass.* 6 Jun. 2003, n. 9085, RDIPP, 2003, 1014 and 16 Dec. 2003, n. 19277, DF, 2004, I, 26. *See* F. Danovi, 'Riconoscimento delle sentenze straniere di divorzio e intervento necessario del p.m.', RDP (2004): 529; F. Tommaseo, 'Riconoscimento di sentenze matrimoniali straniere e intervento necessario del pubblico ministero', FD (2003): 432; L. Querzola, 'Riconoscimento delle sentenze straniere di divorzio e p.m.: un binomio necessario secondo la Cassazione', *Corr. giuridico* (2004): 52.

695. *See* M.G. Civinini, *supra*, 98 et seq. *See also* E. D'Alessandro, *supra*, 67 et seq., with reference to the American notion of issue preclusion.

696. *App.* Bologna 22 Oct. 2007, n. 1134, <www.giuraemilia.it>.

697. *Cass. SU* 23 Oct. 2006, n. 22663; 1 Aug. 2007, n. 16991; 18 Nov. 2008, n. 27338.

enforcement proceedings may be brought in Italy at the time being, and the competent court only has to verify whether the requirements set by Article 64 of Law No. 218 of 1995 are complied with.[698]

Subject-matter jurisdiction is given to the Court of Appeal, which exceptionally in these matters performs the functions of a Court of First Instance. As for territorial jurisdiction, the petition must be filed with the court of the place where the foreign decision has to deploy its effects.[699] If no specific venue can thus be determined, the general provisions on territorial jurisdiction fall to be applied (Articles 18 CPC et seq.).

The 1995 Act did not provide for specific procedural rules for recognition and enforcement proceedings and the case law came to the conclusion that, the ordinary rules for proceedings before the Court of Appeal should apply.[700] As a consequence, recognition and enforcement of foreign judgments in Italy under the 1995 Act were usually (and unnecessarily) rather long and costly. Article 30 of DLGS 150 of 2011, however, now states that proceedings for the recognition and enforcement of foreign proceeding in Italy follow the rules of 'summary proceedings' (Articles 702 *bis* et seq. CPC: *see* paragraphs 343 et seq.).

The petition takes the form of a *ricorso* and it should briefly present the scope and the events of the foreign proceedings where the decision was granted and analyse every single requirement of Article 64 of the 1995 Act (*see* above) with reference to the judgment whose recognition is sought. The plaintiff must also file with the court a certified copy of the decision rendered abroad, in compliance with the applicable international provisions on the legalization of foreign documents or *apostille*.[701] Should such copy not be filed, the petition will be denied by the court.[702]

The plaintiff, however, does not bear the burden of the proof in relation to all of the necessary requirements listed in Article 64.

As a matter of fact, he or she has to show that the foreign court had indirect jurisdiction over the dispute (Article 64 lett. (*a*)), that procedural public policy under Article 64 lett. (*b*) and (*c*) was duly complied with in the foreign proceedings and that the decision has become final in compliance with the applicable foreign law (Article 64, lett. (*d*)). It is up to the defendant, on the other hand, to prove that a conflicting Italian decision exists (Article 64, lett. (*e*)), that prior proceedings on the same dispute are pending in Italy (Article 64, lett. (*f*)), and that the effects of recognition of the decision would run contrary to public policy (Article 64, lett. (*g*)). In a recent decision, however, the *Corte di cassazione* held that, when recognition of a foreign judgment is contested, the investigation on the existence of the grounds

698. *Cass. SU* 18 Nov. 2008, n. 27338.
699. *App.* Rome 12 Apr. 2000, RDIPP, 2001, 126.
700. *Cass.* 14 Jan. 2003, n. 365.
701. *Cass.*, 28 Mar. 2003, n. 4742.
702. *App.* Bologna 28 Sep. 2006, n. 983, <www.giuraemilia.it>.

for recognition should be performed by the court ex officio, taking into consideration the materials gathered in the course of the procedure, with the plaintiff suffering any adverse results when the necessary requirements fail to be thus ascertained.[703]

In the course of the proceedings, an evidence-gathering phase may take place if necessary, that is, if and when the available documents are not sufficient to uphold either the plaintiff's or the defendant's positions.

As it was already pointed out, review on the merits of the foreign decision is no longer possible. As a matter of fact, Law No. 218 of 1995 repealed the code provision which enabled the Court of Appeal, under certain conditions, to perform such review.[704] As a consequence, today, the foreign judgment will be either granted or denied recognition, but the Italian court will never enter into the merits of the case decided abroad.

The court renders judgment on the plaintiff's petition, granting or denying recognition or enforcement to the foreign decision. Partial recognition or enforcement may be granted, should the requirements of Article 64 of the 1995 Act exist only in relation to some of the parts of which the foreign decision is composed.

Should the petition be denied, it is possible to file a further petition, alleging new facts or changes to the juridical situation considered at first (e.g., when recognition was denied on the ground that previous proceedings were pending in Italy, should those proceedings be struck out with no decision on the merits, the petition for recognition of the decision rendered abroad may be filed again).[705] A recognition/enforcement petition may be filed again also when it was originally denied on grounds purely relating to the recognition proceedings themselves.

When recognition of a foreign decision is denied, any interested party may start proceedings in Italy on the subject-matter originally adjudicated upon abroad, as long as personal jurisdiction can be found here.

The Court of Appeal decision may be appealed before the *Corte di cassazione*, on purely juridical grounds. The Supreme Court's role, in this context, is particularly limited in scope. For example, it cannot review the Court of Appeal decision concerning the violation of public policy or the juridical qualification of the foreign decision to be recognized.[706] Moreover, it is not possible to raise objections to the recognition of the foreign decision for the first time before the Supreme Court.[707]

426. As it was remarked in the previous paragraphs, when the recognition of a foreign judgment in Italy is contested or the judgment is not complied with and/or when such decision needs to be enforced in our country, a recognition/enforcement petition must be brought in the competent Court of Appeal. As concerns standing, Article 67 of Law No. 218 of 1995 has a very broad wording: as a matter of fact, it refers to any interested person. In other words, an action for recognition and enforcement may be brought not only by the parties to the foreign proceedings (or

703. *Cass.* 22 Jul. 2004, n. 13662.
704. *App.* Milan 4 Dec. 1998, RDIPP, 2000, 110.
705. *App.* Milan 28 Dec. 1999, RDIPP, 2000, 1081.
706. *Cass.*, 1969, n. 3881.
707. With reference to the violation of public order, *see Cass.* 18 Dec. 1992, n. 13437.

their privies in the title) but also by any subject with a related or connected claim to the one adjudicated upon abroad.

The wording of Article 67 of the 1995 Act also enables the losing party in the foreign proceedings to bring an action for a negative declaratory judgment to verify that the decision rendered abroad does not meet the requirements set by Article 64 and therefore may be neither recognized nor enforced in Italy.

The Court of Appeal will verify whether the decision rendered abroad complies with the conditions set by Article 67 of the 1995 Act (which, roughly speaking, have not dramatically been modified as compared to the ones previously set by Article 797 CPC).

In particular:

(a) the judgment must have been rendered by a judge of competent jurisdiction, in compliance with the principles governing the exercise of jurisdiction in Italy (Article 64, lett. (*a*) of the 1995 Act): in other words, a foreign judgment will be recognized in Italy only if, at the same conditions, an Italian court would have assumed jurisdiction over the dispute (the so-called *competenza indiretta*);
(b) the claimant's petition in the proceedings *a quo* must have been served on the defendant in compliance with the foreign provisions, and the rights of the defence in the foreign proceedings must not have been violated (Article 64, lett. (*b*)): this provision (together with the one set forth in Article 64, lett. (*c*)) requires the judgment rendered abroad to comply with the so-called procedural public policy; in other words, the petition starting the foreign proceedings must have been duly served on the defendant, and the latter's right of the defence must have been safeguarded over the course of the whole proceedings. It is not necessary, however, for the foreign court to have applied the same procedural provisions which would have been applied in Italy at the same conditions: only the safeguard of fundamental procedural rights, such as the ones implemented in the Constitution (e.g., the impartiality of the court, the right of the parties to be treated on an equal footing, the right of the party to be heard by the judge before a decision is taken, and so forth) must be granted;
(c) the parties must have appeared before the foreign court in compliance with the applicable foreign procedural provisions, or they must have been duly declared in default (Article 64 lett. (*c*)): this requirement is effectively a specification of the one sanctioned in the previous lett. (*b*), under the 'safeguard of the right of the defence' caption. In other words, also this requirement falls under the 'procedural public policy' standard of review;
(d) the foreign decision must have become res judicata in the rendering State (Article 64, lett. (*b*), *see* above, paragraph 3);
(e) foreign judgments must not be incompatible with an Italian decision having full res judicata effects (Article 64, lett. (*e*)): this is a traditional requirement as concerns the recognition of foreign decision (the so-called, conflict of judgments exception). Since a given legal relationship may not be adjudicated upon in a conflicting way in Italy and abroad, the municipal decision will always prevail, as long as any available appeal against it has been brought. It is important to stress, however, that this 'exception' has a rather narrow scope. In particular, any logical incompatibility in the reasons of the two decisions is considered to

be irrelevant, since only conflicting practical effects may be considered in this context; this happens, for example, when from the two decisions consequences derive that mutually deny each other);

(f) no prior proceeding on the same subject-matter and between the same parties must be pending in Italy (Article 64, lett. (*f*)): this requirement is deeply connected with the new provision on lis pendens introduced by Law No. 218 of 1995 (*see* paragraph 152). As a matter of fact, when proceedings are started in Italy on a dispute which is already being adjudicated abroad, the Italian courts are now under the obligation to stay the case if they come to the conclusion that the judgment that is going to be rendered by the foreign judge is likely to be granted recognition in Italy. Conversely, when proceedings are previously brought in Italy, the lawmaker has made it clear that they should be respected by other legal orders under the sanction that, should the latter not stay the proceedings subsequently started there, the resulting judgment will not be recognized in Italy;

(g) the effects of the judgment provisions should not violate public policy: this is another traditional requirement in this area of the law. As a matter of fact, every legal order reserves the right not to give effects to foreign normative rules or judicial decisions under public policy considerations. In modern private international law, however, the relevance of public policy, especially in commercial law, is gradually diminishing. As concerns us here, on the one hand it has to be remarked that the notion of international public policy has to be considered. Such notion, which refers to the safeguard of the fundamental principles which set the ethical and juridical basis of the Italian system, is considered to be narrower than the one applied with reference to purely municipal relationship and disputes. On the other hand, Article 64, lett. (*g*) of Law No. 218 of 1995 does not take into consideration neither the foreign judgment in itself, nor its reasoning, but merely its effects within the Italian legal order. It is argued that, from this point of view, public policy considerations may deny recognition to a foreign decision only in rather serious and particular circumstances. As a matter of fact, foreign decisions in civil and commercial matters (with the exclusions of some sensitive areas of the law like family or succession law) will only rarely be denied recognition in Italy on public policy grounds.

427. Special recognition provisions are set out for decisions in matters of status, legal capacity of persons and non-contentious jurisdiction with a stronger influence of private international law (Articles 65–66 of Law No. 218 of 1995).[708]

In these areas, private international law considerations play a very important role: basically, a foreign decision will be recognized in Italy if it spreads legal effects in the country whose law is deemed to be applicable to the merits of the dispute.

---

708. *See* M.A. Lupoi in Carpi & Taruffo (eds), *Commentario breve al codice di procedura civile*, 6th edn (Padua: Cedam, 2009), 2480 et seq.

II. International Treaties

428. As elsewhere, also in Italy different sets of rules apply to the recognition and enforcement of foreign decisions, depending on the State whose courts rendered the judgment and the subject-matter adjudicated upon.

First of all, since Italy is a member of the European Union, the European procedural regulations on the circulation of judicial decisions among the Member States have to be considered. In particular, as concerns civil and commercial matters, in order to recognize and enforce decisions rendered in other EU Member States, the provision of regulation No. 44/2001 (Brussels I) will be referred to. In matrimonial and parental responsibility matters, on the other hand, regulation No. 2201/2003 (Brussels II *bis*) will be applicable (*see supra*, paragraphs 40 et seq.). Moreover, decisions and documents coming from other Member States and which are granted the status of European enforcement orders according to the various regulations applicable (in particular, regulations No. 805 of 2004 and No. 1896 of 2006) will be enforced in Italy as of right, without any *exequatur* proceedings. It is beyond the scope of this monograph, however, to analyse the provisions of these important European regulations. Suffice to say here that a petition for recognition under the Brussels system in Italy takes the form of a *ricorso* to the Court of Appeal, which will grant or deny recognition and or enforcement with a decree. Such decree can be opposed either by the defendant or by the petitioner before the Court of Appeal, which will decide with a judgment. Against such judgment *ricorso* to the *Cassazione* is admitted.

Secondly, it has to be considered that Italy has ratified several bi- and multilateral Conventions in matters of recognition and enforcement of foreign judgments in several areas of the law. The Conventions and international Treaties which have not been superseded by any European regulations, are always deemed to prevail over the application of competing municipal legislation (Article 2 of Law No. 218 of 1995) and will need to be considered by the court ex officio, should a foreign decision fall into their scope of application.[709]

In particular, it is worth mentioning that recognition of ecclesiastic marriage decisions is governed by the 1929 Treaty between Italy and the Holy See, as modified in 1984.[710]

709. For a collection of materials, *see* F. Pocar et al., *Codice delle convenzioni di diritto internazionale privato e processuale*, 3rd edn (Milan: Giuffrè, 1999).

710. *See* Badiali, 'Il riconoscimento delle sentenze ecclesiastiche di nullità dei matrimoni nel nuovo sistema italiano di diritto internazionale privato', RDI (2000): 7.

Part X. Arbitration

Chapter 1. Arbitrability

429. Arbitration is a quite popular method to solve commercial disputes in Italy today. As a matter of fact, it is considered to be an efficient, speedy, confidential and professional (if costly) alternative to lengthy, public and often chaotic ordinary civil proceedings.

From an original dislike, with many restrictions as to the possibility for the parties to oust the jurisdiction of ordinary courts and the effects of the arbitral award, in recent years, a very strong pro-arbitration policy has emerged in Italy, in particular in the latest reforms (of 1994 and 2006 respectively) of the relevant provisions of the code.[711] In 1994, Law No. 25 fully recognized arbitration as an equivalent (private) alternative to judicial proceedings and effectively put the arbitrators' award on the same footing as a judge's decision. More recently, DLGS No. 40 of 2006 completely revised the provisions of the CPC on arbitration, introducing an even more favourable legislation.[712]

As a matter of fact, after the reform of 2006, the autonomy of arbitration vis-à-vis judicial proceedings has been strongly implemented. Today, not only can the arbitrators decide, *incidenter tantum*, any issue which is relevant for the decision of the dispute, even when it falls outside of their jurisdiction, unless this is specifically forbidden by the law (e.g., issues of personal status), but also have the situations where an arbitration must mandatorily be stayed been reduced (e.g., arbitration proceedings must be stayed when the arbitrators raise a constitutional issue to the *Corte costituzionale*, or when an unarbitrable issue falls to be decided with binding effects by a judge) (Articles 819–819*bis* CPC). Moreover, the arbitrators may render their award even when the same or a related dispute is pending before the Italian ordinary courts and, while arbitration proceedings are pending, in order not to interfere with the arbitrators' powers to freely decide upon their own competence, no claim concerning the invalidity or the inefficacy of the relevant arbitration clause may be brought before the judge (Article 819*ter* CPC).

---

711. *See* F. Carpi, 'Libertà e vincoli nella recente evoluzione dell'arbitrato', <www.judicium.it>; C. Punzi, 'Ancora sulla delega in tema di arbitrato: riaffermazione della natura privatistica dell'istituto', RDP (2005): 963; C. Punzi, 'Luci ed ombre nella riforma dell'arbitrato', RTDPC (2007): 395; E.F. Ricci, 'La delega sull'arbitrato', RDP (2005): 951.

712. *See* F. Carpi, *supra*; E. Odorisio, 'Prime osservazioni sulla nuova disciplina dell'arbitrato', rdp (2006): 253; C. Punzi, 'Ancora sulla delega in tema di arbitrato: riaffermazione della natura privatistica dell'istituto', *supra*, 963; C. Punzi, 'Luci ed ombre nella riforma dell'arbitrato', *supra*, 395; E.F. Ricci, 'La delega sull'arbitrato', Rdp (2005): 951.

Besides, after 2006, the possibilities for the courts to review the merits of the arbitral decision have been largely narrowed and largely made dependent on the parties' will.

430. Specific provisions for the arbitration of disputes in certain areas of the law are provided for by various statutes.

Among them, it is worth mentioning Articles 34 et seq. of DLGS 35/2003, which introduced ad hoc provisions for arbitration in company matters (*arbitrato societario*).[713]

Special provisions are also given for the arbitration of labour disputes. In particular, Law No. 183 of 4 November 2010 (the so-called *Collegato lavoro*) recently reformed this area of arbitration law, rewriting Article 412 CPC. The law now allows arbitration clauses to be agreed upon either in collective labour contracts or by the individual parties after the dispute has arisen between them. Moreover, the new legislation, in a rather confusing way, appears to have ruled about as many as five different types of arbitration in relation to labour disputes.[714]

431. A distinction has to be made between an Italian and a foreign arbitration: the former will be governed by the provisions of Italian procedural law and the latter, as a general rule, will be relevant for the Italian legal order only as concerns its final award, subject to recognition and enforcement in our country (*see* at paragraphs 445 et seq.).

As a matter of fact, the code of civil procedure does not specify when an arbitration must be qualified as an Italian one. However, according to Article 816 CPC, the application of Italian procedural law derives from the location in Italy of the seat of the arbitration. It is argued, therefore, that an arbitration having its seat in Italy will be qualified as an Italian one, while an arbitration with its seat abroad will be considered to be a foreign one.[715] Article 816 CPC was reformed in 2006, and its present text leaves the determination of the seat of the arbitration to the will of the parties or, lacking the parties' agreement, to the arbitrators.

If neither the parties nor the arbitrators have expressly established a seat for the arbitration, such seat will be located in the place in Italy where the arbitration clause was agreed upon or, failing that, in Rome.

---

713. *See* P. Biavati, 'Il procedimento nell'arbitrato societario', RA (2003): 27; M. Bove, 'L'arbitrato nelle controversie societarie', GC (2003): II, 473; F. Carpi, 'Profili dell'arbitrato in materia di società', RA (2003): 411; F. Corsini, 'L'arbitrato nella riforma del diritto societario', GI (2003): 1285; E. Fazzalari, 'L'arbitrato nella riforma del diritto societario', RA (2002): 443; F.P. Luiso, 'Appunti sull'arbitrato societario', RDP (2003): 705; E.F. Ricci, 'Il nuovo arbitrato societario', RTDPC (2003): 517; G. Ruffini, 'Il nuovo arbitrato per le controversie societarie', RTDPC (2004): 495; G. Tarzia, 'L'intervento di terzi nell'arbitrato societario', RDP (2004): 349.

714. More details in C. Punzi, 'L'arbitrato per la soluzione delle controversie di lavoro', RDP (2011): 11 et seq.

715. *See also* C. Punzi, *Disegno sistematico dell'arbitrato*, vol. II (Padua: Cedam, 2000), 287 and 291; C. Punzi, *Il processo civile. Sistema e problematiche*, vol. III (Turin: Giappichelli, 2008), 283; P. Biavati, 'Arbitrato internazionale'. in *Arbitrati speciali*, ed. F. Carpi (Bologna: Zanichelli, 2008), 400.

The seat of the arbitration is a very important element because many procedural provisions refer to it in relation to various forms of judicial cooperation and protection of the arbitral proceedings (e.g., when one arbitrator must be appointed or removed by the court).

Arguably, according to Italian law, it should always be possible to determine the 'nationality' of an arbitration, therefore negating the admissibility of the so-called floating arbitration. It should be remarked, however, that in arbitration located in Italy the arbitrators are free to hold meetings and deliberate in a different place than the official seat, and even abroad – Article 816(3) CPC. In other words, when the seat of the arbitration is located in Italy, the arbitral award will still be qualified as an Italian one even though it was deliberated abroad.

However, an arbitration (either Italian or foreign) may be qualified as 'international' when it refers to a dispute related to two or more different legal orders and therefore does not have a purely 'national' character. As a matter of fact, the reform of 2006 eliminated the specific part of the code dedicated to international arbitration, so that now all arbitrations located in Italy are subject to the same rules, irrespective of any foreign connection.[716] As we shall see in the next paragraphs, some specific provisions exist, however, granting a special treatment for arbitrations having some form of foreign connection. Today, the CPC does not even give a notion of international arbitration: one may be drawn, however, from Article 830(2), which provides for a specific provision in relation to the review of an award, when one of the parties, at the time the arbitral clause was drafted, was resident or domiciled or had his or her main seat outside of Italy.

432. One of the peculiarities of Italian arbitration law is that two forms of 'municipal' arbitration are regulated: as a matter of fact, arbitration may be qualified as either *rituale* or *irrituale*, the former being treated as a functional equivalent of judicial adjudication of a dispute, the latter defined as a contractual determination of the parties' dispute.[717] The reform of 2006 has clarified the distinction between these two models of arbitration. In particular, *arbitrato irrituale* – which was originally created by the business practice (and recognized by the case law) to overcome the original rigidity of the rules of the code (and the fiscal implications of *arbitrato rituale*) – was formally recognized by law, with a new Article 808*ter* introduced in the CPC.

In practice, the main difference between these two forms of arbitration concerns the effects of the awards rendered therein.[718] A *rituale* award, as a matter of fact, is granted the same authority and effects of a judicial decision (Article 824*bis* CPC): it has res judicata effects, it can be appealed against before the Court of Appeal and it can be enforced against the debtor, after the *Tribunale* grants an *exequatur*. However, an *irrituale* award is considered a contract, which binds the parties but does not, in itself, have res judicata effects and cannot be enforced *ex se*. Different remedies against an arbitral award are granted, depending on its *rituale* or *irrituale*

716. *See* A. Briguglio, 'La dimensione transnazionale dell'arbitrato', RA (2005): 679.

717. B. Sassani, 'L'arbitrato a modalità irrituale', <www.judicium.it>.

718. *See* E. Fazzalari, 'La distinzione tra arbitrati "rituale" e "irrituale": qualcosa si muove?', RA (1999): 253.

qualification. In particular, after the reform of 2006, an award rendered in an *arbitrato irrituale* may be declared null and void by the judge, in the course of ordinary cognizance proceedings at first instance, upon several specific grounds (e.g., the arbitral clause was invalid, the arbitrators did not follow the parties dispositions as to validity of the award, the contradiction principle was not duly respected in the course of the arbitration, and so on). It is up to the parties to qualify their arbitration as either *rituale* or *irrituale* in the arbitral clause. After the reform of 2006, however, Article 808*ter* CPC makes it clear that, in case of doubt, the code provisions on *rituale* arbitration will apply.

Not every dispute, however, may be decided through arbitration. As a matter of fact, according to Article 806 CPC, as revised in 2006, it is not possible to defer to arbitration a dispute concerning rights that the parties may not freely dispose of (*diritti indisponibili*);[719] the law may also exclude the arbitrability of other types of disputes.

719. G.F. Ricci, 'Dalla "transigibilità" alla "disponibilità" del diritto. I nuovi orizzonti dell'arbitrato', RA (2006): 265; G.F. Ricci, 'La convenzione di arbitrato e le materie arbitrabili nella riforma', RTDPC (2007): 759.

Chapter 2. Arbitration Agreement and Party Autonomy

433. The provisions of the CPC are still mainly dedicated to the *arbitrato rituale*, for which general procedural guidelines are set forth. Of course, ample recognition is granted to the parties' autonomy, and a specific provision has been introduced in 2006 stating that the parties may refer, in their arbitral clause, to an arbitration regulation (both national and international) (*arbitrato amministrato*: Article 832 CPC).[720]

434. In Italian law, to be valid, an arbitral clause[721] must be stipulated in writing (Articles 807–808 CPC), either in relation to a contract, before a dispute arises (*clausola compromissioria*) or as an autonomous agreement, in reference to a previously stipulated contract, most often after a dispute has arisen between the parties (*compromesso*). Article 808*bis* CPC, introduced in 2006, now explicitly allows the parties to stipulate arbitration clauses in relation to specific non-contractual disputes.

In order to avoid interpretation disputes, Article 808*quater* CPC now expressly states that, in all dubious cases, the arbitration clause must be interpreted as to enable the arbitrators to adjudicate every dispute deriving from the contract or the relationship the clause itself refers to.

The validity of the clause does not depend on the validity of the contract it refers to and vice versa, in compliance with the severability principle: Article 808(3) CPC.

---

720. *See*, e.g., E. Ricci, 'Il nuovo Regolamento della Camera Arbitrale Nazionale e Internazionale di Milano', RA (2003): 663.
721. For an analysis of the new provisions of the CPC as concerns arbitral clauses, *see* M. Bove, 'Aspetti problematici nella nuova disciplina della convenzione d'arbitrato rituale', <www.judicium.it>.

Chapter 3. Composition of Arbitral Tribunal

435. According to Article 809 CPC, the arbitral panel may be composed of one or more arbitrators, as long as they make an odd number;[722] the clause must either indicate the names of the arbitrators or specify the way in which they must be selected and nominated. Each party usually appoints one arbitrator; if one of the parties does not choose his or her arbitrator, the counterpart may file a petition to the president of the tribunal of the place where the arbitration has its seat,[723] who will then appoint an arbitrator ex officio.

An exception is made for the arbitration of company disputes: since traditional binary clauses prove rather inefficient in this context, where a plurality of parties is most often involved, Article 34 of DLGS No. 5 of 2003 provides that, to be valid, an arbitration clause inserted in a memorandum of association must defer the power to appoint all of the arbitrators to a third party outside of the company.[724]

The reform of 2006, moreover, introduced specific rules concerning the appointment of arbitrators in multiparty disputes: Article 816*quater* CPC.[725]

Other provisions regulate the way an arbitrator can be substituted (Article 811 CPC) or challenged (Article 815 CPC).

A specific provision (Article 813*ter* CPC) was introduced in 2006 concerning the arbitrators' liability: basically, similar rules are now provided as those relating to a judge's civil liability.[726]

The arbitrators have the right to be paid for their activity, either with the agreement of the parties or with an order of the court (Article 814 CPC). Article 816*septies* CPC, introduced in 2006, explicitly states that the arbitrators may put the further continuation of the proceedings under the condition that the parties advance the foreseeable costs of the procedure. Should the parties not comply with this request, the arbitral clause will no longer be binding for them. In other words, a rather strong device has been introduced to ensure that the costs of the procedure will be covered at least by the party which has an interest in the continuation of the proceedings.

722. If an even number of arbitrator is chosen, one other arbitrator is appointed by the president of the *Tribunale*: Arts 809(2) and 810 CPC.
723. Or of the other places indicated in Art. 810(2) CPC.
724. *See* Boggio, 'Le clausole compromissorie statutarie alla luce dell'art. 34, comma 2, D. Lgs. n. 5 del 17 gennaio 2003', RA (2005): 199; E. Zucconi Galli Fonseca, 'La convenzione arbitrale nella società dopo la riforma', RTDPC (2003): 929.
725. On the problems which arose under the pre-2006 rules in multi-party arbitration when it came to appointing the arbitrators, *see* E. Zucconi Galli Fonseca, 'Qualche riflessione sulla clausola binaria nell'arbitrato con pluralità di parti', RA (1997): 744.
726. A. Briguglio, 'La responsabilità dell'arbitro al bivio fra responsabilità professionale e responsabilità del giudice', GC (2006): II, 57.

Chapter 4. Interim Measures and Preliminary Awards

436. As a rule, arbitrators are not empowered to grant interim measures (Article 818 CPC). According to Article 669*quinquies* CPC, if the dispute is governed by an arbitral clause or if the dispute has been submitted to arbitration of any kind, an interim measure may be applied for to the ordinary judge who would be otherwise competent to decide that dispute. In other words, State judges will support the arbitral panel by releasing those interim measures which arbitrators may not issue themselves.

The rules of Articles 669*bis* CPC et seq. apply to interim proceedings (*see* paragraphs 380 et seq.). In particular, mention to Article 669*octies* (5) CPC must be made, governing the relation between an interim measure rendered *ante causam* and the subsequent proceedings on the merits (paragraph 378). When the beginning of those proceedings is necessary under Article 669*octies* (1) CPC (*see* paragraph 389), the party that was awarded the interim measure is burdened to notify the other party, within sixty days, a declaration stating its intention to bring arbitral proceedings and in which the arbitrator(s) of its choosing is or are appointed).

An exception to the rule above is provided for arbitration in company disputes (*controversie societarie*) under Article 35(5) of DLGS No. 5 of 17 January 2003: whenever an arbitral clause grants arbitrators the power to review a company resolution, they are also empowered to issue an order staying the enforcement of that resolution. This interim order is not subject to any form of review.

437. Arbitrators may decide every issue arising in the proceedings with an order which may be always modified or revoked. They may also decide any preliminary question by way of non-final award (Article 816*bis* (3) CPC). When a non-final or partial awards is given, the deadline to deposit the final award is automatically postponed for 180 days, according to Article 820(4)(c) CPC.

Chapter 5. Conduct of Arbitral Proceedings

438. Proceedings are regulated by the rules the parties themselves have agreed upon before the beginning of the arbitration; otherwise, the arbitrators are free to arrange the procedure, as long as they grant the parties sufficient time to present their case and to reply to the counterpart's defences (Article 816*bis* CPC).[727]

In order to solve a previously controversial issue, Article 816*quinquies* CPC was introduced in 2006, allowing third parties to voluntarily join or to be forcibly joined in the arbitration proceedings only by agreement between the third parties themselves and the original parties and with the arbitrators' consent.

After the reform of 1994, DLGS No. 40 of 2006 has made arbitral proceedings even more independent of judicial interference than in the past: not only can the arbitrators decide, *incidenter tantum*, any issue which is relevant for the decision of the case, even when it falls outside of their jurisdiction, unless this is specifically forbidden by the law (e.g., issues of personal status), but also the situations where a compulsory stay of the arbitration must be disposed have been reduced (e.g., arbitration proceedings must be stayed when the arbitrators raise a constitutional issue to the *Corte costituzionale*, or when an unarbitrable issue must be decided with binding effects by a judge) (Articles 819–819*bis* CPC).[728]

Moreover, the arbitrators may render their award even when the same or a related dispute is pending before the Italian courts and, while arbitration proceedings are pending, in order not to interfere with the arbitrators' powers to freely decide upon their own competence, no claim concerning the invalidity or the inefficacy of the relevant arbitration clause may be brought before the judge (Article 819*ter* CPC).

439. In 2006, a new provision has been introduced, providing for general rules for the evidence-gathering phase before the arbitrators: Article 816*ter*.

In particular, the arbitrators are allowed to hear a witness either before them or directly at the witness' home or office, if the latter gives his or her permission for doing so. Also, a witness may deposit a written statement in lieu of appearing before the panel at an oral hearing. It must be reminded that written testimony is instead still prohibited in judicial proceedings.

The reform of 2006, with an aim at implementing the efficiency of the evidence-gathering phase before the arbitrators, allowed the latter to apply to the competent court to have any unwilling witness summoned before them.

Moreover, the new provision now expressly allows the arbitrators to appoint experts to solve technical issues and to request written information to a public body.

In general, even when the law does not expressly provide so, it is believed that arbitrators may make use of the same means to gather evidence as those admitted in judicial proceedings.

---

727. R. Marengo, 'Lo svolgimento del processo nell'arbitrato', RA (1997): 299.

728. In relation to the rules existing before the reform of 2006, *see* L. Montesano, 'Questioni incidentali nel giudizio arbitrale e sospensione di processi', RDP (2000): 1; P. Nela, 'Le questioni pregiudiziali nel giudizio arbitrale (il nuovo art. 819 c.p.c.)', RDP (1995): 171; F. Danovi, *La pregiudizialità nell'arbitrato rituale* (Padua: Cedam, 1999).

Chapter 6. Arbitral Award

440. The arbitrators are under a duty to render their award within the time limit set by the parties or, failing that, 240 days from the date they accepted their appointment as arbitrators. This deadline may be extended for 180 days when the following procedural activities must be performed (and only once for every type of activity): the gathering of evidence, the appointment of an expert, the rendering of a partial award or the modification of the original composition of the arbitral panel (Article 820 CPC).

The deadline for the award may also be delayed when all of the parties so agree in writing or by the order of the *Presidente* of the competent *Tribunale*, upon the request of one of the parties or the arbitrators.

If the deadline expires before the award has been rendered, any party may serve on the other parties and on the arbitrators a notice stating that she intends to hold the arbitrator in forfeiture. In this case, arbitration proceedings are discontinued, and the arbitrators are liable for the damages the parties incurred in as a consequence of their lack of timely performance. If no notice is served, however, the arbitrators may still render the award with no negative effects (Article 821 CPC). In other words, the parties may no longer wait until the award has been rendered before challenging the arbitrators' forfeiture, as it happened in the past.

441. In rendering the award, the arbitrators should apply the relevant legal rules, unless the parties agreed on an equitable decision (Article 822 CPC).[729]

The Code does not explicitly allow the parties to choose upon the application of a foreign law (or even of *lex mercatoria*) to the merits of their dispute, but it is argued that the possibility for the parties to agree on a choice of law clause in relation to an arbitration derives from the general principles and the specific provisions of private international law.

Article 823 CPC specifies that the award is rendered upon a majority vote; the same rule lists the elements that the award must include (most notably, the award must be signed by all the arbitrators).[730] From the day of the last signature, the award is binding between the parties.

The award must be handed by the arbitrators to the parties. Whenever the award has to be enforced, a copy of it must also be filed in the *Tribunale* of the place where the arbitration seat was located, in order to obtain the *exequatur*. Against the *Tribunale* decision, an opposition (*reclamo*) may be brought to the Court of Appeal (Article 825 CPC).

When the *exequatur* is allowed, an arbitral award is enforced exactly as a judicial decision.

729. *See* Tucci, 'L'equità del codice civile e l'arbitrato di equità', *Contratto e impresa* (1998): 469.

730. Not necessarily at the same time or in the same place (Art. 823, last para., CPC). An award is valid; however, if it was signed by a majority of the arbitrators, when the other(s) did not or could not sign it too.

Chapter 7. Recourse Against Arbitral Award

442. If the arbitrators made material mistakes, the award can be corrected (Article 826 CPC). The award can also be appealed on some specific grounds listed in Article 829 CPC[731] before the Court of Appeal of the place where the arbitration seat was located (*impugnazione per nullità*).

The award can also be reviewed when one of the conditions of *revocazione straordinaria* is met (Article 395 CPC, *see supra*, paragraph 277), and third parties may bring *opposizione di terzo* against it in compliance with Article 404 CPC (*see supra*, paragraphs 279 et seq.).[732]

731. With reference, e.g., to the invalidity of the arbitration clause, the violation of the time limit set for the deposit o the award, for violation of the adversary principle and so on.
732. More details in F.P. Luiso, 'Le impugnazioni del lodo dopo la riforma', RTDPC (1995): 13.

Chapter 8. Recognition and Enforcement of Awards

443. A foreign award is (i.e., an award rendered in an arbitration whose seat was located abroad) must be recognized by an Italian court before it can spread res judicata effects or be enforced in Italy.[733] Recognition of foreign awards is regulated by international treaties and by national provisions.[734]

444. Italy is a signatory of various international treaties in matters of arbitration. The most relevant piece of international legislation in this area of the law is the New York Convention on the recognition and enforcement of foreign arbitral awards of 10 June 1958.[735] Next to this, the Geneva European Convention on international commercial arbitration of 21 April 1961 and the Washington Convention for the resolution of disputes in respect of investment between states and the citizens of other states are also worth mentioning.[736]

445. When no international treaty is applicable (which is indeed quite rare in practice), the provisions of the Italian CPC must be referred to.

This part of the Italian law on arbitration was reformed in 1994 by Law No. 25, which introduced Articles 839 (on recognition and enforcement of foreign awards) and 840 (on opposition to the court's decision on the petition for recognition/ enforcement) in the code. These provisions basically reproduce the text of Articles V and VI of the New York Convention of 1958, thus effectively extending the scope of application of the latter also to awards rendered in States which are not a party to the Convention.

In particular, according to Article 839 CPC, a petition for the recognition of a foreign award must be filed with the President of the Court of Appeal of the place where the other party resides or, if that party resides abroad, of the Court of Appeal of Roma.

A certified copy of the foreign award and of the arbitration clause must also be filed. A certified translation of these documents must be provided as well if they are written in a foreign language.

733. *See* A. Barletta, 'L'exequatur dei provvedimenti cautelari arbitrali stranieri (tendenze e prospettive di riforma)', RDP (2003): 1193.

734. Articles 839 et seq. CPC, which have been introduced by the Law No. 25 of 5 Jan. 1994. *See* Bove, M., 'Il riconoscimento del lodo straniero tra Convenzione di New York e codice di procedura civile', RA (2006): 21; P. Biavati, 'Commento ad artt. 839–840 CPC', in *Arbitrato*, ed. Carpi (Bologna: Zanichelli, 2001).

735. It is beyond the scope to this monograph to enter into any detail of this important convention, on which a vast literature exists. For some Italian contributions, *see* Carpi, F., 'L'esecutorietà della sentenza arbitrale secondo la convenzione di New York', RDP 88, 386; C. Giovannucci Orlandi, 'La convenzione di New York per il riconoscimento e l'esecuzione delle sentenze arbitrali straniere (1958)', in *Essays on transnational and comparative civil procedure*, ed. Carpi, Lupoi (Turin: Giappichelli, 2001), 243–264; A. Briguglio, *L'arbitrato estero* (Padua: Cedam, 1999); Bernardini, 'Sentenze arbitrali e Convenzione di New York', RDP (2006): 89.

736. *See* Biamonti *Italy*, in *International Execution Against Judgments Debtors* 12 et seq. (Campbell, ed. vol. II Sweet and Maxwell).

At this stage, the President of the Court of Appeal can only check the formal regularity of the award, and he will grant the recognition or *exequatur* petition unless he finds that:

(a) the dispute could not be deferred to arbitration according to Italian law;[737] in other words, whether the arbitration concerned a right the parties could freely dispose of falls to be decided in accordance with Italian law, irrespective of the law applied to the merits of the dispute by the arbitrators; or
(b) the award contains provisions which violate Italian public policy.

The President of the Court of Appeal will either allow or deny the petition with a decree (*decreto*).

446. Against the President's decree granting (or denying) the *exequatur*, an opposition may be raised by any interested party, with a *citazione* to the Court of Appeal within thirty days of the date when the decree was either communicated (in case the petition is denied) or served (in case the petition is granted).

The procedural rules provided for opposition to a *decreto ingiuntivo* (Articles 645 et seq. CPC, *see retro*, paragraph 377) apply, if compatible.[738]

The Court of Appeal decision can be appealed to the *Corte di cassazione*.

447. It is the burden of the party that opposes the *exequatur* to show that there are reasons for not enforcing the foreign award in Italy. As a matter of fact, Article 840 CPC lists several grounds for refusing to recognize or enforce in Italy a foreign arbitral award. Such list clearly reproduces the criteria referred to in Article V of the New York Convention of 1958 to serve the main function.

A foreign award will then not be recognized or enforced in Italy if, alternatively:

(a) the parties to the arbitral agreement were, under the law applicable to them, under some incapacity, or said agreement was not valid under the law to which the parties have subjected it or, failing any indication thereon, under the law of the country where the award was made;
(b) the party against whom the award is invoked was not given proper notice of the appointment of the arbitrator or of the arbitration proceedings or was otherwise unable to present his or her case therein;
(c) the award deals with a difference not contemplated by or not falling within the terms of the submission to arbitration, or it contains decisions on matters beyond the scope of the submission to arbitration; however, if the decisions on matters submitted to arbitration can be separated from those not so submitted, that part of the award which contains decisions on matters submitted to arbitration may be recognized and enforced;

737. This provision is in compliance with Art. V, para. 2 of the New York Convention of 1958.
738. *See* E. Zucconi Galli Fonseca, 'L'esecutorietà del lodo arbitrale straniero in pendenza di opposizione', RA (1997): 345.

(d) the composition of the arbitral authority or the arbitral procedure was not in accordance with the agreement of the parties, or, failing such agreement, was not in accordance with the law of the country where the arbitration took place;
(e) the award has not yet become binding on the parties, or has been set aside or suspended by a competent authority of the country in which, or under the law of which, that award was made.

Moreover, in line with the final part of Article V of the New York Convention, the last paragraph of Article 840 CPC states that recognition and enforcement of a foreign arbitral award will also be denied if the Court of Appeal finds that:

(a) the subject-matter of the dispute was not capable of settlement by arbitration under Italian law; or
(b) the award's dispositions are contrary to public policy.

In compliance with the rule of Article VI of the New York Convention, according to Article 840 CPC, the Court of Appeal may stay the recognition proceedings should the award be appealed against before the courts of the State of the seat of the arbitration. It may also, on the application of the party claiming enforcement of the award, order the other party to give suitable security.

Chapter 9. International Arbitration

448. As it was already pointed out, the fundamental provisions on arbitration law is found in the code of civil procedure of 1940.

The original rules of the code did not provide for a specific procedural treatment nor for a qualification of international arbitration.

To recognize the peculiarities of this form of arbitration (and possibly to enhance the role of Italy as a seat for international arbitrations), however, in 1994, Articles 832–838 were introduced in the code of civil procedure to regulate some aspects of international arbitration.[739]

These new provisions were clearly inspired by the rules of the Geneva Convention of 21 April 1961, on international commercial arbitration[740] and aimed at implementing the specific needs of litigation in transnational commerce. In other words, after the reform of 1994, international arbitration was considered to be a form of Italian arbitration, subject to both the general procedural provisions of the code concerning arbitration and also to some special rules, derogating from the general provisions or governing specific features of international disputes resolution.

In particular, Articles 832 et seq. put a stronger stress on the autonomy of the parties and on the de-formalization of the arbitral procedure than the general rules on arbitration, following some principles generally followed in the international arena.

According to Article 832 CPC, as reformed in 1994, an arbitration could be qualified as 'international' when at least one of the parties resided or had its operative seat outside of Italy or when a relevant part of the obligations deriving from the relationship to which the dispute related had to be performed abroad.[741]

Basically, in drafting this qualification of 'international arbitration', the Italian lawmaker had adopted both an objective and a subjective criterion.

The special provisions governing international arbitration in Italy after the reform of 1994 may be summarized here as follows:

- less formal requirements were set for the validity of the arbitration clause; such clause could also be included in the general contractual conditions established by one of the parties, as long as the other party was, or should have been, aware of the inclusion of the arbitral clause therein (Article 833 CPC). In other words, arbitral clauses stipulated *per relationem* were deemed to be valid, and the current practices of commerce were implemented;
- the parties could agree on the rules that the arbitrators had to apply to the merits of the dispute (including the possibility to agree on an equitable decision); should such an agreement lack, the arbitrators could apply the law which they deemed to be the most closely connected to the dispute, adopting a case-by-case approach. In other words, arbitrators were entitled to bypass the traditional mechanisms of private international law. However, they were requested to take into considerations, in their analysis, commercial practices (Article 834 CPC);

739. A. Briguglio, 'La nuova disciplina dell'arbitrato internazionale', GC (1994): II, 83; Luzzatto, 'L'impugnazione del lodo arbitrale internazionale', RA (1997): 19.

740. C. Punzi, 'Il processo civile. Sistema e problematiche', *supra*, vol. III, 283.

741. *See also* C. Punzi, *Disegno sistematico dell'arbitrato*, *supra*, 287 ss.

- the parties or the arbitrators could choose the language of the arbitration, taking into consideration all the relevant circumstances (Article 835 CPC);
- the parties could derogate to the general discipline on challenging arbitrators (Article 836 CPC);
- the arbitral award could be deliberated by a majority of the arbitrators also through a video-conference (Article 837 CPC);
- some restrictions were established to the possibility of bringing appeals against the award (Article 838 CPC).

Little more than ten years after the 1994 reform, the Italian lawmaker drastically changed its attitude towards the regulation of international arbitration in the Italian legislation.

As a matter of fact, in 2006, the *decreto legislativo* No. 40 brought an extensive reform to arbitration law in Italy.[742]

One of the policies of the new legislation was to unify the rules applicable to municipal and international arbitration: in other words, as a general rule, the same procedural provisions now apply irrespective of the presence of some 'foreign' elements in the dispute.

Following the principles expressed in the 'legge delega' (i.e., the Act of Parliament which empowers the Government to approve pieces of legislation) No. 80 of 2005, the *decreto* of 2006, on the one hand, repealed the special provisions of the code of civil procedure dedicated to international arbitration, while, on the other hand, at least in part extended the special treatment formerly reserved to international arbitration to arbitration in general.

As a matter of fact, in 2006, the lawmaker came to the conclusion that it was no longer necessary to adopt different rules for these two types of arbitration, since also 'ordinary' arbitration could now enjoy the same de-formalization formerly adopted only in relation to international arbitration.

Having said this, a special treatment is still reserved to arbitration with a foreign element as concerns the possibility to raise an appeal against the final award.

In particular, as an exception to the general rule, according to the new Article 830(2) CPC, if, at the time the arbitral agreement was made, one of the parties resided or was domiciled abroad, when an appeal is raised against an award and the Court of Appeal allows the appellant's petition, the court may then decide de novo the merits of the case only if the parties agreed about this judicial new decision in the arbitral clause or if they give their mutual consent in the course of the appeal proceedings. This is arguably the only provision of the code now granting a specific provision for an arbitration having some foreign connection (i.e., the residence or domicile abroad of one of the parties at the time the arbitral clause was made).

It is argued, however, that the *decreto legislativo* No. 40 of 2006 had a somehow conservative approach, and that some of the innovative spirit of the provisions introduced in 1994 for international arbitration was lost in their conversion in the general rules on arbitration.

742. M.A. Lupoi, 'Quel che resta dell'arbitrato con elementi di estraneità', RTDPC (2009): 1339.

In particular, after the reform of 2006, as concerns the formal requirements of the arbitral clause, Article 807 CPC now requires that the clause be stipulated in writing (requirement *ad substantiam*), with no exceptions.

No reference is any longer made to arbitral clauses accepted *per relationem*. Nonetheless, it is generally agreed that the parties may still validly stipulate arbitral clauses by making a clear and unequivocal reference to the general terms of a contract containing such a clause (the so-called *relatio perfecta*).

The reform of 2006 did not tackle the most problematic issues concerning arbitration having some foreign elements.

For example, no provision is set to determine the law applicable to the arbitrability of a dispute having some foreign connection.

It is therefore argued that, in Italy, at least as concerns the courts' approach, such issue should be resolved in compliance with the *lex fori*, following the solution which appears to be applied in the context of the New York Convention of 1958, in the light of the relationship between Article II, paragraphs 1 and 2 and Article V, paragraph 2).

As a matter of fact, the notion of 'arbitrability' set by Article 806 CPC (which refers to rights which the parties may freely dispose of) has a strong public policy connotation and therefore had to be mandatorily applied even as concerns international arbitration.

No provision, moreover, is dedicated to the law applicable to the arbitral clause. The principle of autonomy of this clause vis-à-vis the contract it is included into is clearly established in Italian case law. Clear opinion is expressed, however, as concerns the determination of the law applicable to it.

It is submitted that this problem cannot have a unitary solutions: as a matter of fact, some aspects concerning, for example, the validity and the effects normally fall to be submitted to the law governing the whole contractual relationship, while others, having a more procedural nature (such as the formal requirements for the validity of a clause) should, as a general rule, be governed by the *lex fori*.

Finally, after the former version of Article 822 CPC has been modified in 2006, there is no longer any provision in the code of civil procedure enabling the parties to mutually agree on the choice of the law applicable to the merits of the dispute.

This does not imply, however, that a choice of law clause would considered to be invalid in this context: as a matter of fact, it would be astonishing if it would.

It is therefore submitted that today this issue is solely governed by the relevant provisions of private international law at the national, European and international level.

It is also possible (although allegedly unusual) for the parties to agree on the application of the so-called *lex mercatoria*.

The present wording of Article 822 CPC, however, unlike the former Article 834 CPC, seems to exclude that, lacking any express choice of law clause, the arbitrators may of their own motion determine the law more closely connected with the dispute: on the contrary, the new rule clearly states that, when no choice of law clause can be found, the arbitrators decide the dispute by applying the relevant legal provisions.

In other words, the new Article 822 CPC tries to curb the arbitrators' discretion in the determination of the *lex causae*.

Today, therefore, arbitrators are bound to find the law applicable to the merits of the dispute solely by making reference to the Italian rules of private international law.

Today, moreover, the wording of Article 822 CPC also makes it impossible for the arbitrators, lacking the parties' consent, to take into consideration for their decision the practices of commerce and *lex mercatoria* in general.

However, Article 822 CPC enables the arbitrators to render an equitable decision when the parties, 'through any expression', have thus determined.

It is submitted that the present Italian provisions on the law applicable to the merits of the arbitral dispute are somehow too strict and rigid, in particular when one compares them with their international equivalent (*see*, e.g., Article 28 of the UNCITRAL model law of 1985 and 33 of the UNCITRAL rules).

449. International arbitration, however, falls within the scope of application of several international Conventions which Italy has ratified and which supersede any competing municipal provision.

The most relevant piece of international legislation in this area of the law is surely the New York Convention on the recognition and enforcement of foreign arbitral awards of 10 June 1958. Also the Geneva European Convention on international commercial arbitration of 21 April 1961 and the Washington Convention for the resolution of disputes in respect of investment between States and the citizens of other States are worth mentioning. However, it is beyond the scope of this chapter to enter into any detail of these important Conventions.

Part XI. Mediation

Chapter 1. Legislation/Definitions

450. The approach to ADR in Italy is a mixed one. On the one hand, ever since the 1970s, academics have been interested in these matters, to try and find a solution to the ever-worsening situation of civil justice. On the other hand, the lawmaker has been slow in adopting statutes and provisions to help the ADR cultural revolution to take a firm hold in the Italian system.[743]

Having said that, the Italian CPC has always recognized the power of the judge to try and help the parties conciliate their dispute. Law No. 353 of 1990 even made it mandatory for the judge to make such an attempt (when the nature of the case so allowed), but the practical results were so discouraging that, in 2006, the law was changed and now a settlement conference is possible only if all the parties make such a request. As a matter of fact, there is an intrinsic contradiction in mixing the role of judge and conciliator, especially when the judge is overburdened with cases and has little time to dedicate to conciliation attempts. Recently, however, the law has introduced the possibility for the judge to formulate to the parties a settlement proposal: this prerogative, of course, goes even beyond the possibility of helping the parties to conciliate, insomuch as it puts the judge in a position to 'force' such conciliation (*see* paragraph 215).

From the 1970s, moreover, the Italian lawmaker started using conciliation as a preliminary step, before the plaintiff was allowed to bring his or her case to court (*condizione di procedibilità*), in relation to certain types of disputes. The first area where this preliminary attempt at conciliation was introduced was labour law: at first, this attempt was merely voluntary, but in 1998 it was made mandatory. Later on, similar mandatory attempts at conciliation were introduced in other areas, like disputes between consumers and firms providing telecommunication services.

In family law, Article 155*sexies* (2) CC (introduced by Law No. 54 of 2006 and now redrafted as Article 337*octies* (2) CC by DLGS No. 154 of 2013),[744] for the first time, made a reference to mediation, empowering the judge to propose to the parties the possibility of staying proceedings concerning parental responsibility, and

743. *See* R. Caponi, 'Just settlement' or 'just about settlement'? Mediated agreements: a comparative overview of the basics, RabelsZ 79 (2015): 117.

744. *See* Pugliese, 'Problemi e prospettive in tema di disciplina della mediazione Familiare e delle relativa professione, anche alla luce della recente direttiva europea sulla mediazione in materia civile e commerciale', *Familia* 3 (2008): 59; M. Romano, 'La mediazione Familiare tra tentativi di valorizzazione e difficoltà operative', *Familia* 3 (2008): 111; F.R. Fantetti, 'La mediazione familiare nei procedimenti di separazione e di divorzio', *Fam. pers. succ.* (2008): 302.

referring them to a mediator to try and reach an agreement on the issues litigated upon. This is widely considered an important provision, but it is still seldom used because the lawmaker apparently forgot that family mediation is not governed by any specific piece of legislation, so that even the notion of family mediator has no legal delimitation or qualification.

Some Italian courts, however, are using this provision extensively, in litigated cases as well as in relation to joint petitions for divorce or separation.[745]

451. The situation has changed in recent years. As a matter of fact, Italy was under the duty to implement in national legislation the principles set forth by the European Directive No. 52 of 21 May 2008, on certain aspects of mediation in civil and commercial matters. Article 60 of Law No. 69 of 2009, therefore, granted the Government the power to issue a *decreto legislativo* on mediation, following certain guidelines (which were themselves based on the standards set by the Directive).

On 4 March 2010, DLGS No. 28 was thus enacted.[746] This piece of legislation for the first time introduced a general discipline for mediation in Italy, filling an important lacuna in the system.

The main flaw of this important reform was that it seemed to consider mediation more as a tool to reduce the courts' caseload than as the expression of a new cultural approach to litigation. In particular, it appeared rather suspicious of the role of lawyers and Italian lawyers, in turn, expressed very hard opinions on the new *decreto legislativo*, especially insomuch as it made a preliminary attempt at mediation a mandatory precondition for certain types of disputes (*see* at paragraphs 202 et seq.).

745. *See*, e.g., *Trib.* Lamezia Terme 28 Nov. 2007, *ord.*, <www.minoriefamiglia.it>; *Trib.* Lamezia Terme 5 Dec. 2007, *ord.*, FD, 2008, 265; *Trib. min.* Campobasso 10 Dec. 2007, *decr.*, FM, 2008, no. 4, 24; *Trib.* Lamezia Terme 11 Mar. 2010, *ord.*, FM, 2010, no. 10, 70.

746. *See* R. Caponi, 'Italian civil justice reform 2009', *ZZPint* (2009); D. Noviello, 'Considerazioni in merito al rapporto tra mediazione e processo alla luce del decreto legislativo n. 28/2010', <www.comparazionedirittocivile.it>; Amerio et al., *La mediazione nelle liti civile e commerciali. Metodo e regole* (Milan: Giuffrè, 2011); Armone & Porreca, 'La mediazione tra processo e conflitto', FI (2010): V, 95; M. Bove, 'La riforma in materia di conciliazione tra delega e decreto legislativo', <www.judicium.it>; A. Carratta, 'La via italiana alla conciliazione: luci ed ombre nel decreto legislativo sulla "mediazione finalizzata alla conciliazione nelle controversie civili e commerciali"', in *Sull'arbitrato. Studi offerti a Giovanni Verde*, Auletta et al. (Naples: Jovene, 2010), 141; S. Chiarloni, 'Prime riflessioni sullo schema di decreto legislativo di attuazione delle delega in materia di mediazione ex art. 60 legge n. 69/2009', <www.ilcaso.it>; F. Cuomo Ulloa, 'Novità in materia di conciliazione e mediazione', *Contr.* (2009): 640; D. Dalfino, 'Mediazione, conciliazione e rapporti con il processo', FI (2010): V, 101; F.P. Luiso, 'La delega in mateeria di mediazione e conciliazione', RDP (2009): 1257; C. Punzi, 'Mediazione e conciliazione', RDP (2009): 845; G. Raiti, 'La delega in materia di mediazione e di conciliazione delle controversie civili e commerciali ex art. 60 Legge n. 69 del 2009', in *Sull'arbitrato. Studi offerti a Giovanni Verde*, *supra*, 657; G.F. Ricci, *Il procedimento di mediazione di cui al D.LGS. 4 marzo 2010, n. 28* (Turin: Giappichelli, 2010); R. Tiscini, 'Vantaggi e svantaggi della nuova mediazione finalizzata alla conciliazione: accordo e sentenza a confronto', GC (2010): II, 489; R. Tiscini, 'Il procedimento di mediazione per la conciliazione delle controversie civili e commerciali', <www.judicium.it>; E. Zucconi Galli Fonseca, 'La nuova mediazione nella prospettiva europea: note a prima lettura', RTDPC (2010): 653.

Article 4, for instance, obliges the lawyer to inform in writing his or her client about the possibility to mediate the dispute rather than going to court. If that information is not given, the client has the right to invalidate the contract with his or her lawyer.

As it was seen in paragraph 202, a decision of the Constitutional Court (6 December 2012, No. 272) declared many provisions of DLGS No. 28 unconstitutional, in particular those concerning mandatory mediation. After a few months however, the lawmaker brought back such preliminary device, though in a revised form, in order to comply with Constitutional provisions (*see* paragraph 202). Here, therefore, mention will be made to the rules of DLGS 28 as revised by DL No. 69/2013.

The positive influence of mediation in reducing the courts' workload is still under scrutiny. In order for mediation to be effective on a large scale, a cultural change is needed in the lawyers' and in the public attitude towards litigation. Arguably, this will happen in the next future, with a joint effort by universities and practitioners.[747]

452. Article 1 of DLGS No. 28 provides the definitions of some of the most important notions used by the new piece of legislation.

In particular, it specifies that 'mediation' means the activity of a third and impartial person (the mediator), aimed both at assisting two or more parties in searching an amicable agreement to solve a dispute between them and at making a proposal to solve such dispute.

Concerning the mediator, Article 1 specifies that he or she has no power at all to adjudicate the dispute or render binding decisions for the parties. In other words, in the provisions of DLGS No. 28, two different models of mediation are mixed: on the one hand, the so-called facilitative mediation (where the mediator only helps the parties reach an agreement on their own terms), and on the other hand, the so-called adjudicative mediation (where the mediator, if the parties fail to reach an agreement of their own, finally offers them a proposal to solve their dispute, which the parties are then free to accept or refuse within seven days, even though their refusal to do so might have some negative consequences on the costs of future litigation: *see* paragraph 457). As a general rule, such proposal may not refer to any declaration made by the parties nor to any information acquired in the course of mediation (Article 11).

However, 'conciliation' is defined as the positive result of mediation, that is, the agreement which settles the dispute between the parties. In other words, following the guidelines of the EU Directive, mediation and conciliation are considered not as two different types of ADR, but rather as, respectively, the proceedings which the party go through in order to solve their dispute, and the result of such proceedings.

453. DLGS No. 28 of 2010 refers to four different 'models' of mediation:

747. *See* L. Cominelli, *Training Young Lawyers in the European Mediation Framework: It's Time to Devise a New Pedagogy for Conflict Management and Dispute Resolution*, 2 ILJ 163 et seq. (2016).

(1) voluntary mediation: here, the parties mutually agree (without being obliged to do so) to try and mediate a dispute between them, before going to court.
(2) Court-proposed/imposed mediation: after the revision of 2012, Article 5(2) empowers the judge, at any stage of the proceedings (and even at the appeal level) to send the parties before a mediation centre to try and conciliate the dispute;[748] the case is then postponed, and the parties are supposed to file a mediation petition before a centre of their choice; when such a referral takes place, in the original dispute the judge arranges a further hearing in a delay of at least three months, in order to check whether the parties did indeed appear before the mediator and if a settlement was thus reached. It the parties, however, fail to comply to the judge's order, the case will be struck out with no decision on the merits. Practice is showing that some judges apply this form of mediation quite extensively.
(3) Mandatory mediation (Article 5(1*bis*)): this was the most troublesome and controversial type of mediation in the original version of DLGS No. 28. As it was already pointed out (*see* at paragraphs 202 et seq.), the lawmaker had initially made it mandatory to preliminary try to mediate several types of disputes. Lawyers strenuously opposed this innovation (with good reasons, as concerns the high costs of mediation proceedings, even when no agreement was reached). The Constitutional Court, at the end of 2012, declared such mandatory mediation to be unconstitutional, alleging that the Government had gone beyond the boundaries set by Article 60 of Law No. 69 of 2009 (the *legge delega*: *see* paragraph 6).[749] In other words, mandatory mediation fell for formal and not substantial reasons.[750] It was easy for the lawmaker, then, after a few months, with DL No. 69 of 21 June 2013, implemented by Law No. 98 of 9 August 2013, to revise the rules of DLGS No. 28 of 2010, basically restoring the provisions which the Constitutional Court had declared unconstitutional.[751] A few changes were however brought, in order to bypass constitutional problems and the lawyers' opposition to mandatory mediation; according to the revised Articles 5 and 8, therefore, today it is still mandatory to try and mediate certain types of disputes, but what the parties are supposed to do before filing a claim in court is only to participate at least in an informative conference with a mediator. At the end of such conference the parties may decide either to go through with the mediation or to be done with it and proceed before the court. If such is the case, only a nominal fee will have to be paid. In other words, today, the preliminary

748. In the previous formulation of the rule, the judge could only 'propose' to the parties to try and mediate their dispute.
749. Basically, the Constitutional Court argued that neither the European Directive nor the *legge delega* gave the Government power (as delegated lawmaker) to provide for mandatory mediation for certain types of disputes.
750. *See* E. Silvestri & R. Jagtenberg, 'Tweeluik – Diptych: juggling a red hot potato: Italy, the EU and mandatory mediation', *Nederlands-Vlaams tijdschrift voor Mediation en conflictmanagement*, (2013): n. 1, 29.
751. *See also* M. Bove, 'L'accordo conciliativo rivisitato dal c.d. 'decreto del fare', <www.judicium.it>, 1;F, Cuomo Ulloa, *La nuova mediazione. Profili applicativi* (Bologna: Zanichelli, 2013).

condition to starting court proceedings can be satisfied quite quickly and inexpensively. Of course, the lawmaker's challenge is for as many parties as possible to be persuaded by the mediator to try and mediate their dispute. In other words, today, the preliminary condition to starting court proceedings may be satisfied quite quickly and inexpensively. Of course, the lawmaker's challenge is for as many prospective litigants as possible to be persuaded by the mediator to try and mediate their dispute. It must also be noted that some courts are showing a restrictive approach to the new provision of Article 5(1*bis*), going beyond its wording and claiming that, in order for the procedural precondition to be met, it is not enough to simply attend the first conference before the mediator. The parties are thus required to seriously try to mediate the dispute. Moreover, the maximum legal duration of mediation proceedings has been reduced (from four to three months) and road accident cases are no longer subject to preliminary mandatory mediation.

(4) Voluntary mandatory mediation: when the parties contractually try and mediate any future dispute between them, they are then bound to go through mediation proceedings before bringing their case to court. Here, however, such mediation is mandatory only in so far as the parties voluntary agreed so.

Chapter 2. Rights That Can Be Subject to Mediation

454. Not every kind of dispute may be mediated. Following the guidelines of the EU Directive, Article 2 of DLGS No. 2 specifies that only disputes in civil and commercial matters concerning rights of which the parties may freely dispose of (*diritti disponibili*) may be subject to mediation.

Interestingly, the Italian implementation of the Directive does not limit mediation to transnational disputes, but extends this form of ADR also to national cases.

Chapter 3. Mediation Agreement

455. As it was seen in paragraph 453, DLGS No. 28 of 2010 allows 'voluntary mandatory mediation'; i.e., the possibility for the parties to insert in their contracts a 'mediation clause', binding them, to try and mediate any future dispute between them. This form of mediation, however, still appears to be very little used in contractual transactions in Italy.

Chapter 4. Persons/Institutions That Can Act as Mediator

456. According to DLGS No. 28, mediation proceedings have to take place within public or private mediation centres (*organismi di mediazione*) registered and approved by the Ministry of Justice (*see* Articles 16, 18 and 19). In other words, the parties may not directly appoint their own mediator: rather, they appoint a mediation centre which will then assign their case to one (or more) of the mediators registered with them.

The law sets down the requirements a mediation centre must comply with in order to be approved by the Ministry of Justice.

457. In order to become a mediator, a three-year university degree is needed. Also members of professionals 'orders' or associations, however, may apply to become one. Applicants must then attend a formative course and an apprenticeship in a mediation centre. Mediators are expected to attend eighteen hours of professional updating every two years. Lawyers may perform as mediators by statute.

Mediators must be registered in a mediation centre to handle mediations. Every mediator may be registered in as many as five centres.

Chapter 5. Mediation Procedure

458. DLGS No. 28 of 2010 does not regulate mediation proceedings in every detail. On the contrary, it specifies – Article 3(1) – that the proceedings are governed by the regulation of the institution chosen by the party. Such regulation however must satisfy certain minimum standards, namely confidentiality of the proceedings (*see also* Article 9) and impartiality of the mediator, who should also be adequate in granting fair and speedy progress of the mediation sessions. Article 3(3) also specifies that the acts of the mediation proceedings should not be subject to formal requirements. In other words, a deformalized procedure is provided, mostly based on orality and with minimum exchange of written materials.

Some procedural guidelines, however, are fixed by statute. First of all, Article 4 makes clear that, to start the mediation, the interested party has to file an application in an institution of his or her choice. In the revision of 2012, it was specified that the mediation centre must be chosen within the territorial jurisdiction of the court which should decide the case. In the application, the name of the mediation centre, the parties, the object and the reasons for the claim should be indicated. Upon receiving the application, the centre appoints a mediator and sets the first hearing with the party within thirty days of the moment the application was filed.

When he or she is appointed, the mediator is required to sign a declaration of impartiality; he or she should also make a disclosure about facts or circumstances that could make him or her biased. The law forbids him or her from receiving any compensation directly from the parties (Article 14).

The institution sends a copy of the application and communicates the date set for the meeting to the other parties (Article 8). The actual progress of mediation is then left to the regulations approved by the institutions. The law just says that the mediator should make an effort to lead the parties to amicably settle their dispute. If the case may be, the mediator may also be coordinated by 'experts' (whose role in the proceedings is not clear …).

The law also establishes the maximum length of mediation: after the revision of 2012, three months, running from the date the application is filed in the mediation centre.

Article 11(1) of DLGS No. 28 of 2010 enables the mediator, even on his own initiative (if the institution's regulations so allow), to formulate a mediation proposal to the parties; in other words, it is up to the mediator to propose a solution to the dispute. The parties are of course free to accept that proposal or not. However, if the case goes on before the judge, the fact that the winning party refused a mediator's proposal which was substantially confirmed by the final judgment will have an influence on the costs of the proceedings (*see* paragraph 305).

Chapter 6. Settlement Agreement

459. If the case is settled (possibly, with parties' acceptance of the proposal made by the mediator), a report is written and duly signed by the parties and the mediator (Article 11). It may be made enforceable by the *Tribunale*, upon the party's application for *exequatur*, unless it is deemed to be in violation of public policy or mandatory provisions. It may then be used as an enforceable title for generic and specific enforcement and for registering a mortgage (Article 12).

If, however, the parties do not reach an agreement, each of them has the prerogative to bring the case before the competent court.

As it was pointed out above (*see* paragraph 452), in the course of the proceedings, the judge may take into consideration the fact that the winning party refused a mediator's proposal which was substantially confirmed by the judgment, at the time of issue his or her final decisions on costs. The judge may also consider the fact that a party refused to take part in the mediation in order to reinforce his or her opinion on the merits of the case. Moreover, additional costs may be taxed on a party which did not take part in mediation proceedings without good reason.

Apart from this, however, there is an absolute prohibition for the parties to reveal anything that was said or done in the course of mediation, unless all the parties agree to release to the judge these pieces of information. The mediator has a confidentiality obligation and has a privilege against being heard as a witness in the course of the proceedings (Articles 9 and 10).

460. Special provisions on A.D.R. in relation to consumers are provided by Article 141 of the Consumer Code as modified by DLG No. 130 of 6 August 2015. [752]

---

752. *See* P. Bartolomucci, 'La nuova disciplina delle procedure di risoluzone alternative delle controversie in materia di consumo: il D.L.GS. n. 130/15 e le modifiche del Codice del consum0', NLCC (2016): 494. Interestingly, the ECJ, in its decision of c. 75/16, *Menini v. Banca Popolare Società Cooperativa* of 14 Jun. 2017 found that, in relation to Directive 2013/11/UE of 21 May 2013, on the alternative resolution of consumer disputes, national legislation may introduce mandatory mediation as a preliminary condition to bringing civil proceedings, as long as such requirement does not prevent a party from exercising their right to a day in court. However, the same Directive was deemed to be incompatible with national rules requiring a consumer to be assisted by a lawyer in mandatory mediation or which impose a party to show a good reason in order to withdraw from mediation proceedings.

Chapter 7. Setting Aside a Settlement Agreement

461. There is no specific national legislation regarding the setting aside of a settlement agreement.

Chapter 8. International Mediation

462. There is no specific national legislation on international mediation.

Part XII. Assisted Negotiation (*negoziazione assistita*) and Referral of Pending Cases to Arbitration

Chapter 1. Legislation

463. As we have seen in the previous part, mandatory mediation was introduced in Italy as a device to try and reduce the courts' workload. In practice, it has failed to effectively pursue this aim, since only a small fraction of cases are actually conciliated. As a matter of fact, only a minority of civil disputes are subject to mandatory mediation and, in general, parties (and lawyers) still appear to be reluctant to find amicable solutions to their disputes, especially when the respondent is a bank or an insurance company. Since the overall situation did not appear to improve (as fast as it should), in 2014, the Italian lawmaker deemed it necessary to find new ways to encourage litigants to avoid going to court (or, looking at it from a different standpoint, to make it harder for them to find the courtroom's open).

On 12 September 2014, therefore, DL No. 132 was approved by the Government (and later converted into Law No. 162 of 10 November 2014 by Parliament),[753] bringing 'Urgent measures of "*degiurisdizionalizzazione*" and other interventions for dispatching backlog in matters of civil justice'.[754] As a matter of fact, in this statute, a new catchword was invented by the lawmaker: *degiurisdizionalizzazione*, which has no obvious equivalent in English and which may be roughly translated as a process towards the unjurisdictional solution of disputes ('dejurisdictionalization'). In other words, lawyers were given a more active role in the solution of disputes, enabling them to negotiate cases and come up with settlements having full enforcing authority, with no need of a judicial *exequatur*. This might not sound like the invention of the wheel for foreign observers, but it must be remarked that, until *decreto* No. 132 of 2014, though lawyers could of course negotiate disputes for their

753. *See* C. Consolo, 'E' legge (con poche modifiche) il d.l. sulla 'degiurisdizionalizzazione' arbitral-conciliativa, sulle passerelle processuali, sulla grinta esecutiva', GC (2014): 1061.

754. *See Degiurisdizionalizzazione e altri interventi per la definizione dell'arretrato (d.l. 12 settembre 2014 n. 132, convertito, con modificazioni, in l. 10 novembre 2014, n. 162)*, FI (2015): V, 1; D. Borghesi, 'La delocalizzazione del contenzioso civile: sulla giustizia sventola bandiera bianca?', <www.judicium.it>; A. Briguglio, 'Nuovi ritocchi in vista per il processo civile: mini-riforma ad iniziativa governativa, con promessa di fare (si confida su altri e più utili versanti) sul serio', <www.giustiziacivile.com>; B. Capponi, 'La crisi della giurisdizione civile', CG (2014):1277; C. Consolo, 'La giustizia civile: quale volto dei nostri processi fra giurisdizione e ADR?', CG (2014): 1263.

clients, the relevant settlement, even if legally binding for the parties, could not be used as an enforcement title (*titolo esecutivo*) (*see* paragraph 410) without previously referring to the court to have a (summary) decision rendered on that settlement or, since 2005, having their clients signatures verified by a notary public or another public official.

Since 2014, the role of practitioners in the Italian system of civil justice has changed. No longer just the partisan defenders of parties both in and out of court, they are now an integral part of the system for the solution of disputes, with new 'public' powers as regards the authentication of their clients' signatures and the control over the conformity of the latter's agreements with mandatory provisions and public order.

DL No. 132 of 2014 tackles the problem of courtroom's congestion from two standpoints. On the one hand, the idea that parties should be compelled to try some form of ADR before bringing their case to court, which led to the introduction of mandatory mediation (*see* paragraphs 450 et seq.) has been further implemented, with the introduction of *negoziazione assistita* as a preliminary procedural mandatory step in many civil cases. On the other hand, an attempt has also been made at finding a way to actually take cases already pending out of the courtroom to be decided by arbitration: a completely new device for the Italian procedural system which might recall court-annexed arbitration but which is really something different.[755]

755. A. Briguglio, *supra*, 8.

Chapter 2. Referral of Pending Cases to Arbitration

464. Referral to arbitration of civil proceedings pending before judicial authorities is dealt with in Article 1 of DL No. 132[756]. Basically, in civil cases concerning rights which the parties may freely dispose of (*diritti disponibili*), apart from labour and public security disputes, pending before the *Tribunale* at first instance or the Court of Appeal at the time of entry into force of the new provision, the parties may jointly apply to hand over the power to adjudicate the case to arbitrators, under the provisions of the code of civil procedure. An exception is made for tort or monetary disputes for a value of EUR 50,000.00 or less in which a public administration is involved: as a matter of fact, the latter's consent to remitting the dispute to arbitration is presumed, unless it expresses its written dissent within thirty days of receiving the other party's request: in other words, a public administration may be bound to bring the case to arbitration as a consequence of its silence in the face of a remittal request from its counterpart.

When such a joint request is handed to the judge, according to paragraph 2 of Article 1 of DL No. 132, the latter, after checking that the requirements for the application of the provision are complied with,[757] will transfer the case to the President of the local Bar Association (*Consiglio dell'Ordine*) who, in turn, will appoint an arbitral panel of 3 arbitrators for cases of a value of at least EUR 100,000.00 or of a single arbitrator, when both parties so decide, for cases of a lesser value. Some commentators, however, believe that the President of the Bar Association should be involved only when the parties have not agreed on whom to appoint as arbitrator in the first place.[758] However, the (indeed questionable) rationale of the new remedy appears to favour the creation of a necessary connection between the court and local lawyers, so the first interpretation appears to be the most correct one. Actually, the President of the Bar Association is bound to appoint as arbitrators lawyers who have been registered at the local Bar for at least five years and who have previously given their consent to such an appointment: this monopoly of lawyers in court-derived arbitration has been rightly criticized.[759]

According to paragraph 5*bis* of Article 1, the Ministry of Justice is supposed to establish criteria for the appointment of arbitrators in this context, taking into consideration, in particular, the arbitrator's professional expertise vis-à-vis the subject-matter of the dispute and a rotation principle in the assignments of such appointments.

After the appointment of the arbitrator(s), the case proceeds before them. Paragraph 3 of Article 1 makes it clear that this is not a fresh arbitral proceeding but a continuation of the original judicial dispute: as a matter of fact, both the substantial

---

756. Cerri, 'Vedi alla voce: "Degiurisdizionalizzazione" (trasferimento alla sede arbitrale di procedimenti pendenti', <www.judicium.it>; M. Gradi, *Inefficienza della giustizia civile e 'fuga dal processo'* (Messina: Edizioni Leone, 2014), 63 et seq.; A. Sirotti Gaudenzi, *Procedimento arbitrale e rapporti con il processo civile dopo la Legge 162/2014* (Santarcangelo di Romagna: Maggioli, 2015); V. Vigoriti, 'Il "trasferimento" in arbitrato: l'inizio di un'inversione di tendenza', <www.judicium.it>.
757. A. Briguglio, *supra*, 9.
758. A. Briguglio, *supra*, 10; V. Vigoriti, *supra*, 7.
759. V. Vigoriti, *supra*, 7.

and procedural effects of the initiating judicial petition are preserved, and the deadlines expired before the judge may not be reopened before the arbitrators. This is a major difference vis-à-vis 'ordinary' arbitration proceedings, where the parties activities are not bound by procedural time limits.

The arbitral award is expressly granted the same effects of a judgment, thus making it clear that this is what, under Italian law, would be called an arbitration 'rituale' (*see* paragraph 432).

465. The law does not clarify what happens to the judicial proceedings when a case pending before the *Tribunale* at first instance is referred to arbitration under Article 1 of DL No. 132. Apparently, such referral is definitive, and judicial proceedings are struck out with no decision on the merits.[760] This implies that should arbitrators never come up with an award, the dispute will have to be started anew with no possibility to simply reinstate it before the original judge.[761]

This is not necessarily the case at the appellate level: as paragraph 4 of Article 1 makes clear, when an appeal dispute is referred to arbitration and the arbitrators do not render their award within 120 days of the formation of the arbitral panel, the case has to be reinstated within 60 days before the Court of Appeal from which it was first transferred.[762] At this point, the award may no longer be granted. However, if the deadline expires and the proceeding is not reinstated before the Court of Appeal, the case is struck out.

The new provision takes into consideration the higher costs of arbitration as compared to those of judicial proceedings and, in order to encourage the application of this new method to solve a dispute, establishes that the Ministry of Justice will operate, for this context, a reduction of the ordinary criteria to determine an arbitrator's reward.

Commentators have written a lot about this new provision, which appears to have many problematic implications, in particular as concerns the relation between the different phases in which proceedings could now develop, especially at the appeal level. In fact, the possibility for arbitrators to review a judicial decision of first instance and possibly change it with their award is a completely new procedural option that breaks the traditional view of the relations between judges and arbitrators. Until 2014, such relation was one-directional, in the sense that only judges could review, under the conditions set by Article 829 CPC, an arbitral award. Now, such relation has become bi-directional.

466. This new procedural device has proved to be a failure, with no practical applications. As a matter of fact, the basic question which Article 1 of DL No. 132 fails to answer is why should parties who are already involved in judicial proceedings agree to bring the dispute before arbitrators? And why should they do it following the strict requirements of the new provision and not by simply abandoning judicial proceedings and start an arbitration anew?

---

760. A. Briguglio, *supra*, 11.
761. A. Briguglio, *supra*, 11.
762. D'Agosto, Criscuolo, 'Prime note sulle 'misure urgenti di degiurisdizionalizzazione e altri interventi per la definizione dell'arretrato in materia di processo civile', <www.ilcaso.it>, 9.

It has to be considered that arbitration, even with the new tariffs set by the Ministry of justice, is more expensive than a judicial trial, in Italy and elsewhere. Moreover, one of the parties will usually have no interest in accelerating the dispatching of the case by removing it from the slow judicial trail to bring it on the faster arbitration highway. Even more doubts arise when one considers the option to refer to arbitration a case which has already reached the Court of appeal. The main attraction of this option is the possibility to shorten the exceedingly long time which Italian Courts of second instance take to dispatch a case (usually 4\5 years). However, the party that won at first instance will be rather reluctant to move away from the court and enter the realm of arbitration, considering that arbitrators may pay less deference to the first instance decision than another judge would.

Such a procedural option, however, appears to be attractive when all the parties are dissatisfied with the first instance decision and the dispute has a very technical or specialized nature, in so far as all the parties may want to have the case reviewed within a shorter delay by an highly specialized panel of 'private adjudicators'.

Chapter 3. Assisted Negotiation

467. Negoziazione assistita (assisted negotiation) consists of formalized negotiations between the parties and their lawyers to settle their dispute to avoid going to court (or, one may add, in order to bring a pending judicial dispute to a settled end).

When parties settle by way of a *negoziazione assistita*, their agreement is granted full authoritative effects, as regards the enforcement of the obligations taken in such agreement. In other words, parties are encouraged to use this new ADR so that when a settlement is agreed upon but the other party fails to respect it, it will be possible to enforce it directly, without previously obtaining a judgment on the agreement.

It must be remarked that the lawmaker introduced *negoziazione assistita* also as a way to bring a new preliminary barrier to the introduction of a judicial claim. Article 3 of DL No. 132, in fact, specifies that in relation to any dispute concerning damages deriving from the circulation of vehicles and boats and to any dispute, not covered by mandatory mediation under Article 5(1*bis*) of DLGS No. 28 of 2010 (*see* paragraph 450), which concerns a monetary claim, of which the parties may freely dispose of, for a value of EUR 50,000.00 or less, *negoziazione assistita* is a '*condizione di procedibilità*', i.e., a preliminary procedural requirement which has to be satisfied before the case may be brought to court. In other words, with the introduction of preliminary assisted negotiations, today, in Italy, most civil cases concerning a right of which the parties may freely dispose of fall under one form of *condizione di procedibilità* or the other.

468. Negoziazione assistita is a highly formalized method to solve a dispute between two or more parties. The procedure starts upon the initiative of a prospective litigant who, through his lawyer, invites the other party to stipulate an agreement to cooperate in good faith and loyally in order to amicably solve their dispute with the assistance of their lawyers. The other party is, of course, not bound to accept that invitation but her unjustified refusal to do so may be considered by the judge, in subsequent proceedings, when deciding on the costs of the dispute (*see* paragraph 305). When, on the other hand, the invitation is accepted by the other party (who should answer in writing, with the assistance of a lawyer, within thirty days), a covenant is drafted to start the assisted negotiation (*convenzione di negoziazione assistita*).

In such 'preliminary' agreement (which must be recorded in writing) the parties must mention, *inter alia*, the programmed duration of their negotiations (by statute, no more than three months which may be extended for thirty more days with the parties' joint consent).

If an agreement is reached, the relevant document is considered a *titolo esecutivo* (enforcement title) (*see* paragraph 407). The parties' signatures are certified by their lawyers, who also certify that the agreement complies with mandatory legal provisions and public order.

Chapter 4. Assisted Negotiation in Matrimonial Disputes

469. A special form of *negoziazione assistita* has been provided for matrimonial and parental disputes between married parties by Article 6 of DL *legge* No. 132.[763] As a matter of fact, until 2014, in order for spouses to separate or divorce, they had no alternative but to apply for a Court order (*see* paragraphs 335 et seq.). The parties, of course, could agree on the conditions of their separation or divorce, but still such agreement needed to be confirmed in front of a judge and approved of by the *Tribunale*. Through *negoziazione assistita*, however, the parties may now negotiate with their lawyers in order to reach an amicable solution to their separation or divorce and the agreement that they eventually reach is drafted and checked upon by their lawyers, with public control reduced to a minimum. Actually, their agreement is subject to a review by the *publico ministero*: nonetheless, such review is rather limited and might not be so effective, so that the danger that the spouses' or the kids' rights may be somehow restricted is present.

470. The procedure starts with the spouses agreeing to negotiate together with the assistance of a lawyer on each side. Then, if the following negotiation is successful, an agreement is duly signed, with the spouses' signatures certified as authentic by their lawyers. At this point, however, a further requirement is provided for by Article 6 in comparison with 'ordinary' assisted negotiation (*see* above), since, in this area of family law, usually the parties are not in the position to freely dispose of their rights. The parties' agreement, therefore, must be filed in the office of the *Pubblico Ministero*, (*see* paragraphs 95 et seq.) If the agreement does not concern minors or kids who are still not financially independent, the *Pubblico Ministero* is supposed to examine it and eventually grant his 'nulla osta' (i.e., no obstacles to the agreement are found). Otherwise, the agreement undergoes a deeper analysis and the *Publico Ministero* is supposed to either authorize it or not. However, when the PM finds some troublesome aspects in the agreement which make it impossible for him to authorize it, he is supposed to transfer the file to the President of the *Tribunale* who will then call the parties before him and review the agreement with them. When all the necessary steps are successfully dealt with, the agreement has to be handed over to the public registrar to update the parties' civil records.

---

763. F. Danovi, 'I nuovi modelli di separazione e divorzio: una intricata pluralità di protagonisti', FD (2015): 1141; B. Poliseno, 'La convenzione di negoziazione assistita per le soluzioni consensuali di separazione e divorzio', FI (2015): V, 34; F. Tommaseo, 'La tutela dell'interesse dei minori dalla riforma della filiazione alla negoziazione assistita delle crisi coniugali', FD (2015): 157.

Chapter 5. Separation and Divorce Without Lawyers

471. An even faster and more informal way to get a separation or a divorce, moreover, can be found in Article 12 of DL No. 132, which enables spouses with no minor or still financially dependent offspring to simply appear before the Mayor of the place of residence or domicile of either one of them and declare their will to separate or divorce, even without the assistance of a lawyer.[764] In the case of separation, such declaration is immediately effective. As for divorce, on the other hand, the spouses are required to appear before the Mayor a second time, no earlier than thirty days later, to confirm their will to no longer be married to each other.

Article 12 states that the parties' agreement may not contain any '*trasferimento patrimoniale*' (transfer of patrimonial rights). There has been some controversy over the interpretation of this provision. In particular, some commentators argue that it forbids any clause in the agreement having monetary effects: in other words, in light of this very restrictive (and arguably wrong) interpretation, parties may only agree to separate or divorce, with no further agreement on alimony or maintenance. Recently, however, both the Ministry of Home Affairs and the *Consiglio di Stato* have declared that this provision in Article 12 only prohibits the parties from transferring rights in rem in their agreement before the Mayor, while they are free to agree on an alimony payment between each other.

764. G. Casaburi, 'Separazione e divorzio innanzi al sindaco: ricadute sostanziali e processuali', FI (2015): V, 44.

Selected Bibliography

§1. In English

Bernardini, P. *The Italian Law on Arbitration. Text and Notes.* The Hague and Boston: Kluwer, 1998.

Blomeyer, A. 'Types of Relief Available (Judicial Remedies)'. In *IECL, Civil Procedure,* edited by Cappelletti. Vol. XVI. Ch. 4. Tubingen: Mohr, 1982.

Caponi, R. 'European Minimum Standards for Courts. Independence, Specialization, Efficiency. A Glance from Italy'. In *Festschrift fur Professor Nikolaos K. Klamaris*. Athens – Thessaloniki: Sakkoulas Publications, 2016, 151.

Cappelletti, M. & B. Garth. 'Introduction – Policies, Trends and Ideas in Civil Procedure'. In *IECL, Civil Procedure*, edited by Cappelletti. Vol. XVI. Ch. 1. Dordrecht: M. Nijhoff, 1987.

Chiarloni, S., 'Civil Justice and Its Paradoxes: An Italian Perspective'. In *Civil Justice in Crisis. Comparative Perspectives of Civil Procedure*, edited by A.A.S. Zuckerman, S. Chiarloni, P. Gottwald. Oxford: Oxford University Press, 1999, 263.

Cohn, J. 'Parties'. In *IECL, Civil Procedure*, edited by Cappelletti. Vol. XVI. Ch. 5. Dordrecht: M. Nijhoff, 1976.

De Cristofaro, M. & N. Trocker (eds). *Civil Justice in Italy.* Tokyo: Jigakusha, 2010.

Di Federico, G., 'Judicial Independence in Italy'. In *Judicial Independence in Transition*, edited by Seibert-Fohr. Heidelberg: Springer, 2012, 357 et seq.

Fazzalari (ed.). *Italian Yearbook of Civil Procedure*. Milan: Giuffrè, 1991 (Vol. I) and 1993 (Vol. II).

Grossi, S. & M.C. Pagni. *Commentary on the Italian Code of Civil Procedure.* Oxford: Oxford University Press, 2010.

Herzog, P. & D. Karlen. 'Attacks on Judicial Decisions'. In *IECL, Civil Procedure*, edited by Cappelletti. Vol. XVI. Ch. 8. Dordrecht: M. Nijhoff, 1982.

Lupoi, M.A., 'Nowhere Fast? Shortcuts to Judgment in Recent Italian Procedural Legislation'. In *Ways of Implementation of the Right to Civil Proceedings Within a Reasonable Time.* Vilnius: Vilnius Universitetas, 2016, p. 299.

O'Malley, S. & A. Layton. 'European Civil Practice'. In *Italy.* Ch. 53. London: Sweet and Maxwell, 1989, 1352.

Van Caenegem, R.C. 'History of European Civil Procedure'. In *IECL, Civil Procedure*, edited by Cappelletti. Vol. XVI. Ch. 2. Dordrecht: M. Nijhoff, 1973.

§2. MORE SPECIFIC

Amato, C. & C. Perfumi. 'Financial Investors as Consumers and Their Protection: Recent Italian Legislation from a European Perspective'. In *Opinio Juris in Comparatione*. Vol. 3, 2010. Paper No. 3, 1–23. <http://lider-lab.sssup.it/opinio>, online publication, September 2010.

Biavati, P. 'Oral and Written Evidence in Italian Civil Procedure Law'. <www.uv.es/ coloquio/coloquio/informes/ip2ita.pdf>, online publication.

Ballarino, T. & A. Bonomi. 'The Italian Statute on Private International Law of 1995'. In *Yearbook of Private International Law*, edited by P. Sarcevis & P. Volken. Vol. II. Munchen: Sellier, 2000, 99.

Barsotti, V. & V. Varano. 'Legal Education in Italy'. In *Opinio Juris in Comparatione*. Vol. 1, 2010. Paper No. 3. <http://liber-lab.sssup.it/opinio>, online publication, March 2010.

Biavati, P., 'Judicial Cooperation in Europe: Is Exequatur Still Necessary?'. *International Journal of Procedural Law* 1 (2011): 403.

Caponi, R. 'Italian Civil Justice Reform 2009'. *ZZPint* (2009).

Caponi, R. 'The Collective Redress Action in the Italian Legal System'. *ZZPInt* (2009).

Caponi, R. 'The Performance of the Italian Civil Justice System: An Empirical Assessment'. *The Italian Law Journal* (2016): 15.

Caponi, R. '"Just Settlement" or "Just About Settlement"? Mediated Agreements: A Comparative Overview of the Basics'. 79 *RabelsZ* (2015): 117.

Caponi, R. 'Italian "Class Action" Suits in the Field of Consumer Protection: 2016 Update'. <https://papers.ssrn.com/sol3/papers.cfm?abstract_id=2796611>.

Carmignani, A. & S. Giacomelli. 'Too Many Lawyers? Litigation in Italian Civil Courts'. <www.bancaditalia.it/pubblicazioni/econo/temidi/td10/td745_10/en_td_745_10/en_tema_745.pdf>, online publication.

Carpi, F. 'The Parties and the Judge in the New Commercial Proceedings in Italy and the Ideological Choices'. *Civil Justice Quarterly* 25 (2006): 70.

Cavallini, D., 'Judicial Discipline: Different Approaches in Five EU Member States'. In *Handbook of Judicial Politics*, edited by R. Coman & C. Dallara. Iaşi: European Institute Editions, 2010, 125 et seq.

Cavallini, D., 'State Liability for Judicial Wrongs: Impact of Rulings of the European Court of Justice and Debate in Italy'. In *The Culture of Judicial Independence in a Globalised World*, edited by S. Shetreet & W. McCormack. Brill/Nijhoff, 2016, Chapter 21.

Chiarloni, S. 'Civil Justice and Its Paradoxes: An Italian Perspective'. <www.processocivile.org/chiarloni%5Cop0002.pdf>, online publication.

Cominelli, L. 'Training Young Lawyers in the European Mediation Framework: It's Time to Devise A New Pedagogy for Conflict Management and Dispute Resolution'. *The Italian Law Journal* 2 (2016): 163 et seq.

Consolo, C. 'Discretionary Powers and Hierarchy of Judges: Variation on Four Recent Issues Arising from Case law and Legislation (in the Main Civil Law Systems: France, Germany, Italy'. In *Essays on Transnational and Comparative Civil Procedure*, edited by F. Carpi & M.A. Lupoi. Turin: Giappichelli, 2001, 13–28.

Conte, G. 'The Italian Way of Mediation'. *GC* (2014): 163.

Cristina, G. 'Civil Procedure Reforms in Italy: Concentration Principle, Adversarial System or Case Management?'.<www.bancaditalia.it/pubblicazioni/quarigi/qrg66;internal&action=_setlanguage.action? language=en>, online publication, September 2009.

De Cristofaro, M. 'The Abolition of Exequatur Proceedings: Speeding Up the Free Movement of Judgments while Preserving the Rights of the Defense'. *International Journal of Procedural Law.* (2011): 432.

De Luca, A. 'Cost and Fee Allocation in Italian Civil Procedureì'. *Civil Justice Quarterly.* 29 (2010): 428.

Donzelli, R. 'The Role of Coercion in Legal Norms with a Focus on Italian Civil Procedure'. in *La costrainte en droit. The constraint in law*, edited by E. Calzolaio & P. Serrand. Zurich: Lit Verlag Gmbh, 2017, 197.

Ferrarese, M.R. 'Civil Justice and the Judicial Role in Italy'. *The Justice System Journal* 13 (1988–1989): 168.

Ferrari, F. & Bocharova, N. 'The Astreinte in the Italian and Russian Administrative (Judicial) and Civil Proceedings'. *Russian Law Journal* 3 (2015): 8.

Finocchiaro, G. 'Access to the Judiciary under the New Italian Law on the Judiciary System: Critical Remarks'. In *Access to Justice and the Judiciary. Towards New European Standards of Affordability, Quality and Efficiency of Civil Adjudication*, edited by A. Uzelac & C.H. Van Rhee. Antwerp: Intersentia, 2009, 119.

Franzina, P. 'The Proposed New Rule of Special Jurisdiction Regarding Rights in rem in Moveable Property: A Good Option for a Reformed Brussels I Regulation?'. *Diritto del commercio internazionale.* (2011): 789.

Gioia, G. 'Labor Process and Labor Alternative Dispute Resolution in the Italian System'. *Comparative Labour Law & Policy Journal* 34 (2012-2013): 813.

Grossi, S. & M.C. Pagni. *Commentary on the Italian Code of Civil Procedure.* Oxford: Oxford University Press, 2010.

Honorati, C. 'Provisional Measures and the Recast of Brussels I Regulation: A Missed Opportunity for a Better Ruling'. *Rivista di diritto internazionale privato e processuale* (2012): 525.

Lupoi, M.A. 'Brussels II: New Rules for Transnational Matrimonial Disputes'. In *Essays on Transnational and Comparative Civil Procedure*, edited by Carpi & Lupoi. Turin: Giappichelli, 2001, 105–154.

Lupoi, M.A. 'The New Provisions on Contractual Jurisdiction in Regulation (EU)44/2001'. In *Comparative Studies on Business Tort Litigation*, edited by R. Sturner & M. Kawano. Freiburg: Mohr Siebeck, 2011, 122.

Lupoi, M.A. 'Between Tradition and Innovation: The Formation of a Jurist in Italy'. In *The Reception and Transmission of Civil Procedural Law in the Global Society*, edited by M. Deguchi & M. Storme. Antwerp: Maklu, 2008, 93.

Lupoi, M.A. 'Recent Developments in Italian Civil Procedure Law'. *Civil Procedure Review* no. 1 (2012): 25.

Lupoi, M.A. 'Interim Measures in Italian Family Proceedings'. In *Provisional Measures in Italian and Greek Procedural Law*, edited by K. Makridou & G. Diamantopoulos. Thessaloniki: Sakkoulas Publications, 2016, 43.

Lupoi, M.A. 'Nowhere Fast? Shortcuts to Judgment in Recent Italian Procedural Legislation'. In *Ways of Implementation of the Right to Civil Proceedings Within a Reasonable Time*. Vilnius: Vilniaus universitate leidykla, 2016, 299

Selected Bibliography

Marino, C. 'The Wane of Res Judicata in the Italian Enforcement Proceedings'. *ZZPInt* (2008): 29.

Pocar, F. & F. Viarengo & Villata. *Recasting Brussels I.* Padua: Cedam, 2012.

Radicati di Brozolo, L. 'Arbitration and the Draft Revised Brussels I Regulation: Seeds of Home Country Control and of Harmonization?'. *International Journal of Private Law* 7 (2011): 423.

Rasia, C. 'Provisional Remedies in Italian Law System'. In *Provisional Measures in Italian and Greek Procedural Law*, edited by K. Makridou & G. Diamantopoulos. Thessaloniki: Sakkoulas Publications, 2016, 13.

Serio. M-. 'An Italian Perspective'. In *The Option of Litigating in Europe*, edited by Miller & Carey-Beaumont. London: UK National Committee of Comparative Law, 1993, 123.

Silvestri, E. 'Class Actions in Italy: Great Expectations, Big Disappointment'. *In Multi-party Redress Mechanisms in Europe: Squaking Mice?*, edited by V. Harsagy & C.H. van Rhee. Anwerp: Intersentia, 2014, 197.

Silvestri, E. 'The Devil Is in the Details: Remarks on Italian Enforcement Procedures'. In *Enforcement and Enforceability. Tradition and Reform*, edited by C.H. Van Rhee & A. Uzelac. Antwerp: Intersentia, 2010, 207.

Silvestri, E. 'Enforcement of Civil Judgments and Orders in Italy: An Overview'. *Bond Law Review* 12, no. 2 (2000). Article 4. <http://epublications.bond.edu.au/blr/vol12/iss2/4>.

Silvestri, E. 'Notes on Case Management in Italy. *www.academia.edu.*

Silvestri, E. & R. Jagtenberg. 'Tweeluik – Diptych: Juggling a Red Hot Potato: Italy, the EU and Mandatory Mediation'. *Nederlands-Vlaams tijdschrift voor Mediation en conflictmanagement* 17, no. 1 (2013): 29.

Szego, B. 'Inside Italian Appeals: Why Reforms Didn't Work?'. <www.bancaditalia.it/pubblicazioni/quarigi/qrg61;internal&action=_setlanguage.action?LANGUAGE=en>, online publication, July 2008.

Taruffo, M. 'Rethinking the Standards of Proof'. *American Journal of Comparative Law* 51 (2003): 659.

Varano, V. 'Civil Procedure Reform in Italy'. *American Journal of Comparative Law* 45 (1997): 657.

§3. IN ITALIAN

General

Biavati, P. *Argomenti di diritto processuale civile*, 3rd. Bologna: BUP, 2016.

Chiarloni, S. (ed.). *Le recenti riforme del processo civile.* Bologna: Zanichelli, 2007.

Chiovenda, G. *Principii di diritto processuale civile.* 3rd edn. Naples: Jovene, 1980 (reprint).

Comoglio, L.P., C. Ferri & M. Taruffo. *Lezioni sul processo civile.* 5th edn, two volumes. Bologna: Il Mulino, 2011.

Curzio, P., L. Di Paola & R. Romei. (eds.), *Processo del lavoro*, Milan: Giuffrè, 2017

Fazzalari, E. *Istituzioni di diritto processuale.* 7th edn. Padua: Cedam, 1994.

Fazzalari, E. *Il processo ordinario di cognizione*, Vol. I, *Primo grado*. Turin: Utet, 1989; Vol. II, *Impugnazioni*, Turin: Utet, 1990.
La China, S. *L'esecuzione forzata e le disposizioni generali del codice di procedura civile*. Milan: Giuffrè, 1970.
Luiso, F.P. *Diritto processuale civile*. 8th edn, five volumes. Milan: Giuffrè, 2015.
Mandrioli, C. & A. Carratta. *Diritto processuale civile*, 25th edn, four volumes. Turin: Giappichelli, 2016.
Martino, R. (ed.). *La giurisdizione nell'esperienza giurisprudenziale contemporanea*. Milan: Giuffrè, 2008.
Montesano, L & G. Arieta. *Trattato di diritto processuale civile*. Padua: Cedam, 2001.
Proto Pisani, A. *Lezioni di diritto processuale civile*. 6th edn. Naples: Jovene, 2014.
Punzi, C. *Il processo civile. Sistema e problematiche*. 2nd edn, four volumes. Turin: Giappichelli, 2010.
Punzi, C. (ed). *Le riforme del quadriennio 2010-2013*. Turin: Giappichelli, 2013.
Ricci, G.F. *Diritto processuale civile*. 6th edn, three volumes. Turin: Giappichelli, 2016.
Verde, G. *Diritto processuale civile*. 4th edn. four volumes. Bologna: Zanichelli, 2015.

More Specific

Allorio, E. La cosa giudicata rispetto ai terzi. Milan: Giuffrè, 1935.
Andrioli, V. Il concorso dei creditori nell'esecuzione singolare. Rome: Soc. ed. Del Foro italiano, 1937.
Arieta, G. 'Le tutele sommarie. I procedimenti per decreto ingiuntivo e per convalida di sfratto. I procedimenti possessori'. In Trattato di diritto processuale civile. 2nd edn. Vol. X. Padua: Cedam, 2011.
Barbieri, C. & G. Campagna. La nuova esecuzione forzata: opposizione, sospensione, estinzione dopo la l. 30 giugno 2016, n. 119. Bologna: Zanichelli, 2017.
Bartole, S. Il potere giudiziario. Bologna: il Mulino, 2008.
Besso Marcheis, C. (ed.). La mediazione civile e commerciale. Turin: Giappichelli, 2010.
Biavati, P. & M.A Lupoi (eds). Regole europee e giustizia civile, 2nd edn. Bologna: BUP, 2013.
Biavati, P., D. Cavallini & R. Orlandi. Assetti della giustizia civile e penale in Italia. Bologna: il Mulino, 2016.
Biavati, P. Giurisdizione civile, territorio e ordinamento aperto. Milan: Giuffrè, 1997.
Bove, M. Il principio della ragionevole durata del processo nella giurisprudenza della Corte di cassazione. Naples: Edizioni Scientifiche Italiane, 2010.
Bove, M. Modifiche in materia di espropriazione del credito nel d. l. n. 132 del 2014 convertito in l. n. 162 del 2014. www.judicium.it.
Briguglio, A. & B. Capponi. Commentario alle riforme del processo civile. Padua: Cedam, 2007.

Selected Bibliography

Campeis, G. & A. De Pauli. La procedura civile internazionale. 2nd edn. Padua: Cedam, 1996.

Capponi, B. La leggi processuale civile–fonti interne e communitarie (applicazioni e vicende). Turin: Giappichelli, 2001.

Capponi, B. Dieci anni di riforme sull'esecuzione forzata. www.judicium.it.

Carnacini, T. Il litisconsorzio nelle fasi di gravame. Padua: Cedam, 1937.

Carpi, F. L'efficacia 'ultra partes' della sentenza civile. Milan: Giuffrè, 1974.

Carpi (ed.). Arbitrato. 3rd edn. Bologna: Zanichelli, 2016.

Carpi (ed.). Arbitrati speciali. 2nd edn. Bologna: Zanichelli, 2016.

Carratta, A & M. Taruffo. 'Poteri del giudice'. In Commentario del Codice di Procedura Civile, edited by S. Chiarloni (dir.). Bologna: Zanichelli, 2011.

Cipriani, F. (ed.). La riforma del giudizio di Cassazione. Commentario al D. lgs. 2 febbraio 2006, n. 40, capo I e alla L. 18 giugno 2009, n. 69, capo IV. Padua: Cedam. 2009.

Chiavario & Lupo (eds). Commento alla normativa delegata sul giudice unico. II volumes. Turin: Utet, 2000.

Comoglio, L.P. Le prove civili. 3rd edn. Turin: Utet, 2010.

Consolo, C., F.P. Luiso & B. Sassani. Commentario alla riforma del processo civile. Milan: Giuffrè, 1996.

Consolo, C. Spiegazioni di diritto processuale civile. 10th edn, three volumes. Turin: Giappichelli, 2015.

Costantino, G. Riflessioni sulla giustizia (in)civile (1995-2010). Turin: Giappichelli, 2011.

Cuomo Ulloa, F. La nuova mediazione. Profili applicativi. Bologna: Zanichelli, 2013.

Danovi, R. La nuova legge professionale forense. Milan: Giuffrè, 2014.

D'Alessandro, E. Il riconoscimento delle sentenze straniere. Turin: Giappichelli, 2007.

Di Federico, G. (ed.). Ordinamento giudiziario. Uffici giudiziari, CSM e governo della magistratura. Padua: Cedam, 2008.

Ianniruberto G. & U. Morcavallo. Il nuovo giudizio di Cassazione. Milan: Giuffrè, 2010.

Lopes Pegna, O. I procedimenti relativi all'efficacia delle decisioni straniere in Italia. Padua: Cedam, 2009.

Lupoi, M.A. Conflitti transnazionali di giurisdizioni. Milan: Giuffrè, 2002.

Menchini, S. Il giudicato civile. Turin: Utet, 1988.

Menchini, S. Il processo litisconsortile. Struttura e poteri delle parti. Milan: Giuffrè, 1993.

Montesano, L. Lezioni sulla giurisdizione e sull'efficacia delle sentenze. Bari: Cacucci, 1972.

Patti, S. 'Le prove. Parte generale'. In Trattato di diritto privato, edited by G. Indica & P. Zatti. Milan: Giuffrè, 2010.

Patti, S. & L. Rossi Carleo. 'Provvedimenti riguardo ai figli'. In Commentario del Codice civile Scialoja-Branca, edited by F. Galgano. Bologna: Zanichelli, 2010.

Pellegrini, S. Il processo civile e la civile giustizia. Padua: Cedam, 2005.

Pizzorusso, A. L'ordinamento giudiziario. Bologna: il Mulino, 1974.

Punzi, C. Disegno sistematico dell'arbitrato, two volumes. Padua: Cedam, 2000.
Ricci, E. Il giudizio civile di rinvio. Milan: Giuffrè, 1967.
Punzi, C. La nuova stagione della Corte di cassazione e il tramonto della pubblica udienza. *RDP* (2017): 1.
Ricci, G.F. Le prove atipiche. Milan: Giuffrè, 1999.
Saletti, A. La riassunzione del processo civile. Milan: Giuffrè, 1981.
Taruffo, M. 'La prova dei fatti civili'. In Trattato di diritto civile e commerciale, edited by Cicu, Messineo & Mengoni. Milan: Giuffrè, 1992.
Tarzia, G. Il litisconsorzio facoltativo nel processo di primo grado. Milan: Giuffrè, 1972.
Tedoldi, A. Le novità in materia di esecuzione forzata nel d. l. 12/2014. *CG* (2015): 390.
Trocker, N. L'intervento per ordine del giudice. Milan: Giuffrè, 1984.
Vullo, E. 'Procedimenti in materia di famiglia e di stato delle persone'. In Commentario del Codice di Procedura Civile, edited by S. Chiarloni, tome I. Bologna: Zanichelli, 2011; tome II, Bologna: Zanichelli, 2013.
Vullo, E. 'Procedimenti cautelari in generale'. In Commentario del Codice di Procedura Civile, edited by S. Chiarloni. Bologna: Zanichelli, 2017.

Selected Bibliography

Index

The numbers here refer to paragraph numbers.

Index

Index

www.ingramcontent.com/pod-product-compliance
Ingram Content Group UK Ltd.
Pitfield, Milton Keynes, MK11 3LW, UK
UKHW020135290926
15471UKWH00003B/490